# FIGHTING FOR
Afghanistan

# FIGHTING FOR Afghanistan

*A Rogue Historian at War*

SEAN M. MALONEY

NAVAL INSTITUTE PRESS
*Annapolis, Maryland*

This book has been brought to publication with the generous assistance of Marguerite and Gerry Lenfest.

Naval Institute Press
291 Wood Road
Annapolis, MD 21402

© 2011 by Sean M. Maloney
All rights reserved. No part of this book may be reproduced or utilized in any form or by any means, electronic or mechanical, including photo-copying and recording, or by any information storage and retrieval system, without permission in writing from the publisher.

**Library of Congress Cataloging-in-Publication Data**
Maloney, Sean M.
  Fighting for Afghanistan : a rogue historian at war / Sean M. Maloney.
    p. cm.
  Includes bibliographical references and index.
  ISBN 978-1-59114-509-7 (hardcover : alk. paper) 1. Maloney, Sean M., date 2. Afghan War, 2001—Personal narratives, Canadian. 3. Afghan War, 2001—Campaigns. 4. Soldiers—Canada—Biography. 5. Historians—Canada—Biography. 6. Canada. Canadian Armed Forces. Princess Patricia's Canadian Light Infantry. I. Title.
  DS371.413.M35 2011
  958.104'7—dc23
                                                              2011019897

∞ This paper meets the requirements of ANSI/NISO z39.48-1992 (Permanence of Paper).
Printed in the United States of America.

19  18  17  16  15  14  13  12  11     9  8  7  6  5  4  3  2  1
First printing

FOR

Joanne Morey

Ralph Lipoth

Brian O'Grady

Laura Frye

*and*

Matthias Shulte

A teacher affects eternity;
he can never tell where his influence stops.

—HENRY BROOKS ADAMS

# CONTENTS

| | | |
|---|---|---|
| | *Preface* | ix |
| | *Acknowledgments* | xiii |
| | *Introduction:* THE SITUATION | 1 |
| PART *One* | MISSION: CTF AEGIS | 17 |
| PART *Two* | MISSION: TF ORION | 83 |
| PART *Three* | EXECUTION | 225 |
| | *Conclusion* | 305 |
| | *List of Terms and Acronyms* | 309 |
| | *Notes* | 315 |
| | *Index* | 319 |

# PREFACE

In the summer of 2006, the Taliban and Al Qaeda mounted their most ambitious assault on the people of Afghanistan since their loss of power in 2001. Focusing their efforts on four provinces located in Operation Enduring Freedom's (OEF's) Regional Command South (RC South), the enemy initiated a desperate dual with Afghan, American, British, Canadian, Dutch, and other allied forces who were led by a Canadian brigade headquarters and supported by an American division headquarters. It was only through the perseverance, bravery, and flexibility of the soldiers in this coalition that disaster was averted.

Counterinsurgency war, as we have all been relearning since 2001, is a complex mechanism with numerous moving parts operating at many levels, not all of which are visible to the naked eye. In the case of the war in Afghanistan, it is futile to attempt to understand the essence of the war from solely a tactical or a strategic position. The tactical sometimes becomes the strategic; combat cannot be conducted outside the context of national development and (re)construction. The enemy never goes along with the program and rarely separates his operations into the neat packages that we use to describe the levels of war at Western military colleges. Similarly, it is difficult to describe the nature of counterinsurgency war in Afghanistan in a single volume because it has evolved from 2001 to 2010. Afghanistan is a demographically diverse and rugged country. The situation changes annually, even monthly. Midcourse adjustment is the norm. Organizations—and more importantly, people—change. Continuity is extremely difficult to achieve.

*Fighting for Afghanistan* operates from a specific vantage point. In order to capture those moving parts and how they interact, this book looks at the activities of Combined Task Force (CTF) AEGIS, led by Brigadier General Dave Fraser, and Task Force (TF) ORION, led by Lieutenant Colonel Ian Hope. CTF AEGIS was a Canadian-led multinational brigade headquarters that was responsible for five battalion-sized task forces. At the start of our story, only three of these task forces were deployed: a Romanian battalion that handled security for Kandahar Air Field (KAF), CTF AEGIS' main base; an American battalion conducting counterinsurgency operations in Zabol province; and a Canadian battle group operating in Kandahar province. A British battle group and a Dutch battle group were in the process of deploying to the region when all hell broke loose. TF ORION, the Canadian battle group, occupied a central position in this drama both geographically, because Kandahar province is the center of the affected region, and operationally, because of how TF ORION was equipped, structured, and employed in the course of events.

CTF AEGIS and TF ORION deployed in January–February 2006, just after I left Kandahar where I had spent some time with the Provincial Reconstruction Team (PRT) observing its operations. As soon as I finished teaching my classes at Royal Military College that spring, I badgered the chief of the land staff, Lieutenant General Andy Leslie, and the commander of CTF AEGIS, Brigadier General Dave Fraser, to let me return. They bugged the commander of the newly established Canadian Expeditionary Forces Command, Lieutenant General Mike Gauthier, who agreed. Very soon I was on a plane back to KAF. This was an amazing stroke of luck. I arrived just at the time the enemy was escalating his operations. In addition, most of the media had gone home because the operational tempo appeared to be lower and the novelty of the Canadian deployment had fallen away.

My intent was to capture the brigade–battle group "slice" of the action: what it was like to fight in Afghanistan, how the two commanders envisioned the campaign, and what actually happened on the ground. I also wound up closely observing the tactical application of the plans on numerous occasions. Consequently, I spent the summer of 2006 observing operations from the Joint Operations Centre (JOC) at the CTF AEGIS headquarters all the way down to company level, when I joined "A" Company, 1st Battalion Princess Patricia's Canadian Light Infantry (1 PPCLI), and followed them into the Battle of Pashmul. This book is based on my observations and experiences during that time.

*Fighting for Afghanistan* is the third book in an Afghanistan trilogy. *Enduring the Freedom: A Rogue Historian in Afghanistan* looks at the situation in the spring of 2003, and *Confronting the Chaos* examines the conflict in 2004 and 2005. These books are not intended to be a collective definitive history of the war in Afghanistan, but rather are intended to record what it was like during these times, how the war was fought, and what our people—Canadians, Americans, Afghans, and others—accomplished.

Some caveats. This work in no way represents the official views of any Canadian government agency or organization, nor those of any international organization or ally—nor would I ever want it to. Military operations are a human endeavor and by their nature extremely stressful. Not everybody gets along all the time. Every possible human behavior comes out under this level of stress. In some cases, people regret aggressive behavior toward others, bury the hatchet later, and move on. In other cases, they do not, and animosities fester that can have an impact on how events are interpreted. National pride plays a significant role in how these matters are handled, both publicly and privately, in the short and long terms. I was privy to this behavior on numerous occasions. It is not my intent to present a salacious exposé of coalition or personal in-fighting. Understand that this happens on every coalition operation and has since warfare began. When I do discuss disagreements and frustrations, it is with the intent of capturing the facts on the ground and how they affected the situation as it was in play. My comments are not meant to pass some kind of universal judgment on the leaders involved. Mistakes get made. Clausewitz and Murphy wander all over the battlefield.

I also had this manuscript examined for purely operational security considerations. Thankfully, there were very few issues in that realm. A small number of intelligence-related and counter-IED (improvised explosive device) matters were blurred for publication.

My perspectives are by no means the final word on what happened and I willingly admit that I may be proven wrong later. What I recorded, though, is what happened or appeared to be happening at the time I was in the room, in the back of a light armored vehicle (LAV), or flying around in a helicopter. That said, there were a number of inflammatory things said and aspects of serious personality conflicts that I have chosen not to discuss here because it would detract from the story I want to tell. The dialogue herein is as I recall it at the time and is recounted without malice. As usual we must give consideration that no two people remember events exactly the same way.

# ACKNOWLEDGMENTS

Thanks...

To all the men and women who served with CTF AEGIS and TF ORION: without your help and your support at every turn, this book would not have been possible. That even goes to the people I locked horns with on occasion. To Brigadier General Dave Fraser for requesting my presence in Afghanistan, to Lieutenant Colonel Ian Hope for making it all happen on the ground. To Lieutenant General Andy Leslie and Lieutenant General Mike Gauthier and their staffs for supporting my work from Kingston to Ottawa to Kandahar. To Lieutenant General Ben Freakley for talking to me in depth when the heat was off.

To the men of TF ORION's Niner Tac, in particular Corporal David "Stitch" Hayward, Corporal Greg Davis, Corporal Keith Parsons, Master Corporal Greg White, Private Nigel Williams, and especially my phlegmatic driver Corporal Neal Carswell.

To Captain Kevin Barry for his friendship and particularly for his calmness under fire when it mattered most.

To the snipers, especially Billy B. who took an interest in my education.

To Major Kirk Gallinger, for taking me along with "A" Company.

To Company Sergeant Major Pete Leger, especially during Operation Zahar.

To the men of One Niner: Corporal Brian "Gibby" Gibson, Master Corporal Steve Pichovich, Corporal Gerry Strong, and Corporal Chris Raike, plus any atts or dets I've missed.

To Warrant Officer Mark Pickford and Master Corporal Chuck Prodonick, for being consummate professionals.

To Major Harj Sajjan, for his deep insights.

To my brother, Colonel (now General) Hussein, for our friendship.

To Padre Suleyman Demiray, for helping me, Jesus tap-dancing Christ, to see the light more clearly.

To Yusuf Zoi, once again, as ever.

To Major Nick Grimshaw, for his deep insights and support.

To Major Bill Fletcher, for the Gumbad job.

To Captain Jon Hamilton, for his bravery.

To my old friend Major Erik Liebert for explaining the machinations of the PRT and Kandahari politics to me—and holding all those tigers down, including his own. BTFB, Champ—yeah!

To all our interpreters, especially Niaz Mohommad, Ahmad Faizi, Bashir, Sami, Aktar, Aktar's brother, the Sheikh, the Mullah, Aziz, Mohommad Hasan, Mohebullah, Qatr, Usman, Lucky, and Rocky. As the Pashtuns say, "What's old is gold."

To the redoubtable "Q," Captain Quentin Innis, and indomitable Captain Julie Roberge, and Captain Darcy Heddon for their intellectual engagement and their friendship.

To Major Mason Stalker—you've come a long way, baby, since Kosovo!

To Captain Walter Martin and Sergeant Dan Guillaume, for protecting me during Operation Zahar.

To (now) Second Lieutenant Martha Rzechowska, Captain Chris Hunt, and Captain Tom Nield, for the insights, ruminations, and great conversations.

To Lieutenant Colonel Shane Schreiber, Lieutenant Colonel Mark Brewer, Lieutenant Colonel Tim Bishop, and Colonel Chris Vernon for letting me be there when it mattered.

To Pam Isfeld, for her friendship and her attempts to get me to understand and demonstrate by personal example that not all people in the Department of Foreign Affairs and International Trade (DFAIT) are willfully evil.

To Christina Green, Renata Pistone, and Michael Callan for the same, vis-à-vis the Canadian International Development Agency (CIDA).

To Major Randy Graddic for services rendered over the years. We'll always have that mortar attack.

To Major Dave Buchanan, for getting me in when I needed to get in.

To Lieutenant Colonel Simon Hetherington, for listening.

There were numerous and sometimes anonymous people who drifted in and provided something—information, a piece of kit, a helicopter, moral support—just at the time it was needed, and who drifted on not expecting thanks. It is those little things that make the world go 'round.

And finally, to those in the special operations and intelligence world who assisted me in various ways at various times—yet again: I salute you—yet again.

The staff at Naval Institute Press deserves recognition not only for *Fighting for Afghanistan*, but also for *Confronting the Chaos*. Without the support of Rick Russell, Adam Kane, Judy Heise, Susan Corrado, and Alison Hope these books would not have existed—and certainly not in the form they are in. And finally, thanks to my friend and agent Fritz Heinzen for everything.

Oh yes. I almost forgot. There are the critics, particularly the anonymous ones. Every time you do what you do, every snide personal slight, every belittlement, every ad hominem attack only strengthens my resolve to ensure that the efforts of the men and women of the coalitions in Afghanistan are captured in my way, on my terms, and in my words. I invite you to be creative, not destructive. I challenge you to have the intestinal fortitude to try your hand at writing about your experiences for public consumption. Thanks again.

And for those who are intrigued by a nontraditional approach, thanks for taking a chance. Traditional narrative cannot effectively capture what it was like to be there. *Fighting for Afghanistan* is the best I can do to put you into the fight, so you can see our people in action in one of the toughest combat environments in the world.

*Introduction*

# THE SITUATION

What was the situation in early 2006? The people of Afghanistan were in trouble. Recently freed from Al Qaeda–supported Taliban domination with all its accompanying backwards medieval paraphernalia, they were confronted with a revitalized enemy and the weakening resolve of the international community who were, at least on the surface, committed to the rehabilitation of the devastated country.

The United States of America was in trouble. The triumphal takedown of the Hussein regime in Iraq and its replacement with a fanatical insurgency and sectarian violence were draining American resources. Farther east, Osama bin Laden and Ayman al-Zawahiri, the men who had conceived the 9/11 attacks, had not been found, and Al Qaeda continued to scheme somewhere in the twilight world that existed between Afghanistan and Pakistan. Others, sensing American weakness, were starting to feed the insurgencies in both countries for their own purposes. Gulliver was getting pinned down.

The original plan conceived by U.S. Central Command in 2003 was to leave minimal forces behind in Afghanistan in case High Value Target-1 (HVT-1) and High Value Target-2 (HVT-2) emerged from cover, to develop intelligence, and then to prepare a force to go in if it looked like these men and their associates had acquired sanctuary on the Arabian Peninsula or the Horn of Africa. At the same time, a wholly separate war was under way in Iraq. There were new HVTs: Saddam Hussein and his heirs, Thing 1 and Thing 2, were still on the loose. The ledger where national credibility was measured, that one critical commodity in international affairs that every nation needs, was blood-red in the case of the United States. The opposition and the media were circling like sharks. People who in September 2001 claimed that everybody was a citizen of New York now distanced themselves from a president, his administration, and what was an increasingly unpopular war. Conspiracy theories abounded, aided and abetted by fringe and not-so-fringe media, and enhanced with outright disinformation.

At the same time, the one success story in the war against Al Qaeda, Afghanistan, tottered in a precarious state. Though the Taliban had been stripped away and the Al Qaeda infrastructure beneath it had been ripped up by Operation Enduring Freedom (OEF), civil war between victorious anti-Taliban groups was only narrowly avoided. That was accomplished through the efforts of some of the nations contributing to the International Security Assistance Force (ISAF) with help from OEF and those Afghans committed to the stabilization of the country.

But now the European-dominated NATO was in trouble. And, like its American member, the organization was loath to admit it publicly. NATO committed to expand the ISAF stabilization effort throughout Afghanistan and to link it with nebulous development objectives that would try the patience of a Nobel Laureate economic expert. The unpopularity of the war in Iraq, however, prompted skittish behavior on the part of several European minority governments, and the international and domestic media in several countries had linked action to support Afghanistan with action supportive of American efforts in Iraq. The guilt-by-association illogic was so strong that the NATO expansion plan was in jeopardy. It is not melodramatic to assert that the fate of the Afghan people lay in the balance. That fate became inextricably intertwined with something that planners blandly called Stage III Expansion.

The origins of OEF are as straightforward as the origins of the ISAF are convoluted. OEF started as a Taliban-destroying, Al Qaeda–hunting operation that by 2004 inadvertently developed stabilization and development functions. ISAF was a stabilization force designed to secure Kabul that inadvertently developed a stabilization and development function and then leaned toward counterinsurgency and counterterrorism. There were two plans, two leaders, two staffs, two different political authorities, and different rules of engagement, not to mention disparate military capabilities. Any reasonable observer could see that having ISAF and OEF coexist was an outright violation of Unity of Command, one of the principles of

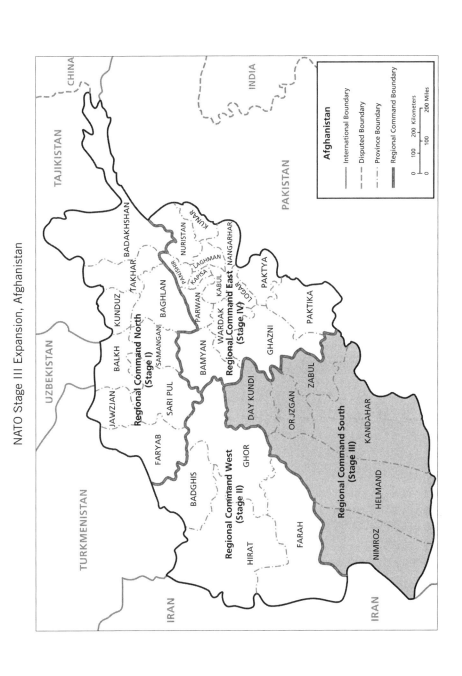

war. The enemy could and would chip away at the fissures between the two. As Napoleon once said, he'd rather fight a coalition than be part of one. In Afghanistan the enemy was fighting two coalitions.

Nations, leaders, and international organizations, however, aren't always reasonable. The situation was aggravated by simplistic analysis in the academic and analytic communities as well as by the media, who declared that ISAF was "UN peacekeeping" and that therefore OEF was "American warfighting." This state of affairs was deliberately encouraged by some who wanted to distance themselves from the United States in the wake of the Iraq invasion. The wording in the mandates assigned to the two missions was frequently used to distinguish between them from a legal perspective. Public perception became firmly focused on the differences between OEF and ISAF, and not on their similarities.

Some elements in the U.S. government wanted out of Afghanistan so they could focus on Iraq, while others wanted to stay with a presence designed to maintain situational awareness so that Bin Laden and Al Zawahiri could be grabbed. The logical path was to have ISAF expand throughout Afghanistan and take over from OEF, with the exception of the HVT-hunting function. The Americans would never relinquish this task to an international organization—not only because of 9/11, but also because of the Bosnian experience where a NATO ally repeatedly compromised the hunt for high-value war criminals in order to embarrass the United States.

So how do you get two elephants to mate? In 2003, NATO agreed to take over PRTs and their protection in northern Afghanistan as a pilot program. This was the first expansion of NATO ISAF outside Kabul and it now divided the country into two separate commands: ISAF and OEF. This move, however, reinforced the public perception of the differences between the missions even though the intention was to eventually replace OEF with ISAF throughout the country. NATO was seen to be progressively expanding into and securing "safe" areas, with the added perception that there was "progressive stability" in the country. Getting NATO countries to shoulder the burden proved difficult. The lineup of NATO nations that wanted to join ISAF with substantial forces was short. Even those few nations would have to be enticed to join.

In early 2004 there was more political momentum in NATO and options were starting to develop. One idea was to NATO-ize all the PRTs in the country, then progressively hand off sectors of the country from

OEF to ISAF. At that point, the American OEF commander would change hats and become the ISAF commander. The block here was, of course, France, who wanted to lead the mission. The Americans refused to turn over control of special operations forces (SOF) and intelligence "enablers" to any French-commanded NATO force, especially when a French government who had taken a very public stance against the United States over Iraq was in power.

To further complicate matters, the level of violence in the OEF operating areas was much higher than it was in ISAF operating areas. This related to the Pashtun ethnic dominance in the OEF areas and their proximity to Pakistan more than anything else, but the public perception was that there was a war in one part of the country and peace in the other. ISAF participation had been "sold" to those publics as a "peacekeeping" mission, so why would a "peacekeeping" mission go into a violent area and fight a war? The perception that there was "progressive stability" in the country ran into a brick wall.

By 2005, OEF had handed off Regional Command West (RC West) to ISAF, putting about half the country under each command. That was Stage II Expansion. The intent was to achieve Stage III Expansion and Stage IV Expansion and hand over most of OEF's functions to ISAF, except for the HVT hunt. And then the effort stalled. None of the Europeans wanted to take control of RC South or Stage III Expansion. RC South was centered on Kandahar, the place media outlets kept telling their audiences was the "spiritual heartland of the Taliban" (debatable), that the insurgency was based here (it wasn't), and where the violence was at an all-time high (incorrect). Most European NATO members were quite happy to operate in RC North and RC West, where there was little or no Taliban-led, Al Qaeda–supported insurgency, far away from the enemy support areas inside Pakistan.

The country that stepped up to the plate was Canada. As of 2005, there was a new government in Canada, one that wanted to repair relations with the United States. It was a government that wanted to move away from the UN-centric "peacekeeping" image manufactured and promoted by the previous government in defiance of Canada's history and her interests. Canada had been continuously committed to the Afghanistan effort since 2001 in various ways, and none of them was in "peacekeeping" capacities. There had been a hiatus after Canada relinquished command of ISAF just before the mission expanded beyond Kabul during which a number of options were under consideration. The Stage III Expansion crisis occurred during this time and the decision was made by the Canadian government to commit a PRT and SOF in 2005 to RC South and then take command of RC South in 2006 under OEF command. Canada agreed to muster support from other NATO countries and then effect a transfer of authority from OEF to ISAF, thus launching Stage III Expansion. The tools to do this would be a Canadian-led multinational headquarters for RC South called CTF AEGIS, and a Canadian battle group and a PRT called TF ORION that would operate in Kandahar province. It was a fitting combination: Aegis, the shield of Zeus, and Orion, the hunter.

The plan was ambitious. The transfer of authority from OEF to ISAF was dependent on whether the American commanders thought that the situation was stable enough to warrant transfer. There was significant American and European political pressure to accelerate NATO expansion in the summer of 2006. The more-prudent American commanders in Afghanistan, however, wanted proof that a non-American force could handle Kandahar before they moved on with Stage III Expansion and then to Stage IV Expansion in RC East, where the bulk of the forces were American. Some of these commanders even wanted an American brigade from the 10th Mountain Division to take over in RC South. There was no certainty that Stage III Expansion even would be carried out in 2006. Canada was now firmly on center stage and the deadly drama was about to begin.

**Enemy Forces**

Who are the insurgents? The answer to this question depends on what year and where in the province we are looking at. The insurgency evolved year to year with different players playing greater or lesser roles. In general, there were the remnants of Al Qaeda's conventional formations and Al Qaeda–supported jihadis. There were the remnants of the Taliban regime's conventional formations and local opponents to the Karzai government who dubbed themselves Taliban. There are the professional killers from Gulbiddin Hekmatyar's HiG (Hezb-I Gulbiddin) organization as well as the highly motivated fighters from the Haqqani Tribal Network (or Organization; HTN). By 2003 an organization called the Quetta Shura emerged to act as a mechanism for these diverse groups so their leaders could discuss and coordinate policy, strategy, and operations.

There are other well-armed entities in Kandahar province that are not part of the Quetta Shura yet pose problems for the security forces and the counterinsurgents. The first of these entities are the various police groups in the province, which especially pose problems when they aren't being paid regularly. The second are the so-called drug barons and their private armies. These narco groups tended to be based on tribe and family, are devoted to making money from the poppy crop, and will align themselves against anybody interfering with their activities.

Similarly, the Pashtun tribal code of Pashtunwali affords various forms of blood revenge between aggrieved parties over the course of generations. Blood feuds involving RPGs and AK-47s are not necessarily Taliban violence, nor are they necessarily insurgent violence.

Consequently, not all violence in Kandahar province is Taliban violence. Every possible permutation of alliances between these groups—Taliban, Al Qaeda, HiG, Haqqani Tribal Network (or Organization; HTO), narcos, police, tribal groupings—exists throughout southern Afghanistan. Every incident, every action, has to be carefully examined to see exactly what the motives are behind the specific use of violence by a particular entity or entities. Some Taliban violence may even serve multiple purposes for different groups. This state of affairs poses significant challenges to any attempt to generalize about the insurgency in Afghanistan.

In early 2006 Afghan analysts, led by the general director of the National Directorate of Security (NDS), concluded a study that confirmed that, in their view, the Taliban threat was much more developed than previously understood, and that it had three phases: strategic survival and reorganization, establishment of foothold bases in remote areas, and mass mobilization using tribal and religious elements.[1] Amrullah Saleh, head of the Afghan National Directorate of Security from 2004 to 2010, and his helpers believed that the Taliban was focusing on several Durrani tribes—the Noorzai, Popalzai, Alikozai, and Ishaqzai, in particular—to get them to shift allegiance and carry the south with them.

The Taliban's objectives, according to the NDS, were "to isolate Afghanistan, discredit the democratic process, and eventually create a parallel government in the villages or the rural communities." Small teams from the Taliban's own areas were sent in to identify progovernment people, intimidate them, and offer to protect poppy fields from government eradication efforts. At the same time, schools were converted to madrassas (a Muslim educational institution associated with a mosque) so that the young could be indoctrinated to submit to the Taliban. All this was protected behind a shield of hit-and-run operations and symbolic targeting.

The enemy fully understood, according to Saleh, the role of the mosque in the fight: "The mosque has served as a tipping point of major political upheavals in the past three hundred years of Afghan history. But this institution has never been as crucial as it has been in the past thirty years." The Taliban also knew how to use "young Pakistan-trained Mullahs to glorify their cause . . . they have chosen the Mullahs as their strategic tool for propaganda and brainwashing of the rural communities . . . there are 107 mosques in the city of Kandahar out of which eleven are preaching antigovernment themes."

Poppy eradication was also problematic: "Big landlords can actually buy the police and much of the destroyed fields belong to poor peasants. They in turn become new recruits of the Taliban." Significantly, "The anti-narcotics campaign of 2006 may give us an image of a determined state in the western capitals, but on the ground we are losing the clash of will—somehow forcing the villagers to be on the side of the insurgents."

The Taliban was estimated to be in the second phase of the insurgency and attempting to transition to the third. Their inability to establish a parallel government at the district level was inhibiting their progression to the third phase; the coalition and Afghan effort, no matter how flawed it was, was a serious impediment to their progress. Yes, the Taliban could mobilize in the rural areas—but could they control all of them all the time? Could they eventually take the urban areas and consolidate them?

Saleh ominously noted, "This war has no tactical solution if we do not fight the Taliban at the theatre level as well and that is to attack their leadership and their headquarters where they are. For as long as neighboring Pakistan remains sympathetic to their cause we will not be able to bring it to a complete end."

Saleh, in general, wasn't wrong. What the analysis missed was the possibility that the enemy might prematurely escalate to near-conventional operations earlier or attempt some form of coup de main instead of progressing in a linear fashion from strategic survival to mass mobilization. There was a historical tradition of something like "foco-ism" in Afghanistan whereby a small group of determined, organized, and armed men create social momentum through the use of extreme and targeted violence against a city in order to generate a fait accompli with the population.² It is safe to say that in early 2006 nobody in the intelligence community thought of foco-ism; it was a discredited, controversial insurgent theory thought only to exist in Latin America. Indeed, there were no firm indicators whatsoever before June that something was amiss immediately outside Kandahar City.

**Friendly Forces**

The Canadian-led CTF AEGIS was an augmented brigade headquarters, whereas TF ORION was a Canadian infantry battalion with armored reconnaissance (recce), artillery, and combat engineers attached. Brigadier General Dave Fraser was "double hatted" as the Canadian theater commander and commander CTF AEGIS.

Although this book deals with the operations of CTF AEGIS and TF ORION, both organizations operated within the larger context of OEF. In Afghanistan, OEF was under the control of an American corps headquarters called Combined Forces Command–Afghanistan (CFC-A). Its subordinate commands included the Combined Joint Special Operations Task Force (CJSOTF), and a division-sized headquarters called Combined Joint Task Force 76 (CJTF 76). The CJTF 76 headquarters rotated between various American divisional headquarters and was augmented with allied staff officers as well as with Americans.

Before CTF AEGIS arrived in 2006, CJTF-76 was commanded by the Southern European Task Force; it controlled two brigade-sized formations: CTF DEVIL and CTF BAYONET. CTF DEVIL was responsible for RC East and included two airborne and one Marine battalion, plus the PRTs in its area of responsibility. CTF BAYONET handled RC South and consisted of three battalions, one of which was guarding the vital Kandahar Air Field in a static role and several PRTs. CTF AEGIS was slated to replace CTF BAYONET in February 2006, so the operational situation that CTF AEGIS inherited is important to our story.

CTF BAYONET, led by Colonel Kevin Owens, operated in a complex volatile environment without enough forces and had to share battle space with the CJSOTF, an organization that was fighting its own war using different methods, not always in conjunction with the conventional forces. In general, the Taliban was hiding in the seams between Farah and

Helmand provinces, in particular in a long mountainous seam that connected northern Helmand, northern Kandahar, southern Oruzgan, and western Zabol provinces. The enemy was also present in three remote areas in southeastern Zabol province. CTF BAYONET assessed throughout 2005 that the Taliban had fractured leadership and was regrouping, but was starting to focus more and more on Kandahar City and increase its use of IEDs. Reconstruction was stalled in the provinces because of a perception of insecurity and the lack of attention given to the rural districts by the provincial governments, especially in Kandahar province.[3]

Unlike CTF AEGIS, CTF BAYONET's area of operations did not include all of RC South: there were five Joint Special Operations Areas (JSOAs) that the CJSOTF was responsible for. The Dutch SOF operated in Registan and Shorabak districts, and a French SOF task force handled Spin Boldak and Maruf districts. Their purpose was to interdict the Taliban crossing the border from Pakistan. The southeastern part of Zabol was another JSOA, with the same task but under the command of U.S. Special Forces. The northern half of Helmand province and all of Oruzgan province were divided into two JSOAs. TF 31, the First of the Third Special Forces Group, operated in that province, working alongside the Afghan National Army (ANA) units they were mentoring and alongside coalition SOF from Australia, Canada, the Czech Republic, and Germany. Consequently, CTF BAYONET handled central and northern Kandahar province, central Zabol province, and central and southern Helmand province. Nimroz province was essentially left to its own devices and had no BAYONET or CJSOTF forces operating in it.

There were BAYONET-controlled PRTs in all four provinces, but there were only two maneuver battalions available, so one of them, 2-503 Infantry (TF ROCK), was stationed in Zabol, and the other, 3-319 Airborne Field Artillery Regiment, commanded by Lieutenant Colonel Bert Ges and reroled as infantry (TF GUNDEVILS), was based in Kandahar. A company-sized recce unit, the 74th Long-Range Surveillance Detachment, deployed to Helmand, while a Romanian battalion protected Kandahar Air Field. American PRTs were located in every province except Kandahar, where the Canadian-led PRT was established in July 2005. Clearly, CTF BAYONET was stretched thin.

CTF BAYONET had three primary tasks in 2005: First, defeat the Taliban and its allies in Zabol, Kandahar, and Helmand provinces. Second, deny the enemy sanctuary inside its area of responsibility. Finally,

BAYONET had to establish secure conditions so that the provincial elections could be held in the fall of 2005.[4] The first task was impossible, given BAYONET's available resources, but was essentially an idealistic end-state established to give operational focus. The second task was achievable, but only for limited periods and only in conjunction with the special forces operating in the northern JSOAs. The third task was achievable, and the provinces in RC South were able to hold elections without a substantial amount of Taliban interference, though voter turnout was low compared to the rest of the country.

None of these objectives, however, directly addressed reconstruction and thus didn't address the grievances in the rural areas that the Taliban were playing on to gain support, though it must be said that all three objectives were supporting efforts to establish legitimate Afghan governance, a precondition to any counterinsurgency campaign. It was only after the Canadian PRT deployed and conducted long-range patrols that CTF BAYONET discovered that the situation in the more remote districts was much more unstable than people thought and that military force wasn't necessarily the best tool to use in all circumstances.

CTF BAYONET held the line as best it could throughout 2005, with TF GUNDEVILS disrupting enemy activity in the northern part of Kandahar province and TF ROCK keeping the Taliban off-balance in Zabol. TF-31 and its coalition partners also disrupted enemy activity in northern Helmand, Oruzgan, and northern Kandahar provinces, but none of the task forces was designed to hold ground, and in any event there weren't enough Afghan security forces to do so. The American PRTs were limited in how much development they could facilitate and tended to do smaller projects that had more of a direct impact on BAYONET's operations. There was no large-scale national development plan yet anyway, though the Afghan National Development Strategy (ANDS) was under discussion throughout 2005.

## Command and Control

The Southern European Task Force was replaced with the 10th Mountain Division's divisional headquarters in February 2006, roughly at the same time CTF AEGIS and TF ORION deployed from Canada to Afghanistan. The new CJTF-76, led by Major General Ben Freakley, commanded CTF SPARTAN in RC East and CTF AEGIS in RC South.

CTF AEGIS operated within the context of CJTF-76, so it is important to explain the nature of this relationship. In general, U.S. Army formations don't like operating with allied division or brigade-sized formations under command, though they generally don't have a problem working with allied battalion-sized units because they can be relegated to secondary supporting tasks. The reasons for this relate to the lack of communications, planning, and logistic interoperability between U.S. Army formations and allied formations. They also relate in part to efforts to protect access to the United States' multibillion dollar intelligence apparatus and other high-value national functions.

For example, American divisional headquarters rigidly expect that the subordinate brigades in the division will obey specific, direct orders and will comply to the letter with a centralized division headquarters-generated plan. The Canadian approach, employed by CTF AEGIS, was more flexible. AEGIS staff examined the nature of the situation in Afghanistan, looked at CJTF-76's intent, and crafted its own campaign plan for RC South to accommodate this intent as well as to address regional conditions. In this view, CJTF-76 was there to support CTF AEGIS with divisional- and corps-level resources, not to micromanage it on the ground. CJTF-76 staffs continually demanded extremely detailed contingency and operations (ops) plans in their format, which occupied a disproportionate amount of AEGIS staff power. This clash of cultures played itself out throughout 2006 as the two formations, their staffs, and their commanders learned to coexist.

CJTF-76 also had its own campaign plan. The commander established his intent, which was expressed by a series of verbs: defeat, dominate, develop, engage/convince, and facilitate. The divisional staff saw what resources were at hand, and then crafted several divisional-level plans that essentially shifted scarce resources back and forth between RC East and RC South to meet the commanders' intent. In general, the CJTF-76 campaign plan focused on sanctuary denial. The divisional staff identified where they thought the Taliban were hiding, and these became the priority targets for the operations. The reduction of the sanctuaries was putatively linked in all these plans to protecting emergent governance structures. During the course of CJTF-76's tenure, there were three such divisional plans: operations Mountain Lion, Mountain Thrust, and Mountain Fury. Each plan was geographically based and sequenced.

Mountain Lion went first in early 2006 in Nuristan a Konar and in Nangahar. Mountain Thrust was designed to go into Oruzgan, northern Helmand, northern Kandahar, and Zabol in June–July, then Mountain Fury would finish things off in Paktika, Paktia, and Kowst in July–August.[5] Part of the effort was to facilitate Stage III expansion from OEF to ISAF.

CTF AEGIS, on the other hand, had its own campaign plan and tried to focus on three areas. The first was governance. CTF AEGIS wanted its units to engage provincial and district leaders in order to generate support for the coalition's presence. The second was security. The Afghan army and police needed to be built up as rapidly as possible. Enemy IED networks had to be hunted down to reduce the strategic information operations pressure being brought to bear on the coalition. Third was development. CTF AEGIS wanted to strengthen linkages between the development agencies, the provincial and district authorities, and the NGOs. A precondition for development was to conduct detailed economic, demographic, and tribal recces and analysis so that situational awareness in the rural parts of RC South could be improved.[6]

In effect, there were two different ways of achieving the same aim—one American and one Canadian. It came down to who controlled what resources and how they were employed: the "boots on the ground" conventional and Special Operations soldiers, and the enablers. Conducting operations without the enablers was not an option.

## TASK FORCE ORION

Commanded by Lieutenant Colonel Ian Hope, TF ORION was based on 1st Battalion, Princess Patricia's Canadian Light Infantry. The Deputy Commanding Officer (DCO) was the methodical Major Todd Strickland. Major Mason Stalker handled the ins and outs of the Tactical Operations Centre. There were three infantry companies, "A," "B," and "C." "A" and "C" companies, commanded by Major Kirk Gallinger and Major Bill Fletcher, respectively, both came from 1st Battalion, but "B" Company, commanded by Major Nick Grimshaw, was brought in from 2nd Battalion. Initially, "A" and "C" companies were fully mechanized and mounted in the LAV III eight-wheeled mechanized infantry combat vehicle (MICV) armed with 25-mm cannon. "B" Company was equipped with G-Wagon patrol vehicles but then received eight LAV IIIs. A new armored patrol vehicle, the RG-31 Nyala equipped with a Remote Weapons System, also arrived in-theater while ORION was deploying.

There was a four-gun battery of M-777 155-mm guns from 1 Royal Canadian Horse Artillery (1 RCHA) under Major Steve Gallagher. A combat engineer squadron drawn mostly from 1 Combat Engineer Regiment was led by Major Trevor Webb. Normally, a battle group structure like this had an administration company to handle logistics, but in order to save money those positions had been taken away and given to the National Support Element (NSE). There was a significant amount of doctrinal angst about this.

An armored recce and surveillance troop from the French-speaking 12e Régiment Blindé du Canada was also present. Commanded by Captain Brian Flemming, the troop was equipped with eight Coyote recce vehicles, which possessed mast-mounted sensor systems and turrets equipped with 25-mm cannons.

In a controversial move, the entire Kandahar PRT was placed under the command of TF ORION. The PRT was similar in structure to the previous PRT.[7] The PRT had "OGDs" (Other Government Departments)—USAID, the civilian police (CIVPOL); Canadian International Development Agency; and representatives from the Department of Foreign Affairs. There was a Civil–Military Cooperation (CIMIC) organization (similar to a U.S. Army Civil Affairs unit). The idea was that "B" Company would provide mobile force protection to the PRT, so it was initially mounted in G-Wagon armored Mercedes vehicles, some of which sported a machine-gun turret, and not in LAV IIIs. When the previous PRT commander was repatriated early, Major Erik Liebert from 1st Battalion Princess Patricia's Canadian Light Infantry took over until Lieutenant Colonel Simon Hetherington could be brought into theater in July.

There were several Canadian organizations present in Kandahar that didn't report to TF ORION but that supported it or worked with allied units in various ways. The NSE handled administrative and logistics support to Canadian units in Afghanistan. Commanded by Lieutenant Colonel John Conrad, the NSE controlled maintenance, recovery, supply, and all the other vital sinews of war, plus the military police.[8] A signals squadron unofficially dubbed TF MERCURY handled all the signals support for the NSE, and TF ORION. A detachment of 2 (Electronic Warfare) Squadron equipped with Mobile Electronic Warfare Teams (MEWTS) provided significant support to TF ORION and allies.

Major Mark Godefroy headed up the All-Source Intelligence Center (ASIC) in a special separate compound where the "secret squirrels" went about performing the dark arts of intelligence collection, collation, and dissemination. There was also the Tactical Unmanned Aerial Vehicle (TUAV) detachment. The TUAV unit commanded by Major John Casey was manned by a mix of gunners and air force personnel. The TUAV in this case was the CU-116 Sperwer unmanned aerial vehicle, of which there were nine deployed from a compound on the periphery of Kandahar Air Field.

PART *One*

# MISSION: CTF AEGIS

This time, it didn't start with an Airbus. It started with Air Canada and a fortuitous meeting with Major General Stu Beare and Captain Mike Duggan, in Pearson International Airport in Toronto. I'd known Stu for years and watched him and his staff in action in Bosnia in the waning days of the Stabilization Force (SFOR). We talked about my experiences with the PRTs and the challenges they were having coming up with a force. I learned that, since I had left the PRT earlier in the year, there had been substantial changes. As I left to catch my flight, Stu said, "Have a great trip! And for Christ's sake don't get hurt! You're the only guy we've got recording all this."

I was jammed into economy with the rest of the aerocattle. As a government employee I wasn't entitled to be pampered and didn't really expect it, but sleeping on the marble floor in Vienna waiting for my connection was going too far. On the flight over the jabbering blue-haired lady with the English accent kept asking annoying questions. The questions stopped and I took the pause as an opportunity to slip on the noise-cancelling headset I brought with me and to drift away on some Hans Zimmer submarine music.

I had a stopover at Wolfgang Amadeus Mozart International Airport. There was Mozart everything, everywhere. I immediately consumed a Viennese espresso to blank out the visually screaming artwork that ordered me in a Schwarzenegger tone of voice to "Shop Me, Amadeus!"

The coffee shop was packed. A cloud of smoke hung over the tables and I contemplated hauling out a cigar to contribute to the carcinogens when an attractive lady approached and asked if she could sit with me: there was nowhere else to sit. Her name was Irene and she was Swedish.

"So, Irene, what do you do?"

"I'm a nurse."

"Where do you work?"

"I'm with the Swedish Army in Mazar-e Sharif in Afghanistan."

It was a day for coincidences. And it's always fun to talk with nurses, especially nurses like Irene who had served in Afghanistan, Darfur, and Kosovo. I learned that the camp at Maz had been hit with an outbreak of a gastrointestinal bug, taking 111 personnel out of service. Fever. Chills. Diarrhea. Emergency stocks of rehydration solution had to be flown in and rations deployed when it was learned that bad contractor-served food was the problem. Another strike against alternative service delivery. As every military historian knows, disease causes as much or more damage to a deployed force than enemy action. Nice to see nothing had changed in the twenty-first century.

I'll spare you the details of my arrival in KAF via C-130. By 2006 it was getting routine for me so I slept most of the way. I was assigned a transient bay in a tent between Canada House and the helicopter landing area part of KAF. I bumped into Dr. Anne Irwin from the University of Calgary who was conducting a sociological study and spending time with "C" Company. I went to ground around 2200, then was awakened by the siren at 2300. I groggily put on my body armor and rolled under the cot. But then I had to urinate so I walked over to the porta-john next to the bunker. A small group was already under concrete so when I was finished I joined them. Anne was there.

"Ho hum," I said, "Another stupid and ineffective rocket attack. Where did it land this time? The shit pond?" The more experienced people present and I had a good laugh. "Nah, it landed near the gravel pit. I didn't hear anything—no noise, no explosion." AH-64 Apache attack helicopters were lifting off to try and find the rocketeers. Maybe "CSI KAF" would discover that Hadji had eaten chicken before he fired the rocket . . . after the AHs were done with him. Or if the Romulans, as the Romanian battalion guarding KAF was called, killed him.

The soldiers were playing *Grand Theft Auto* on their PlayStation Portables in the bunker, while others chilled to their MP3 players. We chatted about video games. "You know," one said, "the soundtracks are getting better and better. It's like playing in a movie." I agreed: "Have you heard the soundtrack for the movie *Black Hawk Down*?" "Yeah!" Another said. "It reminds me of this place! I play it when I'm in the field." We talked about the music of Hans Zimmer, who specializes in movie soundtracks, and Rupert Gregson-Williams, who did the soundtrack for the game *Battlefield 2: Modern Combat*. Zimmer and Gregson-Williams always incorporate music from the geographic locale where the movie or game is happening into their soundtracks. The movie *Black Hawk Down*, for example, blends American rock with traditional Somali music, while the soundtrack from *The Peacemaker* has haunting music from Bosnia. I developed an attachment to the music of Afghan singer Ahmad Zahir the last trip and I let his music play in my head in the dark.

There was now a 100 percent roll call for Canadian personnel. A rumor started, fueled by a report in Al Jazeera, that two Canadian soldiers had been captured by the Taliban. The Canadian NSE was all cranked up. As the shit smell from the sewage pond wafted over us and a dust storm started, I chatted with a group of young soldiers who were with the Electrical and Mechanical Engineers (EME).

"There probably isn't anybody captured," one said. "The Taliban most likely are exploiting personnel effects found in a wrecked vehicle. That's why we've started to recover the wrecks."

"So they can't be exploited for I/O (information operations) purposes?"

"Yeah. Like, if they take pictures of them and put them on the net."

"So you guys in EME go out and recover the vehicles?"

"Oh yeah!" they all said simultaneously, "That's our job! We go outside the wire too," they told me proudly.

Outside the wire. That was a new term for me here. Outside the wire was clear, but what did being inside the wire mean? I asked.

"Well, some people are saying that people inside the wire aren't really at the same level of risk as those guys outside the wire."

Okay, here we go again. This goes back to when Christ was a corporal. In World War II, it was the rear echelon. In Vietnam, it was the derogatory term Rear Echelon Mother Fucker, or REMF. But was KAF really a "rear area"?

The war here had changed since I was here last and that was less than six months ago. Tim, one of the EME soldiers, explained the types of operations he was involved in. "There was this LAV early in the tour. It was stuck during an operation and there was no recovery, so two A-10s came in with 500-pound bombs and tried to destroy the vehicle. The locals salvaged the 25-mm gun and even the remains of the engine. On another occasion, a G-Wagon that was unrecoverable was destroyed in place. We were on another operation when an RG-31 Nyala had to be destroyed by dousing it with gas and then firing a 66-mm LAW at it."

My head whirled. I had just spent time with the PRT, poking around the more remote corners of Kandahar province as part of a low-level counterinsurgency effort. Nothing like this was going on then. Tim and his friends were describing events right out of the World War II. Destruction in place? Denial to the enemy? Those were concepts I learned during the Cold War if it looked like our vehicles were about to be captured.

"We were in this remote village, I'm not sure where," Tim explained. "This LAV was stuck and we came in to get it. The locals told us that we had to be out of there before dark, before the Taliban came and hurt them. They mobilized the entire village to help dig out the LAV and then clear a path so we could get the wrecker in to right the vehicle. They were cool: they helped us. An old man guided us out of the village complex himself."

"So you guys went in with recovery vehicles, set up a perimeter, and did the recovery?"

"Yeah. We have to be ready to fight back, right? We're not getting our balls cut off."

Vehicle recovery as a combat operation. Things had changed in Kandahar province. Dramatically. The "all clear" came an hour later. But sleep? That was, as the actor playing Robert McNamara in *Thirteen Days* says, for the weak. I wasn't going to get much over the next two months.

Anne Irwin and I had coffee.

"What's with this inside the wire/outside the wire stuff? That's new to me."

Anne explained that she had detected an informal hierarchy that developed among the troops. There was a pyramid of prestige. "It goes from being inside the wire, to being outside the wire. If you're outside the wire, it then progresses to going out on combat operations, then to being under fire or IED attack. If you're wounded in the fighting, that's the next level."

"You know what the problem with this model is, Anne?"

"What?"

"The tip of the pyramid is getting killed in combat. That's the ultimate in the informal prestige structure here."

There wasn't much more to say. Despite the fact we were both civilians, Anne and I worked outside the wire. It would be interesting to see where we fit into the pyramid.

## Combined Task Force AEGIS Modus Operandi

My first stop was to CTF AEGIS headquarters, located in the same building that Colonel John Campbell's headquarters occupied in 2003. I was looking for Brigadier General Dave Fraser's office and I encountered Major Dave Buchanan, his executive assistant, who ushered me in. Dave welcomed me to AEGIS and took me around to meet the staff. Like many of the Canadian officers at AEGIS and ORION, I had known Dave Fraser for some time; I had met him while I was writing the history of our mission to Kosovo. TF ORION, for example, was based on the lead Canadian infantry battalion that went into that Serbian province in 1999, so the junior officers from that time were now running things. Dave's deputy chief of staff, Lieutenant Colonel Shane Schreiber, was a dangerous intellectual I knew from the Land Forces Doctrine and Training System, and Lieutenant Colonel Tim Bishop, the chief of staff operations, was another old friend from my days at the University of New Brunswick. It was a reunion of sorts.

I was introduced to Colonel Chris Vernon, British Army, who was the chief of staff; Lieutenant Colonel Steve Williams, U.S. Army; and Lieutenant Colonel Mark Brewer, Australian Army. Colonel Van Den Bos from the Dutch Army, the deputy commander, wasn't in, but I was introduced to the rest of the ops staff, including Lieutenant Colonel Peter Williams, Canadian Army; and Major Randy Graddic, U.S. Army. Pam Isfeld from Department of Foreign Affairs and International Trade was the political adviser (POLAD), while Christina Green from CIDA was the development adviser (DEVAD). It was from my interactions with all these people and many others that I learned how AEGIS did business.

On the surface, CTF AEGIS looked like a brigade headquarters, but the similarity was superficial. Military historians engrossed in the conventional wars of the twentieth century have fixed ideas about military structure and leadership, but any attempt at comparison between, say, a brigade headquarters operating in Normandy in 1944 and an organization like CTF AEGIS is problematic. Yes, AEGIS had the traditional "bureaux" that would be familiar in a brigade from 1944: personnel, intelligence, operations, and logistics. AEGIS, however, wasn't a maneuver brigade reporting to a maneuver division. It was a static multinational headquarters that had to coordinate functions that either didn't exist or weren't important in a 1944 setting.

The division and corps, respectively CJTF-76 and CFC-A, with their SOF, high-tech fires, air support, and enablers all had to have the ability to communicate with AEGIS, so there were aviation coordination, SOF liaison, and fires deconfliction cells. There also were new organizations dedicated to something called "effects."

AEGIS had to maintain situational awareness on aid and development across provinces in RC South. That meant, in theory, that the efforts of four PRTs, the progress of the four provincial development committees (PDCs), and the operations of the Afghan Ministry for Rural Reconstruction and Development (MRRD) had to be coordinated with AEGIS battle-group military operations. Thus, the DEVAD.

Afghanistan is, of course, a sovereign country that abuts other sovereign countries. Consequently AEGIS had to have its own ambassador of sorts to track provincial, national, and regional trends because they affected AEGIS operations and to provide the commander and staff with advice. Visiting Afghan leaders and ministers had to have a point of contact. Thus, the POLAD.

The always-smiling and friendly Pam Isfeld was AEGIS' POLAD. With significant experience in the Balkans, Africa, Russia, and Afghanistan, Pam's job was to keep Dave Fraser abreast of political developments affecting Afghanistan in general, and anything that might have an impact on military operations in particular. The POLAD was to keep track of how AEGIS' operations related to the primary international documents justifying the coalition presence in Afghanistan—the UN Security Council resolutions, the Bonn Agreement, and the emergent Afghanistan Compact. The POLAD also had a role in monitoring Security Sector Reform. Japan, for example, was a massive donor nation and a lot of its money was being spent in RC (South) on the Highway 1 projects. Similarly, Pam also kept an eye on what was euphemistically called "national-level impediments to reform." For the most part, this dealt with the behavior of the Afghanistan government and its agencies. The POLAD was the commander's means to interact with the diplomatic community in Kabul so its members could be leveraged to help solve problems as they arose between coalition partners and between them and the Afghan government.

The Afghan security forces operating in RC South had their own command structure. AEGIS had to coordinate with 205 Corps, the headquarters commanding four Afghan National Army brigades in the region, none of which was up to full strength. AEGIS also had to interact with the plethora of Afghan police units, of which there were at least four different types in each province: border police, highway police, national police, and standby police. And then there was Pakistan. During 2006 OEF rekindled its on-again, off-again relationship with the Pakistani security forces (PAKMIL). AEGIS had to liaise with PAKMIL, too.

CTF AEGIS was multinational, but dominated by Canada, the Netherlands, the United Kingdom, and the United States. The headquarters positions in AEGIS, like any other multinational headquarters, depended on who contributed what to the coalition. The highest-ranked national officer not only did his AEGIS job, but also represented his nation and its interests, all of which had to be coordinated and addressed. There were significant military and national cultural differences that at times demanded a conciliatory as opposed to a commanding approach in order to smooth ruffled national feathers. These cultural differences could sometimes be as deep as the differences between Westerners and Afghans. In short, an organization like CTF AEGIS needed a leadership style more like Eisenhower's than Patton's—and it still had to function as a tactical-level or even an operational-level headquarters. The traditional levels of war were blurred here in ways that would be unrecognizable to those studying traditional twentieth-century warfare.

Lieutenant Colonel Tim Bishop invited me in to the JOC. "This is where we keep situational awareness on the whole region," he explained. Like any operations center, the room was full of screens, computers, phones, radios, and desks. Tim sat in the small room where he could see everything. "We do two briefings a day. I deal with the here and now, manage the 'hair on fire' contingencies, put in the bids for assets."

"Put in bids?"

"Yeah. CJTF-76 and CFC-A only have so many ISTAR and SOF resources, so we have to bid for them. The '3–5' shop handles future ops out to thirty days, while the '5' looks several months out. Shane Schreiber and Chris Vernon handle contingency operations, deconfliction, and operations that are occurring three to four days out. We feed all of them, plus the intelligence shop, J-2, and the Joint Fires Effects Coordination Center

[JFECC]. *Everything* has to be carefully coordinated here. We work for an American headquarters, not a NATO headquarters like we did back in Bosnia, and there are significant differences."

I could see there were a lot of moving parts here at AEGIS. The more moving parts, the higher probability that something would break, especially if it wasn't well oiled.

As a military historian I am uncomfortable with use of the term "effects-based operations" (EBO). To me, EBO have always existed in history; the use of this new term amounts to entrepreneurial theory gaining a foothold in the Pentagon and then proliferating into allied armies. And what exactly was EBO? There were different interpretations as to what it was, what it was supposed to be, what it was supposed to accomplish. AEGIS, however, worked out its own unique effects-based approach and Lieutenant Colonel Peter Williams was going to explain it to me. "It's all about the commander's intent," he told me. "What end-state do we hope to achieve? What resources—kinetic or nonkinetic—are going to get us there? Is end-state a verb or a noun?" Kinetic, in this case, meant the use of lethal resources while nonkinetic meant the use of nonlethal resources.

"It takes a long time to see the effects of the nonkinetic piece. Battle damage assessment [BDA] isn't as apparent for nonkinetic operations, but we feel that it is the nonkinetic operations that will have the greater impact."

"What exactly do you mean by nonkinetic operations in the context of AEGIS operations?" I asked.

"Nonkinetic operations engage CIMIC. They engage I/O and media operations, which is our ability to get our story out first, to be truthful, counter falsehoods, and maintain the moral high ground. Good situational awareness is critical in the media front; we have to be tuned in. Major Quentin Innes is our media 'quick reaction force.' The situation is such that the media will call Q first before other sources. We try to use a combination of kinetic operations with a nonkinetic follow-up."

Peter explained that there were problems with coordination: "We've had to clean up after SOF operations sometimes. The British have their way of looking at EBO: they are working on nonkinetic effects teams that comprise medical, CIMIC, and psychological operations [PSYOPS] people. The Americans are prescriptive in their approach. They separate kinetic and nonkinetic. CJTF-76 will call down here and say, 'You will do *this* now' at location X."

CTF AEGIS was a new organization and, being Canadian-led, had little experience with PSYOPs and CIMIC, and even less experience combining the two. One of the greatest deficiencies in the Canadian Forces was its reluctance to engage in PSYOPs and CIMIC. This related to the Cold War outlook and anti-intellectual climate that gripped the army in the 1970s and 1980s that produced a generation of really good battalion commanders who could kill lots of Soviets in West Germany but that had problems adapting to the stabilization operations of the 1990s. AEGIS' Canadian officers all cut their teeth in the 1990s and had some experience with PSYOPS and CIMIC from Bosnia and Kosovo and were moving away from the past. Peter sketched it out:

> It's all in the sequencing when you hit targets. For example, we have access to medical resources from CJTF-76. They deploy Village Medical Outreach (VMO) missions. We have CIMIC teams that use Quick Impact Projects (QIPs), to spend money on small local projects. There are the I/O people who deal with the media. We conduct our Key Leadership Engagements [KLEs] where we interact with local leadership. These are all nonkinetic EBO tools.
>
> The JFECC here at AEGIS gets the commander's intent, and ensures that nonkinetic as well as kinetic tools are used in the plan. The JFECC also handles kinetic operations coming in from CJTF-76 and higher. This is the high-value target (HVT) and medium-value target (MVT) kill/capture operation. Priority One now is the IED cell leaders, makers, and facilitators. They task SOF onto them. Our best hope right now is to disrupt them. We'll get a "to do" list from CJTF-76; it's prescriptive with no priorities. They want to "engage fighting-age males" across the whole area of operations, but it's not clear what exactly that means or where we prioritize it.

When I spoke with the AEGIS staff, I asked them what they thought about the balance between kinetic and nonkinetic operations. As many of them saw it, both had to work together at all levels and weren't supposed to be stovepiped. Some of the staff saw elements in the CJTF-76 staff as being obsessed with the HVT/MVT hunt piece controlled at their level; those staff elements then followed up those operations superficially with nonkinetic operations using resources that belonged to them or that came from units in the provinces. Everything else, apparently, was a secondary effort to those elements in the CJTF-76 staffs. And this wasn't just the Al Qaeda leadership hunt—this was a broader campaign to target *all* insurgent leaders, at all levels. I also learned that this was in part driven by the demand by echelons above reality for measureable kinetic effects against terrorism. This sort of McNamarism frightened me because it didn't really address the nature of the insurgency but could give a short-term and supposedly measureable false impression of "success."

Dave Fraser elaborated on this problem. "American objectives here relate to Al Qaeda—the Taliban is essentially 'noise' to them. They are focused on regional stability—Pakistan and India and especially the nuclear weapons [in those countries]. Iran is a problem but less so right now." Dave also explained to me something I was already familiar with: that there were American agencies working in diametrically opposed directions when it came to the counter-narcotics issue. If the center of gravity was the people and a large number of those people were dependant on poppy cultivation for their livelihood, was it wise to conduct counter-narcotics operations in areas where we needed support? Nobody in the post–Operation Iraqi Freedom world was willing to provide constructive criticism of American efforts. The Americans were tired, sensitive to criticism, and not interested in hearing it. Indeed, Dave had instructions from the chief of the defence staff to help repair relations with the Americans, so he and his staff had to be circumspect about any form of public or private criticism—it could be taken the wrong way. I had not seen the Americans wounded in such a way since the Iranian revolution and subsequent hostage crisis. They didn't know who their friends were any more and trust was at a premium. This even extended to personal relations.

Dave and his staff at AEGIS had to work around this mindset, and it wasn't easy. The CJTF-76 commanding general (CG), Major General Ben Freakley, had his own outlook, which at times clashed with what AEGIS was doing or wanted to do. The same could be said of his operations staff, who seemed to have their interpretation of things, too. In the post-Iraq climate, few in CJTF-76 wanted to admit it when things were not going exactly to plan and, in the American legalistic cultural context, somebody had to be blamed. It was easier to blame an ally.

On other occasions, the CG was incredibly supportive of what AEGIS was doing. There were people who were quite willing to slag the CG (and did so to me on occasion out of frustration) but he was also working in a complex environment with CFC-A, U.S. Central Command (CENTCOM), and the Rumsfeldian Pentagon breathing down *his* neck. Mistakes were made, tempers flared. Everybody saw the forceful side of the CG. What few, a very few, saw at the time was how deeply affected Ben Freakley was when soldiers were killed; Canadian deaths bothered him as much as American deaths.

What Dave Fraser wanted to do was establish broad objectives and then establish the general effects (that is, tasks) that were needed to achieve those objectives. The JFECC fed the process that added the detail to what the target would be. Operations, both kinetic and nonkinetic, were then conducted with appropriate inputs from the intelligence and I/O cells. Effects were achieved, measured, assessed, and fed back to Dave. It was a bit of an OODA (observe, orient, decide, and act) loop and, similar to the intelligence cycle, it followed a decide, detect, deliver pattern. He thought that the EBO stuff coming out of Rand was gobbledygook. "The trick is how to optimize the development and diplomacy pieces here," he said. EBO theory was too focused on shooter-sensor relationships. What was a "shooter" analogy when it came to development? How did long-term effects fit into EBO?

Dave Fraser explained to me one of the mistakes he had made. In his original organizational concept, he saw the battle-group companies acting as "delivery systems" for nonkinetic operations conducted by the PRT; his visits to Zabol influenced this approach. Dave and his staff knew instinctively that a counterinsurgency war is about people and wanted to address the people first, thus the twinned battle group–PRT. The Glyn Berry assassination and the subsequent retreat by Canada's OGDs and the reduction of American Commander's Emergency Response Program (CERP) money meant there was little to deliver, yet the structure remained the same. Dave believed in retrospect that the PRT should have remained a separate unit and should have an enhanced mentoring function with the provincial government. He also believed he should have pushed for more ANA units. Without ANA and with a dysfunctional PRT, TF ORION became focused more and more on unilateral maneuverist operations in the province instead, which was attractive to certain elements in CJTF-76 but not productive when it came to mentoring the Afghan national security forces.

Lieutenant Colonel Shane Schreiber, of course, had to translate what Dave wanted to do into action. Shane and I frequently engaged on how best to conceptualize the war in RC South. We had a number of brainstorming sessions in his office and Shane came up with what I called the "Schreiber-gram." He equated the AEGIS campaign plan with theory: there were three lines of operations—reconstruction, security, and governance. These three were mutually supporting. There were direct relationships between them. In theory, these three lines swept upward toward the objective of establishing Afghanistan as a state that could protect itself from outside interference and to economically prosper for the benefit of the Afghan people(s). The reality, of course, was different. The reconstruction arrow swept down and crossed the security arrow as it swept up. Governance was a sine wave wobbling its way outside the other two arrows. The three lines of operations were mutually exclusive and there was this inverse relationship between security and reconstruction. Shane and Ian Hope came up with the "Schreiber-Hope-gram" that was shaped like a stool: all three legs—reconstruction, security, and governance—had to be of equal length if the situation was to stabilize. The situation as it deteriorated throughout early 2006, however, forced AEGIS and ORION to focus more and more on security, despite what everybody wanted to do.

"What we are doing here is chemotherapy," Shane explained. "Is the cure going to be worse than the disease? Are we treating the symptoms or the disease?"

This was the problem with Operation Mountain Thrust. CJTF-76 crafted a plan and now AEGIS had to accommodate it despite its own campaign plan. The attempts to reconcile the two became the backdrop to everything I was about to witness over the next two months.

Operation Mountain Thrust's objectives, as the AEGIS staff understood them, were to defeat the Taliban in what CJTF-76 planners called "sanctuaries" and then extend Afghan governance to those areas, with the larger objective of facilitating ISAF Stage III Expansion. There were a number of key tasks that related to different phases of the operation. Kill/capture missions were to be conducted against a list of vetted leadership MVTs, especially IED facilitators, no matter what phase the operation was in. Similarly, interdiction operations on the border in Kandahar province were to be conducted to deter or prevent enemy reinforcement in the Mountain Thrust target areas. Phase I (A and B) were a series of shaping operations in Zabol, Kandahar, and Helmand provinces. These included detailed special recce operations in northern Helmand, Oruzgan, northern

Kandahar, and Zabol, plus the interdiction of Taliban infiltration into the major population centers of Qalat, Lashkar Gah, and Kandahar City. In Phase I-B, the main effort was to shift to Helmand using SOF to clear the way for Phase II, Decisive Operations. In Phase II, the main effort was to defeat the Taliban in the Bagran Valley and in Oruzgan using Combined Joint Special Operations Task Force–Afghanistan (CJSOTF-A). Phase III was to conduct restoration and stability operations in those operating areas and then hand those areas over to Afghan authorities.

What did this mean for CTF AEGIS? In theory, RC South and not the divisional headquarters in Bagram Air Field (BAF) near Kabul should have crafted the details of a plan based on CJTF-76's intent. The SOF and enablers should have been cut to CTF AEGIS and the mission executed and led by CTF AEGIS. The reality was that Mountain Thrust was a divisional plan using mostly CJSOTF-A resources executed in CTF AEGIS' area of operations, with CJSTOF-A commanding its own part of the operation and CTF AEGIS commanding two battle groups in a supporting role—TF ORION in Kandahar and TF WARRIOR in Zabol. At the same time, the Dutch and British battle groups would be deploying and were supposed to come under AEGIS' command. TF ORION had to secure to deployment routes to their respective provinces of these battle groups to Oruzgan and Helmand provinces while supporting all the objectives of Mountain Thrust. Development? Mentoring? There wouldn't be any time for that, given Mountain Thrust's time lines and the lack of troops, or given any of the other long-term nonkinetic aspects that needed to be done.

## CTF AEGIS: Nonkinetic Tools

Deploying battle groups and enablers against the enemy—that is the traditional purpose of a brigade group headquarters. In fact, this activity occupied a substantial proportion of the CTF AEGIS effort. There were, however, two particular nonkinetic tools also wielded by AEGIS: development and I/O. If the battle groups were kinetic tools designed to influence the enemy, development and I/O were the nonkinetic tools designed to influence the population.

One of the problems that AEGIS and CJTF-76 struggled to deal with was where development fit into planning. "Development" in this case was a catch-all word for the creation and advancement of infrastructure, expansion of the local and regional economy, and the structural means to maintain it all. The effects-based approach used by CJTF-76 tended

## Schreiber-Hope Counterinsurgency "Grams"

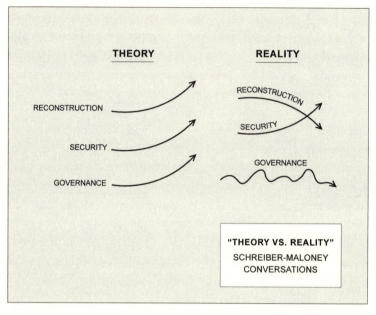

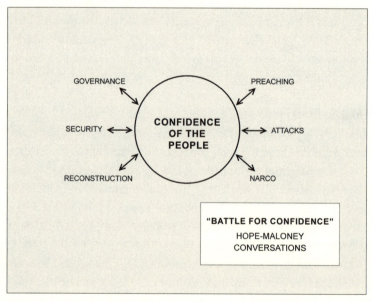

toward civil affairs (or Civil–Military Cooperation [CIMIC], in Canadian doctrine) which is related to but distinct from development. These operations were designed to enhance military operations in the short term vis-à-vis the relationship of the operations to the population. They emphasized QIPs and effects mitigation. For example, if there was collateral damage during a kinetic operation, Civil Affairs (CA) or CIMIC would provide relief and compensation to the affected population after operation completion. In other words, the effects being generated from this approach were short term.

The only means to achieve long-term effects was through national and community development, but there was significant confusion on how exactly to transition from CA or CIMIC to development at all levels of the operation in Afghanistan. This problem played itself out through the PRTs, where CA and CIMIC slammed into development. And then what kind of development? NGO-led development? Government of Afghanistan–led development? Indeed, many in the non-Afghan development community thought development should be completely separate from the military and tried to distance themselves from CTF AEGIS and the PRTs.

CTF AEGIS had a DEVAD, Christina Green. Christina was from the CIDA, though she took pains to explain to me that she didn't *represent* CIDA in this capacity. Christina had experience in Iraq as well as in Afghanistan and was well suited to the task of being development's devil's advocate in AEGIS' military-dominant staff. "My job is to provide support and advice to the commander when AEGIS had dealings with the development environment," she explained. "I deal with the Afghan line ministries, the Afghan national development programs, the UNAMA [United Nations Assistance Mission in Afghanistan], and the NGOs. I also keep an eye on American CERP funding, plus what CIMIC is up to, all across RC South." With no staff, Christina had to be part of the effects planning process for future operations, and at the same time provide Dave Fraser with development situational awareness. The differences between what AEGIS wants to accomplish and what CIDA would like to accomplish in a similar situation were minimal, Christian told me. "CIDA calls it 'resource-based management,' while AEGIS calls it 'effects.' In this case, AEGIS wants visible, tangible effects, particularly in the areas of economic development, job creation, and projects. Both have the same goal, but their timelines are different."

A lot of CTF AEGIS' development activity was CIMIC-like "Hearts and Minds," but the development spectrum also included humanitarian assistance and reconstruction. One of the main problems was that CTF AEGIS didn't control most of the money that flowed into the provinces from the various aid sources, but the push was on from higher echelons to demonstrate that there was progress. The UN, NGOs, private donors—many of these didn't want any association with either the military forces or the government. Development and aid activities were conducted without coordination. "A ton of development is conducted under the radar screen, despite the security situation. It's all low-key; it has an 'Afghan face.'" Christina explained that this didn't fit into AEGIS' conceptualization of development and they weren't sure how to explain it to higher headquarters, specifically CJTF-76.

Why was this the case? Glyn Berry's assassination resulted in CIDA retracting from Kandahar province. "This was an inadvertent benefit. It forced the Afghans to do the work. It forced the building of local capacity first. Usually this comes later in the development process. Normally, international organizations work with the locals, then the local people build local capacity, then the international organizations wean them off it and then exit the picture with a big I/O flourish." I asked Christina what the biggest obstacles were. "Iraq is literate, Afghanistan isn't. This poses problems in any interaction between Western European bureaucracy and tribal structures. That's why an Afghan face at the district and community level is so important." That was what Michael Callan was trying to accomplish with the defunct Confidence in Government (CIG) program: use the *shura* (consultative decisionmaking) system, use the mosques, let the Afghans do it with their style, not ours, "We are trying to get all the PRTs in RC South to embrace local governance. The process is important, and we have to develop faith in the process. Hell, the military is not unlike a tribal system!" Christina exclaimed.

The bulk of the money coming into RC South in the first half of 2006 came from USAID, followed by CERP, and then by a trickle from the National Solidarity Program (NSP). USAID resources were focused on commerce and industry, community development, education, governance, water and sanitation, health, and energy. CERP resources tended to be directed toward infrastructure.

One of the problems I'd noted was the tenuous connection between what was going on in the provinces and what was happening in Kabul.

Christina traveled to Kabul monthly to deal with the various commands and development agencies, and the Afghan government. But there were enough problems down here in RC South: "We have to have donor coordination meetings, where the CIMIC people are theoretically supposed to handle coordination and deconfliction. We're trying to get the PDC to meet, but it's difficult." The Guv, Asadullah Khalid, wasn't interested and was focused on security issues. UNAMA was having problems dealing with the PRT or the PRT was having problems dealing with the local UN rep, an ex-KGB Russian who accused certain national development agency representatives of being spies. As usual, UN people thought they should be coordinating everything.

Michael Callan's CIG initiative was subsumed by the National Solidarity Program (NSP). The NSP, run from Kabul, wanted to establish community development councils to get aid directly to districts and communities. The main block here was the provincial-level leadership. As a result, only five districts in Kandahar province received any NSP aid—Dand, Maywand, Zharey, Arghandab, and Kandahar City. The amounts spent were very small—in one case, less than $40,000. The rest of the districts received no NSP money at all. There were two reasons for this state of affairs: the lack of provincial capacity to deliver the aid, and the security situation. The idea was to use the PRTs to "assist" the provincial governments in supporting the NSP, but that would take time.

The development problem was a major preoccupation with the staffs of all headquarters and was closely related to Stage III Expansion. The impression I got was that, despite Major General Freakley's insistence that nonkinetic operations were critical in gaining the support of the Afghan population, the CJTF-76 staff wasn't too interested in development issues. Instead, it was interested in, as they put it, "setting the conditions for Stage III Expansion"—a short-term problem requiring a short-term solution, which was mostly kinetic with nonkinetic effects mitigation. Development could be left up to ISAF. Since AEGIS was the organization that would handle the transition from OEF to NATO ISAF, it was an important vantage point to view strategy evolution and to determine where development would fit in. As a result, AEGIS hosted exploratory meetings. I met Lieutenant Colonel Tim House, a British colonel, during one such meeting where the details of ISAF's new strategy were discussed.

Because of my background in tracking the war since 2003, Pam Isfeld and Christina Green invited me to contribute to the discussion. Tim House readily agreed.

In early June 2006, ISAF issued new strategic guidance. Using what was informally called the "ink spot" or "ink blot" approach, regional commanders were to identify "bubbles of excellence," to be called Afghan Development Zones (ADZs), consolidate them, and prepare to expand them in the future so they could connect them all up and squeeze the Taliban out of each province, district by district. The initial areas were to be the progovernment districts in each province, where development resources would be prioritized.

"Whoa! I've heard this before. Is somebody at ISAF channeling Sir Gerald Templer of Malaya? Or pirating the work of a group of American planners who floated the idea of Regional Development Zones [RDZs] back in 2003? This sounds like rubber-encased circular motive facilitation device reimagining to me," I said. Indeed, Pam told me of the RDZ's fate: "It's like they built the storefront but didn't have anything to put in it," Pam explained. "Now we have the money from the IMF [International Monetary Fund] and World Bank and we have the Afghan National Development Strategy [ANDS] to feed the development program."

"Commander ISAF wants early effects as soon as ISAF takes over RC South," Tim House said. "I/O is critical here so we have to identify zones where we can get early progress, zones that have strategic location, and where the tribal demographics can facilitate our ability to access the population and deliver security." The security-reconstruction-governance pillars would drive activities in each zone. The tools would consist of the PRTs, the provincial coordination centers (PCCs), the coalition and ANA maneuver forces, and the PDCs. The idea was to use the Afghan national security forces to secure the governance and development centers, protected by coalition maneuver forces close in, while SOF would disrupt enemy activity outside the zone(s).

I put up my hand. "I have a question."

"Dr. Maloney?"

"This will entail abandoning key terrain, or other areas where we have had previous successes. What will we be giving up? How are we going to explain this in the I/O realm? We're engaged in Operation Mountain Thrust right now. We're going to lose people during those operations and some of those operations involve securing areas that might not be compatible with the RDZs. Are we going to walk away from all this during the transition to Stage III?"

Colonel House demurred. He already knew where this was going. There was a clash between CJTF-76 and ISAF on this matter developing. We both knew that neither OEF or ISAF had the forces to control every district in every province and that there would have to be reprioritization under the new regime. "Yes, this is a problem," House said. He went on, "And what exactly do we mean when an area in the RDZ is 'secure'? What are the criteria? We may have to view the development of the ANSF [Afghan National Security Forces] as a line of development itself. Their presence is critical to securing the RDZs."

"And the enemy is already targeting 'soft' police forces and facilities," an intelligence guru interjected.

The Danish J-9 representative, Lieutenant Colonel S. Knudsen, noted, "The PRTs are already an 'ink spot'; it is critical that the provincial capitals be included. We already have a strategy. We can't withdraw from those areas. So what will the relationship be between the 'PRT ink spot' and the 'district ink spots'? And what time frame are we looking at? Three–five–ten years?" Surely we weren't going to walk away from successful PRT work....

Lieutenant Colonel Mark Brewer had another way of looking at the situation. "Yes, there will be tension in transition from OEF to ISAF, but I think that Mountain Thrust will contribute to security, even if we leave those areas that will lie outside the RDZ. Think of it as the large version of SOF disruption outside the RDZ." Mark's point was valid: Mountain Thrust was supporting the deployment of the Dutch to Oruzgan and the British to Helmand. Where the ISAF plan was problematic was the ability of the ANSF to stand up and secure the zones. One contributor stated baldly, "COMISAF's vision of the ANSF is not attainable in the short term. We need a whole new police force, and another whole brigade of ANA to implement this in Kandahar province."

Christina looked at it from a development perspective and was seriously concerned. "How are we going to handle the donors? What if their priorities interfere with our priorities? How do we convince the donors to go along? They have plans to concentrate and deploy resources. They may be outside the ADZs." This situation was compounded by what Tim House called the "Independent Republic of Helmand" problem, where the close integration of national development agency operations and national military operations might produce a national synergy that would work at cross-purposes to the new coalition priorities. We had all seen this happen in Kosovo. And then there was the ANDS. What would happen when the government insisted that the provincial governors play ball and it worked at cross-purposes to their local interests? The POLADs and DEVADs were going to be busy. . . .

An additional danger was the possibility that the rural population might flee their districts and settle in the ADZ. This could lead to intertribal fighting over scarce resources, land, and water access inside the ADZ. A variant on this was the possibility that somebody might deliberately order such a migration and depopulate the agrarian rural districts and leave them to the Taliban—and those hunting them. This wasn't Malaya, though, and it wasn't in anybody's best interest to template that model in its entirety to Afghanistan. OEF and ISAF were not colonial entities and shouldn't behave as such. The British could get away with that in Malaya in the 1950s—we couldn't in the twenty-first century.

There was no doubt that the ADZ concept was imperfect, but what emerged in the meeting were a number of positives. First, there needed to be one strategy for Afghanistan, not two or three or four, and this one was better than a plethora of half-baked strategies. Second, to be successful, the concept had to be linked to the ANDS—the "connective tissue" existed in the form of the provincial development committee, the provincial coordinating center, and other semimoribund mechanisms that could be reanimated with some mentoring. Third, OEF and ISAF simply didn't have the resources to control all the districts in every province. We might not even have the resources to "secure" all the good, supportive districts. The whole effort at this point was to keep the enemy disrupted, to hold on to and develop what we had, and to shield police forces and local governance as they slowly improved, while ensuring that we had domestic political support in our home countries for continued operations. From one perspective, CTF AEGIS was part of this larger effort to buy time.

I was present when Ehsan Zia, the minister of the MRRD, paid a visit to AEGIS. Minister Zia, who had a background as a professional NGO worker in the years after the Soviet pull-out, knew the danger of having a strictly Kabul-centric view of what was happening in the south, so he and his entourage wanted as much information as possible about CTF AEGIS and its role in the development effort, as well as an assessment of the problems endemic to RC South. Colonel Chris Vernon explained the

AEGIS' three lines of operations, but the conversation shifted abruptly into the opium problem when some of Zia's entourage started asking questions about what role AEGIS played in eradication. Colonel Vermeij, the new deputy commander, deftly dealt with this: "We will make enemies of the people if we use coalition forces against the narcos. Our focus here is rebuilding, not eradication. Our biggest problem right now is that we can sweep through the rural districts, but we can't stay in them."

To avoid having the conversation fixated on the narco issue, Chris Vernon explained the ADZ concept that ISAF would employ in the future, pointing out that the exact locations had not yet been agreed on. "The government of Afghanistan must make the decisions and be seen to make decisions, not us," Chris emphasized. Minister Zia nodded slowly and steepled his fingers. "As for kinetic operations," Colonel Vermeij went on, "we will have to do this on behalf of the government, at least until capacity is built with the security forces. Trust must be established with the population. We will have to do more patrolling, but not using armored vehicles. We will be using dismounted patrols in Oruzgan province," he explained.

"That said," Chris interjected, "General Richards and President Karzai must accept that we cannot be everywhere. The main threat right now is in 'the seams'—northern Helmand, Oruzgan, northern Zabol, and now in Panjwayi and Zhari down here in Kandahar. The border infiltration routes come in from Zabol, Spin Boldak, and the Helmand River valley. The main enemy bases are in Baluchistan, specifically the city of Quetta. The enemy infiltrates the country in small numbers and without weapons."

"What would improve the situation regarding the border?" one of Zia's staffers asked.

"We have a relationship with the Pakistani Army corps in Baluchistan, but what we really need is international pressure on Pakistan immediately. Incidentally, the same infiltration routes are used to export opium in the other direction," Colonel Vermeij pointed out. The messages of the meeting were clear. Expectations in Kabul had to be reduced. The coalition forces couldn't be everywhere and this affected development expectations. Kabul also had to understand that the reach of the government in Helmand would remain limited for some time and there was no point in pressuring AEGIS on that matter. The former governor and the chief of police were challenging the current governor, Engineer Daoud, for power.

The governors in Kandahar and Zabol had better working relationships with their security forces. The PRTs played a major role in these relations. Helmand was in trouble. CERP money was virtually nonexistent now so even QIPs weren't being done any more, let alone development.

Vermeij explained what was going on in Helmand. "American, Dutch, and Australian SOF have shaped the battlefield to assist with the Dutch deployment task force [DTF]. The DTF will bring a lot of money, but the problem will be establishing relations with the new governor. We will use the PRT to collect information on what the population needs and feed it to him. It's important that the people in the province understand that the DTF is going to stay. We'll then move on to the district level, but first we have to gain the confidence of the people. The Australian and Dutch SOF will handle the northern passes while we do this and will work with the ANA." Chris added that Oruzgan also had a former governor who was a problem.

"How do you view the situation in Dai Kundi province?" Minister Zia asked.

"We see it as a success story. It's predominantly Hazara [an Afghan ethnic group] and thus cannot be infiltrated or controlled by the Taliban. We have police liaison with Dai Kundi and they tell us that it's stable, and the Hazara have their own defense forces. They don't need the coalition forces, apparently," Vermeij added.

Zia nodded: he had already known the answer. "Can we expand the police in RC South?"

Chris pointed around the map. "Well, the main problem with the police is that they're weak. There is no money to pay them. We understand they haven't been paid here in three months. Corruption is rife because of this. President Karzai hasn't signed off on the police reforms yet. The Afghan National Police (ANP) are way behind the ANA: there is American money and DynCorp training at the Regional Training Centre (RTC), but the force is immature. The governors tend to use the police as a private militia. We need the right combination of good governors and good police chiefs."

Minister Zia shifted the conversation to more development issues. "One of the problems as I see it is that the government needs more visibility with the people. The people need to see Afghans when projects are opened, not the NGOs. The symbolism is important: we need something to unify the people after this long war. We want them to be involved in the hard work and not have it all done by others."

"The problem, sir, is that the governors have no DEVADs or staffs. Here Asadullah Khalid runs things with four cell phones. There is no bureaucracy," Chris said.

"So I need to get my people down here to work with your J-9 and then work with the governors. How will that work?"

"We already have a mix of programs in progress: the QIPs, CIMIC, and CERP, but we need to get the NSP down here. The PRT is acting as a focus and coordination mechanism more and more, so the NSP could work with the PRT and the governor," Christiana interjected.

"I have concerns about the overuse of the PRTs," the minister said. We need something more permanent, not a lash-up. The process needs to be more systematic. How do we get more government of Afghanistan involvement in the PRTs? The PRTs were never set up to be permanent structures. They were a short-term bridge. What about the PDCs?"

This was an area people didn't want to get into. The issue at this time was that some of the governors, particularly in Kandahar, were more security focused and weren't as interested in the provincial development committee, so the PDCs languished. Because the governors were appointed by President Karzai, there were limits to how much criticism could be openly directed at them by the minister or other staffs.

"Our other weak area is letting the people know that the government is helping them. How do we educate the people?" It was clear this was a ministerial rhetorical question, but it pained him that NGOs were getting the credit; this was bad for morale. There was a consensus that the current I/O approach wasn't working.

Chris picked up on this point. "The money isn't getting here. We are competing with the Taliban and the Taliban is winning the economic fight: the Taliban can find and buy people in the rural areas better than we can. There are a lot of young men out there with nothing to do. We have the economic might of the Western world and we can't provide them with jobs." Chris was correct, and Christina followed up: "Large-scale national projects done by contractors don't employ that population. If we don't do something now, we're going to lose them." QIPs were "holding the fort" but only for so long. "The locals want something, but we need to ask them what it is. We should be providing those things, not the Taliban," Chris emphasized.

As Minister Zia took all this in and continued with his tour, I thought about the I/O problem. I/O, as I would discover, underpinned everything and was built into all planning activities in one way or another, deliberately or accidentally. Like development, however, I/O was something new and caught between the need to immediately react to events and the need to pursue longer-term objectives in the country. Perceptions could lose the war—and nearly did later in the fall of 2006.

Squadron Leader Andy Thayne from the RAF Regiment was in charge of I/O for AEGIS but unfortunately he was going on leave. Over a curry lunch at the British dining facility, he introduced me to his team, which included Major Quentin Innes, the redoubtable "Q," from the PPCLI. Captain Julie Roberge, a public affairs officer from the Canadian headquarters, was going to take over from Q when *he* went on leave. I also met Captain Tom Nield, an American PSYOPS specialist who worked at TF ORION.

"Information operations" itself was a loaded term subject to a variety of interpretations depending on what army you were in or what government department you worked for. I/O covered a spectrum of activities. The commanders might have an understanding of an effect they wanted to generate and I/O was one of those tools, but not all staffs were used to incorporating it into their activities. This problem manifested itself in both AEGIS and ORION.

At TF ORION there was an I/O officer, but the constant staff shortage generated by the leave process meant that he was employed in duties deemed more important—like ops. Then one of the ORION staff who had some experience with I/O during his time with the SFOR in Bosnia held the seat temporarily. Eventually, Captain Tom Nield of the U.S. Army was brought in: he had experience with the Tarin Kot PRT up in Oruzgan. In the American system, Tom was used to coordinating public affairs, PSYOPS, and civil affairs in support of a unit's operations, a role that was uncommon in a Canadian battle group in 2006.

To illustrate the difference between the Canadian and American approaches, the PRT arranged to have several airdrops of material assistance to a rural area. The regular Canadian system would efficiently process the request and get the air force to drop the containerized delivery system pallets into the target area. Mission complete. In the American system, the I/O officer would examine the region where the drop would take place, determine what the tribal groupings were, establish what the commander's intent was, and generate a possible effects list based on who was on the receiving end. Are the people at the other receptive to the government and its message? What do the people in that region need and want as opposed to what we have to deliver to them? The Canadian process at the battle-group level didn't systematically incorporate these information points into the operation: it just carried out the drop and didn't measure or track the long-term effects. Perceptions had to change. It wasn't just an airdrop of food and building supplies: it was a nonkinetic weapon that generated effects. As ORION got more experience on the ground, however, there was more and more understanding of I/O. Still, it took time because it wasn't really part of Canadian doctrine.

CTF AEGIS was more systematic about I/O because it was a multinational headquarters that had allied officers experienced in the I/O functions and because it came from services that regularized it in the 1990s. There were, however, similar challenges at AEGIS when it came to I/O. The Canadian Forces at this point had not come to grips with the relationship between public affairs and I/O and this problem was reflected in Afghanistan. Public affairs is a political function in the Canadian system, though uniformed members carry it out for reasons related to obscure management changes during the Trudeau era, in the 1970s. Consequently, public affairs is highly centralized and under the shadow of the primary organs of the elected and unelected government in Ottawa. The speed of modern technology makes this worse. This system doesn't care about allies, and it doesn't care about the enemy. All it cares about is protecting the existing government from criticism. And criticism from domestic media is far, far more important to these people than criticism from, say, the Taliban.

They tried to have separate public affairs offices in the Canadian national headquarters, at CTF AEGIS and at TF ORION. Public affairs officers, however, had to deal with Afghan, Pakistani, American, Italian, Spanish, and every other NATO-member press corps, not just with Canadian media. Oh, and the enemy was conducting propaganda and I/O against AEGIS and ORION too . . . but public affairs didn't want to sully itself with I/O. That was nasty stuff for PSYOPS, which Canada, by the way, didn't have. People like Captain Julie Roberge, a Canadian public affairs officer who worked at AEGIS, were caught in the middle. The more Julie understood how integrated PSYOPs and public affairs were in the real life of the deadly world of Afghanistan, the more she tried to explain that things had to adapt. Public affairs people got upset and tried to keep the two separate.

The reality was that AEGIS couldn't have separate functions for dealing with international media, local media, Canadian media, and enemy media. It had to be seamless, mostly because of the need for speed, but also to keep the messages consistent. Q understood: he was an infantry officer and wasn't subjected to the public affairs–PSYOPS problem to the same degree Julie was. Q knew that he had minutes to react and get the word out into the mediasphere after an incident had occurred. The Ottawa public affairs people didn't get it and could never react quickly enough, so the enemy would always retain the advantage if it were left up to them. And why did all this matter? It was all about influencing the population to side with the government of Afghanistan and the coalition forces. The people in Ottawa were worried about keeping the elected officials in power, though one could be generous and suggest that some of them understood that maintaining Canadian public support for the mission was important too.

What did a typical I/O "battle" look like in 2006? On one occasion, a senior mullah from the Kandahar Ulema Shura, the main religious body in the city, was run down by an ANA truck and severely injured. Q and the I/O staff had to investigate, come up with a statement, and deliver that statement to the appropriate news outlets in less than thirty minutes. If they didn't, the Taliban could issue a statement of its own claiming that coalition forces deliberately killed the mullah, which would force AEGIS to issue a denial and put AEGIS in the position of having to prove to the population of the city that it had nothing to do with the accident. If this wasn't handled deftly, the Taliban could augment its message and rioting could break out, just as it had in Kabul earlier in the year. People would die and the coalition forces would be diverted from their other tasks.

Another example: the Taliban proliferated a message in the city that the reason there were so many civilian casualties during IED attacks was because coalition vehicles were armored and the blasts deflected into the crowded streets, not because they, the Taliban, initiated such attacks in the first place. Only in Afghanistan could passive armor protection become the subject of an enemy I/O attack, but the I/O staff had to craft some form of response. Q discovered that the Quetta Shura issued fatwas against coalition actions that were transmitted through the mullahs. Q developed a relationship with the Kandahar Ulema Shura and got them to issue counter-fatwas condemning Taliban suicide attacks.

The I/O staff at AEGIS also was confronted with the "new media," something that wasn't understood by the Ottawa denizens. In the spring of 2006, Taliban propaganda DVDs appeared throughout the city. These gruesome products depicted Mullah Dadullah Lang executing "informers," and showed the horrifying execution of two teachers, with their school burning in the background. Q didn't want his people exposed to these DVDs because of the possible long-term psychological effects, but somebody had to develop a response. Nobody at AEGIS had the ability to counter enemy I/O on the Internet—that was left up to echelons above reality. How exactly do you counter a snuff film? Most people in Ottawa didn't believe that this sort of behavior was possible between human beings and seemed to pretend it didn't exist. Focusing efforts on establishing a radio station was one way of diverting attention from this harsh reality.

The presence of Canadian media in the area of operations generated substantial trouble as well as tangible benefits. On the downside, the AEGIS I/O people were confronted with the outright manipulation of a Canadian reporter by the Taliban. This reporter interviewed a handful of people who all conveniently blamed Canada for the bombing of a bus loaded with interpreters who worked at KAF—that is, if the coalition forces weren't here the bus wouldn't have been bombed, that sort of logic. On another occasion, Canadian media interviewed the father of a man killed by the Taliban in that same bus bombing, who spoke out against the people who killed his son. He was later abducted by masked, armed men and disappeared.

Not to be outdone, the vaunted BBC acted as an enemy I/O tool. Some I/O staff jokingly called it the "TBC." Late one night in Afghanistan, the BBC website reported that a coalition airstrike in Helmand province hit a school and killed two hundred children. There was a flurry of activity in the JOC. The story was hardcopied to prevent its Orwellianization as the airspace deconfliction staff searched for the incident high and low. Nothing. Helmand Task Force (TF HELMAND) was asked to investigate, just in case it was some sort of SOF activity. Nothing. There was no airstrike, and there were no civilian casualties. At all. Yet here was the most respected news organization in the world reporting that it was fact . . . and not just in English, but in Pashto, and Urdu, and Farsi, and

Arabic. By some British mechanism, the BBC had pulled the story within thirty minutes. But it was too late. The story was re-reported elsewhere and there was no way of countering it.

As I understand it, an informal investigation revealed that a Taliban spokesman duped a stringer who passed it to a representative who knew the cousin of somebody in the BBC and it became "news," a not-uncommon process the more I talked to British officers experienced in dealing with the BBC in the Balkans. There was some speculation that elements or individuals in the BBC permitted this unvetted story to proceed because they were against the American intervention in Iraq. If you check the BBC website archives, you will find no record of it. Down the Memory Hole. Never forget: Eric Blair (George Orwell) worked for the BBC. . . .

INTO THE ABYSS?
Kinetic operations could also contribute to I/O . . . and here's how.

It was a dark but not a stormy night. There was nothing taking off from the usually frenetic KAF runways—no C-17s, no CH-47s. It was quiet, with the exception of generator hum. This was highly unusual. Was there early warning of a rocket attack? What was going on? Then, without warning, there was this incredible noise that everybody agreed sounded like a space shuttle booster taking off. It was loud, and the airframe of whatever it was instantaneously disappeared into the night, a flame orange blip in the distance. Then, as if time had temporarily been suspended, everything returned to normal: C-17s took off, CH-47s landed. Later on that evening, a number of six-wheeled trucks with armored cabs unobtrusively drove into a compound on the camp and the crews went for coffee at Green Beans.

I was in the JOC one night talking to a Canadian staff officer who was explaining various aspects of JOC operations when the U.S. Air Force airspace deconfliction rep, a sergeant with so many chevrons on his ACU (Advanced Combat Uniform) sleeve that it was a question of how many decades he'd been in as opposed to singular years, leaned over and said, "It's *Dr. Strangelove* time."

"Who is it?"

"It's DARTH 20.[1] He's prosecuting a TST [time sensitive target]."

This sort of engagement happened every so often. With little or no warning, aircraft would appear in CTF AEGIS' battle space and go after TSTs.

"Where's he going?"

The USAF NCO used a laser pointer to indicate a location somewhere in Helmand province. DARTH 20 was a B-1B (strategic bomber) loaded with twenty-four joint direct attack munitions (JDAMs). I surmised that one or several "enablers" had located an enemy leadership target and that he or they would be "prosecuted" with the bomber's payload.

"Higher wants to know if there are HELMAND TF or other RC South units near that location."

There was some activity.

"No. He's clear to go in."

A JOC gofer went and woke up Dave Fraser, who came in his PT (physical training) gear.

"Who's he after?"

"Looks like Number Four."

The B-1B was now only minutes away from the target. The action had to be split between the JOC and another room where the strike could be observed with an enabler that happened to be in the area.

The B-1B released a pair of 1,000-pound JDAMs onto the target compound. "Nobody could have survived *that*," somebody said. But then reports came in that there was movement in the strike site, so two more JDAMs were expended. Then a fifth.

"Higher is asking if we can conduct the BDA," one of the desk officers said. Dave contemplated this for a minute.

"No, we don't have the resources. And the enemy knows we do BDA so they might set up an ambush if we go charging in there tonight, which will force us to commit forces we have tasked for the ongoing operation. Hold off and observe for now," Dave instructed. "Maybe later. Unless they have aviation we can use," Dave grinned, knowing full well that the higher headquarters wouldn't cut helicopters to AEGIS to do this task. Any air assault in there would need attack helicopter support, which AEGIS would have to borrow. Then there would be the explosive ordnance disposal (EOD) resources. . . .

The JOC was clinical, silent, no fuss, no panic. I had watched the calm, calculated assassination of Number Four. Fuck him.

I attended the handover briefing in the JOC one evening. A Canadian staff officer who I knew well was on duty when word was passed to him that something was up. He shifted and looked at a computer chat room. "It's a HIMARS [high mobility artillery rocket system] stand up!" he chortled and rubbed his hands. "You've got to watch this." Somebody was going to get whacked. I could picture several six-wheeled trucks with armored cabs exiting a compound and deploying to their firing point. The HIMARS was essentially half a multiple launch rocket system (MLRS) mounted on a truck body. It could fire MLRS rockets or guided missiles. This particular missile type was extremely fast and highly accurate; it relied on GPS for guidance. There were several advantages to using HIMARS. First, it could respond quickly, especially if there weren't any aircraft in the area. Second, it was cheaper than, say, a B-1B. Its only downside was range. It could cover some targets, while aircraft covered others. To our dismay, the system was stood down for whatever reason.

The next day I was in Dave Fraser's office. He was pissed off. "*This is what I have to deal with!*" he said disgustedly. This particular incident made it into the public domain many months later when somebody leaked Predator imagery to the media—in this case it depicted about two hundred Taliban in ranks being addressed by a commander somewhere in Afghanistan. The Predator, which was armed at the time, was not cleared to attack them for a number of reasons related to rules of engagement.

"So why not hit them with a HIMARS instead? They'd die faster," I joked.

Dave Fraser nearly went white. "You know about HIMARS?"

"Come on. I used to be armored recce. I know an MLRS launcher when I see one, like the ones driving around here. Pretty neat system. Too bad Canada doesn't have them."

"Well, it's not there. You didn't see it."

So, you ask, why am I writing this? I spoke with General Freakley later and asked him why HIMARS was such a big secret. He looked at me with that quizzical look he has that implies but doesn't state you're mentally deficient. "I don't know what the big deal is," he said. "Dave Fraser fired off nearly my entire ops stock of HIMARS! I had to go to CENTCOM and get more! Everybody had to have heard them all being launched!"

At the time, HIMARS and other systems were a big deal. It was imperative to keep certain capabilities under wraps, especially from the media, because whatever the media saw, the enemy saw. Then the Canadian air force proudly explained in great detail how they had been moving U.S. HIMARS for the Americans using Canadian C-130s.[2]

I asked Major General Ben Freakley and others to explain to me how the whole system worked. As I understood it, CJTF-76 held the Combined Joint Prioritized Kinetic Target List, and CTF AEGIS had their own Prioritized Kinetic Target List. The people on these lists were the Taliban, Al Qaeda, HiG, and HTN leaders: for the most part they were Tier III and Tier IV leadership, mostly what were classified as MVTs. CJTF-76 and CJSOTF were permitted to hunt them down and kill/capture them. The HVTs were reserved for the Other Coalition Forces, the "Men in Black," who had their own resources and would appear out of nowhere.

Each name had to be vetted by a high-level targeting committee. It had lawyers on it as well as operational commanders and intelligence people. It was a painstaking process to get a name on the lists. I suspect that the lists had to be approved by President Karzai. I gather we didn't want to kill somebody that could be PTSd (National Reconciliation Program, or Program Takhim-E-Sohl) and we didn't want the program misused to kill political rivals.

Any enabler could go after the vetted targets, but the limitations of the coordination process and the sheer number of hunting organizations were revealed in the Azizi strike in Panjwayi district in the spring of 2006. The Other Coalition Forces did Azizi, but then didn't tell AEGIS where it was so effects mitigation couldn't be done in a timely fashion. There were a lot of civilian casualties, Ben Freakley explained, because the Taliban HVT and his close protection party deliberately hid among the civilian population in the town as the Other Coalition Forces and its AC-130s hunted him. It was Azizi that really drove home the need for closer SOF coordination, but it was still a work in progress in the summer of 2006. There was, in his view, far too much needless compartmentalization.

My concern, from a counterinsurgency point of view, was collateral damage. It was one thing to have eyes on the ground, to track an individual and then shoot him with a Barrett sniper rifle or to use a Predator's Hellfire to take out the target's SUV. It was another to take an aircraft or missile, respond to an enabler hit, and drop bombs or fire off warheads. There are different levels of decreasing precision-sniper rifle, Hellfire, JDAMs—even though they are all precision systems. What if there were other people in a compound that had nothing to do with the target? Was the whacking of an MVT with a JDAM or HIMARS worth the collateral damage? That was an interesting judgment call. Effects mitigation with

CIMIC and development aid might not be enough to assuage a population steeped in Pashtunwali.

I asked a number of the protagonists about this problem. The consensus was that the MVT was notorious enough. For example, if he was an IED facilitator that had mutilated and killed allied people or cut people's heads off for the Internet, the gloves were off. Several explained to me how the targeting system worked to reduce the possibility of collateral damage, which obviously I can't go into but appeared to be extremely ethical to me. In some cases, they wouldn't shoot. In one case I observed, they didn't shoot. Not all these men were gung-ho General Jack D. Ripper replicants, but some were. It boiled down to a clash in cultures: the twenty-first-century descendants of twentieth-century American airpower theory and a technological Phoenix Program against the twenty-first-century descendants of nineteenth- and twentieth-century Commonwealth imperial policing coupled with 1990s concepts of postconflict nation building. Here we were trying to reconcile all of them. Enablers and shooters: it was an instantly gratifying, seductive, and comfortable way to wage war, but for us to succeed in Afghanistan, the system had to be carefully integrated with the other tools, and not left to its own devices.

## Aviation and Air Support Issues

Another challenge facing CTF AEGIS was the provision of aviation (helicopters) and fast air (jets). There were a lot of aircraft based out of KAF but almost none of them was under AEGIS' direct control. AEGIS could not access some of the national assets but could bid on others. The CTF AEGIS aviation cell explained all of this to me in great detail.

The Dutch machines were not OEF-tasked: they were ISAF-tasked, even though the Dutch were moving into Oruzgan province before Stage III Expansion and the shift from OEF to ISAF control in the south. AEGIS, being part of OEF, could not directly task those machines, which included six AH-64 Apache attack helicopters, plus CH-47 Chinook and Cougar transports. Their priority was to transport the DTF to Oruzgan and provide top-cover escort to Dutch convoys.

The United Kingdom had a whole air wing at KAF and out at Camp Bastion in Helmand. HELMAND TF had CH-47 and AH-64D Longbow Apache attack helicopters; these belonged to 16 Air Assault Brigade. In KAF, there was a clutch of CH-47 Chinooks, some more AH-64Ds, a handful of Lynx, and a half-squadron of GR-7A Harrier close-support aircraft. All these aircraft were under national control: AEGIS could not move British AH-64s to cover a Canadian convoy, for example, or provide fire support to TF ORION.

The United States had U.S. Air Force and U.S. Army aircraft but their command relationships were even more complex. The U.S. Air Force HH-60s were to be used strictly for combat search and rescue and, in a pinch, medevac—they reported to a wing in BAF but had a det (detachment) at Kandahar. A-10 Warthogs came in from BAF, while B-1B bombers based somewhere in the Middle East periodically orbited the battlefield; these were controlled by the American Combined Air and Space Operations Center somewhere else and requested through CJTF-76. The MQ-1 Predators belonged to another organization altogether: the 62nd Expeditionary Reconnaissance Squadron, or Flying Jackalopes (the jackalope, of course, is a mythical animal) were, like the B-1Bs, a theater-level asset controlled from CENTCOM's forward headquarters in the Middle East. Indeed, MQ-1s and other assets moved seamlessly back and forth between Afghanistan and Iraq, and places in between. The same applied to the AC-130U gunships that had a relationship with the SOF world.

The problem with MQ-1 operations vis-à-vis AEGIS was the high level of classification of the MQ-1 imagery. Not all countries were cleared to see it and those that did had to enter a special room to do so. This limited how information collected by that system could be used in a timely fashion in 2006.[3]

The U.S. Army helicopter organization was TF KNIGHTHAWKS, which consisted of CH-47 Chinooks, AH-64 attack helicopters, and UH-60 Black Hawks. Part of KNIGHTHAWKS was under the tactical control of AEGIS, but there were all sorts of caveats. The organization, overall, was uncomfortable dealing with a Canadian-led multinational headquarters and cited the lack of Canadian experience with helicopters and potential misunderstandings over the lack of knowledge of U.S. Army procedures. Conversely, there were elements in AEGIS, ORION, and other organizations that viewed the KNIGHTHAWKS as unwilling to meet AEGIS halfway, as cautious and risk-averse, and that thought they would only get involved in what they viewed as high-risk operations if they could be convinced that there was some high payoff. Out in the field, however, American helicopters and Canadian ground forces tossed aside these issues and got the job done, as I witnessed on numerous occasions. There was also a pair of Australian CH-47s, but they were tasked to support their Special Air Service Regiment in Oruzgan.

The real bone of contention wasn't between KNIGHTHAWKS and AEGIS—it was between AEGIS and the U.K. Helicopter Task Force. A slice of 16 Air Assault Brigade made up HELMAND TF–3rd Battalion, The Parachute Regiment battle group; the U.K. PRT; the logistics units; and the helicopters. The BRITFOR headquarters—the senior British national headquarters in-theater led by Brigadier Ed Butler—was also 16 Air Assault Brigade HQ. Keep in mind that CTF AEGIS was a brigade-sized headquarters, and in theory the U.K. battle group and PRT were supposed to report to it. The U.K. helicopters did not—and, as we will see, there were conflicts between AEGIS and BRITFOR on a number of issues such as who was really running the war in RC South. Indeed, as I understood it from talking to British staff, the British government gave specific instructions to BRITFOR that British helicopters were not to exceed a certain number of flying hours per month. I was told that this was to save money and that the limits were imposed by the Chancellor of the Exchequer. So let's say a British AH-64 was permitted X hours per month. If those hours were used up by, say, the nineteenth of the month, the aircraft had to sit idle on the runway, no matter what the operational situation was, until the first of the next month. Canadian soldiers, in theory, could be fighting and dying somewhere in RC South and, in theory, those AH-64s would not be allowed to come to the rescue.

Now, before I cast any more aspersions on the British government for this idiocy, let me take a shot at my own government. Why, you ask, are there no Canadian helicopters deployed with CTF AEGIS? Well, somebody in the Canadian government decided in the early 1990s to get rid of all of Canada's CH-47 Chinooks and sell them to the Dutch. They also got rid of all of our recce helicopters (which were, incidentally, armed with 7.62-mm Gatling guns). They also jettisoned the Twin Huey tactical transports. Why? As the story goes, Quebec needed jobs, the Mulroney government needed votes, and somebody thought that an executive version of the Bell 412, built in Quebec, could somehow replace all three types of aircraft. (How a Bell 412 replaces a Chinook beggars the imagination.) These people convinced a whole other group of politically intimidated people to go along with them. Canada wound up saddled with an underpowered executive helicopter that had to be massively retrofitted so it could conduct military operations, and at the same cost it would have been to acquire the vastly more capable and proven UH-60 Black Hawks.

It remains unclear as to exactly why the Griffons were not deployed in 2006, but cost was probably one of the prime factors. The Chrétien government cancelled the Cormorant helicopter project in the 1990s because of more ridiculous politics. Had these aircraft been available in 2006, they could have alleviated some of Canada's lift problems. Indeed, I flew in Royal Navy Sea Kings that had their antisubmarine warfare gear removed, had guns put on, and were performing well in the thin air around Kandahar. Lack of creativity? Lack of money? Lack of political will? Take your pick.

One of the AEGIS staff told me, "We have to build a matrix of what can be used when. I have to admit we have problems beyond the norm here. There are command and control problems, there are national caveats. There are different rules of engagement. And then there are egos—*massive* egos—that present serious roadblocks. The demand for data, the micromanagement, makes the process lethargic. And the enemy, by the way, knows this. They know they have X minutes from initiating an action to when we show up. They know our processes are slow."

This situation was aggravated by bad blood that emerged while I was in-theater. An American soldier, wounded in an ambush, died before a helicopter could make the "golden hour." (If wounded are evacuated to the hospital in less than an hour, their probability of survival exponentially increases.) The helicopter tasked to extract the American wounded was a British Chinook, and for whatever reason it took more than three hours to medevac the kid. CJTF-76 raised hell over the incident. It didn't matter what the truth of the matter was, or why the helo was delayed: there was an entrenched belief in American circles that the soldier had died because of British incompetence, and that if KNIGHTHAWKS were supporting the operation they would have been on time. The fact that the British Chinooks were associated with CTF AEGIS in some way cast a shadow on AEGIS as well and generated collateral mistrust, again regardless of the facts. Dave Fraser's staff did what they could to mitigate the damage.

On the other hand, relations with the Royal Air Force's IV(AC) Squadron were pretty good. AC stood for "Army Cooperation." IV(AC) could trace its roots back to World War I, when it provided recce and close air support to ground troops over Flanders. I got the brief from Wing Commander Ian Duguid and Flight Lieutenant Daniel Stuchfield.

"We fly the GR-7A here, but we're waiting on the GR-9A to come into theater," Wing Command Duguid said as he pointed to the slide showing a Harrier in flight. "Our role here is to conduct preplanned attacks, close air support, and recce. The bulk of our missions are recce and close air."

"Are you an OEF or ISAF resource?" I asked.

"We work with both. The ISAF missions are mostly defensive, low-tempo tasks and involve route recce, bridge recce, and that sort of thing. For OEF, it's the opposite: high-tempo, offensive warfighting. We also do 'show of force' missions to provide an air presence, which has a deterrent effect on the enemy. We'll be coming in at one hundred feet (thirty meters) and use a lot of sound and noise. We have noticed, however, that lately the enemy isn't running away—they're staying in place."

"Is there an anti-air threat?"

Flight Lieutenant Stuchfield took the floor. "There is a MANPADS [man-portable air-defense system] threat-infra-red SAM-7, -14, and -16. Sometimes we pick up Iranian and Pakistani systems near the border areas. The Taliban even tried to use an RPG against a Harrier during a show-of-force mission. We heard they were working on the fusing of the round to have a go next time. We have no reported use of MANPADS against fast air at this time. They do use RPGs against helicopters. They tried against an American UH-60 yesterday."

The GR-7As weren't the most sophisticated systems available when it came to weapons, however, but they were there and Canadian CF-18s were not. The GR-7As were essentially bombers with no gun. In one configuration, they had a laser for targeting but it was for estimating distance and not for guidance. They had "dumb" bombs: 500-pound Mk-82 bombs fused for airburst or impact, plus a CRV-7 rocket pod, carrying Mach-3 high-explosive rockets. The U.S. Air Force A-10s and the U.S. Marine Corps AV-8B Harriers had the LITENING pod (precision targeting pod system), which did range estimation and guidance. Duguid and Stuchfield really wanted that system. Their existing laser-guided bomb (LGB) system could handle laser guidance or drop a JDAM, but they needed two aircraft to do the job if lasing was used. U.S. aircraft carried one LGB and one JDAM. The American enhanced PAVEWAY II was a "drop and forget" 1,000-pound guided bomb; with the LITENING pod, one plane was needed. IV(AC) Squadron could, however, operate at night with forward looking infra-red (FLIR) night vision goggles to provide green daylight.

The RAF Harriers provided a lot of support to Canadian ground forces in Kandahar province and were held in high regard, especially by TF ORION's "C" Company after Operation Jagra in June 2006.

## AFGHAN NATIONAL ARMY CAPACITY BUILDING

Colonel Tim House of the British Army handled what CTF AEGIS dubbed "J-37" matters that, in layman's terms, were the interface between AEGIS and the coalition entities engaged in working to improve the Afghan security forces. Tim, who had experience doing the same thing with the Mozambiquan Army so it could fight the Mozambican National Resistance in the 1990s, walked me through the players in this particular drama. "First, there are the embedded training teams or ETTs—you're familiar with them. They report to TF PHOENIX in Kabul. PHOENIX is based on a U.S. National Guard brigade that reports to Combined Security Transition Command–Afghanistan (CSTC-A), which belongs to CFC-A. The ETTs work at the kandak, or what we call the battalion level.[4] Confusingly, ISAF deploys operational mentoring and liaison teams [OMLTs], which are similar to ETTs but report to NATO." Already this was problematic: two separate coalitions doing the same task. "Oh, and both OMLTs and ETTs operate in the same area at the same time," he added. To make matters even more interesting, CJSOTF had its own program going, but I'll come back to this later. Another layer were the Regional Command Assistance Groups (RCAGs), which handled the ETTs for each regional command and reported to TF PHOENIX in Kabul.

CTF AEGIS' campaign plan was originally based on having a kandak in each province, twinned with the national battle group and the PRT. The idea, again, was to have the battle group mentor the kandak. However, Tim explained, the ANA laydown was much less than anticipated. Between the end of January and June, there were supposed to be a corps headquarters (205 Corps), three brigade headquarters (one each in Helmand, Kandahar, and Zabul), four infantry kandaks, a combat support kandak, and a combat service support kandak, with more on the way.

The actual laydown as of June 2006 was nothing remotely like that. 205 Corps HQ existed, as did the brigade headquarters. 2nd Brigade in Zabul mustered three infantry kandaks, a combat support kandak, and a combat service support kandak—Zabol was solid with its ANA. Kandahar, on the other hand, was far from solid. There was a battery of D-30 guns in forward operating base (FOB) Martello, a weapons company in

Spin Boldak. One infantry company was over in Helmand. One infantry kandak, the combat support kandak, and combat service support kandak were in Camp Sherzai outside KAF. Three infantry companies, including the recon company, were detached to SOF operating from Gheko, and thus outside AEGIS' influence. Helmand was in bad shape: there were two depleted infantry kandaks and a combat service support kandak—and that was all.

Then there was Oruzgan province, which was supposed to be under Dutch command. But the Netherlands was going to be in that province under the auspices of ISAF, so they wanted Dutch OMLTs, not American ETT-mentored kandaks. But there weren't enough kandaks for Oruzgan, either.

None of the deployed Afghan units was at full strength and all suffered from a lack of equipment. Indeed, an Afghan company was usually sixty personnel, not ninety to a hundred, like Western forces. The support functions were in worse shape. This, coupled with the problems with the PRTs, severely limited AEGIS' ability to carry out its campaign plan. Where was the ANA in the south after four years of mentoring and training? And why did Zabol seem to have a disproportionate amount of available forces? Zabol was the smallest of the provinces. The situation was not good. Really not good.

The state of the ETTs was interesting, Tim explained. "The Americans are short of manpower. Do you realize there are a pair of U.S. Navy submariners leading an ETT in Helmand province?" And I used to joke with Navy people that we could cut back on Navy funding because Al Qaeda and the Taliban didn't have any submarines. . . .

A planner I knew who spent time at CENTCOM explained what he thought some of the problems were. "USSOCOM [United States Special Operations Command] and CENTCOM are competitors in Afghanistan. There are institutional obstacles to partnering U.S. SOF and U.S. conventional forces in-theater. Both entities fought over who controlled the new ANA kandaks coming out of the training system: they were originally trained by the 19th and 20th Special Forces Groups, but TF PHOENIX was turned over to a National Guard infantry brigade. USSOCOM wanted priority so they could use kandaks in irregular warfare. This wasn't Tier I JSOC black ops: this was the traditional ODA [Operational Detachment Alpha]-indigenous force relationship, like in Vietnam with the Meo-U.S. Special Forces relationship."

Conversely, CENTCOM saw the ANA as a regular army to be trained and deployed as such with ETTs who weren't necessarily U.S. Special Forces personnel. Oruzgan province, for example, was a big JSOA until the Dutch deployed. It was a SOF playground and had been since 2002: the ODAs and associated Afghan Militia Forces (AMF) fought the war their way in there. The bottom line for CTF AEGIS was that only Zabol province had an Afghan kandak working with conventional forces: Helmand didn't and neither did Kandahar. There was supposed to be a kandak permanently twinned with TF ORION, but it wasn't in the province: it was in Oruzgan with the U.S. Special Forces. Again, there were competing views on how the war should be fought, and both views were operating at the same time.

But what about quality control? What was going on in the kandak training system? I flew up to Kabul to meet with Major Paul Peyton and Captain Errol Maceachern, two of the nineteen Canadians who worked at the Kabul Military Training Center (KMTC), better known as Camp Alamo. We drove into the camp, which was across the street from Camp Warehouse, the ISAF Kabul Multinational Brigade HQ that I'd been to regularly over the years. "In the past six months we've put seven kandaks through our part of the system," Paul said as he showed me around the training area. "The current TF PHOENIX is a National Guard unit from Oregon. We are part of the training assistance group (TAG) that works under them. They report to CSTC-A, while the KMTC reports to the Afghan Ministry of Defense."

"Where does the TAG fit in the training process?"

"A typical Afghan solider gets an initial seven weeks at a training brigade, and then does an advanced individual training course that lasts another six weeks. The top people are tested and sent off to do, say, recce training or artillery or NCO selection. The TAG handles collective training—we do that here. Then the British handle the NCO School, which is an additional five weeks for those who qualify." Paul and Errol explained that almost all of the officers were former AMF commanders; the French handled officer training, but the training was considered substandard by many who worked in the TAG and the ETTs. The officers, when they're ready, met their NCOs for the first time for the two weeks of collective training with the TAG. And that, according to Paul, was the problem. "There is currently no experience injected into a newly generated kandak. This has had a significant impact on the credibility of the leaders and consequently the confidence and capability of the kandak." Getting the TAG and its higher headquarters to understand that that bond had to be developed earlier was a problem. In many ways, the Canadians and British were mentoring the TAG as much as they were mentoring the Afghans. The Afghan Ministry of Defense was an issue: they didn't want to assign an officer too early out of fear that they might desert if the kandak is assigned to the south. That was indicative of a serious problem. The problems in the south were affecting the willingness of the trainees to learn.

"We do the squad and platoon collective training here," Errol told me as we drove out to one of the ranges. "We try our best to train these soldiers to fight, and get them to start training their own people." The Afghan officer's ability to understand the soldiers' welfare was generally poor and there were serious quality-of-life issues. Discipline amounted to physical abuse. "We do intervene, by the way," Paul took pains to tell me. "In one case we had an NCO beat a soldier, so other soldiers from his same village were ready to lynch the NCO. The Canadian sergeants intervened in what became a Mexican standoff."

One of the major deficiencies Paul and Errol noted was the complete lack of feedback from the field. The ETTs and OMLTs had no means to pass on what was going on to the TAG, so the TAG couldn't evaluate its effectiveness and improve training. Other deficiencies included the lack of IED training, no night operations training, and no company level ops training. In other words, the deploying kandaks could barely operate at the platoon level. It was as if the ANA training system was some sort of sausage factory that pumped out warm bodies to occupy static positions and neither function nor think at a higher level. This was very different from my experience with Major Brian Hynes' ETT in Kabul in 2004. Something happened between late 2004 and 2006 that affected the quality of the kandaks, but what that was, exactly, was unclear.

If the exit strategy for the coalition was a functional ANA, we had a long, long way to go. Everybody I spoke with—American, British, or Canadian—blamed the KMTC staff, but knew there were larger policy problems. There was a lack of leadership and direction. The mission wasn't clear. Were the coalition troops supposed to mentor the KMTC staff to build an institution, or were they there to provide combat training for deploying kandaks, or both? Nobody knew, but the guys at the "coal face" defaulted to getting soldiers ready to fight, because that was what they did best. There were obvious problems between the muddled relationships between CSTC-A, KMTC, the Afghan Ministry of Defense, TF PHOENIX, and the TAG. It was less than functional and contributed to problems getting trained Afghan soldiers down south and into the fight.

I watched Sergeant Joel Turnbull instruct a platoon conducting live fire with their Hungarian AK-47s. He worked through an interpreter, which wasn't easy at the best of times. Sergeant Turnbull used a hockey stick as a pointer to designate arcs of fire to the trainees. "We add a bit of the Canadian method here," he told me during a smoke break. The other Canadian trainers agreed and told me about the close relationships they built up with the Afghans and the influence they gained over time through team building. "It's so . . . us," one said. "Remember Kandak 52?" The guys all nodded vigorously. "This was one of the first coherent kandaks we worked with. The troops were sent to a holding kandak after training. There was a flap and the RAF was going to fly in some of them as filler to an ongoing operation in Helmand province. The guys who weren't selected *deserted* the holding kandak and stowed away to join their buddies." There were, indeed, lions among the lambs.

I also learned, however, that the Afghan priority for quality kandaks wasn't the south: it was around Kabul and the northern Afghanistan areas. I think, based on my experiences in 2004, that there was still residual mistrust between the higher-end power brokers . . . and a whiff of coup d'état was still in the wind. Or they were needed, like 209 Corps in RC North, to keep a lid on private forces that were still undergoing the disbandment of illegal armed groups (DIAG) process.[5]

What did all this mean for CTF AEGIS? Zabol had a lot of resources and probably would be in good shape. Oruzgan was a SOF playground for the time being. The ANA presence in Helmand was minimal. In effect, TF ORION would have to go nearly alone in Kandahar province—the existing companies of the depleted kandak could only send a handful of platoons to the fight. And that was it. We needed more Afghans down south, but they weren't coming.

The situation also highlighted a flaw in that Canada lacked the ability to mobilize "influence resources" in Kabul to apply pressure to get kandaks brought into Kandahar province. If this were an American formation, it would have plugged into a vertically and horizontally connected array of U.S. organizations and duked it out by bidding for more resources against other organizations. CTF AEGIS was a tactical- and operational-level headquarters that was not part of that system, and had no experience with that system. It was competing with another brigade in an American division, which in turn was competing with CJSOTF, and then with the other regional command (under ISAF). And CTF AEGIS had no "friends at court" in the Afghan Ministry of Defense—U.S. contractor MPRI was mentoring that ministry. The Canadian embassy was next to useless in this regard.

As a side note, Lieutenant Colonel John Conrad, the National Support Element (NSE) CO, saw how deficient the Afghan combat service support kandak was in Camp Sherzai. He offered to have the Canadian NSE, which was not under AEGIS' command, act as an ETT to improve combat service support kandak's situation. Paul Peyton and the Canadians at KMTC were logistically supported by the NSE and conveyed the sorry state of logistics training back to John, who came up with various ways and means to help out the ANA in Kandahar, even if it was low impact and at a low level. Every little bit helps, and, with Afghan culture, relationship-building and continuity is important.

CTF AEGIS had a good working relationship with the 205 Corps commander, Major General Raoufi.[6] A tall, thin, laid-back man, Raoufi's challenges were nearly beyond imagination. He was working to get another kandak down to Kandahar province in time for upcoming operations in Zharey and Panjwayi districts while at the same time trying to fix the leadership of his 1st Brigade HQ. He met regularly with Dave Fraser.

"The new unit we are bringing here is untested," he said as he pointed to his papers that were written in Dari. "I want the 1st Brigade unit that is here to mentor and guide them. 205 Corps has more combat experience than any other corps in the Army, but the northern corps have none. This will take some time, however." Raoufi was concerned about premature commitment of untried forces.

Raoufi was also working on rebalancing the 205 Corps forces. He knew there were too many of those forces in Zabol and that more were needed in Helmand, but an enemy attack on the ANA in Zabol that destroyed several fuel trucks had the potential of pinning those forces in that province. The governor was a factor here in pressuring the ministry of defense and Raoufi to keep kandaks in Zabol. Raoufi had to keep Highway 1 open from the boundary of RC East to Kandahar City. There were rumors that the highway police had deserted their checkpoints in

Zabol, a situation that would nearly guarantee that forces couldn't be redeployed to Sangin, Helmand—which redeployment the British were pressuring him and his superiors in Kabul to do.

There were coordination problems with the police, of course. The army and police did not get along: the ANA viewed themselves as professionals and viewed the ANP as reuniformed AMF. They weren't wrong. The ANP in Zabol were short of supplies of all kinds, so Dave Fraser asked Raoufi to consider providing the police with the stuff needed to hold the road so he could plan for a possible Sangin deployment. Dave really wanted to get Esmatullah, the regional chief of police, and Raoufi together in one room so they could sort it out, but that wasn't going to happen today. . . .

## The Afghan Police Forces and Capacity Building

The police force was even in worse shape than the army was. In 2005 there had been the Afghan Uniformed Police, Afghan Border Police, and Afghan Highway Police; we generally just called them ANP. They weren't all real police. Many of them were, in fact, DIAG'd former militia personnel who still held allegiance to various power brokers in the province who had been "legitimized" by being given a uniform and a patch.[7] In theory, they belonged to the Afghan Ministry of the Interior (MOI)—there were other national-level police: the Counter-Narcotics Police, the Standby Police, and something called the Special Police. The MOI was being "mentored" by the Germans as they requested this "pillar" during the 2001–2002 Bonn process. There were some nascent CIVPOL mentor teams operating in Kandahar in 2006, and there was a U.S. contractor–manned RTC that reported to Kabul, but it wasn't clear what relationship they had to CIVPOL activity at the PRT, or to AEGIS' ANSF capacity development people, or to anybody else at this point in the game. From where I stood, the whole system was figuring out exactly who was where and who commanded them. OSC-A and the Germans were, at the time, also overhauling the police with the National Police Reform Program.

Dave Fraser, Tim House, and Colonel Paul Calbos were working on the new policing command structure and how it related to CTF AEGIS. There was a PCC located next to the Governor's Palace and, in theory, there was going to be one for each province in the south. These gave the police, intelligence, and military representatives a place to coordinate with themselves and with the political authorities; this was right out of the British experience in Malaya, Kenya, Cyprus, and Oman, and was a sound concept, given the right personalities. Now the idea was to form a regional version of the PCC—in this case, an RCC. Paul Calbos was mentoring General Esmatullah, the designated regional chief of police. The MOI was learning that all was not well "down south" and wanted more involvement in policing. Up to now, everything was being run at the governor level.

An assessment conducted by one entity and vetted by the J-37 staff concluded that the Afghan forces were essentially resupplying the enemy. Afghan national security forces supply convoys were plundered by the Taliban. The amount of lost fuel and ammo was, in a word, "astonishing." The Afghan MOI was asking for coalition military police to escort the resupply convoys. Well, AEGIS had military police but they were doing traffic control at KAF, and there was a small detachment at the PRT that was helping with mentoring the police alongside the CIVPOL detachment. "Is the stuff going to the black market or the enemy?" Dave Fraser asked. Tim House explained that the bulk of the missing ammo were RPG rounds, so it was probably going to the enemy.

The list of policing problems was long and distinguished. Esmatullah was confronted with a near-post-apocalyptic environment. There was no justice system—that is, no judges, courts, lawyers, or even court buildings. What law did they use? There were three or four, depending on where they were supposed to lock people up.

Esmatullah didn't even "own" the police in the four southern provinces. The "police" were a mix of DIAG'd AMF personnel wearing police uniforms; partially trained police that had passed through the RTC in Kandahar; and whoever in the rural areas was armed and declared themselves to be police. There was no quartering plan, and there was a rudimentary logistics system. In several meetings I attended it became clear that the police needed something like the ETTs or the OMLTs that worked with the ANA. The Canadian PRT was trying to do something like that, but after the Glyn Berry assassination, skittish bureaucrats in Ottawa were afraid to allow the CIVPOL to go "outside the wire" (but they did anyway).

But the regional chief was skittish, too. Colonel Paul Calbos explained that he was a Hazara, and had little or no standing in the tribal politics of the south. He was seen as an outsider. The governor, Asadullah Khalid, got a $300,000 police budget per month and pretty much did what he liked with it, regardless of what Esmatullah thought the priorities should be. He didn't want to play ball with Esmatullah. Dave Fraser, working through Pam Isfeld, was able to contact President Karzai, who in turn called down to Asadullah and told him to cooperate. The big question was, were the police a federal entity, a provincial entity, or a private entity? The provincial district police chiefs all had allegiance to the Guv, who appointed them in the first place: it was a nepotism and patronage buffet. And of course the president appointed the governors. The only way to play this game was to come up with even more money, train a police force that had a higher allegiance, and slowly "chessgame" those patronage appointments out of the way. Otherwise, police violence could look an awful lot like Taliban violence. . . .

ORUZGAN PROVINCE
CTF AEGIS was responsible for non-SOF coalition operations in Oruzgan province, which had several international as well as operational complexities. In 2002 Operation Full Throttle was mounted to kill/capture Mullah Omar near Deh Rawod, with tragic results for a large wedding party: this had ramifications throughout the region at the time and memories were long. In 2005, Oruzgan was a JSOA, where five twelve-man ODAs, an Operational Detachment Bravo (ODB, the company-level command element for the ODAs) from TF-73, and three associated Afghan kandaks and other small allied SOF elements kept the Taliban off balance. Oruzgan is mountainous with several large valleys and was a perfect sanctuary area. It was also a transit route that ran from northern Helmand, through Oruzgan, to Zabol, and then to Pakistan and back again.

In the original 2005 plan, a NATO-member battle group and PRT working under CTF AEGIS was supposed to take over from the U.S. Special Forces in Oruzgan; similarly, another NATO-member battle group and PRT would do the same in Helmand. However, when the time came to deploy, CTF AEGIS had only TF ORION and the American battle group, TF WARRIOR, in Zabol under command. Britain and the Netherlands were supposed to commit to Helmand and Oruzgan, respectively, but the political decision making in London and The Hague wasn't cooperating with the AEGIS time line.

The exact moves in this diplomatic ballet are beyond the scope of this book, but when AEGIS and ORION deployed in January 2006, Britain and the Netherlands were still locked in debate. The Dutch case was a major problem: they had a coalition government and a small party didn't want to deploy to Oruzgan, citing the 1995 Srebrenica massacre as a reason not to get involved. The Euro-rhetoric flew fast and furious: if the Dutch didn't deploy, NATO was finished and would have no credibility, and so on and so forth. Eventually, the decision was made in February, and the British agreed to deploy right after the Dutch did.

The Dutch deployment, therefore, was highly politicized before the lead elements of the DTF hit the ground in Kandahar in the spring. Dutch casualties would be a sensitive issue. Any form of combat involving Dutch forces would be a sensitive issue. As with Canada's commitment to ISAF in 2003, the Dutch mission was disingenuously billed as a "reconstruction" mission, something akin to "peacekeeping," and not counterinsurgency. To make matters even more interesting, the Dutch were adamant that operations would not start until all their forces were in place—no rolling start with partially committed forces. Everything had to be in Oruzgan before they would begin.

That affected CTF AEGIS in numerous ways. Oruzgan had no major airports and the Dutch only committed a single C-130 transport, so the Dutch forces had to land at KAF, mount up, drive down Highway 4 into Kandahar City, get through the city unscathed, then drive north up the (partially paved, at that time) Tarin Kot Road, through Shah Wali Kot district where the enemy had a number of sanctuary areas, and then into Tarin Kot, the provincial capital of Oruzgan. The DTF—that is, the Dutch engineers and contractors who would build Camp Holland—would precede TF ORUZGAN, which would deploy with its 1,600 troops sometime in the summer of 2006. How was CTF AEGIS supposed to get nearly two thousand Dutch personnel into Oruzgan without taking casualties? If the enemy hit the Dutch convoys hard, they might be able to turn public opinion in the Netherlands against the mission and stop the deployment, which in turn would have massive knock-on effects in ISAF, and then in NATO and between NATO's members. Given the problems the Dutch were having with their coalition government, this attenuation of their mission was a very real possibility.

One of the first steps was to establish a presence in Shah Wali Kot district. TF ORION took over the former GUNDEVILS platoon house in Gumbad to keep an eye on the rugged "Belly Button" feature out of which Mullah Tahir and his band of merry psychos operated. At the same time, resources were provided to pave the Tarin Kot Road from Kandahar City to Tarin Kot. This would take time: tribal entities along the route all had to have "buy in" or the road wouldn't get paved. That took several months, and the project was partially completed. By January the Kandahar City–Tarin Kot border section was paved.

Both projects laid the ground work for the decision to establish FOB Martello, just off the Tarin Kot Road in Shah Wali Kot. FOB Martello was to act as a stopover and support point for the deploying Dutch forces, but was to be manned by TF ORION because there were no other forces available. This in turn had knock-on effects on what TF ORION could or couldn't do throughout the province, because a portion of the battle group had to man the base. And what happened if the enemy attacked the FOB? That might draw in even more forces. These were the sort of dilemmas CTF AEGIS and TF ORION had to deal with. What were the priorities given finite resources? Escort development representatives around the province, or man and defend FOB Martello? Pursue gender-equality projects, or pave the Tarin Kot Road?

The Dutch task force was scheduled to arrive in April, with the main body of troops arriving in June–August. At the same time, CJTF-76 was planning Operation Mountain Thrust, which would incorporate several operations in Oruzgan. One of the intentions of Mountain Thrust was to use SOF in Oruzgan as a "shaping" operation to take the heat away from the Dutch before they deployed. Starting in mid-May and running into early July, SOF mounted a number of suboperations, the most important of which focused on the Chora Valley and the routes in and out of Tarin Kot. With the Australian SAS Regiment in the lead, and with the Dutch Korps Commando Troops (KCT) participating, enemy forces were significantly "degraded" so that the first convoys could get up north to the Camp Holland site. MQ-1 Predators roamed around hunting Taliban leadership targets. During one of these actions, Lieutenant Marco Kroon from the KCT won the Military Order of William, the Netherland's highest medal for courage, when his team was surrounded and besieged. These operations formed the background to TF ORION's northern operations in June–July.

CTF AEGIS also performed another role in assisting the Dutch. The Netherlands only authorized one C-130 Hercules transport to assist with the move of the DTF and OTF to Tarin Kot. Because the CTF commander was Canadian, and because he was "double-hatted" as the senior Canadian commander for the theater, he could draw on Canadian air transport resources. Consequently, several Canadian C-130s moved Dutch troops to the rudimentary airfield at Tarin Kot and airdropped supplies to other allied forces during the shaping operations in the province.

For the most part, the deployments went off with very few attacks. Day in and day out, a pair of Dutch AH-64 Apaches provided top cover as the truck convoys wound their way past the Dala Dam, up into lower Shah Wali Kot, past FOB Martello, and onward to Camp Holland. A Dutch mechanized infantry platoon equipped with MICVs later joined the Canadians at FOB Martello to free up troops for use elsewhere.

### The Zabol Provincial Reconstruction Team

Brigadier General Dave Fraser was heading up to Zabol province to take a look at the American PRT and invited me along. "I like what the Americans are doing up there. It's a different approach," he said as we slung on our body armor at the TF KNIGHTHAWK heliport. Two grayish UH-60s were already turnin' and burnin' as I grabbed my pack and followed Dave over to them. We were off, flying on a southeastern route from KAF, then east into the Rode Maruf mountains, with their brown, copper, and reddish rocks that defied the sun's hammering heat. The two Black Hawks flew the contours in the canyons, one of those flights over the geographically complex and beautiful terrain where you temporarily start to believe in God again.

The approach to Qalat took us into a landing zone (LZ) compound that abutted TF WARRIOR's headquarters. We were met by Captain Steven Wallace, U.S. Army, the FOB commander, and Major Frank Strueck, the task force commander. The situation in Zabol was different from the other provinces, and that was not surprising because of the differences in the terrain. Zabol was bisected by the Kabul–Kandahar highway running the length of it from northeast to southwest. There were mountains to the north, which ran into Oruzgan and northern Kandahar provinces, and the Shinkay Valley, which connected to Pakistan, to the south. Lieutenant Nolan briefed us on the current operation. There was an IED cell and an ambush group operating from the hills to the south of the highway near Sha Joy. Their modus operandi was to sortie at night, lay the devices, and retreat to the hills. TF WARRIOR deployed its scout platoon and had caught six Taliban from this cell the prior night.

The bulk of TF WARRIOR's TICs (troops in contact) were in a goose-egg–shaped area south of Highway 1, south of Galam. TF WAR-

RIOR arranged for a VMO in this area and about five hundred people showed up for treatment. Historically, the VMO discovered, this area had been a Taliban training center and the capital of Zabol during the regime's existence. The Toki tribe predominated, who were fairly educated. They didn't like Hazaras; when Kabul sent ANA and ANP units that had Hazaras in them, there were problems. It wasn't that straightforward, however: some in TF WARRIOR believed that the current governor tacitly supported the Taliban and that there was a deal going on. Taliban were strong-arming the shopkeepers in the region for cash and supplies, but once the Americans and the ANP got interested, this stopped quickly—a little too quickly.

Nolan explained that orders had gone out from the Quetta Shura to Taliban units and cells in Zabol in June that said, approximately, "You're not doing enough. Get off your ass." When there wasn't enough activity to suit the Quetta Shura, it sent in two Taliban commanders, Mullah Asidullah and Mullah Malam, to "motivate" the troops. CJSOTF thought they caught them both in an orchestrated ambush, but the BDA was inconclusive. It was also evident that the Quetta Shura viewed the population in most of Zabol as not pro-Taliban. To make matters worse for the enemy, the Taliban in Zabol were heading to Helmand province. These particular Taliban were broke and needed cash, so they were going to join the poppy harvest in Helmand to get paid. The Quetta Shura was unhappy and there was pressure on the cells in Zabol to increase the level of violence. There were indicators that Asidullah was alive, but on the move. He refused to stay in one place for more than a day or a night. If he was constantly on the move, he couldn't plan and he couldn't execute. TF WARRIOR credited their PSYOPS with this: they had a campaign going with the mullahs who relayed to Taliban sympathizers that the TF WARRIOR commander, Frank Strueck, *personally* wanted to kill Mullah Asidullah. This, according to sources, had a profound effect on Mullah Asidullah, who was getting jumpy. TF WARRIOR was waiting to pounce when the opportunity presented itself.

I got the impression that Zabol was no longer "Indian country" as it had been in 2005. Nolan explained that they saw a significant increase in the number of school kids, from none to the hundreds. Once school facilities were completed—and they approximated a typical school room circa the 1930s in Canada or the United States—they were filled to capacity. PRT carpenters worked with local people and mentored them in construction techniques. The main problem was ensuring that there were proper toilet facilities in the schools, something the locals weren't used to....

AEGIS' interest in all of this was related to the transfer of authority that was going to take place in Zabol. Romania was going to deploy a battalion to Zabol and the American battalion was going to leave. The Americans would keep the PRT, however. RC South's interest was in keeping Highway 1 open. The PRT was integral to the Zabol stabilization effort.

Major McGlaughlan, USAF, was the PRT commander. "Call me 'Beave,'" he insisted. I asked him how the effort was organized in Zabol. "TF WARRIOR has an NCE, the battalion, and the PRT. The battalion is big and actually has about 1,600 people in it: three infantry companies and three independent platoons all mounted in Hummers, an MP platoon, an engineer platoon, a battery of eight 105-mm guns, and forty intelligence personnel.

"The PRT consists of one hundred people, including Department of State, USAID, eight civil affairs officers, and a forty-man security force. The comms, intelligence, drivers, cooks, and so on are all USAF personnel. The NCE has access to brigade-level assets, like Tactical HUMIT Teams, PSYOPS, and snipers."

Beave explained that the PRT handled large development projects, while the battalion dealt with smaller projects. Both drew on the same Commanders Emergency Response pot of money. The other government departments like the Department of Justice and the Department of State dealt directly with their Afghan counterparts; USAID worked with the PRT on the large projects, but had its own funds. "The PRT has to 'deconflict' so that we don't have 'fratricide' between the two organizations," Beave explained. His PRT had a development "targeting" board, and it had the same problems as the Canadian PRT. It took informal and personal means to solve many problems that were forced on the operators by their respective bureaucracies. The battalion and the PRT had an effects board at the NCE level so that they could synchronize their operations. I assumed that information and intelligence also flowed into a single organization at the NCE level.

There was a meeting scheduled between the Americans, the district chief, and the ANA commander in a district on Highway 1. There we got an Afghan perspective on the security situation. The district chief with red and black hair, a black beard, and a brightly colored skull cap was drinking a big orange pop: the ensemble made him look like a really violent clown. "The enemy is still out there, even though he isn't creating damage," he told us through the interpreter. "The enemy will attack the highway and the district center. We foiled the last attack by the presence of the ANA and the Americans. The Taliban will continue with ambushes but its direct attacks have dropped off in number."

"What is the situation with the police?" Dave Fraser asked.

"We have seventy officers, but only fifty-five have identification with pictures. They haven't been paid for three months. If they are not paid, the Taliban will pay them. They will go home to the hills. If I lose the ANA here, I will be unable to maintain the situation. I need fuel, weapons, ammunition, and money. I have rations from the Americans, but we are only able to get fuel on a monthly basis. My men use weapons seized from the Taliban." So the police had to forage for weapons from the enemy? That wasn't a good sign. Throughout the discussion, we learned that there was virtually no help from the government. There had been an ambush that killed three police officers and destroyed two vehicles. These men were buried right outside the gate of the compound and the burnt pickup truck in the field was one of the ambushed vehicles.

It turned out that Major Frank Strueck had recently been able to secure funds for the police, and they had just started to get paid. The district chief, though, thanked the coalition forces for their assistance throughout the meeting. "The enemy wants this district to fail: they attack our road engineers. But the enemy has been foiled, and they now are taking sanctuary to the south in the mountains. That is good."

"What are your development needs?" the team asked.

"We need Highway 1 paved. We need reliable bridges. If we had buses, people could move around and work. At least we are better off than the districts in northern Kandahar," the district chief smiled. "We have a lot of civilian traffic here. If we have roads and bridges, there will be work. People will stay and not go to Pakistan. More schools. More police stations. We need garbage collection at the bazaar."

When we were having lunch, Beave told me about the trade school that the PRT sponsored. Several National Guard soldiers who had civilian construction skills came up with the idea of teaching techniques to those locals that were interested. In time the PRT was able to mentor the provincial government ministry responsible for reconstruction into formally accepting the idea. The soldiers took on Afghans who were interested in the building trades and they worked together on the smaller projects. There were few NGOs here and none had the capacity or interest in the trade school. As Beave explained, there was another agenda in play. Indolent youth were a prime recruiting ground for the Taliban. If they had something to do, if they had the means of making a living, they would be less inclined to join up. "Employed youth don't become fighters," he said.

The governor in Zabol had a vision where Highway 1 was paved, and there were lateral paved roads north and south that ran off the highway into the rural areas. As road construction progressed using local people, he wanted to establish a clinic next to the bazaars in each community, and then later, a district center next to the clinic. The roads would then connect these islands of governance and commerce to form a lattice, with Highway 1 as the "backbone." Stability, presumably, would follow, while the kinetic forces killed the enemy.

The main obstacle to this was the UN. The UN arrived in Zabol with their way of doing things, including a contract process that ensured that contractors in Kabul or Pakistan got the contracts for local reconstruction. This pissed off the local people. It was entirely possible that violence directed at construction personnel wasn't Taliban violence but local violence. Or somebody with a relative in the Taliban convinced them to ambush a construction party . . . and the various permutations of that theory thereof. USAID, incidentally, wasn't free of similar problems in Zabol province. American accountability legislation didn't take into account overt nepotism and patronage. It was akin to the narco problem and the detainee problem. To what extent can Western governments legally alter how they do business in a different culture? Can there be one law that governs behavior in both North America and Afghanistan? Where, exactly, is the point of compromise? And will the critics and media and political opposition back home allow it or will they insist that Western approaches and legal processes be forced onto Afghanistan? This was the nub of the problem.

We met with the Zabol chief of police, who looked like Lee Marvin with a white beard. He had been a counternarco cop in Khost province, not an easy job. He provided us with further insight into the policing situation. When asked questions, he answered with clipped, Soviet-like answers that came through even in translation: "The government's authority is the people in the districts" and "We respond in a joint, coordinated fashion to enemy provocation." It was obvious where he learned his trade. Like his counterparts elsewhere in RC South, the chief's main issue was pay for his men and ammo. There had been no money for three months. He understood that General Esmatullah was new in the position and that he couldn't even supply *himself* yet, but the chief still sent him regular reports.

"The enemy will attack in the next six months and we will have to respond lacking 85 percent of our personnel and weapons. We need more people. I need people I can trust. I can't trust the district police chiefs. The problem is that the MOI can't get people to come here. All of my existing people will succumb to pressure." The chief then explained in detail that he needed them all removed . . . and he had a list. He *had* to be ex-KHAD (Khadamat-e Etela'at-e Dawlati, Government Intelligence Service). I mean, lists?

The conversation shifted to a discussion of larger police policy. Ten provincial police chiefs were supposed to have been fired (that is, nearly 50 percent of the provincial police chiefs in the country). Four were displaced and not fired, for human rights violations. Just then an aide, in a clean uniform, came in, saluted (!), and passed the chief a paper. He nodded, and the aide saluted and left.

Then the chief slipped up and started a sentence in English and immediately switched to Pashto. I was able to speak with the chief one-on-one. He had over the years served in Herat, Konduz, and Feyzabad; he even had a postgraduate degree in policing. "I have been a police officer for 41.5 years. I have fought for two things: against corruption and against narcotics. If we had the equipment, the fight would be ours," he asserted. He was, he said, optimistic that the problems would be overcome, that the PRT and TF WARRIOR had always responded when needed and together they would be successful. I could almost hear the band playing *The Internationale* in the background. I really believed that the chief was sincere. He had me convinced he was serious. Afghanistan needed a whole generation of men like him. But where were they going to come from?

On our way out of Qalat, I saw a lot of construction under way. This was a province that was going somewhere, but could the effort be sustained over the long term? And how would the enemy react to an increased target set relatively closer to the Pakistani border than, say, Oruzgan? Only time would tell.

## The United Kingdom and the Helmand Task Force

The situation with the deployment of British forces to Helmand province and their relationship to AEGIS was a challenge in many areas. When I first hit the ground, a staff member told me that the British forces were in the process of "a complete meltdown of their command and control system here." This surprised me greatly. When I was at the Royal Military College of Canada, I taught all the classic British counterinsurgency operations—Dhofar, Cyprus, Kenya, Borneo, Northern Ireland, and Malaya. That collection of experiences, with their successes and failures, was the basic body of information on a Commonwealth army fighting that style of warfare. To hear that things were not going well for the British over in Helmand . . . I was taken aback.

Until, of course, I was able to familiarize myself with what had been going on. Once the British government agreed to deploy in February, the usual process of shaping operations, recce, infrastructure construction, and force deployment went into gear. Again, the British weren't new at this: they had deployed with OEF in 2002 and with ISAF in Mazar-e Sharif in 2003. They had run a PRT up in Maz. They also had antagonized their German neighbors over in Feyzabad with their use of SOF against people involved in narcotics, uncoordinated operations that produced unintended consequences.

There also had been special operations "shaping operations" in Helmand. These were more or less an operational and infrastructural recce operation carried out by American, British, and Canadian SOF in the spring. There were some U.S. ETTs working with the ANA's two kandaks. It looked like things were okay from mid-2005 into spring 2006.

The U.K. PRT was established in Lashkar Gah sometime in April 2006, while BRITFOR flowed in. TF HELMAND consisted of the PRT; 3rd Battalion, the Parachute Regiment commanded by Lieutenant Colonel Stuart Tootal; and a light armored squadron from the Household Cavalry equipped with Scimitar vehicles. BRITFOR, which was the British national command and logistics element that was *not* under CTF AEGIS' command, was based on the brigade HQ for 16 Air Assault Brigade and was led by Brigadier Ed Butler. The British helicopter unit, equipped with CH-47 Chinooks and AH-64 Apaches, also belonged to BRITFOR.

TF HELMAND had to drive from KAF up Highway 4, through Kandahar City, west along Highway 1 past Zharey district, through Maywand district, and into Helmand province. The British convoys had to move through the Canadian area of operations, but they had different rules of engagement and were not under AEGIS' command. There were incidents where the wrong people got shot by troops who weren't fully acclimatized. The fallout from those situations had to be addressed by the Kandahar PRT, which distracted it from other tasks. To make matters worse, a level of guilt-by-association built up over time so that in 2007, when a British convoy overreacted and shot and wounded more than thirty people in the city, the population nearly turned on the Canadian Forces in the city.

There were grievances in Helmand that existed prior to the HELMAND TF deployment. In 2002, U.S. SOF made deals with the tribal groups in Helmand in order to get assistance in the fight against the Taliban. These groups, most of whom had connections to the Akhundzada families, were anticipating something on the order of $2 million in cash for their efforts, or nonefforts, as the case might be. When the USAID and U.S. State Department got involved later, they told the principals that Helmand would get $2 million in aid—and that it would be distributed by the governor. This, needless to say, didn't go over well and damaged relations between the Helmand power brokers and the coalition forces. There were sporadic spurts of violence, but nothing on the order of what happened later.

The real trouble for CTF AEGIS started during harvest season in the spring of 2006. As part of the British government's communications strategy to convince critics in Britain to support the redeployment of British forces from Maz to Helmand, the mission was billed by British politicians as a "peace-support" operation that would have collateral effects on the domestic situation in the U.K.—namely, counter-narcotics operations in Helmand would take heroin off British streets. A similar communications strategy had been used in the Mazar-e Sharif deployment. The Taliban, seeking fissures wherever they could find and exploit them, now had one. The message was now, "The British, the ones who oppressed you in the 1800s, are now coming here to take away your livelihood!" At the same time, one of the main narcotics clans in Helmand had a break in relations with the HiG organization, which was now allied with the Taliban. The Taliban could play a reconciliation role between the two groups and improve the synergy of the insurgency in Helmand.

Sure enough, when the Afghan Eradication Force (AEF) arrived in the spring to eradicate the poppy fields, large swaths of the population shifted into the "alienated" column. What the average farmer saw was an Afghan security force with American advisers backed up by British troops moving onto his land and plowing up his plants—with little or no compensation. None of this, by the way, was influenced by CTF AEGIS.

The Taliban was present in the province, but not in great numbers. They tended to hang out in the mountainous north adjacent to Oruzgan, and to some extent in Farah. They had their people farther south, but when I visited Afghanistan in 2004 and 2005 there did not appear to be a significant level of insurgent violence. Indeed, the Americans had only a company and a small PRT to keep an eye on things. The enemy, however, attacked the isolated Bagran Valley district center in north in March 2006 and took it over; the enemy forces came out of two small mountainous zones in Farah to do that job. When the British showed up, they provided more targets for the enemy to attack, which attracted more enemy forces, who then allied themselves with the aggrieved parties in common cause.

To prevent a recurrence of the Bagran Valley deal, HELMAND TF was instructed by Division (CJTF-76) to distribute 3 Para into "platoon houses" that were to be located in proximity to the district centers throughout the northern part of the province at Sangin, Now Zad, Kajaki, and Musa Qala. This, in theory, would provide a security presence at the district level and permit aid programs to be carried out, but it was not the original plan that the HELMAND TF deployment was based on. Colonel Charlie Knaggs, the HELMAND TF commander, wanted to secure their bases in Lashkar Gah and Geresk, work on the governance and development lines, and then move north later. Keep in mind how big Helmand province is—also keep in mind that the two ANA kandaks in Helmand were not capable of anything larger than platoon-level activity. The helicopter force was now supposed to resupply those platoon houses. The 3 Para platoons, being light infantry, were mounted in unarmored Land Rovers and had limited mobility compared with TF ORION.

HELMAND TF also had to contend with the artificialities imposed by the ISAF-OEF relationship. We knew the enemy had these locations inside Farah province, but Farah was in RC West and under ISAF command. The forces there were Italian, Portuguese, and Spanish. A Canadian officer I know acted as a liaison to RC West and came away less than impressed. RC West refused to mount effective operations against those Taliban zones in Farah. They were, they claimed, too far from their bases and, in any case, they were on a peace support operation and not doing counterinsurgency. When pressed, RC West mounted the poorly but appropriately named Operation Turtle, but it stalled out when the Spanish force hit an IED. Frustrated, CFC-A deployed a U.S. Special Forces ODB to work with the ANA's 209 Corps in RC West and get them into shape, but that would take months. In any event, Farah was far, far away from the provincial capital of Lashkar Gah, which itself was not yet secured. Governor Daoud insisted that securing it was the priority.

The politics surrounding Governor Daoud and his relations to the British effort in Afghanistan, I suspect, would resemble the plot of a Robert Ludlum novel. As I understood it at the time, Daoud was championed by the British in Kabul and was essentially imposed on the province by President Karzai. This imposition displaced other leaders who were more closely connected to the Helmand power structure and, of course, its narcotics trade. I was told on several occasions that some events in Helmand were designed in part to embarrass Daoud and had little to do with insurgent activity. Again, the barest outlines of this problem existed in early 2006 and there is no way that the deploying British forces had anything like a full understanding of those dynamics. Once again, the counter-narcotics agenda was a prism that distorted the realities of the situation.

On the command and control front, relations between BRITFOR and AEGIS were tenuous. I believe, looking back at it, that Brigadier Ed Butler really wanted his own separate command in Helmand, one that didn't report to AEGIS. As one officer put it, Butler was ambitious, had served in the SAS (Special Air Service), and wasn't afraid of locking horns with Major General Ben Freakley. Playing second fiddle to a Canadian general whose operational experience involved stabilization operations at the battalion level in Bosnia and who wasn't interested in contorting the needs of Afghanistan to meet British domestic political needs might have posed problems. I don't know for sure, but this was the impression I took away from people at AEGIS. Butler was the only player in the 2006 drama who wouldn't talk to me at the time and it was clear from his nonverbal communication with me that he regarded the presence of a historian (especially a Canadian one that he couldn't control) with some suspicion.

What I do know for sure was that there were other command issues in the British camp. Butler may have been commander of BRITFOR, but the forces deployed in Helmand were supposed to respond to CTF AEGIS. Colonel Charlie Knaggs was supposed to be the HELMAND TF commander and was supposed to have a command relationship to Dave Fraser. 3 Para, however, belonged to Butler's 16 Air Assault Brigade, not to Charlie Knaggs' lash-up headquarters, and 3 Para's CO Lieutenant Colonel Stuart Tootal and Butler were old friends. It doesn't take a rocket scientist to figure out what the implications of that arrangement were.

The British deployment was predicated on the more benign environment of a peace-support operation, but what they ran into was something very different. That situation set the stage for several deployments from Kandahar province and Zabol province to prop up the British position, and, in some cases, even relieve and rescue surrounded British forces. CTF AEGIS was confronted with a situation whereby its campaign plan could not be carried out, in part because of the constant need to shift scarce forces to Helmand. Those forces, in theory, were needed to provide security for the population and reconstruction and aid projects in their home provinces. CTF AEGIS' objective of facilitating the reconstruction and governance effort and shielding that effort from Taliban interference in some ways became more and more subordinated to British domestic political requirements.

## COUNTER-NARCOTICS MATTERS

Counter-narcotics was massively problematic for AEGIS. The main problem was that all the nations contributing to the counterinsurgency effort in RC South had conflicting counter-narcotics policies. In the broadest sense, counter-narcotics policy and the means by which it is carried out formed one division of opinion. Counter-narcotics could involve, for example, an alternative livelihoods program to replace the poppy crop with another one, like saffron. Or it could include the eradication of poppy via its physical destruction during late growing or early harvesting season in the spring of the year. The American policy was split: the State Department and the Drug Enforcement Administration favored eradication, but the Department of Defense and the Other Government Agency did not. Britain was pro-eradication, but the Dutch were not. Canada did not favor eradication and pushed for a variety of creative alternatives. ISAF, being European-dominated, was pro-eradication, but OEF's CFC-A was not.

As for the Afghans—well, which ones? Kabul wanted eradication because its reconstruction donor countries wanted it. The provincial governors—that depended on their situation province by province. The governors generally paid lip service to the counternarco policy and set up what were collectively called "governor-led programs." The intention was to have the governors be the "face" of eradication. Nobody seriously considered the possibility that some of the governors might actually *be involved* in the narco trade; that was too horrible to contemplate. In any event, Kabul told the governors to put together an eradication plan, cajole mullahs and tribal elders into providing public support, and then verify eradication with *"Untouchables"*-like verification teams. No consideration was given to the insurgent situation by those in Kabul pushing all of this. It was as if the insurgency didn't exist.

Overall, there were two drug processing and trafficking syndicates in the south: the Helmand group and the Ghazni group. The Ghazni group had contacts with the Tajik Mafia in Kabul, who had links to Russian organized crime. The Helmand group had links to the plethora of narco groups operating in Pakistan that also had connections to Al Qaeda and the Taliban. Keep in mind that the narco problem wasn't new and that those links went back several decades. In the old days of the jihad, HiG was the organization that dealt with the Helmand group; in the late 1990s, it was the Taliban.[8] Both groups had a variety of links to the provincial governments in the south.

Sometime in 2005 the United States and the United Kingdom decided to fund the AEF (also known as TF EAGLE). Obviously, it was poorly named because its purpose wasn't to eradicate Afghans: it was to eradicate poppy. The AEF consisted of Afghan police, Afghan army, DynCorp pilots flying UH-1H helicopters equipped with Gatling guns, tractor operators, and ex-U.S. military operators, many of whom had experience in Colombia with U.S. State Department–funded programs. The Afghan military contingent also had an U.S. Army ETT that reported to TF PHOENIX via the RCAG. The AEF had no relationship, command or otherwise, or even formal liaison staff to CTF AEGIS or CJTF-76—except for this ETT anomaly.

When I arrived in Afghanistan in 2006, the debate over the role and use of the AEF was still raging. Because Oruzgan province was going to be under Dutch and therefore ISAF control, there were plans to use the AEF to conduct eradication there. The U.S.-commanded CFC-A said "no way" because Oruzgan would not be under ISAF control until sometime in July or August.

When the British agreed to take Helmand province and deploy a PRT and battle group, they also brought with them their counter-narcotics policy, which involved eradication. Once HELMAND TF stood up, the AEF deployed alongside Governor Daoud's eradication force that was also prepared to conduct eradication. Daoud was a governor favored by the British, facilitated into power by the British, but one that clashed with the existing provincial power structure. Both eradication task forces went to work . . . and then encountered serious armed resistance. The presence of the American ETTs with the AEF made it look as it OEF, and by extension AEGIS, were pro-eradication. This had predictable results. The Canadian-led coalition forces, which had no intention of conducting poppy eradication, were now tarred with the same brush as the AEF. Consequently, it wasn't long before Taliban agitators appeared in the south with the message, "The infidels are here to take away your livelihoods. We will help train you to fight them, brothers!"

To pour gas on this raging blaze, governor-led eradication was subjected to bribery, extortion, and tribal political pressures at all levels. If a poppy farmer had the cash, he coughed up and maybe the AEF tractors became a little less efficient. Or maybe he was the cousin of somebody on the provincial council. But his neighbor didn't get or couldn't afford such protection and became resentful. And guess who showed up to exploit these grievances?

The bad info ops that came out of this was that the whole mess reinforced the perception in the population that (a) the government of Afghanistan was corrupt, (b) ISAF and OEF supported government corruption, and (c) the Western powers only care about their domestic agendas, and don't really care about Afghanistan or its people. The self-evident nature of this problem during a counterinsurgency war should have been obvious but it remains astounding that the pro-eradication elements continue years later in their sheer bloody-mindedness, making new enemies and reinforcing old ones—again, in a land where Pashtunwali rules. And they can't claim they weren't told: almost all of us involved in the war at that time told them so long before 2006.

When the AEF went to work in Helmand in March–April 2006, it got shot at by organized, well-armed personnel.[9] In one instance Canadian artillery that deployed to Helmand with an infantry company to support an expanded presence in Sangin came under pressure to provide fire support to the AEF when it was attacked on the other side of the Helmand River. This caused a certain amount of consternation back at

CTF AEGIS. AEGIS didn't like being manipulated by the pro-eradication elements into cutting across policy already established by OEF, CFC-A, and the Canadian government.

In effect, the counter-narcotics fight undermined the counterinsurgency fight in southern Afghanistan on several levels. It was a European and U.S. law enforcement lobby agenda ("We can't give in on Afghanistan eradication, because then we'll have to give in on Colombian eradication," I was once told by a American drug cop) imposed on Afghans and the government of Afghanistan. It in no way stopped or even hindered the flow of cash to narco elements embedded in the Afghan provincial governments. What it did do was demonstrate to the average Afghan that the coalition didn't understand, or didn't want to understand, what the hell was actually going on out there. And, I venture to say, it emboldened those involved in such activities to expand their ability to acquire money into other activities, which made matters worse over the course of the next few years. All anybody heard was the media and think-tank mantra about the "Narco-Terror Nexus," and *nobody* questioned it. Indeed, the so-called analysis, if taken to the next logical step, should have made it the "Narco-Terror-Afghan-Government Nexus." But that was a little too unpalatable because it would undermine the less-sophisticated argument that suited a variety of purposes in the media and academic communities.

There were some Machiavellis who believed that selective eradication could be used, very carefully, at the district level to put pressure on narco elements in the provincial governments. The idea here was to focus some eradication operations on those who already bribed officials to get them to ignore their crops, and get them mad at the current officials. At the same time, the message would be heard by the officials who might change their ways. It was another form of "chessgame," but I never found an example where this worked. The aggrieved parties went to the Taliban—or the Taliban went to them.

THE ONGOING PROBLEM OF PAKISTAN
In May 2006 the media asked the AEGIS chief of staff, Colonel Chris Vernon, about the relationship between the Taliban insurgency and Pakistan. A subsequent *Guardian* article read,

> Colonel Chris Vernon, chief of staff for southern Afghanistan, said the Taliban leadership was coordinating its campaign from the

western Pakistani city of Quetta, near the Afghan border. "The thinking piece of the Taliban is out of Quetta in Pakistan. It's the major headquarters," he told the Guardian. "They use it to run a series of networks in Afghanistan." The Afghan president, Hamid Karzai, echoed these comments by accusing Pakistan of arming the insurgents. "Pakistani intelligence gives military training to people and then sends them to Afghanistan with logistics," the Pakistan-based Afghan Islamic Press news agency quoted him as saying. Col Vernon said the Quetta leadership controlled "about 25" mid-level commanders dotted across the Afghan south.

This set off the proverbial international shitstorm. The Islamic Republic News Agency screamed, "Pakistan on Friday described as ludicrous remarks by British Colonel Chris Vernon, chief of staff for southern Afghanistan, that Pakistan is allowing Taliban to use its soil for attacks in Afghanistan." Chris got a personal phone call from "higher"—a British "higher," *very* "higher"—that told him approximately to shut the fuck up.

It emerged later that Britain was engaged in an extremely sensitive investigation that required Pakistani cooperation. The results of that operation resulted in the arrest of twenty-four suspected terrorists in the United Kingdom and the unraveling of a plot to attack with liquid explosives airliners departing Heathrow. The plot was conceived and funded by a network in Pakistan that apparently siphoned off money from relief funds established to help with the relief of the 2005 Kashmir earthquake in order to pay for the materiel and personnel needed for the operation.

But were Chris' comments in fact ludicrous?

- The enemy was commanded by the Quetta Shura, and it met in Quetta, Baluchistan, which technically was part of Pakistan.
- I was told that Afghan businessmen who lived in Quetta but had connections in Kandahar were coerced into funding Taliban activities and using their businesses to facilitate the entry of personnel and ammunition into the RC South provinces. Other Quetta businessmen, both Pakistani and Afghan, needed no coercion and willingly supported the insurgency. Some had supported the Taliban in 1996 when criminal violence got out of hand and interfered with their ability to conduct commerce along Highway 4 and Highway 1 in Afghanistan.

- The madrassas in and around Quetta are heavily infiltrated with radical Islamists. This in part is a result of failed educational policies under the Bhutto government that reduced funding to secular schools in the early 1990s.
- While on numerous operations, I saw our forces uncover weapons caches that had RPG, 82-mm, and 107-mm rounds in them. These weapons had Chinese and English markings, not Farsi or Russian. The ammo was new, not rusted or chipped, and therefore did not come from old 1980s Mujaheddin stockpiles. Pakistani Army ammunition carries English and sometimes Chinese markings.
- The Taliban casualty evacuation (CASEVAC) "ratline" ran from hidden clinics in the districts, sometimes to Kandahar City and Chaman, or back to Baram Chah and then Quetta. I understand that some wounded were even evacuated by air from Pakistan to hospitals in the Gulf, which was not a new procedure and had occurred in the 1980s.
- The internally displaced persons (IDP) camps in Kandahar province were other entry points for Taliban infiltration. Taliban personnel pretending to be returning refugees easily blended in with the IDP populations in the Pakistan camps and then got a free ride from those camps near Chaman all the way to camps north of Zharey district and another camp between Panjwayii and Kandahar City.

At the same time, there were some examples of improved cooperation with PAKMIL late in July. The Taliban base area at Baram Chah south of Helmand was under serious scrutiny. When the Taliban activated its CASEVAC chain during the battles in Sangin, Nawa, and Garmser, the coalition forces detected them moving the wounded to the border with an escort force. There was a firefight between retreating Taliban and Pakistani forces, and the Pakistanis asked for close air support. A B-1B arrived, but because the Pakistan force had no certified JTAC the plane couldn't engage. The B-1B buzzed the Taliban, unnerving them and allowed the Pakistani tactical commander to take advantage of the disruption. Initial BDA was estimated to be fifty enemy dead.

We have to move beyond our traditional conception of what constitutes a state. We have been doing so since the 1990s, but the apparent ambiguity of the coexistence of the Taliban, Al Qaeda, and Pakistan defies conventional reasoning and has the potential to lead to various forms of conspiracy theory.

Colonel Chris Vernon's remarks were not as counterproductive as many at the echelons higher than reality thought. The Kandahar City audience welcomed his confirmation of what they already knew was the case. He's a hero to many of them, as our I/O people learned later. The stature of the coalition forces increased in that target population after his remarks, and did not decrease.

## CASUALTIES OF WAR

The most difficult aspect of war to discuss is casualties, what the analysts glibly call "the costs of war." The immediate and long-term effects of having one's friends killed or mutilated in combat are integral to any personal account of war. Memoirs capture these emotions on an individual level, but analytic historical accounts sometimes seem bloodless. And nobody ever talks about the effects of war on administrative staff. Derided in Vietnam as REMFs and by some in Afghanistan as people who live in comfort and don't go "outside the wire," I found in my travels and discussions that the war had profound effects on the J-1 staff, the people who handled personnel administration. Most soldiers are not comfortable talking about emotions at the best of times. Some of the J-1 people were conflicted and weren't sure if they had "earned the right" to be upset because they hadn't experienced IED attacks, direct fire, and so on.

This emotional terrain is so rocky that some people wanted to express how they felt to me but didn't want to be identified. And that is fully understandable. For example, I was in the dining facility (DFAC) near the Canadian headquarters having lunch when one officer came in, and, in a parody of grace, prayed to Satan instead. Now, was this done for the benefit of the padre who was present as a joke, or was it something else? He also whistled Christmas tunes in July. I suspected it was more than black humor. It was his way of dealing with the war.

He was having a smoke one day and we started talking. "You know, I have to be present when the Mortuary Affairs people do the final cleanup of the bodies before they are put in the coffins, sealed, and shipped home." He took a long drag on the cigarette. "The Mortuary Affairs unit here is American: it's from Puerto Rico. They are very caring, and very respectful. I don't know how they do it. When the close protection party

G-Wagon was blown up with that massive IED, the remains of four guys were put into five bags. Mortuary Affairs had to do the sorting. I had to be there when they had figured it out. It was like a human jigsaw puzzle. I was also there one time when they were mopping up the blood. I was literally ankle-deep in blood once. Not many people can say that." He took out another cancer stick and tapped it on the pack. The conversation just trailed off. It would affect him in one way or another for the rest of this life and he knew it. There was nothing more to be said.

Major Darcy Wright and I got to know each other on various excursions with Niner Niner, General Fraser's tactical headquarters (TAC HQ). Darcy, who is an infantry officer from 1 PPCLI, worked as the J-1 for CTF AEGIS, so he dealt with all nationalities who contributed to the mission and who lost people. Darcy felt each and every one of those, not just the Canadians. He was responsible for picking up the personal gear and effects of the men who had been killed from the smaller troop-contributing nations, the ones who didn't have an NCE. Darcy once had to identify a friend of his who had been killed in a LAV rollover. His staff had to collect the data on each and every casualty, including the wounded, and decide how to handle notification of the next of kin. I asked him how this affected his staff.

"We have had to develop a disengagement from the task. Early on, it was all novel. It really, really takes a toll on your soul. Some of my people find it really difficult to go to the ramp ceremonies. I really hate the thugs, the enemy. I have an increasing hatred for the enemy with each death I have to deal with. I also have more and more respect for the Afghan people, who have endured this for decades. We now share a mass of misery together. My staff is closer than before—all ranks. I have to handle the documentation for all casualties and I also deal with Mortuary Affairs." Darcy explained that on one occasion he helped the Puerto Rican National Guard soldiers reassemble a soldier after an IED attack and he had to suppress all of his emotions and get the job done as quickly as possible. "They are spectacular. They are so respectful and wash the bodies very carefully and ensure the safety of all personal effects," he explained. "But the wounded: they take a greater toll on the staff, especially psychologically. The dead are dead—we respect that. But the worst are those who are paralyzed, or have traumatic amputations. My staff has a certain amount of isolation from the other troops, which doesn't make it easy with the 'inside the wire/outside the wire' bullshit. You know, Nic

Goddard was my next-door neighbor back home." Why should it affect Darcy less than those who were there when she died?

"Then there is 'safe little KAF.' You know, since you've been here this summer, we've had eighteen seriously wounded people from the rocket attacks here. And those are shrapnel wounds, skull fractures, and facial lacerations. 'Outside' you can shoot back. Here, we have to go for the bunkers. The randomness of it can affect people. My people exhibit resignation and apathy now because there are so many attacks. I anticipate that some people will have problems reintegrating when they get home. We've hardly had any 'freak outs' here. There's a lot of mission focus and that helps. I'm worried about what will happen later."

I wanted Darcy's impression of TF ORION and the casualty issue. "TF ORION is a finely honed killing machine," he said. "When it comes to casualties, there is none of this 'officer–other ranks' thing. The proportion of casualties is about equal. Two officers killed and three wounded out of twenty-six, and seven killed and fifty wounded out of eight hundred men." Nobody was being used as cannon fodder and the officers led from the front. As it should be. "And guess how many soldiers have been returned home for disciplinary reasons from the Canadian contingent of two thousand people? Two." That was incredible. The numbers of disciplinary repatriations for a typical six-month Canadian SFOR tour in Bosnia was usually in the double digits. And here was TF ORION in Month Five of a counterinsurgency war—with two!

During my time in KAF, I also was able to gain insight into the mental health situation. It was distressing to learn that there were still competing schools of thought about treatment. One school of thought was to keep battle stress or traumatic stress casualties in-theater, treat them at KAF, then return them to their unit for the rest of the tour. The other school of thought was demanding near-immediate evacuation and treatment outside the theater of operations. Obviously, if someone was psychotic or suicidal, than the latter approach was perhaps best, but that was the exception and not the rule. From what I saw, it was better that soldiers worked it out among themselves as a team—it was better to "get back up on the horse." Otherwise, everybody working "outside the wire" or "inside the wire," including me, would have been evacuated at one time or another and there would be nobody left to do the job.

PART *Two*

# MISSION: TF ORION

We need some "connective tissue" here. I've just described AEGIS' moving parts and some of the challenges the headquarters was confronted with in 2006. Before we get into more detail, let's review TF ORION's movements prior to that year. Ian Hope and his staff met up with Lieutenant Colonel Bert Ges from TF GUNDEVILS on 1 February for a ground recce of the area of operations, and by 10 February TF ORION's soldiers were conducting a joint familiarization process for the tactical commanders. A LAV III from "A" Company hit an IED near Pada, wounding four Canadians. This event served as a wake-up call that Afghanistan wasn't Bosnia, Cyprus, or Somalia.

By 24 February TF ORION was up and running and the TF GUNDEVILS left for home. The ORION Tactical Operations Center (TOC) was located in a collection of plywood shacks that were near the improvised JTF-2 CQB training area. On 27 February AEGIS took over from BAYONET and occupied the old CTF-82 headquarters complex.

Operation Counterstrike, established by BAYONET for counter-rocket operations in the hills outside KAF, was replaced by Operation Pharos, that employed the sniper teams and Coyotes from TF ORION. At this point, a Romanian battalion, the 341st Infantry Battalion (TF WHITESHARKS) handled KAF security. It required augmentation for proactive measures, however, so from time to time ORION would work with WHITESHARKS. The battle group really wanted to do a multiple-company sweep through the northeastern communities (contingency plan Normandy) as a first "shake-out" operation, but this was vetoed from higher.

The sniper teams kept getting "rumbled." There was just too much civilian traffic in these areas and a lot of curious kids. After one insertion north of Highway 1, one team was mortared. Eventually, ORION's efforts to support KAF security were rolled into Operation Rocket Man.

## Operation Sola Kowel: "A" Company in Shah Wali Kot District

"A" Company, led by Major Kirk Gallinger and Company Sergeant Major Pete Leger, became responsible for the former GUNDEVILS area of operations in upper Shah Wali Kot district. In March, FOB Martello hadn't been built yet and tactical infrastructure was limited to the Gumbad Platoon House, situated next to the district center. Gumbad is a rocky, mountainous area: its primary feature of interest was the Belly Button, a collection of small mountains with a small valley in the center. It would have been a perfect citadel a hundred years ago—and probably was. Isolated, with its own water supply and long observation distances, the probability of finding enemy activity there was high. "A" Company settled in and started a patrol program with lots of local leadership engagement and CIMIC assessment activity.

TF GUNDEVILS had been chasing around a Taliban leader named Mullah Tahir who had access to several insurgent bands operating in Shah Wali Kot, through northern Khakriz district, into Neish district, and Mianashein district. The American task force had a series of escalating running battles throughout late 2005. Now that TF ORION was on the ground, Operation Sola Kowel was mounted to disrupt the Taliban, establish better rapport with the population, and generate some breathing space for the construction of FOB Martello and improvements to the Tarin Kot Road. Sola Kowel was a shaping operation so that the Dutch task force could get into Oruzgan province.

Kirk Gallinger's company rotated a platoon through the Gumbad Platoon House. For Sola Kowel, though, another "A" Company platoon and other enablers like Steve Gallagher's M-777 guns were brought in, while "C" Company was readied for the operation. The scheme of maneuver was to have "C" Company screen to the north and east of the Belly Button, while "A" Company scaled the mountains and swept the "bowl." There was another operation scheduled for the area, but it was a CJSOTF mission designed to take out a leadership target. Originally "C" Company was going to assist with that other operation, but the weather stopped the helicopter insert, so Bill Fletcher and his men became part of the screen.

The kickoff of Sola Kowel was marred, tragically, by two events. The first was a vehicle accident on 2 March that killed two soldiers from "B" Company: Master Corporal Tim Wilson and Corporal Paul Davis. The second was the attempted murder of Captain Trevor Greene on 4 March. Trevor, a CIMIC officer, was working in the Shinkay-Nari Wala area. He and his team stopped to conduct a leadership engagement. After twenty minutes of conversation, a young man walked up behind Trevor, pulled out an axe, and drove it into the back of his head. The security party opened up and killed the attacker. Another individual prepared to throw a grenade, but he was discouraged from this action by fire and withdrew. Trevor was medevac'd and barely survived. The shocked locals claimed the attacker was crazy, but other information pointed toward the probability that this was a deliberate attack encouraged by a Taliban leader. Subsequently, when "C" Company was deploying north of the Belly Button, the enemy attacked a clearly marked Bison ambulance with a remote-controlled IED. There were no injuries in that incident.

"A" Company started its maneuver to and through the objective areas. Captain Martin Larose (Kirk and Pete were on leave) took "A" Company up the Belly Button in an arduous night climb and swept through the bowl. There were indications that the enemy had previously used it as a rest area, but there were no weapons caches. Both companies spread out and conducted leadership engagements in the communities, while CIMIC gathered as much information as possible so the area could be assessed for projects and development. These operations continued throughout March.

At the same time, local mullahs started getting "night letters" from the Taliban, after which there was increased IED use in Shah Wali Kot with two remote-controlled IED attacks conducted in the Gumbad area. Somebody new was in town. In the face of this increased threat, "A" Company continued to push out to the communities and surveyed what would become FOB Martello.

Upper Shah Wali Kot remained a hotbed of insurgent activity and the worst was yet to come. On 22 April Dave Fraser's close protection party was traveling through the district on the way back to KAF when the enemy detonated a remote-controlled mine stack. The massive explosion nearly obliterated the G-Wagon, and killed Corporal Matthew Dinning,

Bombardier Myles Mansell, Corporal Randy Payne, and Lieutenant Bill Turner. Bill was on his way home on leave and had hitched a ride.

## Operation Katera: "C" Company in Sangin District, Helmand Province

The situation in Helmand province heated up just as TF ORION was preparing to get a grip on governance and development lines of operations. U.K. SOF initiated their first recce operations at the end of February in preparation for the TF HELMAND deployment. Elements of TF-73, the U.S. SOF task force, also deployed around this time and established FOB Wolf just south of Sangin. The CJSOTF was getting more and more information that enemy leadership targets were starting to coalesce in this area. The TF-73 elements started to get into TICs with these well-armed and organized groups. In early March a major ambush killed a senior NDS commander, the Sangin district leader, and a bunch of ANP. Toward the end of March, TF-73 was getting into more and more contacts all around Sangin, one of which resulted in the death of Sergeant First Class Christopher Robinson from 2nd Battalion, 20th Special Forces Group. FOB Wolf was renamed FOB Robinson (FOB ROB). At this point, that was the only coalition presence in northern Helmand.

At the same time, the AEF arrived and started poppy eradication using methods that, according to Ian Hope, were "ruthless." TF ORION was instructed by CTF BAYONET to prepare a contingency plan to assist the AEF in extremis. This posed problems, because it was not Canadian policy to support eradication. After some high-level politicking, ORION was relieved of the task . . . sort of. The division HQ, CJTF-76, normally maintained a platoon-sized airmobile quick-reaction force (QRF) in the south: platoons from the various battle groups and battalions rotated through the role and it was Canada's turn. Finally, 7 Platoon from "C" Company parked its LAVs and sat next to the American helicopters awaiting any emergency that required them.

When insurgent forces attacked FOB ROB on 29 March, the QRF deployed by helicopter to reinforce the position at last light. The Canadian platoon was thrown into the line as the enemy attacked from the north and the west in a coordinated fashion. Poor fire coordination and confused command and control between the SOF, the ETTs, the Afghans, and the QRF platoon produced a situation where a SOF 7.62-mm machine gun raked the Canadian and American ETT positions, killing Private Robert Costall from 1 PPCLI and Sergeant 1st Class John T. Stone from the Vermont National Guard. This was the first time the insurgents had been bold enough to mount an operation of this scale and expertise. There were questions as to whether this was Taliban, specialists from elsewhere such as HiG, or the private army of one of the annoyed narcos.

In any event, the FOB was reinforced with a Coyote surveillance system and a Canadian LAV company. Bill Fletcher's "C" Company moved out, accompanied by the TF ORION's Niner Tac because of the long-range communications requirements. A det of M-777 guns, plus the forward control station for the Sperwer TUAV and a supply echelon, formed the rest of the force, which would stay in the Sangin area for more than a month.

ISTAR reportage confirmed that Koo Agha was the main bad guy in the Sangin area, but that there were others flocking to him. This organization started to ambush columns on Route 611, the main service route from Highway 1 to Sangin. The LAV company threw them for a loop and ISTAR reportage indicated that the various groups kept passing the buck because nobody wanted to engage the Canadians. Seven Platoon got first blood. Spotting fighters in an ambush position on a hill, they engaged with 25-mm, killing them all and destroying a pickup truck. Then mortars started hitting around FOB ROB. Helmand was hot and here was the proof.

The SOF ODA in the base initially refused to go out with "C" Company: they were pissed off that they were under investigation for the friendly fire killing of Costall and Stone. "C" Company went out anyway. The target was Koo Agha. ISTAR platforms were layered and fed to the forward observation officer (FOO), Captain Nic Goddard, who coordinated fire plans to support the series of cordon and searches designed to trap the enemy leadership. Bill Fletcher conducted a series of diversionary moves with the LAVs while Nic Goddard used the TUAV to try to acquire targets. "The [ISTAR] hits were coming fast and furious," Bill explained. "The green tanks are here! The green tanks are here!" A dismounted insertion went in and found bomb-making materials. But Koo Agha was gone. Another operation, Operation Bator, had the ODA working with "C" Company finally—but again the operation was a dry hole. The target, Mullah Zahir, wasn't there. Bill Fletcher believed that Operation Katera "completely discombobulated them around Sangin"—

for the time being. It probably helped draw off insurgent resources from countering the initial British lay-down to the south.

## "B" COMPANY: ZHAREY AND PANJWAYI DISTRICTS, KANDAHAR PROVINCE

"B" Company was an anomaly compared to its counterparts: it was a mixed company of vehicles: G-Wagons, some with the gun shield kits and some unarmed; and LAV IIIs. B Company crews were a mech infantry company that also had LAV III training, but were now working alongside the OGDs, transporting them in G-Wagons. "My primary function is to provide force protection, both static and mobile, to the PRT *and* be responsible for all things inside Kandahar City, plus Zharey, Maywand, and Panjwayi districts," Major Nick Grimshaw explained to me. With his able second-in-command Captain Jay Adair and CSM Wayne Kelly, Nick's responsibilities expanded exponentially throughout the spring of 2006. Like the PRT company I had been with in 2005, "B" Company was supposed to be a delivery system for the OGDs. "After Glyn Berry was killed, those guys were seldom leaving the gates, so I also became responsible for the joint PCC at the Governor's Palace. Those guys had access to sources that we could never hope to have." "B" Company handled all QRF tasks in the city, like if an IED went off. Nick also patrolled along Highway 1 north of Zharey district.

> We did a lot of information gathering. We found that there was considerable progress in Panjwayi, especially after the road was paved. We'd conduct dismounted patrols in there and buy stuff from the stores in Bazaar-e Panjwayi. I could drive right up through Pashmul to Highway 1 without any problems. We also hooked up with the ANP, Captain Massoud. The Afghan National Highway Police [ANHP] had checkpoints along Highway 1 and they started getting hit. We'd take the RCMP [Royal Canadian Mounted Police] and military police from the PRT and do assessments. We'd help the ANHP with force protection improvements while the ANHP assessed their policing capabilities. We became suspicious—some of the checkpoints never got hit, but others did.

As part of its information collection operations, "B" Company also started to conduct low-level counterinsurgency operations on its own in

Zharey and Panjwayi districts. There was also a four-man CIMIC team with the company led by Captain John Angus that they started to use. Nick determined, "It was no good just to go to a village and say, 'Oh, we need eight wells and we need a school,' and so on. We tried to reinforce district governance. They needed to come to us with a consensus, give us sheets signed by the district leader and then we would take those to the PRT. Unfortunately, it was early days and the focus [of the PRT] was on Kandahar City. The PDC wasn't meeting yet, and there was lots of district favoritism."

"B" Company would work with the police—either Colonel Tor Jan's people from the PRT or Captain Massoud's people from Standby Police Unit 005—and conduct cordon and search operations in both districts. "We did the outer cordon, the police went in, lined up all the males of fighting age, the district chief of police and district leader arrived and decided who should be detained, who was a foreigner, and so on. However, we lost the ability to gain intelligence from them because we didn't detain them—the Afghans did."

Nick and his men determined that all was not on the up and up, however. "There was an NDS guy in Maywand who spoke to us in confidence. He told us that people were being detained who were not insurgents. They were growing poppy for the wrong guy or running guns for somebody else. This was a battle for power and influence in the districts and separate from the Taliban. The district leaders are appointed by the governor, and they aren't elected." More specifically, this was a battle for influence along Highway 1. There was money to be made from illegal "tolls" and the movement of contraband.

It took some time for Nick and "B" Company to suss all of this out. "We were poking around down at the school in Mushan, in western Panjwayi district, when we got a panicked phone call from the district leader saying the ANP were under attack at How-z e Madad, on Highway 1." Four Platoon and "B" Company HQ rolled into a firefight but it wasn't clear who was who. It turned out, "The ANP were doing poppy eradication, going into certain villages. Maywand and Zharey ANP would pick out key villages, go in and threaten to eradicate a field, and extort money unless they complied." Of course, local people would fight back. Were they Taliban? Or not? And how could our forces know?

The one cop that everybody trusted was Kadr Jan, a man of courage and integrity. He was killed accidentally in a confused situation where there were three brands of ANP from Maywand, Zharey, and Panjwayi; "B" Company; the governor and his close protection party; and an AH-64 Apache. However, many believed that Kadr Jan had been set up to fail and ultimately to be killed by those in the Kandahar power structure who were afraid that he would investigate them next. Tragically, the AH-64 shot him up because of a command-and-control breakdown during the operation.

On 14 April there was a big TIC in Zharey district between the ANP and the Taliban. By chance, fourteen Taliban were killed in the engagement, including some enemy leadership. On 24 April the ANP captured an important MVT and leader from the Baqi Network, Mullah Ibrahim. Another operation on 29 April netted fifteen Taliban detainees, five enemy KIA, and seven enemy WIA.

By the end of April, Nick was concerned about activity in Zharey and Panjwayi. "The indicators were there that there were more and more insurgents coming in. The PRT OGDs and other NGO sources in the area were saying, 'Hey, I heard this, I'm a little concerned.' We then started getting reports from people about IEDs. We saw a lot of fighting-age males moving east from Helmand into Kandahar. There were certain indicators that we became aware of, like when we rolled into a village. If women and children started leaving, we knew there'd be a gun fight. We got attuned to this."

Consequently, "B" Company asked for, and got, a VMO mission. "B" Company and the ANP would secure a village, and medical personnel from across the coalition, including Afghans, would hold a clinic. Operation Bravo Barca took place on 10–11 May. According to Nick Grimshaw, "We did [VMOs] as often as we could, both for information gathering and to demonstrate physicality, you know, tangibly demonstrate to the locals that we're not a bunch of thugs or a bunch of astronauts pouring out of the space ships, that we're there to provide assistance to the Afghans. We did about half a dozen of these."

The increased importance of the two districts west of the city led to the establishment of Patrol Base Wilson (PBW) on Highway 1. This compound housed two platoons from "B" Company, the Zharey ANP, and the Zharey District Center. Over time it grew to be a major staging base for district operations, and a way point for forces headed to and from Helmand. "It was important for us to maintain a presence out there," Nick told me, "so the CO left it up to me. It was either going to be in Zharey or Panjwayi, so we improved both district centers but chose Zharey. I left 4 Platoon with the PRT and 5 and 6 Platoons went to PBW. Our move to PBW was illustrative of the fact that there was a growing insurgency and a significantly more determined and tenacious enemy in the area."

Better access to the people in the districts led to increased reports of enemy activity in Nahlgam, Sangsar, and Sia Choy in Zharey district. On 14 May 2006 the infamous Mullah Baqi, leader of the Baqi Network, responsible for suicide IED terrorism inside the city, was killed with three of his men in a TIC near Sangsar in Zharey. There was substantial ISTAR reportage after that indicating that Mullah Dadullah Lang and four other Taliban senior leaders were over in Maywand district and trying to figure out how to replace the Zharey and Panjwayi leadership. All of this and more led to two follow-on operations.

## OPERATIONS BRAVO GUARDIAN AND YADGAR: ZHAREY DISTRICT, KANDAHAR PROVINCE

Major Nick Grimshaw and Captain Jay Adair from "B" Company, were looking at some HUMINT (human intelligence) provided by ANP sources in mid-May. The poppy harvest was over, opium was making its way to market, and money was changing hands. There were reports of insurgents coming into Zharey district and setting up shop in the vicinity of Pashmul. "It was like somebody flicked a switch, and the insurgency was on," Nick explained. "It was off the scales for this area." Nick, however, was on leave so Jay took over. Operation Bravo Guardian was a dismounted operation into Zharey that was designed to rattle the enemy's cage on 17 and 18 May.

In this operation, "C" Company maneuvered into screening positions from Highway 1 to southwestern Zharey, while "B" Company, accompanied by the ANP, crossed the Arghandab from Bazaar-e Panjwayi and headed toward Pashmul. Fifteen Taliban were captured around Pashmul, but the force then started taking fire from a nearby compound. Two AH-64s were brought in and engaged. The enemy was seen fleeing to the northwest. "B" Company gave chase and started searching compounds to root out the enemy fighters, who were seen fleeing into the "triangle," an area west of Pashmul. Jay Adair readied "B" Company to go in and clear it when ISTAR reportage indicated that enemy fighters had entered the mosque in Pashmul. Then 2 Platoon got hit from two sides with RPGs, which produced three casualties, so 3 Platoon moved to support. The Apaches, however, were "bingo" fuel and had to head for KAF, so Nic Goddard called in 155-mm fire from the M-777 guns. As Captain Andrew Nicholson told me later, "Nic started a fire mission. She wanted to use the Excalibur round, a precision-guided 155-mm shell because it was a built-up area. She didn't get a chance to finish. Four RPGs hit the LAV III from both sides. There was no penetration, but a ricochet from the shrapnel killed Nic."

Eventually a B-1 bomber came on station, but then there were authority problems at brigade. These related to the estimated damage that the bombs on board would cause. A 500-pound bomb was then dropped on the center of the compound. Payback for Nic Goddard.

The death of Captain Goddard was a shock and, because she was the first Canadian female officer to be killed, it became a major media event. Many of the officers and soldiers I got to know over the summer were very concerned about how she would be portrayed. "She was an artillery officer first," Major Steve Gallagher said. "We don't want the gender thing overriding that," another officer insisted, "There's been far too much of that crap. Nic was one of us, not some feminist figurehead."

Operation Bravo Guardian flowed into Operation Yadgar: Ian Hope wanted to keep the pot stirred in Zharey. On 23 May "B" and "C" Companies deployed to two staging areas (PBW and the Panjwayi district center) at night, while the TUAV and other means were focused to see if the enemy had any warning of the moves. ISTAR resources indicated that the enemy had backed off in and around Pashmul after Bravo Guardian and thinned out back toward Sia Choy. When 2 Platoon moved in to do a cordon and search west of Pashmul in the morning, they were engaged with RPGs and small arms. The enemy broke contact, but four hours later 2 Platoon was engaged again, taking one wounded. A JDAM dropped onto a target compound and 155-mm rounds were brought down. Both companies dug in for the night and sent out ambush patrols, but there was no further contact.

Ian Hope's assessment of the situation was telling and prophetic:

> The enemy has chosen his ground well in that he can hide in any of the hundreds of large compound complexes in these districts, or in the deep troughs between the tall grape vine furrows that rise four feet (1.2 meters) high and allow any number of men to lie down under complete cover. There is also an intricate system of deep

irrigation trenches that he can maneuver on. . . . It is my assessment that there is still considerable enemy in the Zharey-Panjwayi area; they are confident in their ability to fight, and they do not want to give up this ground. . . . The nature of the terrain—very narrow roads, bounded by ditches and walls, combined with the lush orchards that obscure views and fields and fields of deep grape furrows—makes vehicle and dismounted movement very difficult. Temperatures exceed 120 degrees F (50 degress C) at midday. Each compound complex poses a considerable clearance problem.

## TIER I SOF AND EFFECTS MITIGATION

Around 2340 hours on 17 May, as TF ORION was operating in Panjwayi and Zharey districts, a temporary JSOA was declared in Panjwayi district near Talukan. TF ORION had a platoon in contact near Pashmul when this notification came in. From 0200 to 0300 hours on 18 May, TF ORION was treated to a noise and light show that lasted an hour. AC-130 gunships blazed away, AH-64s orbited the area, and B-1 and B-52 bombers dropped JDAMs. Elements of a Tier I SOF team were inserted. When TF ORION checked in with AEGIS, they learned that a TST had just been "prosecuted." It was an enemy leadership HVT. There had been credible ISTAR reportage that a senior enemy leader was present and the Men in Black went in. On 22 May the same thing happened again, this time in a JSOA established around the village of Azizi, near Nahlgam in Panjwayi district.

In this case there were significant civilian casualties in the course of the second operation. Major General Ben Freakley explained to me that the AC-130s caught more than one hundred enemy moving at night in the open and went to work. This force and presumably the leadership it was protecting went into the compounds and started fighting from them, using the civilian population as shields. There were more than sixty civilian casualties; they started to arrive at Mir Wais Hospital right after the attack.

The problem was that AEGIS and ORION didn't know exactly where the casualties were coming from. This wasn't just a human life issue—it was an I/O issue. The media got riled about the "bombing of civilians." AEGIS and ORION were taking heat for an operation they had nothing to do with and that they couldn't effects mitigate with CIMIC . . . because the Men in Black weren't around to ask. When AEGIS finally demanded a detailed grid from "higher," "B" Company found out it was wrong, which delayed humanitarian assistance even longer. The I/O damage was mitigated to some extent by the Guv, who went with the media to the hospital and proceeded to harangue the wounded. The message? "You people brought this on yourselves because you didn't call the police and tell us where the Taliban was. Your men are cowards because they let the Taliban into your compounds." Counterintuitive message to Westerners, completely appropriate to Afghans.

Major General Ben Freakley at CJTF-76 used the incident in an attempt to gain better coordination with other SOF forces. It is unlikely, however, in a culture steeped in Pastunwali, that the inhabitants of Azizi will ever support coalition forces again. TF ORION now had to "wear" the long-term effects of something they weren't responsible for and couldn't control, and that they couldn't explain to the media, who wanted someone to blame.

Contrast this with a later operation. An IED cell leader was detected by various ISTAR resources, so the British SOF went after him one night in Zharey. An AC-130 tracked numerous enemy fleeing the area—the bait, as it turned out. The leader surrounded himself with children from that village and walked out using them as human shields. What would you do? He's going to kill more coalition soldiers, but if we kill him, we kill kids. The SOF team chose not to engage. All of those moral and ethical dilemmas we learned about in school while growing up ("We have rations for four people, but there are six in the lifeboat . . . and three have pistols") had to be addressed by commanders on the ground. Not the media. Not the academics. Not the politicians.

These operations were further indicators that all was not well in Panjwayi and Zharey, but the Tier I world, echelons above reality, had no intelligence feed to conventional forces, so AEGIS and ORION had to figure things out. The Tier I forces weren't into assisting in building the intelligence picture for a couple of districts: they were solely focused on killing enemy leadership. However, the frequency of the Tier I operations added to TF ORION's belief that there was a build-up of enemy leadership in Zharey and Panjwayi—but nobody knew why, exactly. The most likely target of these two operations was Mullah Dadullah Lang, who apparently got out into Maywand district to the west and then into the Registan Desert to avoid the SOF strikes.

So why was Mullah Dadullah Lang in the area? Sometime before this, the Quetta Shura met to consider future operations in southern Afghanistan.

Objectively, the Taliban operations in Shah Wali Kot weren't enough to distract coalition forces away from Highway 1–Zharey–Panjwayi. A Taliban build-up in Zharey could be used to interfere with the British deployment into Helmand, and such a force could be used to create a staging area to go after Kandahar City. It is not a coincidence that ISTAR reportage indicated the enemy prepared six hundred fighters to move into Zharey–Panjwayi, reconstituted its leadership network after Baqi was eliminated, and even asked HiG for additional "experts" in early June. A man of Mullah Dadullah Lang's stature would have been needed to broker all of the local- and operational-level deals necessary to facilitate this activity.

**Other Developments**

At the same time, rocket attacks were stepped up against KAF. In April and May there were five attacks, but two of these occurred nearly back-to-back on the nights of 27 and 29 May. The 29 May attack consisted of an unprecedented six rockets. There was also a major shootout in Helmand between a French ETT-mentored Afghan company and insurgent forces operating east of Highway 611. This was a particularly nasty ambush. The French and Afghans were escorting engineer equipment up to improve FOB ROB. This twenty-vehicle column came under attack and was broken up into four parts and cut to pieces. At the same time, and it wasn't clear how, French SOF (1er Régiment Parachutiste d'Infanterie de Marine; 1st RPiMA) got involved in the extrication of the ETT's casualties and then got into trouble during the extraction. Adjutant Joel Gazeau and Senior Corporal David Poulain were killed by the insurgents, both apparently after being captured, tied up, and gutted alive in front of captured Afghan troops. A British QRF arrived by helicopter and beat back the ambush force.[1] There were up to fifty ANA and ANP casualties, and at least one other French SOF soldier was wounded. The infamous Koo Agha took credit for this debacle. Helmand was heating up—again.

As these early operations demonstrate, TF ORION was stretched thin—*really* thin. Lieutenant Colonel Ian Hope's task force had double the area to cover than the previous battalion and, to boot, kept having its forces dispatched over to neighboring Helmand province for long periods. The terrain ORION had to work in was incredibly diverse, from mountains in Shah Wali Kot to the prairie-like open Dasht to the close-in cultivated areas of Zharey and Panjwayi and the urban desolation of

Kandahar City. And, as we will see, the political, social, and tribal terrain was even more complex.

## Preparations for Operation Jagra and the Opening of FOB Martello

There was a lot of frenetic activity on 10 June. The Guv, Governor Asadullah Khalid, came in the night before around 2200 to see Dave Fraser over at CTF AEGIS. He was, apparently, in a panic. He had information that eight hundred Taliban were coming into the Panjwayi and Zharey districts. Dave Fraser and Ian Hope, and General Ben Freakley on the Tandberg videoconferencing system, discussed this development.

At the morning battle update briefing, the planned Operation Mountain Thrust operations west of the Belly Button in Khakriz district were temporarily called off. The briefing indicated that there were seven hundred Taliban infiltrating Zharey district along with six Land Cruisers carrying ammo. A cell was there to support the infiltrators with IED placement on Highway 1. Massoud's HUMINT net was reporting that there were "new" Taliban coming in equipped with hitherto unseen mortars and heavy machine guns. General Freakley became really interested and was prepared to deploy MQ-1 Predators to support any operations in Zharey.

There was some speculation as to enemy motives: The Taliban had to offset the opening of FOB Martello, which would be an I/O victory for the coalition. They might attack the proceedings. They might lay IEDs on the Tarin Kot Road. They might even mount operations from Zharey. It wasn't clear. There had been some rounds fired at a convoy on Highway 1 and when CASEVAC arrived they were shot at with RPG and small arms fire, but there wasn't a lot of overt enemy activity there right now. Maybe they were trying to put us to sleep and then strike.

The initial coalition planning was based on the belief that the enemy thought we were totally focused on FOB Martello. Ian's concept of operations involved taking an infantry company and infiltrating it at night into Zharey to probe around and see what turned up. The main problem was lack of route clearance packages (RCPs), the IED-detection equipment that was needed to lead any vehicle movement on unproved roads. Canada didn't have the kit and there were only so many American RCPs. One wouldn't be ready until 11 June. Should TF ORION wait for it? The same with the Canadian M-777s, the only artillery in RC South. Should the operation be conducted without guns, or should we wait to shift a pair of them so they were in range? There were only four. Any probe into Zharey had to take into account the availability and coordination of resources, usually called "enablers" by the staff, Major Mason Stalker and his people in the TOC) had to check for the availability of engineers and the RCP; CASEVAC and other medical resources, including bed space availability in the Role 3; the availability of fast air or attack helicopter support; the availability of artillery; and, most important, the availability of ISTAR resources: Coyotes, UAVs, electronic warfare and others. It wasn't enough just to have an infantry company available in LAVs: if all, some, or none of the enablers was available, this affected a risk matrix. If the risk matrix was too high, the operation would not be approved or would be delayed.

This approach appeared to be at odds with intelligence-driven operations, but it really wasn't with a good staff. The staff had to be quick and they had to know the disposition of all the enablers at all times. At the same time, this placed the burden squarely on the battle-group commander's shoulders. He had to make a decision: go or no go. If a commander was risk-averse, nothing got done and the availability matrix might be used as an excuse: "We can't go without X." On the other hand, if some enablers were available, but not all, the commander had to use best judgment. Was the operation worth the risk? How much risk was acceptable? No one else could make that decision. Those who criticize commanders' decisions need to understand these factors. A lot will be driven by personality. Bureaucrats and politicians who worried about casualties loved commanders that were risk-averse. So did the enemy.

The change in the situation affected where the leadership would be. General Fraser was going to FOB Martello, Ian wasn't. The Guv wasn't sure yet. The TF ORION staff worked up its contingency plans.

I was up early for breakfast. The only free space in the DFAC near Canada House was next to a Canadian, who turned out to be Major Bob Harold. Bob was an ammo tech, responsible for the care and storage of all the deadly downrange stuff. We talked about the progress of the war, and the nature of it. "You know, I heard there was a eight-year-old girl in the Role 3 [hospital]. She'd been caught in the cross fire that resulted in the wounding of four Taliban," Bob told me. The nurses were having a struggle dealing with the wounded, detained Taliban fighters, knowing what they'd done and having to care for the results. Apparently the girl asked for a knife so she could kill the detainees. We finished up and greeted the hot dawn.

Today was the inauguration of FOB Martello, named after the forts that protected my hometown of Kingston, Ontario. This was a big deal, and, like everything in the war in Afghanistan, there were multiple objectives. The Dutch DTF was starting its move to its bases in Oruzgan province. They would have to travel on Highway 4, through the city and then north on the Tarin Kot Road through the hot districts of Shah Wali Kot and Mianishien. The Tarin Kot Road also was being paved. A decision was made to build a FOB just off the Tarin Kot Road to exert a coalition presence in the area. This FOB would act as a way over for the DTF convoys if necessary; and it would provide a coalition presence in a region that hadn't had one since the early days of the war when SOF operated around there. The FOB could be used to project power into those districts as necessary. On the down side, manning and defending the FOB would take scarce resources away from other things. Still, the strategic aim of facilitating the Dutch deployment, keeping in mind that getting the Dutch to commit to OEF in Afghanistan was a feat in itself, overrode other requirements.

Of course, having an FOB in disputed territory like this made it a magnet for enemy action. The decision was made to have an elaborate ceremony inaugurating the opening and invite all the local leaders and mullahs as a gracious display of hospitality. Coupled with this were several I/O messages: We are bringing substantial firepower with us. We are bringing development assistance. Please cooperate and let us know if the enemy is moving around your areas.

I found myself on a U.S. Army Chinook loaded with I/O, CIMIC, and other personnel headed for MARTELLO. Two men who I would get to know well were on that flight: Major Quentin Innis from 1 PPCLI, and Captain Tom Nield from the U.S. Army PSYOPS. The usual escort of AH-64s orbited around us as the Chinook clawed its way through the hot air over Kandahar City. We circled the Tarin Kot Road and then landed on it. It was oiled but not yet paved. Three LAV III vehicles raced to the makeshift LZ to pick us up and we bounced back to the FOB.

Built in a bowl FOB, Martello was a substantial but undeveloped facility: there were Canadian LAVs and Dutch MICVs on run-up positions on the HESCO Bastion walls. There were no permanent buildings: the troops were in two-man tents. The shitter was a two-holer built of plywood and there was a constant lineup at it. The dust was fine, like moon dust. Dust clouds billowed as we walked and got into everything. Engineering equipment I'd never seen before, but that I learned was an RCP, was lined up. There was a pair of M-777 155-mm guns and their tractors there, plus 81-mm mortars. Coyotes and other vehicles equipped with mast sensors kept a sharp eye out for the enemy. I also saw Afghan D-30 artillery pieces.

There was a big *shura* tent, plenty of refreshments . . . and a new, clean RG-31 and LAV III facing the tent as if on display. The media then arrived via Bison. I saw some familiar faces, like Christy Blatchford of the *Globe and Mail*, and Mathew Fisher from the Global-controlled newspapers. A TV camera was set up on a tripod; it was from Kandahar TV. Another helicopter came it: it had Brigadier General Dave Fraser on board. There were elders and mullahs from all the surrounding villages present, about twenty of them. Canadian soldiers in arid Canadian disruptive pattern (CADPAT), body armor, and weapons acted as stewards, as if it were a mess dinner, distributing water and confections. Our intelligence personnel discreetly photographed the elders and attempted to put faces to names.

I asked Q what was taking so long.

"Well, we can't start without the governor, Asadullah Khalid. He's driving up with his bodyguards."

"No chopper?"

"No. The Guv likes to see the people on the way, get out of the palace, that sort of thing."

There was a bit of a commotion. The Guv had arrived, but he wasn't being permitted into the FOB by the Dutch gate guards because of his private security guards. This was a major faux pas on the part of the Dutch. The Dutch, once they learned who he was, cajoled him, but it was a matter of serious face. Asadullah refused to enter the FOB until General Fraser came down personally to let him in. They had insulted the Guv and nothing could start until this was resolved. The problem here was that they insulted the Guv *in front of* the local leaders.

Dave and entourage walked the five hundred meters down the hill to deal with the situation: the crowd followed. Asadullah was standing next to a white SUV, young, bearded, and animated, talking to the local people who were very curious as to what was going on. Dave made all the right public apologies and we walked all the way back up the hill to the tents. This was astute politics, on both parts. We preached the need for an "Afghan face" all the time and that we were guests in support of the government and so on. We weren't occupiers. Here was a chance to demonstrate it. Our people correctly realized it wasn't worth getting upset over and made the appropriate moves to enhance our standing with the population. It really looked like Asadullah Khalid was in charge, that he could command the visitors with their firepower and resources. It made for great theater.

I saw a man wearing arid CADPAT, a subdued crescent on his epaulettes, and a white skull cap. He was intoning a prayer in English that was translated into Pashto by one of the interpreters from the PRT. A Canadian mullah??? Yes. This was Padre Suleyman Dimeray who gave his blessing to the proceedings. It was like grace before meal. The locals all prayed, everybody bowed their heads, and the *shura* started. The FOB was officially opened first. The elders and mullahs petitioned the Guv, who heard all of the grievances and distributed platitudes. This process took some time.

It was a simple affair, and its immediate effects were hard to measure. It was one more piece in the I/O puzzle, one increment in an area that the coalition really didn't have a lot of information on. Think of the FOB as a sensor, not just a mounting base. It allowed AEGIS to check the pulse of the upper part of the province. It also became the scene of operations later on in the summer.

### Problems in Kandahar Province: North or West?

Lieutenant Colonel Ian Hope had a meeting with the Guv and wanted to check in at the Joint Coordination Center (JCC), so I went along. Ian always took his Niner Tac vehicles and LAVs when he did a run into the city. We sped along Highway 4. I was in one of the air sentry hatches talking to Ian on the intercom system. "I wanted to put the TF ORION headquarters in the city itself, but I wasn't allowed to," he explained. "I wanted my people away from the airfield. Too many amenities. It promotes a base mentality that we don't need here. We're at war. It was also easier to react to events in the city, but there was concern that too much coalition presence in the city would be bad I/O, make us look like occupiers. The PRT is different, though." Bashir was with us to interpret: he smiled.

There was concern over the enemy buildup in Panjwayi and Zharey districts west of the city. A developing theory was that the Taliban was going to mount a "spectacular" against a target or targets inside Kandahar City, possibly against the Governor's Palace, the PRT, or Sarposa Prison. Such an attack would be a major enemy I/O victory.

Zharey and Panjwayi districts, of course, were critical areas. The northern boundary of Zharey was Highway 1, which ran west from the city to Helmand and then to Herat. Cutting it off jeopardized commerce not only in the province, but also in southern Afghanistan and the region. In January–February of 2006, just as AEGIS and ORION were deploying, a major SOF operation was mounted into the district. A member of an enemy IED cell rolled over on his colleagues and the whole thing was taken out. Then operations in May killed the infamous Mullah Baqi and his lieutenants. The enemy was building up in the district again, trying to recoup his losses.

The tribal makeup and politics of Zharey and Panjwayi were extremely interesting at this time. An Afghan friend of mine once explained to me why the place was so complicated when we were having a smoke at PBW. "The separation between Zharey district and Panjwayi district took place in 2004. Before that, it was all just Panjwayi. After the separation, almost all the reconstruction and aid went to Panjwayi and not Zharey. Panjwayi was better-organized, had lots of grapes they needed to get to market, and was much more active at pursuing aid." He butted his cigarette. "The people in Panjwayi got the road paved, but Zharey had ongoing water rights problems. They were into grapes and poppy. They were divided all the time. At the same time there was a tribal imbalance in Zharey, governance was immature, and there was a lot of jealousy internally and directed at Panjwayi." He lit another and breathed it in. "And then there's Mushan, in the westernmost part of the district. It's all about poppies there. Mushan is neither fish nor fowl—nobody wants it. The Noorzai are down there."

Captain Zia Massoud from Standby Police Unit 005 (who we'll meet later) had a different take on things. He recognized the Durrani–Ghilzai split, but explained that there were five tribes that swung back and forth between the two confederations, depending on who was in power. "The tribe has priority, even over Islam," he said. "Ninety percent of the Noorzai and Alozai are Taliban, and 50 percent of the Achechzai and Shabulzai are also Taliban. There is also a split in the Durrani between the

Barakzai and Achechzai that causes problems. It doesn't matter who is in power," he emphasized. "The Popalzai tend to be progovernment." Of course, President Karzai was Popalzai.

In other words, there were ample cracks in the edifice that the Taliban could gain leverage on and keep the area in a constant state of turmoil. The two districts were a mélange of nearly every Pashtun tribe in southern Afghanistan. Any inequitable delivery of reconstruction resources would generate grievances and be fertile ground for conflict—and that had already occurred, setting the place on a trajectory that we might not be able to divert, and were in no position to fully understand under the pressures of what amounted to a serious enemy buildup and the demands to support Operation Mountain Thrust way up to the north.

When CTF BAYONET was in charge in 2005, the coalition was seen to be backing the Barakzai (led by then-Governor Gul Agha Sherzai). Now, we were increasingly seen to be supporting the Popalzai. In early 2006 the main problem areas were Highway 4 and Shah Wali Kot–Zharey and Panjwayi wasn't a problem. An early indicator that there was a problem was a Highway 1 checkpoint attack that resulted in a search of a compound in Asheque on Highway 1. Canadian officers Major Harjit "Harj" Sajjan and "B" Company commander Major Nick Grimshaw saw the district chief of police and the district elder attempting to steal a motorcycle from a local person. My old friend Sergeant Wali from the PRT police applauded as Harj intervened and returned the motorcycle. Word got out that the coalition was standing up to corruption. This increased the stature of the coalition in the Asheque area. "Corruption?" Nick and Harj asked rhetorically. They were more interested in the goings-on in Zharey and Panjwayi, especially along Highway 1.

With some probing, facts slowly emerged. Habbibullah Jan, a member of parliament and major power broker, worked with the Sherzais to fight the Taliban back in 2001 and had control over a private army that was later designated 530 Brigade of the Afghan Militia Forces.[2] The "530 Compound" was situated near a key bottleneck on Highway 1 between Kandahar City and Zharey district. Rezik Sherzai, Gul Agha Sherzai's brother, had the contract for Highway 1 security and Habibullah Jan was "subcontracted" for his stretch of the highway, where his men also supplemented their income with illegal "tolls" on the route.[3] Gul Agha Sherzai also did a lot of school construction in Zharey and Panjwayi districts, considered preferred districts during the Sherzai period. Incidentally, our old friend Haji Agha Lalai was the primary power broker who handled things in Panjwayi.

When Asadullah Khalid was appointed governor and Ahmad Wali Karzai was elected in 2005, Habibullah Jan lost the security contracts to United States Protection and Investigations (USPI), a U.S. State Department–favored security contractor. The USPI then started getting hit all the time . . . in Alikozai territory along the highway. The "haves" became the "have nots" and resented being out of work. The poppy eradication program was also a factor. Habibullah Jan was involved in narcotics production and paid bribes to avoid eradication. With him no longer a buffer to protect the drug farmers, the possibility of eradication disturbed elements in the population. The Taliban then showed up and told the people they would help them fight the "police."

This generated a number of damaging perceptions. When the "police" got hit in the area doing "selective eradication" or "toll collection," they complained to Haji Saifullah, the district leader over in Maywand west of Habibullah Jan's territory, who then called the Guv and told him, "The Taliban are attacking the ANP. Help!" at which point Asadullah Khalid would call up the Canadians to ask for help. In some cases we rushed out to fight and villagers thought the Canadians were resisting the corrupt ANP, which increased Canada's stature with some of the population. In other areas stature decreased: people believed Canadian troops supported corrupt police and officials. Nick Grimshaw and Harj Sajjan discovered other corruption issues: construction dollars artificially inflated the market, and there were contract bid disputes that produced several points of friction between the haves and the have-nots in Zharey. The Taliban exploited this with its I/O: "Look how the corrupt bastards are ripping you off! We can help!"

Asadullah Khalid launched his own operation back in April with Massoud's Standby Police Unit 005, who then got into a TIC. TF ORION rushed out but they were unsure who they were supposed to engage. That was the turning point, when Ian, Harj, and Nick started asking what was really going on. The Guv then publicly called the Canadians "cowards" for not "helping," but higher Afghan authorities came down and told him to stop it with the troops and start being a governor.

Asadullah Khalid greeted us in his chambers. He was tired and under some strain. We talked about the opening of FOB Martello and his trip to the northern districts. "I went up to Mianishien district to look for the

Taliban," he said. "They have left Mianishien empty. They don't have enough people there to mount operations. They must be on the move."

Ian explained that he intended to mount an operation into Zharey as a probe as soon as possible. The Guv explained that he'd met with the district leaders in Khakriz, Mianishin, and Shah Wali Kot. The enemy forces in the north totaled some three hundred to four hundred fighters. But where were they? "Are there still Pakistanis coming in to help them?" he asked Ian. Ian told him that there were Punjabi speakers in the area up north. That meant that they were probably Kashmiris, who were experienced fighters from the Kashmir insurgency in that disputed zone in India. "I have heard there are Arabs in Panjwayi and Zharey, about eighty guys, plus some Taliban from Zabol," the Guv passed on. He was in a quandary and couldn't make up his mind about what to do. There was a threat in the north and a threat in the west, but there were only so many resources. He wanted to hunt down the Taliban in the northern districts now, but Ian was trying to convince him that there was a problem to the west closer to home that was the priority. Ian wanted police, specifically Standby Police Unit 05 under Captain Massoud's command, to go into Zharey with TF ORION. And he needed a commitment today. Ian needed time to coordinate air support and other resources from the Americans: if there was no police commitment, then asking for the enablers was a waste of time. All the moving parts had to be in place.

The Guv used a buzzer to summon some aides. He was behaving like a military governor, not like the governor of an American state or the premier of a Canadian province. He was leaning toward a commitment but it would take some more convincing. We had to meet with the chief of police in the province on another issue, this one involving a planned operation into the northern districts.

We moved over to the JCC, which was in a compound co-located with the Governor's Palace. Captain Darren Hart, the Canadian liaison officer, greeted us. General Aziz, the police commander for the province, was about to arrive. Hart explained to me how the JCC worked: "We synthesize everything here with the Afghans when we plan joint operations. Intelligence flow from both countries comes in here. Our job is capacity building, showing them how to do the synthesis, where it fits with planning. In time the JCC will be Afghan-run with very little coalition input." The JCC also had its own command post and communications. Hart explained that the NDS funneled most of its information into the JCC, so it wasn't all just coming from OEF systems or resources.

The Khakriz district police chief and General Aziz came in. The district police chief was informed that there would be an operation going into his district in about four to five days. It would be a big operation, Ian told him. It would last six to seven days and kill a lot of enemy. Where exactly did the district chief think the enemy was in Khakriz? "Well, they are in Chenar and Tambil," he said, and described the area west of the Belly Button feature. "The Taliban have radios, and they see everything that moves." He indicated on the map where he knew two enemy observation posts were located. With the flat terrain between Khakriz district center and Chenar, they could see us for klicks and klicks (km). They weren't manned at night, he explained.

"How does the enemy move?" I asked him.

"The Taliban travel from Pakistan, to Maruf district, into Oruzgan province, then south through these four passes in Nesh district, south to Kandahar City through my district or west to Helmand province through my district." The JCC staff confirmed with the chief where all these places were, to make sure nothing was being lost in translation. (Sometimes the same name was used for two different places.) Ian sketched out a rough plan: the situation suggested an airmobile landing to the north of where the enemy was, while three units in LAVs converged on the target from the south from three directions. In a spirit of capacity building, Ian wondered aloud, "Who will do the block? Who will do the killing?" Blocks were needed to the west and east to catch anybody trying to get away from the onslaught. "Should the police do it or should TF ORION?" The group mulled that over.

Captain Hart and I talked about some of the problems with the police. There weren't enough ANA forces in the province, so police had to be used to support operations. I was told by someone else that the planned Afghan kandak, the one that was supposed to be twinned with TF ORION, had been poached by U.S. Special Forces. Part of a kandak from northern Afghanistan, from 209 Corps, would be deploying, but not soon enough for these operations. The regional police commander, who commanded the police area that equated to RC South, along with eighty-six other major police leaders across the country, had just been purged by Kabul for corruption and incompetence. This occurred after the Kabul riots in 2006. Consequently, the police were in some disarray.

General Esmatullah was inbound to be the new regional commander; he would be accompanied by a Colonel Paul Calbos, his U.S. Army mentor. But Estamullah wasn't in Kandahar City yet.

General Aziz and Ian agreed that TF ORION would chase, while the police would observe and report. Ian could synchronize his operations. First, he wanted to do the operation into Zharey, while the JCC planned the Khakriz operation. Once Ian was finished in Zharey, the JCC would brief him on the northern operation, and he would modify it as necessary and then execute it.

"We really need JCCs in the adjacent provinces so we can coordinate information flow," he told me. "The enemy uses the seams between the provinces to move and we can't have these artificial divisions stopping us from conducting operations."

"So the Kandahar JCC is unique?"

"Yes. We have nobody to talk to in Oruzgan, Helmand, or Zabol. The TF GUNDEVILS had a PCC when they were here but there was confusion. Was it supposed to coordinate information collection between the coalition and the Afghans, coordinate operations between the coalition and the Afghans, or act as an operations center for joint operations? There are distinct differences."

It was at this point I met Major Harjit Sajjan, a Canadian Sikh from British Columbia. Harj, with his turban, beard, and low-key approach, was a policeman from British Columbia. When Dave Fraser heard about Harj's experiences dealing with organized crime and gang activity, he was brought south from Kabul.

Harj explained to me how he worked. "My responsibilities were vague at first. General Fraser had me work with Asadullah Khalid, but I also worked at the PRT to assess emergent Afghan policing issues. The JCC had already been established by the Americans, but it was only a coordination cell: it had no continuity, no resources, and no focus. I discovered that there was a goldmine of information flowing into the palace." Ian Hope decided to put more resources into the JCC and make it a permanent position that included the deputy battle-group intelligence office, a signals detachment, and an intelligence operator. This took about two weeks to ramp up. "Ultimately, 80 percent of TF ORION's intelligence comes from the JCC, not the ASIC back at KAF," Harj explained.

One of the most interesting individuals working with TF ORION was Captain Zia Massoud. The gregarious Massoud spoke colloquial

English and was Tajik, from up north. He had attended Communist-run schools when he was young in the 1980s (I used to whistle *The Internationale* and he'd join in), but then was evacuated to a refugee camp in Iran when things got really bad. He joined the Northern Alliance and fought in the north against the Taliban in the 1990s. Massoud had been brought into the ANP after the collapse of the Taliban. A member of the NDS in Zabol, he decided it was too much like KHAD for his liking and transferred. He was put in charge of a Standby Police unit—in this case Standby Police Unit 005. The Standby Police have no real equivalent in our system. They were a sort of paramilitary auxiliary, but they wear ANP uniforms and are led by ANP officers. Massoud was tasked with establishing checkpoints inside Kandahar, so he brought a core of people from up north. To do the job, though, he also had to recruit locally, which eventually posed problems. The lack of trained police in the province meant that Standby Police Unit 005, which was of variable strength but peaked at three hundred, was used more and more as a militia force to support coalition operations. They were a stopgap until something better came out of the pipeline (now four years after Bonn).

Massoud used some of his local recruits to handle the checkpoints, and then used his northern core and his better local people to act as a QRF. He ostensibly reported to the regional police commander and then Kabul, but there were complications. The Guv was an old friend of Massoud's from the Northern Alliance days—and the Guv wanted 005 under his personal command to act as his close protection party and to defend the palace, since the DIAG process was slow and he didn't have a vetted close protection party.[4] Apparently. . . . At the same time, Massoud ran his own HUMINT networks in the province, which appeared to be separate from the NDS network. Sometimes the information flowed into the JCC, but other times it did not. Why was this the case?

There were problems in the intelligence architecture supporting AEGIS and ORION. One of the problems was the perception at TF ORION that the J-2 shop at CTF AEGIS and the ASIC that belonged to the Canadian TF AFGHANISTAN HQ did not provide timely intelligence to TF ORION. There were numerous reasons for this perception, but it was clear to me that the need for fast-reacting operations could not be met at the time by the existing architecture. This Canadian architecture was based on restrictive Cold War–era compartmentalization of source information and analysis that in turn was based on the fear that the Americans would shut off the pipeline to Canada not only at the tactical level, but also at the strategic level, if the relationship was "compromised." This had occurred at various times with the Americans shutting off the pipeline to the Australians and the Dutch.

I also found out later that the ASIC generally ignored the JCC, in part because some ASIC people refused to accept that a person working on finding ways for improving the ANSF couldn't be viewed as an intelligence collector. Harj attended the weekly security meeting and learned that the meeting could become a tool as well. Over time he developed rapport with all of the security "players" in Kandahar. The NDS said "no" at first, but later changed its mind. There were in fact two meetings: the first included everybody, including the international organizations operating in Kandahar. The second included just the uniformed Afghan and coalition members. Harj was able to send two pages of solid intelligence to TF ORION per week. The quality of the information was awesome. I found out later that elements in the ASIC didn't like this because they viewed it as "single source" Afghan information and didn't trust it until they could "wash it" through their processes. To me, ground truth information from Afghans that we have developed a rapport with beats stuff coming across a computer hooked up to a bunch of American systems. And, as I learned later, there were technical issues with wiring the TF ORION TOC with the real-time systems they wanted. Some entitites preferred to keep everything centralized in a separate secure compound that was about five hundred meters from the ORION TOC.[5] Information had to go through a laborious process: when it arrived, Ian and his staff couldn't act on in a timely fashion because the intelligence was so stale.

In many cases, Harj and the JCC would predict events based solely on JCC information—and then those events would happen. For example, the Afghans believed that something would blow up in Maruf district. The JCC briefed Dave Fraser and Chris Vernon. AEGIS sent it to the ASIC, who dismissed it as single-source reportage, and claimed nothing would happen. Maruf blew up one month later, forcing AEGIS to move an American infantry company from Zabol province to deal with it. From then on, Harj sent intelligence directly to AEGIS, to ORION, and to the ASIC with his analysis attached.

Consequently, TF ORION developed its own intelligence to supplement what it got from the J-2 and the ASIC so that it could be more agile and react to enemy developments. Some of that intelligence came from the

JCC, some from Massoud's network, and some from informal connections developed between TF ORION and allied SOF organizations. I perceived that there was a lack of confidence at TF ORION in the ASIC products. On the other hand, some in the ASIC thought that TF ORION was being "played" by corrupt provincial government officials and wanted to vet all intelligence coming into TF ORION first. Once again, there was the element of risk versus timeliness in play that the battle-group commander had to contend with.

I met with Ian as Massoud filled us in on developments in Zharey and Panjwayi. "The enemy now has two cooks in a compound in Zharey," Massoud said as he gestured at the map. "He is moving in using Corollas and motorcycles, in small numbers. Those cooks can feed several hundred fighters, or they wouldn't have brought them in. Usually they live off the people, but the people are pissed off with the Taliban and don't want to supply them. I'm also watching 'businessmen' and 'gardeners' come in. They bring the money. My sources also tell me that the new fighters are not well trained: they are mostly Noorzai from Spin Boldak. Some cannot even control their weapons effectively and spray their ammo around."

"Yes," Ian agreed. "The ambush yesterday against Outlaw 26 [the RCP from a convoy from the American 2-82nd Infantry Battalion] was poorly executed. The Americans took a chunk out of them, but they're reconstituting."

"I think they have a new objective," Massoud said. "They want to keep us busy in Panjwayi, then focus their operations up north. Maybe they're no longer interested in attacking Kandahar City." That was an ongoing debate. The Taliban might be using Zharey as a way point to move this bunch up to Shah Wali Kot or Khakriz. The idea that they would attack Kandahar City, though, remained attractive. The enemy didn't believe that the coalition would use airpower in built-up areas because of the fear of civilian casualties and collateral damage. Ian thought out loud: "We need an I/O campaign that can 'explain' to the enemy that we can [use airpower] as a deterrent. The enemy has been telling people in the Panjwayi and Zharey mosques that we won't, so the people don't turn on them." If we do hit them with air, and there is collateral damage, however inadvertent, this could be used as I/O to rally the people against the Taliban.

"I have other information," Massoud added. "A Stinger has reportedly been brought into Panjwayi." "Stinger" in this case didn't necessarily mean the FIM-92 missile launcher: it had become Afghan shorthand for any MANPADS system. "As far as I can tell, there are about one hundred hardcore fighters, and maybe eight hundred armed but untrained support people. They have been armed from old caches from the Taliban days."

"Yes, and we have reports that HiG has some fighters there too, to stiffen them up. What about their reporting network?" Ian asked.

"The enemy is using cell phones and local people. They also are confiscating people's cell phones to deny us information from areas they are operating in." Massoud looked at me. "The enemy made a list of cell phones and who they belonged to. They called all the numbers in the directories. If a government person answered the phone, they killed the phone's owner. At one point I had ten sources in there and soon I was down to two." Massoud gave out cell phones that used prepaid cards. The sources could use the phones all they liked but would only get more cards if they provided accurate and timely information. Sometimes Massoud's unit captured Taliban fighters but then abruptly released them, apologizing for "mistaken arrests" and giving them cell phones as gifts. Some of these fighters called in information, while others communicated with their comrades, not knowing that Massoud and his people were watching who they were talking with to build their picture of the Taliban organization. They called this the "catch and release" program. The enemy leaders will never know how many of its people were providing timely and accurate information to the Afghan government and coalition forces. It was significant in 2006.

## OPERATION JAGRA: ZHAREY DISTRICT 12 JUNE 2006

Operation Jagra was the assigned code name for the Zharey district probe. To observe Operation Jagra, I accompanied TF ORION's Niner Tac, the mobile tactical headquarters for the battle group. Niner Tac consisted of three LAV III command variants: the battle-group commander's LAV III; G-19 or "Golf One Niner," which was the artillery battery commanders' LAV; E-19 or Echo One Niner, the engineer squadron commanders' LAV; an RG-31 Nyala, owned by the regimental sergeant major; and 9-W or Niner Whisky, the CO's G-Wagon that was mounted with electronic countermeasure (ECM) gear. Major Steve Gallagher, the gunner, and Major Trevor Webb, the engineer, weren't always with Niner Tac: for example, a FOO with his LAV was sometimes substituted for G-19. In essence, Niner Tac had nearly the firepower of a LAV platoon even though it was a command element. This became significant later when home leave reduced the operational strength of the battle group by nearly one-third.

I got my protective gear and kit and went over to the Yard, where Niner Tac marshaled before each excursion, for the briefing. Master Corporal Greg White, or "Whitey," was the Niner Tac Master Corporal responsible for organizing road moves and the headquarters setup. He came equipped with elaborate Haida tattoo work and a great cynical sense of humor. The driver was Corporal Dave "Stitch" Hayward, an unflappable former competitive swimmer. The gunner was Corporal Davis, a friendly cigar smoker with wraparound shades. There was Signalman Nigel Williams, a former Canadian Football League football player ("No Tillman jokes out of you!"). The regimental sergeant major was on leave, so Captain Kevin Barry took over the RG-31. He was the operations officer for Niner Tac. Kevin was a highly experienced former warrant officer who had been commissioned from the ranks. Corporal Keith Parsons, who loved his "chaw," was his driver.

"Doc, I'm putting you in Niner Whisky," Whitey announced. "Oh, by the way: It's the least-protected vehicle in Niner Tac!" He laughed evilly. "I was told you were a crew commander in a previous life and we're short on people, so you're now the codriver." Corporal Neal Carswell, a quiet-spoken South African–born reservist from British Columbia, was the Niner Whisky driver. We shook hands and I loaded my kit.

"I don't understand." Whitey was giving me the gears. "What's the difference between a journalist and a historian, anyway? You both write books."

"It's easy. Journalists make you famous—for a little while. Historians immortalize you forever," I told him.

A new regional police commander, General Esmatullah, was inbound and would be joining us. Esmatullah was a Hazara Shi'ite who had sided with the Communists in the 1980s. He owed nothing to anybody and had a reputation for being tough and focused. He was accompanied by his U.S. Army mentor, Colonel Paul Calbos, wielding his Heckler & Koch MP-5.

After picking up Captain Massoud, we proceeded to PBW. By 1030, it was hitting 104 degrees F (40 degrees C) outside as Niner Tac reversed course back east down Highway 1, taking the Bazaar-e Panjwayi turnoff to backtrack along the highway to the Panjwayi district center. These movements were part of the deception plan. Niner Tac looked like an infantry platoon moving around, and not the tactical headquarters. We were joined by a Coyote recce patrol who had recce'd a site behind and above the Panjwayi district center on a ridge that overlooked the entire Zharey district. There was a destroyed T-55 tank sitting there. The 12 RBC Coyotes and the G-19 artillery LAV deployed their sensor masts and equipment, while the Niner Tac crew unfolded the comms gear and tent.

Within minutes we had heard that the enemy had seen "tanks"—that is, armored vehicles—but they weren't sure what was going on and they were asking their reporting net for more information. An hour later, the ANA, moving around the village of Seyyadin, was fired on by a twenty-man Taliban group who apparently were escorting a HiG leader. We heard the Taliban ordering a withdrawal from this contact. It looked like that group was a close protection party for the leader and they weren't interested in engaging.

The situation as it stood at 1130 had "B" Company in a screen between PBW and Panjwayi district center, with the ANHP in a series of vehicle checkpoints along Highway 1.[6] "C" Company was moving south from Highway 1. Ian wanted a Predator or an AH-64 so they could hunt the HiG leader, but none was available. All coalition elements on the ground reported that there was a noticeable lack of children or women in the areas they were in. This was usually a sign that there was enemy present.

Captain Massoud had four cell phones attached to his belt and an earpiece in his left ear. He was getting information from his sources. "One of my people is reporting the presence of 'blacks' in the district. They may be Arabs from Africa."

"Or they saw Williams!" Davis quipped.

There was another contact at 1230. I looked at the map: all it said was "numerous ditches." The 1:50,000 map wasn't detailed enough to depict the complexity of the terrain in Zharey. Niner Tac needed imagery with the routes superimposed on them so the staff could plan.

"The enemy knows about the LAV and tries to stay in areas that we have trouble getting in to," Stitch explained. "I've been able to squeak the LAV through these confined areas, but we have to plan every move in there carefully. There's no place to turn around."

Ian was using the turret optics to watch what was going on in the district below. I could see the White School, which denoted Pashmul, but Seyyedin was difficult to make out from here because the terrain was cluttered. We were about ten kilometers from the action. The LAV engine had to be turned on every so often to keep the power up; it amazed me that the staff could think and plan and completely ignore the noise.

G-19 was asked to prepare a fire mission and called up a det of two M-777 155-mm guns that Major Steve Gallagher had had repositioned for this operation. Artillery was used as a "cut off" in these actions—that is, rounds were dropped on likely enemy retreat routes to "encourage" them to stay in cover so they could be engaged and destroyed with the infantry. There were two more contacts: ten enemy in the open on one and seven in the other. The Afghan forces were engaging the second group, while Bill Fletcher's "C" Company engaged the first. Bill's artillery FOO, Golf-11, then started taking fire as they prepared to call in rounds from the M-777 guns.

Then word came in from 3 Platoon: there were two friendly casualties. The platoon commander was waiting for the artillery before he carried out the assault. This was unusual. The enemy was staying in place to fight, in this case in a grape-drying hut. This wasn't hit-and-run. He was staying to fight.

One of the recce Coyotes then had a contact, ten more enemy moving into a building complex. The ANA moved off to clear them out. Ideally, artillery should have been brought to bear, but the ANA radios and the radios of their accompanying American ETTs were incompatible with the artillery net. It was now 1330 and the temperature had climbed into the low 120s F (50s C). It was hot as hell.

Bill Fletcher had his two platoons in contact. A Predator now had eyes on the battlefield and was observing a reinforced compound that had sandbags all over the place and enemy in it. Ian wanted to know if there were any women or children present before dealing with the compound. Just then, Massoud announced that forty Taliban had been seen. He went to the map and pointed to a grid. However, the two Canadian casualties, it turned out, were categorized as "urgent" and a "Nine Liner" request for medevac helicopters went out to TF KNIGHTHAWK. The report came over the net: tourniquets were tied on, there were thigh and back wounds, an arm wound with a round through the bicep. The casualties were lucid and alert. Then the M-777 guns fired and rounds crashed down on the target compound.

This medley of activity is normal. There are so many simultaneous actions taking place that the battle takes on a rhythm all its own. It's like

Jack Kerouac riffing with words. It's staccato at times, then it wanes, then it's staccato again.

Word came in that close air support was now available and it was equipped with laser-guided bombs (LGBs). Massoud was processing more information. Unit 005 had captured some bad guys: and the bad guys told Unit 005 about a reinforced compound near Salavat in Panjwayi district. Then the radio announced that there was a heat stress casualty that needed evacuation. TF ORION now had three wounded, but we could hear the medevac UH-60 and its escorting attack helicopter in the distance. Massoud told Ian that his men had captured a Taliban carrying IED-making equipment. This fighter wasn't part of this action and was trying to get away so he could continue his activities. This was bonus points for Operation Jagra. The enemy could be spooked into moving and then could be scooped up. Massoud's other informants claimed that forty Taliban fighters were moving away from the fight toward Mohammad Khah.

"Here it comes!" Stitch called out to me. I couldn't hear the plane, but I saw the detonation of the LGB and the pillar of smoke and dust. The Taliban fighting in the grape-drying hut had just been whacked by an RAF GR-7 Harrier. The Harrier's partner aircraft had the laser designator mounted and guided the munitions onto the target. There were some delays getting UAV coverage. The Sperwer couldn't fly in the heat of the day and somebody else owned the Predators. General Freakley came through, however, and there was an MQ-1 Predator orbiting Zharey district. Its sensor crew on the ground back in KAF spotted five enemy moving away from the original contact area. Captain Massoud's sources reported that there were eight severely wounded enemy hiding in Babaghday, and another group of enemy wounded in Chaharshakhey: these were six kilometers west of the fight. The enemy was running west, trying to get into the wider, denser part of Zharey to hide and evacuate. It seemed to be all over by 1720 hours.

One of Massoud's sources knew a local doctor in Panjwayi district area and discovered that twelve wounded fighters had been taken from the battle in Zharey to him; all subsequently died before they could be treated. The picture that emerged was that there were an estimated two hundred Taliban fighters in the Seyaddin–Zangabad–Shabozhey area in Panjwayi occupying grape-drying huts and a compound. They weren't doing anything—yet.

Operation Jagra, 11–14 June 2006

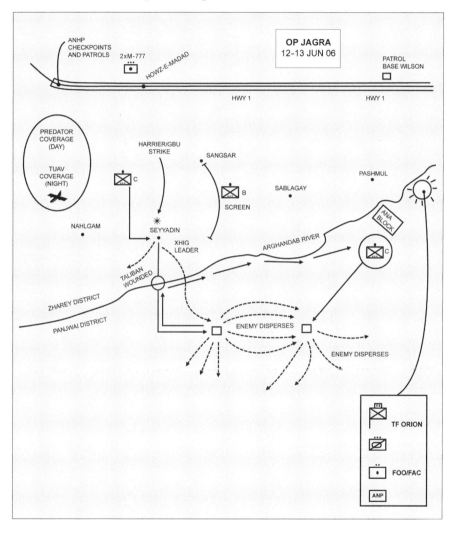

"We need to get eyes on, get a look." Kevin moved through the options: Pred, Falconview, Sperwer. "Move the QRF to the Panjwayi–Zangabad road. That's about a platoon plus. Now do we go in by vehicle or by foot?" The sun was setting, the wind was blowing, and it was still hot. I could hear the call to prayer in Bazaar-e Panjwayi. We had our own "call to prayer"—the O Group (Orders group). And we brought our own "minarets" with us—the Coyote masts. A row of twelve Kutchi camels accompanied by two kids walked by after watering in the Arghandab River.

The enemy was talking about the battle. He had repeaters hidden in the hills for his communications system, so it was difficult to tell exactly who was talking where. The Taliban had its own slang for our vehicles. The LAV III was a "Green Monster" or "Dragon." American Hummers were "Turtles," while the Coyotes were "Limbless Trees." Helicopters and aircraft were "Mosquitoes." Coalition forces were "White Cancer." Williams, of course, was offended by this name.

"The enemy is tired of walking today," Massoud announced, as Ian and Kevin searched for more ISTAR resources. "Okay," Ian said, "We can do a night move. The ANP and our people will link up at the Panjwayi district center and then move out and attack at 0430. No lights, blackout drive. How many police do we have?"

"Thirty as the Zharey QRF, another thirty as the Panjwayi QRF, and thirty more with 'C' Company. Colonel Hakim [the police commander] has another ten as his close protection party."

"Okay, have a platoon from 'C' Company move up the wadi and link up with the ANP. I'm concerned we might get probed, so get a Coyote to sweep back into Panjwayi district. Is the coffee ready?" Ian looked at Williams.

"I don't make coffee for anyone," Williams said menacingly and Ian mockingly took a step backward. We all laughed and made jokes about the scene in *Black Hawk Down* when one of the Rangers complains about making coffee during Desert Storm. The ants were eating the remains of the individual meal packs (IMPs) and small dust storms whirled in the heat. I saw a graveyard in the distance: piles of rocks on the surface with ragged colorful flags whipping in the wind. Bashir explained that one out of every five graves there was a dead Arab Al Qaeda from 2001.

Night routine started and coffee was made. We talked in low tones as we looked out over Zharey district in the starlight. At 2350 hours a silent, red-orange bloom appeared in the darkness over near Zharey district center. It was followed by the sound of an explosion. Illumination rounds were fired by the Canadian 81-mm mortars, but there was no contact with enemy forces. I found the most comfortable rock in Panjwayi district. It conformed perfectly to my head and I fell asleep.

I awoke at 0450 to a full moon. I checked in with Kevin, who was already up. There had been no contact during the night, but the enemy had been seen recce'ing the Niner Tac site. One of them was seen driving a stake into the ground, probably to be used for rocket or mortar ranging. The LAV turret silently tracked back and forth, scanning the Arghandab River with thermal imagery (TI) equipment. The Coyote mast sensor had been set to scan 360 degrees and the sensor operator set an alarm to alert himself if anything moved at two hundred meters distance from the site. There were foot patrols on the perimeter; a patrol was sent to remove the stake.

There had been problems, however. "C" Company vehicles had been getting bogged down all night, which produced delays in the plan to go into Panjwayi. Resupply was also taking place all night.

Niner Tac had a laptop computer that was connected to a satellite antenna smaller than a pizza box. This link could be used for VOIP (voice over Internet protocol) contact with the TOC, but most importantly imagery could be downloaded to it from certain ISTAR resources as JPEG files. The TOC had been instructed to look at and analyze the possible target in Panjwayi. The JPEGs showed two grape-drying huts and a pump house. The intelligence people had determined that there was a possible tunnel entrance. It conformed to the description of the target area from Massoud's source. Another source indicated that there were an estimated one hundred fighters camped out to the west of this position.

At 0705 the force was put on thirty minutes' notice to move, but two LAVs were not serviceable out of ten in "C" Company, and another was stuck. Massoud had a source that told him the enemy had eyes on the stuck LAV, but they held off firing for some reason. And there was more information on enemy activities the previous night: a Taliban ambush group, a different ambush group from the one based in Pashmul, reported losing twelve personnel and most of its RPGs and PKMs (machine guns). It still wasn't clear what the fireball was last night. It was possible it was an inadvertent enemy detonation of some kind, or an illumination round that didn't go off until it was close to the ground. The police reported that small groups of civilians, in twos and threes, were moving west in Zharey. Was it the enemy exfiltrating? No. It was migrant workers going to work. It also was possible that the locals were leaving because they feared there would be more violence in the district as a result of the presence of enemy personnel. On a previous operation more than four hundred locals left Zharey district, some packed into dump trucks.

Ian was mulling over a new plan. He wanted to go after the enemy in Panjwayi district, but it was getting too light. The idea was to move "C" Company up the Arghandab River wadi, and then from Bazaar-e Panjwayi to the grape-drying hut and pump house (Target 1), then sweep the second enemy position to the west (Target 2). ISTAR resources were called away to another operation, however, and there were issues getting eyes on to the target areas. A pair of U.S. Army UH-60s were available, however, and an LZ was prepared at Niner Tac's position. While we were waiting for the UH-60s to arrive, Nick Grimshaw's "B" Company captured a Taliban operative on Highway 1: he was equipped with a digital camera and, as it turned out, had gunpowder residue on his hands. This last was discovered using a field test kit the soldiers carried. Then Massoud's informants called in a report that ten Arabs had been seen in Pashmul near the school; they apparently used the school as cover while they ate and moved on. Other informants reported that three white pickup trucks carrying twenty enemy wounded were on the move somewhere in western Zharey. They stopped and asked local people for water.

The UH-60 landed while its companion orbited. We moved to the bird from the side to avoid the forward-canted rotor and clambered on board. We were off in seconds, flying low over Panjwayi and Zharey districts. I used this opportunity to familiarize myself with the unique terrain. Both districts were matrices of three- or four-foot (0.9 to 1.2 meters) deep grape-growing trenches that surrounded grape-drying huts made of dried mud, that had hardened over the years and now were like concrete. There were narrow roads and walls from three- to six-feet high (0.9 to 1.8 meters) along both sides of the roads. The irrigation streams had trees growing amidst them, which offered natural cover. The whole place reminded me of bocage country in Normandy. Then there were the community compounds, all of them walled and interconnected. Some fields were walled to keep livestock in and predators (the four-legged kind) out. This was complex terrain and the maps didn't do it justice. The two districts were bisected by the Arghandab River and a row of sharp hills, with the Registan Desert to the south.

The idea was to have the helicopters do a sweep of both districts and not stay in one place too long: Ian didn't want to call attention to the area he was interested in. We were so low I wondered if we were deliberately trying to draw fire. At one point we did see two Afghans equipped with AK-47s, but they didn't fire at us. The UH-60s headed back to Niner Tac.

Ian changed the plan: "C" Company would move southwest along the wadi and then around the hills and hook in to Target 2, then move to Target 1. The other route would take too long. The recovery effort in the wadi, in any event, might have compromised the operation. It slowed "C" Company's move in. No movement was seen on either objective. No weapons were seen anywhere. There was no contact. There was nothing in the grape-drying hut on Target 1. It turned out, after talking to local people, that the enemy had moved out during the night and dispersed. Massoud's people now reported Taliban presence in three villages west of the target areas: Mushan, Kowzai, and Handji Muhammad Gul. They were wearing local clothing but had PKM and AK-47 small arms. Ian wanted "B" Company to rapidly move a force down Highway 1 to the western end of Zharey district, then south to the Arghandab River, then to cross the wadi and set up a blocking position at the westernmost end of Panjwayi district. "C" Company would reconstitute and head west to force the enemy into the arms of "B" Company. There were still no ISTAR assets: they were all busy elsewhere. Massoud then reported white pickup trucks were being used to shuttle enemy fighters from east to west in Zharey. "B" Company might have to stop in Zharey and let these forces run into them.

There was better ISTAR information coming in. It turned out the action yesterday was conducted by eighty-five enemy, who took forty KIA and thirty WIA. This was why the enemy was withdrawing from the area. Even Massoud thought these numbers were high: his sources could confirm only twenty enemy KIA and twelve enemy WIA. There were other enemy present, however, but it looked like he was trying un-ass the area. Why?

ISTAR resources reported that one enemy commander passed on to another that a "baby camel" had been killed in either the LGB attack or other actions yesterday. Ian and the staff speculated that this was an enemy leadership MVT. The Taliban didn't have a multilevel hierarchical structure—that is, platoon-company-battalion-brigade command. There were fewer leaders, so when one was killed, it had a more catastrophic effect on the targeted force. If the enemy was a mix of hardcore Taliban and auxiliaries, the hardcore might stay and fight but the auxiliaries would disperse or flee.

"B" Company didn't get any contact as it swung south. "C" Company didn't get any contact either as it moved west. Word was now coming down that CJTF-76, General Freakley, had had enough of the Panjwayi–Zharey operation and was putting pressure on CTF AEGIS to move north, but Ian wanted to continue as long as he could. We rendezvoused (RV'd) with Bill Fletcher and "C" Company's two platoons, one of Nick Grimshaws' platoons from "B" Company, plus their ANA platoon and ANP, in a laager west of the White School in Pashmul. The Afghans, all of them bearded, were smiling: it was their first major action this tour.

Ian and Bill looked at the situation. The enemy had gone to ground somewhere in Zharey. How best to beat the bushes? The most likely enemy locations were the bazaar at Howz-e Madad, on Highway 1, and a built-up area south of PBW, which were labeled Objectives A and B. Part of the force, "C" Company and the ANA, would move toward A through the southern part of Zharey, while the echelon, augmented from the "B" Company platoon, would move north as if it were going back to PBW. Instead of stopping for a cordon and search at Howz-e Madad, "C" Company and ANA would move onto Highway 1, race down the highway, link up with "B" Company's platoon, and initiate a surprise cordon and search of Objective B. A collateral objective was to get the enemy to chatter so ISTAR could build up a picture. The "C" Company group's vehicle crews were to stop periodically and wave maps around and make arm gestures as if they were lost: observant enemy would pick up on this and laugh on their means, which would help us to identify where they were.

We were also about to lose Captain Massoud. He had been in some pain and was due for a root canal; he had to go back in to the city. Before he left, though, he checked in with his network again. When combined, the reports suggested that there were around fifty enemy left in eastern Zharey and all were in the Pashmul area. Some proportion of these were Punjabi speakers, though there were some Baloch speakers working with them. Massoud thought this was a close protection party for a Taliban commander named Abdul Halla Baluch, known to operate in Zharey and Panjwayi. In addition, there was still an ambush group moving somewhere along south of Highway 1. Massoud looked at one of his phones with a scowl.

"I've just lost a source. He was seen on the phone. They'll probably slaughter him now."

"Have you ever heard the enemy talking?"

"Oh yes. On one operation in the north, one Taliban said to another commander, 'The coalition forces are hurting my brain!'"

Operation Jagra was rapidly reaching its culminating point by Day 3. Contacts dropped off and it appeared as though the enemy soldiers were caching their weapons and blending in to the population or exfiltrating singly or in twos and threes. I learned that back in 2005 TF GUNDEVILS developed information on a Taliban ratline that ran from Zharey district to Panjwayi district, and then east from village to village into the southwestern suburbs of Kandahar City. The PRT in 2005 had assisted with information collection on this ratline because it was connected to several corrupt police district commanders in that part of town. This ratline also included safe houses and graveyard weapons caches. At least some of the rocket attacks against KAF came from sites southeast of this ratline. From Zharey there were enemy lines of communication going all the way back to Pakistan. And of course all roads led to Quetta, ultimately.

There was no more contact except for the seizure of enemy weapons in a car on Highway 1. TF ORION forces returned to base to prepare for Operation Mountain Thrust.

Operation Jagra was essentially a probe. It demonstrated that there were more enemy in Zharey than had been believed and that they were up to something more than just ambushing convoys or traffic on Highway 1. The enemy stood and fought before melting away. This was notable and new. The forces simply did not exist to occupy both districts, however, and with the pressure on from CJTF-76 to get TF ORION up north, the enemy was free to reconstitute his presence in Zharey. TF ORION demonstrated it could go anywhere, anytime, but the enemy just moved out of the way. The inability of a company plus to cover all enemy avenues of exfiltration and dispersion was examined by Ian and his staff for the future.

## THE PTS-ING OF MULLAH IBRAHIM

After attending a battle update briefing at TF ORION's TOC, Ian told me that we had just taken into custody a significant Taliban leader, but the details were sketchy about how it happened.

"Okay, who is it?"

"It's one of Mullah Baqi's best friends and possibly the leader of the cell that killed Glyn Berry."

I was intrigued. Mullah Baqi led a Taliban network in Zharey district that harassed the coalition when I was here in 2005. Baqi was a Taliban commander who openly debated with Mullah Omar about the efficacy of suicide bomb attacks, particularly attacks that led to civilian casualties. Omar was wavering, but Baqi wasn't, and neither was Mullah Dadullah Lang, the emergent senior Taliban military commander in RC South. They were convinced that suicide IEDs were the way to go.

The Baqi network was sophisticated. It was functionally structured into a "trigger" unit for ambushes, a mining unit that laid landmines, an IED unit that facilitated suicide operations, and an intimidation unit that distributed "night letters" and conducted selective assassinations of political figures. Money flowed to it from Pakistan, apparently from Inter-Services Intelligence (ISI; Pakistani secret service) sources. It acquired weapons from both Pakistani and Iranian sources. The network's IED cell operated mostly along Highway 1 out of Zharey district, but also went into the city to do "jobs." It was responsible for the attack on 19 May 2005 against TF GUNDEVILS 6, Colonel Bert Ges. Three attacks in August 2005, including a bicycle bomb, also were the work of this cell, in addition to ambushes along the highway.

The madrassa-taught Baqi was from the Kakar tribe and had close connections to ISI and particularly to Mullah Obied, who was a member of the Quetta Shura. A driver in the Taliban times, he had left Afghanistan during the OEF onslaught in 2002 but had been reinserted into his home district of Panjwayi later on to organize the fight against OEF.

Baqi's shadowy organization had several subcommanders, but in a successful SOF operation, Baqi had been killed along with a number of his subordinates in May 2006. Ian explained that the man in custody was Mullah Ibrahim, a known subcommander and close boyhood friend of Mullah Baqi. An informant eventually turned him in. I took a sharp breath in. Ibrahim. That was a major catch. And alive.

"So where is he?"

"In the Role 3."

"The hospital? Why?"

"He's dying of jaundice, but he doesn't realize it. He thinks he's just sick. This is the perfect opportunity to get him to PTS."

PTS was a program that apparently replaced or supplemented the earlier Taliban reconciliation program. Each province had an Afghan PTS coordinator. In this case it was our old friend Hajji Agha Lalai, the provincial council rep from Panjwayi, of all people. The coordinator, ideally a respected man in the community, encouraged Taliban commanders to change sides and bring their fighters over to the government. It was a formal and very public process, for obvious I/O effect. The PTSing commander had to be vetted by the program in Kabul, and had to provide information as well to demonstrate his sincerity. That was the nonpublic part of the program. Major Quentin Innis kept track of the PTS program so it could be rolled into and coordinated with his I/O program. It was, as usual, all very synergistic in nature.

Why did we have him and the NDS didn't? I figured they would have pumped him dry of information first. This whole thing was a bit weird. Apparently, Mullah Ibrahim was picked up by the police and delivered to the Governor's Palace, where he was kept in custody by the Guv's close protection party. Then for some reason Ibrahim was dumped off at the main gate at KAF. After our people had confirmed his identity, he was admitted to the Role 3, who wouldn't permit any interrogation because of medical ethics. It was a classic ethical dilemma: he had information that could save lives, but coercive methods couldn't be employed. In any case, his PTS was deemed by some to be more important.

It turned out that Captain Massoud's network of informants in Panjwayi was able to provide Standby Police Unit 005 with Ibrahim's location. Massoud told me that the men from his unit who had caught the Taliban commander were crying with joy when they apprehended him. Indeed, one of the men had lost family members to Ibrahim's IED cell and wanted to kill him outright. Massoud dissuaded his subordinate but was concerned that some of his men would kill Ibrahim if he was released. To make matters more interesting, a delegation of 150 villagers from Panjwayi petitioned the governor to let Ibrahim go. Massoud said to me with some disgust, "Yes, let him go. To the other world! Let him go to the Forever Jail!"

I also learned that Mullah Ibrahim was afraid of being killed at night in his bed by coalition SOF, that the kill/capture campaign really played on his mind and contributed to his willingness to cooperate. He viewed incarceration by Afghans as preferable to being taken out by the Men in Black or being turned over to the Americans and sent to Guantanamo Bay. He knew what Gitmo was and it freaked him out. That aspect of the whole Guantanamo Bay problem never makes it to the public domain, and it's something Amnesty International and Human Rights Watch don't understand: exaggerated stories of what goes on in Gitmo have a positive PSYOPS effect in-theater. Mullah Ibrahim was a case in point.

Mullah Ibrahim was now caught up in politics. Ottawa was pressuring Dave Fraser to dump Ibrahim and hand him over to the NDS. This related to the problems of detainee policy, problems Ottawa still hadn't sorted out yet. Ian and Q argued that a PTS now, the first big one, would have a significant, immediate tactical I/O effect they could exploit in Panjwayi district. Second, it would empower Hajji Agha Lalai, who could use it to bring even more Taliban into the PTS program.

The exact date of the PTS handoff had to be coordinated carefully to satisfy all agencies. Q and Julie Roberge needed to bring the media together and produce a show for the radio. Hajji Agha Lalai needed to be present: this was a big "win" for him and it would enhance his prestige and demonstrate he was a "player." Kabul was interested. And there was still Ibrahim himself: how sincere was he? Would he play us all off against each other? How much positive control would we have at the PTS event? These were all questions under discussion.

Ian was intrigued with Mullah Ibrahim, I could tell. He explained how he visited him on a regular basis, but kept the conversation limited to farming and Mullah Ibrahim's love of chocolate. He asked me if I wanted to join him on his next visit. Of course I wouldn't pass up a chance to meet the enemy face to face.

We walked over to the Role 3, met up with Bashir, our interpreter, and passed through the plywood lobby. In an isolation room were two hospital beds, one occupied by a silent brooding wounded Taliban, the other by a one-legged man who looked about fifty. There were two bored MPs—one Canadian, one American—watching movies on portable DVD machines.

"Do you want him isolated, sir?" one asked. Ian said yes, so noise defenders and goggles were administered to the wounded fighter to isolate him. For the first visit, I stayed in the background and Ian chatted about grape farming and grandchildren. Ibrahim had that "woe is me" look the Pashtuns get when they're caught with their hand in the cookie jar—or blowing people into bits. That "tell" alone was an indicator. He was calm, and deliberate. It was an anodyne conversation, but I could tell Ian was itching to know more. And what came out of the conversation was that Mullah Ibrahim's voluntary PTS wasn't a done deal yet. I think he sensed that there was debate over what to do about him and he was reexamining his options, how to play people off against each other.

As we were leaving, I heard a nurse mention the name Niaz Mohommad to one of the other staff. Niaz had interpreted for me in the past and I knew his family well.

"What's wrong with Niaz? Is he sick?" I asked.

The nurse paused. "You know Junior?"

"Sure."

"He was severely wounded in an ambush a week ago."

I was stunned.

"Can I see him?"

"Let me ask."

In due course, she came back. "He'd really like to see you. It'll help with his morale."

I went into the ward and I nearly lost control. Here was Niaz, the six-foot-plus tall smiling Niaz that I knew, lying on a hospital bed . . . with bandage-wrapped stumps below the knees and a red filled drain tube coming out of one. He was in obvious physical and mental pain. I choked back the lump in my throat and struggled to maintain my composure.

"Niaz?"

"Dr. Sean! Welcome back. It is good to see you, brother."

"What happened?" I stammered.

"An RPG. I was in a G-Wagon and it was hit. There was this hissing and burning. . . . Dr. Sean, please don't be upset. At least Allah didn't take my hands." He was starting to lose control too. I sat down and just stared at him, completely powerless to do anything, wanting more than anything in the world to have access to a billion dollars to invent a scientific process to grow body parts back.

"You are back to watch the war again?"

"Yes."

"Are you with Colonel Ian?"

"Yes. He's a good friend of mine."

"Dr. Sean?"

"Yes?"

"Fight for me! Please keep fighting for . . . me." He leaned forward, pleading, then drifted off, exhausted. Up to 2005, my engagement with Afghanistan was academic in nature, with a dash of 9/11 payback in the ingredients. In 2005, with the increase in IED attacks against the Canadians—my people who were trying to help the Afghans make a better Afghanistan—it became personal. Now, it was somebody I knew. That solidified my personal involvement in the war even further. I was no longer a mere casual observer: I was a participant in ways I hadn't been. And on this trip this new status would increase even more in ways I couldn't imagine.

Ian and I had a cigar at Green Beans.

"You know we can't interrogate him, right?" Ian asked.

"Oh yeah, I get that loud and clear. But you know, I have a legitimate need for historical information. Ibrahim fought in the jihad against the Soviets, right? Is there anything unethical about asking him about that?"

"No."

"And if the conversation drifts into other topics, with his consent, that's okay too?"

"I don't see why not. I'll check with the Role 3. Who do you want to interpret?"

I almost asked for Niaz, but Bashir was good and I trusted him. This was an opportunity to get into the head of the enemy. I prepared a list of questions to act as a basis of discussion. Ian would introduce me and withdraw.

I went back to the Role 3 the next day. As I entered the plywood lobby and was waiting for the nurse, I looked at a wall chart depicting the snakes of Afghanistan. I focused on the viper. I was about to deal with a human viper.

Mullah Ibrahim was resting comfortably, for somebody that had so much blood on his hands. He greeted us and lifted up his stump and slapped it: he was missing a foot and ankle, but the calf muscle was mostly there. He didn't have the woe-is-me look this time. He looked more confident than before. This was, by the way, a problem with captured Taliban who had in the past fought the Soviets: they knew we wouldn't do anything to them that in any way resembled what KHAD did to them: electroshock, severe beatings, rape.

"May God's peace be upon you, Mullah Ibrahim. I am Dr. Sean Maloney, a military historian. I am in Afghanistan to learn about the jihad against the infidel Communists and of course to see my friends help the people of Kandahar."

"And peace be upon you, Dr. Sean. Welcome."

"I need your help understanding things here, and you are from here and know a great many things. Is it okay with you if I ask you some questions?"

"I will answer your questions as best I can." He wasn't even wary. Of course, he would assume I was an intelligence guy trying to get info out of him. I assumed he knew that, so. . . .

"Where are you from?"

"I am from Panjwayi district. Mullah is my name: I am not actually a mullah. I still don't know how I was caught alive," he ruminated.

"I believe it was God's will," I said. "If God wanted you to die, it would have happened."

"Yes, it must be. The will of God is above all."

"I had a dream last night," I said. "God told me in the dream that you, Mullah Ibrahim, were to be an instrument of God's will here in Kandahar. And God wants peace."

He was startled by this. After some time, he said, "You are correct. I agree. I think Colonel Ian thinks so too."

"The children in Panjwayi district deserve to grow up in peace. Don't you agree?"

"Yes, I agree with you." It wasn't forced, but there was something else there. I had to keep remembering that this wasn't some kindly grape farmer: this was a murderous terrorist, whose operatives had something to do with the loss of my friend Niaz's legs.

"Do you have any jam or fruit? Colonel Hope said he'd send some."

"I'll see what I can do . . . after we talk."

I asked him how he organized to fight the Soviets. "The Islamic Shura Council told us during the time of Babrak Kamal that there was a jihad against the Soviets. I was eighteen years old."

"What tactics did you use?"

"We killed them on our own, one at a time. We killed police, government officials, party members, Russians. We killed them all. Then Pakistan started to help. Reagan helped. We then were organized into groups of eight: each group killed police and took their weapons. In time, the Afghan government people and the police started to help us—like now the police help the Taliban. The next phase involved the organization of the Afghan refugees in Pakistan. The government helped with that."

"Was the ISI involved?"

"Oh yes."

"The CIA?"

"No. It was the ISI. They had their own authority, their own policy. It was independent of the government. Like now. The ISI helps the Taliban."

That was the first time I'd heard anyone admit to this. I kept going.

"What motivates people to fight?"

"We were afraid of the USSR, now we are afraid of the USA. We will keep the U.S. busy and make them tired, then they will leave the region. The Pakistanis want the same thing."

Mullah Ibrahim was talking as if he was still part of the movement, not somebody who was about to PTS.

"I don't understand. You are Afghan, yet you serve Pakistani interests."

"I was forced to leave when the Taliban collapsed. I tried to stay but the government wanted me to pay money. They tried to take money from me. I was forced to pay. So I left for Pakistan eighteen months after September 2001." I learned later that it had been a tribal rival who sided with the Gul Agha Sherzai regime that had harassed him.

"So how did you become Taliban, then?"

"When the Taliban came, they knew me from the time of jihad. I helped them get arms when they came. Then a Taliban friend asked me to join. I accepted and went to Mianishien. Later we captured Kandahar from Rabbani."

"What was it like the first time you killed a Soviet soldier?"

He laughed, as if he were remembering old times with his family at the beach. "I shot a tank at two hundred meters with a rocket launcher near the Kandahar City jail. There were body parts everywhere. Nobody was left alive." He smiled. He also claimed to have destroyed twenty-two Soviet armored vehicles.

"How did you feel about that?"

"I was happy killing Communists and Russians." It showed.

"How do you feel about killing Canadians?'

"How would you feel if *we* invaded *you*?" he retorted.

"We're not invaders. We're here to help the Afghan people."

"Like you helped after the Soviets left?"

"That's not true. The Pakistanis and the OIC [Organization of the Islamic Conference] interfered with the UN when it tried to help. Rabbani, Sayyaf, Dostum—it's not *our* fault they started a civil war, so don't blame us! Then you people started dealing with the ISI!"

Mullah Ibrahim contemplated this.

"Yes, then we started dealing with the ISI. Gulbiddin [Hekmatyar] tried to stop the Taliban, but we needed help and we got it. ISI got Gulbiddin Hekmatyar to change sides. Then there was Al Qaeda. The ISI has become powerful."

He kept going.

"Sayyaf and Rabbani brought Osama bin Laden here to help them at Jalalabad. Then the Arabs showed up after Kabul was captured. Then the Arabs came to Kandahar."

"So what role did you play in all of this?"

"I didn't do any fighting. I wasn't a soldier," he dodged. He was starting to get evasive.

"Come on—you're a leader, a respected leader, in Panjwayi district."

"I was drawn into the leadership circle. It had Salaam Rahim, Hajji Riis, and Mullah Omar in it."

"Did you meet Abdul Azzam? bin Laden? Ayman Al Zawahiri?"

"No, but I dealt with Abu Khobaib in Kandahar City. He was involved with Hajji Agha Lalai back then." Aha. So he had already known the PTS coordinator. . . .

"What about your relationship with Mullah Baqi?"

He brightened up. "We were friends as children. I led Baqi in the old days, but then the Taliban put him in charge after the collapse. I became a fighter and I had a group of experienced fighters. We decided to fight the Americans. That started in 2002. Mullah Omar and we decided to do this." It was evident, however, that Baqi's death disturbed him. Ian said that when he broke the news to Mullah Ibrahim, he became distraught. Whenever I mentioned Baqi after that, he was visibly disturbed.

Our conversation swung all over the place, but Bashir and I compared notes afterward and I can best sum it up like this: Mullah Ibrahim was not well educated, but he was wily. In some cases he was spouting propaganda shit he heard in Pakistan. He is a fighter—and he likes fighting. It doesn't really matter who he's fighting. It was also clear he likes killing. It doesn't matter who, as long as they are foreigners and the killing can be legitimized by the religious authorities. I came away from the whole experience feeling like I'd just been dealing with an unrepentant SS officer circa 1946. Yet, at the same time, he would PTS for his own motives. Or even out of superstition: Bashir said to me afterward, "I think he thinks you really *are* a messenger from God."

"Really? Come on."

"Yes, really: it was his tone and the way he reacted to your 'dream.' He may actually regret what he has done."

"I don't know. I think he's a psychopath."

To give you further insight into Mullah Ibrahim's character, he harassed the nurses at the Role 3, who called him "Papa-T." He deliberately pissed all over the place, which forced the staff to insert a Foley catheter into his urethra. I gather he didn't like this too much. . . . They knew he wasn't some kindly old man. I even had to remind a naive young MP when I was there that Mullah Ibrahim didn't deserve his sympathy, that he'd had Canadians and Afghans killed and mutilated through the actions of his IED cells. I could see the mental attempts to reconcile the image and the reality within this solider, who clearly hadn't been confronted with cynical, evil reality before and was having trouble processing it. It reminded me of Hermann Goering making friends with his American MPs.

The next day. It was nearly show time. Would he or wouldn't he PTS? It still wasn't clear. I went with Ian, Q, and Julie through the cleaned-up terminal at KAF, past the Afghan Border Police and their U.S. Border Patrol mentors. The media were assembling outside, security was tight. It was all ANA and ANP, no Canadian or other coalition troops in sight, though there was a well-armed QRF inside the terminal, just in case. The tone was upbeat. It was a sunny day, and people were smiling. There were Canadian, American, international, local, and Pakistani media. Priority seating was given to the local and Pakistani media, which produced some grumbles from others but tough shit. It wasn't their show. There was a table with an Afghan flag on it: Hajji Agha Lalai came over and sat down, followed by other Afghan dignitaries. Julie and Q kept out of the line of sight of the cameras: Ian was the only coalition face present at the table. His visage was carved out of stone. I stood at the back with Captain Tom Nield, who was watching the media as much as the proceedings. I gather that Hajji Agha Lalai had just had a long, long talk with Mullah Ibrahim.

Then Mullah Ibrahim limped to the table supported by one of the police. He had his artificial leg put back on. He had also by this time dropped the woe-is-me look and was completely impassive, looking down like he was on his way to be executed. He was wearing a gray and silver pajj (Pashtun turban) that wasn't quite wrapped correctly. Hajji Agha Lalai moved the microphone over to him on the table.

"I'd like to thank God first and Canada second for saving my life."

The rest of the press conference amounted to a recantation of the use of violence, severing connection with the Taliban, and a call for fighters to stop the violence. Mullah Ibrahim signed the PTS document. Then the media got to ask questions:

"Were you tortured to sign this document? Are you under duress?"

"No. I'd like to thank Colonel Hope for being so kind to me."

Captain Tom Nield leaned over and said, "On a silver platter."

The I/O team started to exploit this immediately: flyers were printed up, posters distributed, radio and TV spots pumped out. This PTS was on record, which meant it could be used again and again as necessary in different media: flyers, newspaper, radio, and in the mosques. First, it was a message to the enemy. Second, it was a message to the population that important local Taliban commanders were changing sides and maybe they should get off the fence too. Third, it was a demonstration to the international media that their cynical analysis that everything was collapsing in Afghanistan and that the Taliban was unstoppable and resurgent was wrong. It was also personally satisfying to those involved. A significant enemy leader in Kandahar province had been neutralized—and he had neutralized himself, publicly.

But what of his fate? I understand that Mullah Ibrahim was flown to Kabul to a safe house soon afterward and then was admitted to hospital. I heard he died of liver failure two months afterward. None of us shed any tears. When I was in the city, I met with an Afghan friend of mine who was familiar with the affair. "Allah has blessed you and us with the death of Mullah Ibrahim," he exulted.

## THE KANDAHAR PRT

I had a special interest in the Kandahar PRT, having spent part of 2005 with the previous incarnation of it led by Colonel Steve Bowes. I left the

PRT days before Ambassador Glyn Berry, the Department of Foreign Affairs (DFA) representative, was assassinated with a suicide IED. The effects of this assassination were profound and were still having an impact in the summer of 2006 when I returned.

The Kandahar PRT, as originally established a year earlier, was a 250-person organization that reported to the American brigade headquarters responsible for RC South, CTF BAYONET. CTF BAYONET inherited an undermanned and overfunded American PRT from 25th Infantry Division in the spring of 2005 and wasn't sure how to use this unique organization so they essentially let Colonel Bowes and his team experiment with what they thought a PRT should do.[7]

The PRT became an ethnic, tribal, demographic, economic, and political recce battalion with the fledgling ability to mentor the provincial government so it could develop governance capacity. It delivered nonkinetic attacks using money provided by national development agencies: USAID, DFID, CIDA, and, to a lesser extent, the OGDs. In effect, the Canadian-led PRT was starting to develop a picture of what was *actually going on* in Kandahar province, not what people *assumed* had been going on. The PRT could do this because it had its own force protection company that acted as a "delivery system" for the nonkinetic attacks and long-range recce patrols. Most important, the PRT made personal contacts with rural people in ways that hadn't been done on a systematic basis previously.

Two things happened that altered this state of affairs. First, Glyn Berry's assassination gave skittish bureaucrats in Ottawa, many of whom were opposed to the Afghanistan mission and wanted to save Africa instead, an excuse to pull their representatives out of the mission in Kandahar. The DFA and CIDA representatives, Erin Doregan and Michael Callan, essentially were instructed not to go back until the security situation had "improved," with the bureaucrats knowing full well that it probably wouldn't.

The major blow here was to Michael Callan and his work. Michael had identified a major gap in how to improve governance in the rural parts of the province and crafted a plan called Confidence in Government (CIG) as a prototype to address the issues of getting developmental aid directly to the communities and the districts, thus avoiding the potentially corrupt, nearly nonexistent bureaucracy—while at the same time working to establish a bureaucracy that was as noncorrupt as possible to move the money from the federal level to the provincial level. He had made incremental but real headway with the provincial authorities during his time in Kandahar.

This absolutely critical project was now shut down. There was nearly $10 billion of aid money about to flow into Afghanistan through the Kabul "funnel" at the top, but the "spout" at the bottom in Kandahar was plugged.

CIDA insisted on ridiculous security measures. Michael now had to go by helicopter from the PRT to KAF and couldn't go downtown to deal with the provincial government. AEGIS, let alone the PRT, had trouble getting helicopters, even though there were several squadrons of CH-146 Griffons sitting around in Canada. The provincial leaders had to come to see Michael—at the PRT! Just consider how humiliating that was for an Afghan tribal leader.

The second problem was the PRT's relationship to AEGIS and TF ORION. When I left the PRT in 2005, there was concern that the AEGIS organizational plan ignored the PRT's unique structure and modus operandi. Under CTF BAYONET, the PRT was an independent maneuver unit that reported to the brigade and coordinated with all of the other brigade fighting units, like TF GUNDEVILS and SOF units operating in the province. The plan that emerged from Ottawa now had the PRT reporting to TF ORION, the battle group, and not to CTF AEGIS, the headquarters. This "twinning" concept came endorsed from several high-level Canadian military leaders, but Brigadier General Dave Fraser explained to me that he endorsed it based on what he had seen the Americans doing up in Zabol province on one of his recces.

The idea was that the PRT would lose the force protection company, but that the battle group would provide protection from detached elements from its infantry companies. The PRT would lose its EOD team, public affairs officer, and intelligence staff, another bad move. I could see that somebody was looking to save manpower and thought that it was somehow economical to do this, but it stripped the PRT of critical capabilities.

Someone had decided, and that was the way it was going to be. What that person (or those persons) didn't understand was just how integral the force protection company was to PRT operations. Nobody could move without it. Nothing got done without an escort, in the rural areas and particularly in the city itself. The PRT staff now had to ask somebody else to escort them to do their job. What if that somebody had a higher priority provided by a higher commander? What if it was somebody who was focused on kinetic operations and didn't understand nonkinetic operations and just decided that PRT operations weren't as important? What if the enemy changed his approach? And what if the battle group got moved to another province to conduct operations for a protracted period? The campaign planning didn't anticipate these things when it came to the PRT.

The new PRT was supported by "B" Company 2 PPCLI, but time and again "B" Company had to focus on Zahrey district and keep Highway 1 open. PBW was where they hung their hat, not the PRT. The PRT essentially had an infantry platoon instead of a company, which reduced the ability to go out on patrols by two-thirds. Combine this with the skittishness of the OGDs and the PRT became limited in what it could actually do. Then "Phoenix," the USAID representative, got frustrated and essentially moved in with the SOF—taking her checkbook with her. Matthijas Tut from DFID then changed jobs and worked for the Dutch DTF helping them get into Oruzgan province.

The state of play when I returned in June was not good. The PRT was still hamstrung, though somebody was trying to reattach the Achilles tendon. I learned that an old classmate of mine was now at the PRT, trying to keep it going. The gargantuan and pumped Major Erik Liebert was holding several tigers by the tail long before I hopped a Bison resupply convoy to Camp Nathan Smith in northeastern Kandahar City. I found out that the former PRT commander, who replaced Steve Bowes, was returning to Canada and it wasn't clear yet who was replacing him. Thus Erik and the multiple tigers. I knew Erik, who incidentally is an infantry officer, was the man for this. Nobody could bullshit Erik. Not even the Afghans.

When I arrived at the PRT, Erik crushed my hand and immediately invited me into a meeting he was having about the state of health care in the province. A British Army doctor was there: he and his men were essentially a medical recce for Helmand province and needed to know what was going on next door. A USAF medical officer from Kabul was also present for orientation. They had dropped in on Mir Wais Hospital and were astonished to find a sixteenth-century level of medical care. There was still no support by the Kabul government, and there was no pay: the doctors all had second jobs. The supply people in the hospital had connections with the black market, so USAID wouldn't engage. The Red Cross and Red Crescent did run a surgical ward but that was it. There was no helicopter LZ. "We see lots of machines that go 'ping,' but not a lot of delivery," one of the Royal Medical Corps officers, referencing Monty Python, explained.

The United Arab Emirates (UAE) was willing to pump money into the hospital and the mosques, but the mechanisms didn't exist yet to absorb and then spend the money. "We're getting swamped with money at the PRT, but we can't spend it all," Erik told me. "For example, USAID will pay for $10 million of a $25 million road-building project, CIDA has $15 million to spend, but it's like getting elephants to mate. We have to meet so many different donor standards before donors will deliver. The donors use this state of affairs in an attempt to influence decision making, which shouldn't be the objective of the exercise." Erik and his staff spent most of the time deconflicting different groups, providing aid and managing their disparate requirements. The UAE had medical supplies piling up on the docks in Pakistan, but there were problems in moving it forward to Afghanistan. The longer the stuff stayed in the warehouses, the more likely it was to wind up in someone else's hands. Erik wanted to get the Afghan Ministry of Health in Kandahar, the people running the hospital, and the UAE together.

There was something called the Polyclinic in the city, but not much was known about it. There was also an ANA hospital: it had 250 beds, six doctors, and a surgery. The Kandahar City prison also had a clinic with a staff, though its level of medical care was thirteenth century, not sixteenth century.

Astonishingly, none of these institutions appeared to communicate with each other or share resources. The USAF officer told us this wasn't unusual. He discovered that there were a lot of people in the Afghan Ministry of Health in Kabul who were drawing paychecks but had no clue what was going on down in Kandahar. He explained that the ANA surgeon general had a better organization and better health-care delivery than the rest of the government did. Was a military solution going to be the only one until capacity could be built? There was a Jordanian military hospital that had 110 staff and its own 130-man force protection company. Should it be moved south? Even the British allowed its personnel to be treated by the Jordanians. There was an Egyptian field hospital at BAF that had a strong relationship with the ANA hospital in Kabul. There was real Muslim-to-Muslim solidarity there, apparently.

Erik was concerned about the long term. It wasn't enough to have a temporary solution. There had to be protracted health-care delivery and the Afghans eventually had to provide it. He was trying to establish some kind of medical coordinating board at the provincial level so all of these entities could simply talk to each other and exchange information. That alone would be the basis for bigger and better things as the people got to know each other and cooperated: ANA docs could help with a clinic at Mir Wais, while Mir Wais docs could go on VMO missions, and so on.

One problem was the International Committee of the Red Cross (ICRC). Forget the mythology and humanitarian image of the ICRC for now. The ICRC reps at Mir Ways were disinclined to cooperate with any PRT initiatives. They argued that they were "neutral," that the PRT was a combatant, and they shouldn't have anything to do with them. This was unbelievable. OEF was there in Afghanistan at the invitation of a democratically elected government certified by the United Nations, shielding capacity building to make Afghanistan a better place for its people. And the ICRC wanted to be "neutral'? This mentality, by the way, extended to other NGOs and wasn't a new problem. How the hell could an organization like the ICRC possibly be "neutral" in a war with the Taliban—who demanded that the population they controlled forgo medical treatment because "Allah will provide"?

Erik was looking for synergies that could be realistically employed sooner rather than later with the resources he had, but that would have a longer-term effect. To rationalize an irrational situation, he and his staff established four interlocking lines of operations. The first was security: money and resources would be expended on ANP infrastructure, equipment, and training. This was considered to be the most critical priority. The second was health. The security effort could only be sustained with proper medical backup—the ANA hospital, the prison hospital, the polyclinic—all had roles to play in sustaining the police. That would have a spillover effect on the population in the short and long terms in terms of security generally, which would permit the expansion of more health services later. The third line of operation was education. Education undermined Taliban population control, but what it also did was support, if carefully coordinated, feeding programs in areas that were hard-hit.

An example of this was to use QIP money to build or refurbish schools and provide their required paraphernalia, and also to distribute cooking oil through the female students. The more girls that went to school, in theory, the more cooking oil could be distributed by the World Food Program (WFP)—WFP had a funding crunch and needed help with distribution. UNICEF was conducting teacher training but had no resources for construction. Deploying coalition reconstruction resources meant that security forces would have to go along too.

Finally, the PRT had to focus on support to tactical operations. The battle-group infantry companies needed monies for effects mitigation and local QIPs. This would be like CERP except that it would be deployed by the company commanders. The company commanders would identify a QIP, CIMIC would consent, then CIMIC and the PRT would brief the principals, who would determine whether additional analysis needed to be done and, if so, who would do it. The PRT would then provide the expertise, contracting and otherwise, to make it happen. The priority for the work, however, was to be Afghan First, followed by an Afghan NGO, then an international NGO or organization, and then the PRT if necessary. The idea was to get as much Afghan buy-in and participation as possible.

One of the problems was that Canadian CIMIC, unlike American civil affairs, was still evolutionary in Afghanistan. In 2005 there had been a handful of CIMIC people at the PRT. Now there were CIMIC teams working within the battle group *and* the PRT. There was no real coherent doctrine for CIMIC ops at this time. Did CIMIC support tactical ops, or did it do projects, collect data on local conditions, or all of the above? Nobody was sure, and the lessons from the previous PRT had not been incorporated into the 2006 rotation, which was formed and trained in the summer and fall of 2005. This was yet another muddled area that had to be rationalized under the pressure of operations in Kandahar province. Who, exactly, got to set priorities on CIMIC use? Ian Hope? Erik Liebert? And how did all that fit in with the development people at CTF AEGIS like Christina Green? To compound matters, 25 percent of the CIMIC personnel that were to be deployed to Afghanistan were left behind one week before the force left Edmonton for a combination of disciplinary and administrative reasons.

The PRT also was saddled with another serious problem. There was mounting criticism in the Canadian media and analytical community that there wasn't enough "development" being done and there was too much kinetic activity, which meant therefore that the enemy was "resurgent." This cart-before-the-horse logic implied it was our fault the enemy was resurgent, which was bullshit. The enemy, as we have seen, changed how he was doing business and we were trying to adapt to it while at the same time factions within two Canadian government departments didn't really want to be in Afghanistan and had their own agendas that were mostly linked to Africa. It was at this time that the argument emerged in the academic community that Canada should pull out of Afghanistan and go into Darfur with the UN, an absurd and naive proposition. The elected government, however, had to contend with the criticism, so now they were insisting that there be measurable development progress in Kandahar province.

The PRT was in no position to suddenly improve development overnight; there was pressure on Erik and his people to "be seen" to be improving things in a visibly measurable way. It was a nearly impossible demand, given the conditions I have described above, and throwing more money at the problem wasn't a viable solution. The PRT was essentially instructed to spend lots of money: the amounts spent would become the measure of success, not the long-term effects or the screaming need to mentor the Afghans and let them run their own country. The issue here was the absorptive capacity of the provincial government and the federal line ministries in Kandahar province; these were negligible at this time. CTF AEGIS wanted real, tangible results too, but they were being pressured from higher. The outside criticism and the demands would continue well into the fall of 2006, despite all of the good things the PRT was in fact trying to do but couldn't explain in public forums. Instead of telling the critics to go to hell and explaining the complexities of the situation to them, elements in the Canadian government kowtowed to the critics and tried to meet conditions that just couldn't be met.

As usual, the demand by the media and the critics for short-term instant gratification at the expense of mentoring was about to generate more Afghan dependency on the international community. There were Afghans that knew this and were appalled by it. Others, incidentally, were prepared to massively profit from the state of affairs. The potential psychological, not to mention I/O, fallout was immense. The enemy could exploit the state of affairs by declaring this was just more "occupation" activity by foreign forces at the expense of the Afghan people(s).

Erik and his people were finding out other disturbing and unintended effects from previous reconstruction activities in the province. The American approach involved, in part, the use of Commander's Emergency Response Program or CERP money. This allowed American commanders to do QIPs, in addition to what USAID and the development community were doing. CERP money was generally used to support a project that would have an immediate effect on ongoing operations. However, with the demands to be seen to be doing something and the simplistic metrics that went into "proving" that something was being done, CERP monies sometimes went into projects that couldn't be sustained. For example, building a school using CERP was a flawed proposition: that school had to be stocked, maintained, staffed, and protected. CERP would only pay for its construction. If there was no follow-up, it would become a burnt-out shell. But it became a statistic that proved money was being spent in a positive fashion, regardless of what happened later. CERP was better suited to things like road construction or other infrastructure projects that required minimal maintenance. The PRT staff referred to CERP money as "heroin": short-term glow, long-term pain.

To add a further layer of complication, the Americans had supported the Durrani confederation in Kandahar province at the expense of the Ghilzai confederation. In the case of reconstruction aid, most of the CERP money had gone to "reliable" Durrani tribal companies and individuals. This was understandable in the early days when the Durrani were believed to be mostly anti-Taliban and the Ghilzai to be pro-Taliban. But now, when we were trying to achieve stability in the province, the Ghilzai could no longer be isolated. They had to be brought into the system. How did the PRT effect mid-course guidance to balance this situation out when something like 90 percent of the reconstruction aid was going to Durrani affiliates? The solution wasn't clear in the summer of 2006 but it was another aspect to the problem that Erik and the PRT staff had to deal with.

THE PRT AND POLICING ISSUES: CIVPOL

I hooked up with Corporal Bob Hart and Superintendant Wayne Martin from the RCMP who I had met the previous year. Bob introduced me to the other members of the CIVPOL team at the PRT: Constable Ross Davis from Charlottetown, Prince Edward's Island; and Staff Sergeant Al McCambridge, Constable Marc Biage, and Constable Randy Noseworthy, all from the RCMP. "An improvement from *two*," Bob said, "but we need more. A *lot* more." There were some changes in the past five months since I had been to Kandahar: Colonel Tor Jan and his PRT police had been registered, put through the RTC, and legitimized. There was a new provincial chief of police, and a new position, the regional police chief, had been established. The ANP in the province now had a 24/7 duty staff that had links to the JCC. Notably, the U.S.-led CSTC-A had established a police mentor program for these new leaders. Colonel Paul Calbos, a U.S. Army officer whom I would meet on occasion, was the regional-level mentor.

On the down side, there were problems at the PRT. "Foreign Affairs money dedicated to security capacity building—there isn't enough of it and the bureaucratic bullshit we have to go through to get it isn't worth it," one of the cops explained. "It's an Ottawa problem. The DFA and CIDA people here are okay." DFA put up $8 million, but Treasury Board, the Ottawa bean counters, refused to release it until October 2006. CIDA had $100 million for reconstruction, so was it possible that the CIVPOL could access CIDA money? Yes. Initially. Then DFA said no, that their policy was that money couldn't be spent on *items*, only on *programs*. Police reform in Afghanistan was a DFA area, so now DFA and CIDA were locked in a bureaucratic battle in Ottawa. Gavin Buchin and Renata Pistone, the DFA and CIDA reps at the PRT, tried their best to make things work.

Then there was the prison issue. No legal system is sustainable without incarceration capacity. The Afghan facilities were medieval, so somebody in Ottawa had the idea to get the CIVPOL to mentor the emergent prison system. The RCMP didn't want anything to do with that at all. Corrections Canada did that job back home, but then there were issues in getting Corrections people to deploy to Afghanistan.

That said, the CIVPOL cops got out whenever they could to work with their counterparts in the field. Even after Glyn Berry was assassinated and CIDA and DFA were grounded, RCMP officers still went "outside the wire"—men like Staff Sergeant Al McCambridge, who mentored police substation commanders and who conducted joint patrols with the Afghans and the Canadian Military Police detachment at the PRT. "We mentor them on small unit tactics, vehicle checkpoint operations, and searches," Al explained. "Initially we wanted the PRT police to improve their skills so our security would be improved, but then we saw the need elsewhere in the city." This coincided with the replacement of three-quarters of the police substation commanders that occurred in January–February after Glyn's killing. I was told there were still problems in getting the German-led police "pillar" to work. The Germans visited sometimes, but there were ministerial restraints in Germany about working in the field.

An ad hoc policing conference was set up by AEGIS around this time to get a grip on the diverse policing authorities in the province. These included the PRT, DynCorp trainers, the RTC, the CSTC-A mentors, and the military police. This got everybody in one room, something that hadn't happened before. The UNAMA police adviser wanted in too, but the main players in police reform were Germany and the United States. The United States gave the ANP $280 million and eight thousand vehicles, for example. Canada's contribution, through DFA and CIDA, amounted to twelve vehicles and no cash.

"Canada will have to spend more money to be a player here in policing," I was told by one observer. "The Glyn Berry killing was used as an excuse by DFA and CIDA *not* to spend money. Glyn and Erin [Doregan] had their priority list of what needed money, including police reform support. It didn't coincide with the politically correct DFA priorities that focused on gender equality programs. Now they don't have a counterargument from here and are going forward with the Ottawa priority list."

Astounding. Here we were, in the middle of a counterinsurgency war where the police were the key to local security, and DFA was prioritizing gender equality issues? We were back to security versus development. Like nothing had changed since December 2005. "What's it going to be?" my colleague asked rhetorically. "Women's schools or police reform? There's no point building a school if you can't stop it from being burned down."

On the plus side, the CIVPOL guys had successfully completed a number of projects ranging from weapons training and distribution to motorcycle training and distribution to an IED first-responder course, plus the usual vehicle checkpoint training. The real issues, though, were infrastructure improvements, plus the critical need to create a reliable communications system. The list was a long one, and it would take a concerted effort to give the police forces the basics to do the most rudimentary tasks.

## OPS IN KANDAHAR CITY

Because of its contacts and activities, the PRT also was a lens to see into what was going on in Kandahar City. I was particularly interested in the security aspects, so I met with several Afghan friends, including the redoubtable Yusuf Zoi. The policing situation, they told me, wasn't good. They explained that the chief of police's office was penetrated and unreliable, that elements in the ops staff were compromised. One high-level police official was being blackmailed because some family members had stolen drugs from a lock-up in Kabul. They hadn't been caught, but the blackmailing elements knew about it and used it to control him, to the detriment of coalition operations.

On the plus side, I heard the details of a joint ANP–NDS operation, run without coalition input, that nearly netted a Taliban leader who ran an IED facilitation network. The mission didn't achieve its objectives, but the coordination between the two organizations was getting better. The NDS input into the JCC was quality stuff. Some Afghans had found the means to bypass the more corrupt officials and police to get things done. I heard about a counterdrug police unit that took matters into its own hands and started to operate outside the law, such as it was, because they were frustrated by the corruption. My Afghan friends wanted more RCMP to help them professionalize the police. They told me Bob and Wayne had had a positive effect and had even inspired certain ANP. For example, back in 2005 Bob and Wayne pulled their hair out (figuratively—Wayne is bald) over the Afghans' inability to remove a corrupt, pedophile police district commander who controlled the district where the "Golden Arches" were located on Highway 4 between KAF and the city. This guy was now out of the picture by July 2006 and, "Hey presto!"—suicide IED attacks at the Golden Arches dropped off—not totally, but significantly.

"The real impact, though, has come from the British Spetsnaz," one of my friends explained. The fact that SOF was active in the city was not surprising. In the spring, the PRT noticed that something just wasn't right in the city. School authorities didn't want coalition forces going to their schools on humanitarian activities; later the pattern of attacks in the city changed. The confidence level in the city dropped. Erik, Nick, and Harj believed that the bulk of the threat was emanating from outside the city, but there was a definite psychological effect radiating inward. The population was picking up on something that the coalition forces were missing. In time, the British SOF were brought in to work on the problem.

They came in, however, without a robust intelligence capability but, in time, elements of the U.K. Special Reconnaissance Regiment (SRR) were deployed to improve analysis.

What was interesting was the contrast in how different SOF units operated. There had been complaints received at the PRT about the collateral effects of direct action operations conducted by Canadian and American SOF. The damage was minimal but, as one of my Afghan friends said, "Giving a widow an MRE and some bottled water doesn't help her get the door and gate fixed." Some of these people approached the PRT for compensation and there wasn't a mechanism to address it initially, because there was little or no SOF–PRT coordination—especially between the Canadian entities. It was a smaller version of what was going on in the rural areas. The lack of coordination between some SOF and the conventional forces created these fissures; those fissures, if there were enough of them, could be exploited by the enemy for I/O purposes. "The Canadian and American Spetsnaz are really violent, and cause a lot of damage," Rashid said.[8] "The British Spetsnaz are quiet, and sometimes they don't even shoot. They use stealth." There had been three significant British SOF raids that netted IED facilitators and no shots were fired at all. The PRT didn't usually have to remunerate local people after British operations, but they apparently did after Canadian operations.

I learned later that the British SOF was a combination of the Special Boat Squadron (SBS) and the SRR elements put together into TF-42. It generally operated in the city, but also worked in Helmand. Indeed, two members of this task force were killed on the eve of the Battle of Pashmul and their identities and affiliations were reported in the press, which was unusual.[9]

TF-42 had to coordinate with the PRT, the NDS, and with the ANP. A series of talks led to a draft city security plan, which in part was the impetus for the deployment of Standby Police Unit 005 to Kandahar. In theory, Massoud's unit was to establish a series of permanent checkpoints in the city at key points: these checkpoints went about their business acting as a presence and deterring enemy movements or actions. When the SOF and the NDS or other information sources developed a target in a particular district, the checkpoints then served as cut-offs to isolate the area. Then the SOF or the NDS would conduct a direct action on the target building. In theory, "leakers" would be caught in the police net. At least three successful operations had been conducted using this technique.

The larger intent was to force the enemy out of the city as much as possible, particularly the IED cells and the facilitators. Smashing up people's homes and then not compensating them properly did not positively contribute to this process, especially when a certain percentage of targeting information tended to come from the population. Word travels quickly in Kandahar City.

### "B" COMPANY'S WAR: ZHAREY AND PANJWAYI DISTRICTS

Given the importance of Zharey and Panjwayi in relationship to Highway 1 and Kandahar City, I asked Ian why he didn't build a FOB in Pashmul, then introduce police into Zharey to support governance efforts. He said he thought Patrol Base Wilson (PBW) served essentially the same purpose. Some argued that there weren't enough Afghan forces to man another FOB. PBW was already established along Highway 1 and served as a launch pad for influence operations into Zharey. Major Nick Grimshaw and "B" Company fought that war.

"B" Company was inundated with IED in the first week of June. Four IEDs, including remote-controlled and pressure-plate versions, were discovered before they could be blown. Then there was a suicide vehicle attack in Kandahar City on 4 June that killed four locals and wounded twelve. The next day there was another suicide attack against TF ORION. Then, on 6 June, two more IEDs were found on Highway 1. The NDS were able to apprehend an IED maker, who led them to a cache. Zharey wasn't alone—on 7 June two remote-controlled IEDs were found on the road near Zangabad in Panjwayi district. There had to be a new crew in town. The only way to find them was through information gathered by the police from the population, a process that was becoming more coordinated. On 15 June, however, the Zharey district police chief was killed in an attack on a bus that killed nine and wounded eighteen.

The reconstruction line of operations became problematic in the two districts. "Niaz Mohommad was the district leader in Panjwayi, but then he became the district leader in Zharey." Nick pointed to a personality chart.

> He wouldn't make decisions without Haji Agha Lalai saying it was okay. Haji Agha Lalai had many, many, contacts. All of the reconstruction that's occurred in Panjwayi is a result of his influence. He employs his tribe's allies, in this case the Popalzai. He

Captain Zia Massoud contacts his HUMINT net against the backdrop of the shrine in Khakriz. Captain Kevin Barry and Lieutenant Colonel Ian Hope are in the background. (Author)

Lieutenant Colonel Ian Hope, Captain Kevin Barry, and I (not pictured) have a smoke during the Khakriz operation. (Author)

Niner Tac is alerted when a possible suicide car bomb approaches the column near Lam in northern Ghorak district. (Author)

The damage taken by the 9-W G-Wagon after a suicide car bomb attack. The fuel tanks were holed, and the armor penetrated right where Captain Zia Massoud would have been sitting. The window is armored glass nearly three inches thick—and it was starred. (Author)

Coming back from Chenartu Valley, One Niner stops for a smoke. Company Sergeant Major Pete Leger, Corporal Chris Raike, and Master Corporal Steve Pichovich, with Major Kirk Gallinger in the turret. (Author)

"C" Company and the ANA secure the Gumbad subdistrict center in preparation for a VMO operation. (Author)

Captain Julie Roberge talks to the locals lining up for medical care in Gumbad during the VMO. (Author)

Company Sergeant Major Pete Leger and Major Kirk Gallinger at daylight the first morning of Operation Zahar. This picture was taken seconds before we came under fire. (Author)

As Company Sergeant Major Pete Leger and I moved forward under fire, the LAV in front of us was engaged with an RPG that struck the wall. The LAV opened up with 25-mm . . . (Author)

. . . as did the LAV-III and G-Wagon right behind us. (Author)

The A-10s tried to hit the enemy as they shifted positions. This bomb went short nearly four hundred meters and landed in front of us. (Author)

Master Corporal Mark Pickford, Corporal Chuck Prodonick, Corporal John Gute, plus an unnamed medic and a sapper after pulling back for some rehydration during Operation Zahar. The temp was around 110° to 120° F (40° to 50° C). (Author)

Part of "A" Company moves forward to clear out an annoying enemy marksman working the seams. (Author)

Major Kirk Gallinger confers with his platoon leaders, Lieutenant Ben Richard and Captain Kevin Schamuhn, before moving on to the next objective. (Author)

Brigadier General Dave Fraser and his staff at the height of Operation Augustus in Helmand province, July 2006. (Author)

was exercising favoritism toward certain tribes, which you have to understand if you are going to operate in that area. He would drive around without bodyguards and nobody ever took a shot at him. Habibullah Jan told me he's convinced that Haji Agha Lalai is Taliban: "Isn't it interesting that he can drive wherever he wants in Kandahar province and nobody takes a shot at him? Isn't that interesting?" he'd ask rhetorically. Then Haji Agha Lalai told me the same thing about Habibullah Jan!

There were problems getting PRT support for initiatives in Zharey and Panjwayi.

I was dissatisfied with the Canadian reconstruction efforts so I brought the USAID representative on as many patrols as possible.[10] Canada was not able to put its money where its mouth was. We were saying we were there for reconstruction but to this day we still have problems with that. Where USAID could say "we built that clinic, that school, paved that road, we're working in this province," we were still trying to get our ducks in order from CIDA and all the other departments that were involved. Michael Callan couldn't even go out there. The CO at the PRT had a certain budget, but he was restricted in how he could use it. General Fraser at AEGIS didn't have a reconstruction budget. It was just ludicrous. You can't win a counterinsurgency without spending a certain amount of money.

Major Erik Liebert, when he took over the PRT, helped improve things as best he could, with the limits imposed by the lack of interagency coordination and the glacier-like Ottawa bureaucracy.

Nick and "B" Company continued to push the VMOs out the door, but then their recces started to get engaged. In one TIC, four Taliban ambushers were taken out. "We did a really good [VMO] in Nahkoney. The clinic had been burned out some time ago and we wanted to get in there."[11] I smiled. I was there with the PRT investigating the burnout back in December 2005. "We wanted to demonstrate that yeah, you could burn a clinic down, but we're still going to come here and make an effort to provide medical support to the community. It was all really positive. The district leader showed up to meet with the local leaders, and we treated this young girl who had a bad cyst and lesions on her foot. We tried to maintain that theme of actively providing assistance."

The Taliban, on the other hand, were using elements in the police to provide medical support for their wounded. Nick explained,

> Lieutenant Dave Ferris called me up from a checkpoint west of Howz-e Madad and said that something was suspicious at one of the ANHP checkpoints. There were two guys, one in uniform, one not. Dave checked their cell phones and one of the guys had the phone numbers of Taliban insurgents that had just been detained a couple of days ago during an operation in Zharey. There was a hole in the back of the checkpoint building, lots of tire tracks, and there was a whole bunch of medical equipment and bloodstains on the floor. The medical equipment didn't belong to the ANHP.
>
> These guys got hostile with Dave. He recommended that the chief of the ANHP come down here and evict them, because he's obviously Taliban. This caused a shitstorm. I rolled out with 6 Platoon thinking this could get ugly. We were publicly accusing the ANHP of supporting the Taliban. Then two pickup trucks full of guys with guns showed up from the west, from Maywand. Their commander said he was from Maywand, but I hadn't seen him before. He said he heard that the coalition was taking over an ANHP checkpoint and he wanted to know what was going on.

The obvious issue to Nick and Dave was, "If you're from Maywand, than what the hell are you doing in Zharey?" Nick told him to work through his chain of command—that is, the ANHP chief in Kandahar City.

"They looked loaded for bear, and like Taliban without the black turbans. But they were outgunned. My guys were extremely vigilant and nobody was going to fuck around with us at that point. Then they took off. Then the station commander for the checkpoint arrives—from the south in Zharey district, with two trucks full of guys. It was like a Mexican standoff where his guys are surrounding him with guns at the ready and 6 Platoon has their fingers on their triggers." The station commander comes over and rips open his shirt: "You've defaced me in front of my troops. How can you accuse me of supporting the Taliban?" "You need to calm down," Nick said. He claimed it [the tire tracks and blood stains] was all from a vehicle accident a few days ago.

Nick and Dave confronted him with the evidence—the cell phone—and asked who the doctor was that treated the accident victims. He had no answers. Nick told him, "If you fire a single shot at us on the way out, I'm going to level this place." He was later relieved. "The Taliban's communications network was unbelievable. We had more indicators that the Taliban were wearing ANP uniforms and using ANP trucks. We didn't stop ANP trucks on the highway because they're ANP, right? We were supposed to be working alongside them."

Standby Police Unit 005 also had problems with the local police, Nick added. "Massoud's QRF police were located at PBW, and they did not get along with the Zharey police at all. There were allegations that they were trying to kill each other. . . . [N]one of them had uniforms but they all had more guns than they knew what to do with. We eventually evicted them. Even the NDS that were there were not conducting themselves in a favorable manner. The NDS were not cooperating with the police, not sharing information, Later, another NDS guy showed up from Kandahar who was a good tactical questioner."

What Nick was observing was the breakdown of the most important part of fighting an insurgency—the consolidation of local reportage and its assessment and dissemination by the police and intelligence units upward and downward in this chain of command so that it could be acted on by the appropriate forces. The inability to attain this synergy in Zharey led to longer-term problems over the years. Yet the will to improve the police and intelligence system was being undermined from power brokers in the province because it might interfere with their economic- and power-based interests. The Taliban insurgency took full advantage of this disunity and exploited it to the maximum long before we even figured out what the game actually consisted of. Nick Grimshaw, his men, and Harj Sajjan were piecing this puzzle together when it was swept aside by the demand for more kinetic operations to confront the growing enemy near-conventional build-up.

In theory, the ASIC should have been doing this analysis but was more conventionally oriented, KAF-bound, and focused on feeding the Ottawa beast. There was a definite requirement for specialists to assess, in detail, local power structures: who was who in the zoo and their exact relationships with each other. It was beyond the capacity of the ASIC to do so at this point. "B" Company and the JCC knew more about what was happening in Zharey and Panjwayi than any structure back at KAF did.

Nick Grimshaw, his second-in-command Jay Adair, and Harj Sajjan worked hard to make up for these deficiencies. Out of these discussions emerged a series of platoon- and company-sized operations later called "maneuver to collect" operations. These were undertaken at some risk: "B" Company was not prioritized for close air support or Predator support. Sometimes it had access to the M-777 guns if they were within range. The Sperwer TUAV was ineffective during the day because of the heat. That said, one or two platoons, a section of engineers, and some military police, and whatever Afghan security forces they could cajole into going along, would move from PBW into Zharey or Panjwayi districts to generate enemy communications traffic or movements. That data would be used to validate HUMINT collected by Harj Sajjan and the NDS, and then synthesized into a bigger picture of enemy activity and intentions in the two districts.

During these operations, Nick, Jay, and their platoon leaders—Lieutenant Kelly Catton, Lieutenant Konrad von Finkelstein, and Captain Dave Ferris—attended every *shura* they could, conducted what we call KLEs with local power brokers, and used the small four-man CIMIC detachment led by Captain John Angus to identify as many projects as possible to be fed back to the PRT. Nick was hampered by the limited amount of money he had available and figured he could generate more goodwill with more money. That said, "B" Company got to know Zharey and Panjwayi districts extremely well and had the pulse of what was going on. The presence and maneuver in there generated a significant number of "walk-ins" who provided information on the enemy and his movements. Relationships were built; arguably, they were stronger between the locals and "B" Company than they were between the locals and the provincial government or coalition formation headquarters.

It was from this web of contacts that patterns started to emerge to "B" Company in PBW. Whenever there was a contact with enemy forces, they invariable fought, broke contact, moved to a secondary position, fought, then broke contact and backed off to a strong point area or faded away. On one of these operations in Pashmul, the enemy fell back on a cemetery area before splitting up. Wali Jan, the Zharey police chief, received several pieces of information from informants who kept referring to "the cemetery with the big hill" that functioned as a Taliban strong point. Another operation produced similar information. Then Harj Sajjan had a detainee captured on Highway 1 who "sang like a canary" about enemy dispositions—near a "big cemetery on a hill." Some sources also referred to it as "the factory." Whether this referred to drugs or IEDs, nobody was sure. Because of the Operation Mountain Thrust operations, UAVs were not available to check this out. When the Sperwer TUAV was used, its noise signature gave it away and the enemy went to ground.

All of this information, however, correlated with separate information collected by Captain Massoud's network which fed the Guv and TF ORION via the JCC. When the Guv complained to Ian Hope about mounting problems in Zharey and Panjwayi districts, "B" Company's efforts provided more than enough confirmation: the enemy was operating in Pashmul in strength and he was preparing to fight. This ran counter to the conventional wisdom at CTF AEGIS and, more importantly, at CJTF-76, whose staff was busy with Operation Mountain Thrust.

BATTLE FOR THE MOSQUES

Flash forward to 2007: I was in the TF AFGHANISTAN HQ and I saw the padre's office and poked my head in. There was an older Protestant padre sitting there. "Yes?" he said in an irritated tone of voice.

"I'm looking for Suleyman Dimeray."

"Why?" he shot back.

"Because he's the best I/O weapon we have in Kandahar and I need to talk to him," I said.

This older man of the cloth instantly became irate and turned red in the face, shouting, "PADRES AREN'T WEAPONS! WE'RE SPIRITUAL ADVISERS!!!" He made some remarks about prima donnas and preferential treatment.

"Then you don't get what's going on here!" I walked away.

Flash back to 2005 to the PRT. It occurred to me during all the debate over tribal rivalry and mapping that nobody was looking at the mosques. That was to be expected to a certain extent: the Western cultural view perceives a separation of church and state, whereas Islam does not. For the most part, Western armies conducting I/O focused on radio, newspapers, and television. From my travels, however, I viewed the mosque as an I/O medium that the enemy was dominating. Few at that time did and were quite content to stay within the boundaries set by their SFOR experiences in Bosnia.

In 2006, however, somebody was starting to think about it. I met with Padre Suleyman Dimeray on my jaunt out to FOB Martello. We eventually and coincidentally met up again in the back of a hot Bison traveling from KAF to the PRT. I asked Suleyman what he was seeing in the religious sphere in the province.

"The Islam here is a mix of *hanifi* and *wahabbism*, but for the most part the people here don't know the religion," he explained. "They can't differentiate between moderate and radical aspects of Islam. When I first got here, I also found that there was a surge in Sufism in the city. That's not surprising, since Afghanistan was a seat of Sufism in the past. It's just been underground. It [Sufism in Kandahar City] definitely needs more study."

Suleyman Dimeray, brought over as an adviser to Dave Fraser, now worked with the PRT. His task was to engage the religious leadership in Kandahar province. Suleyman was originally from Turkey, but had settled in Edmonton in 1993. When he was studying at the University of Alberta, he met military chaplains and became interested in joining the CF. He arrived in Kabul on a Technical Assistance Visit in 2004 when Colonel Walter Semianow was commanding TF KABUL. Walt wanted religious advice and had to battle with the chaplain general's office to get Suleyman to deploy. There were significant and nasty politics in the padre's world over the imam's disposition: there was some allergic reaction to the "CF imam" label. This sort of thing really distressed him: a padre's denomination didn't matter, and all padres administered to all soldiers. A padre was a padre, but others didn't see it that way and had prejudicial blinkers on.

In any event, he was here in Kandahar and probing into a world the rest of us couldn't get into. That world was fairly scary. "There's a circular problem here in Kandahar," he sketched out. "First, there is an ignorance of Islam itself. Then there is a pride here that they *do* understand Islam. Third, there is freedom, freedom from outside academic Islamic influences. And finally, there is a lack of morals here: everyone is an opportunist. It's a weird fusion of Islam, too."

"How is that?"

"The people really believe they are the 'best' Muslims. The people pray, but they don't mean it. In theory, Islam is there to brake the excesses, but it doesn't work here. There is a lack of leadership. Islam has been subordinated to power."

"Well, Islam was misused by the Taliban. Is it really surprising that they continue to misuse it?"

"No, not really. The enemy uses the mosques as I/O tools. We *must* contain them because that is how they are spreading their influence. Here in the city and in the country."

So what was the state of play in Kandahar province? We had to determine that before developing countermeasures. It is important to understand that, historically, the mullahs and religious leaders in the Pashtun regions had lesser status. This was because the Abdu Qais Rashid, the original Pashtun leader, apparently received his orders directly from the Prophet, therefore was the first among equals in the religious affairs of his confederations. Pashtunwali, for example, trumped Sharia law in southern Afghanistan. The mullahs' role was to provide legitimacy for the tribal leaders. This changed in the 1980s when traditional culture was disrupted during the Soviet occupation and then again when the Taliban took over. The Mullahs gained increased status and power. With the return of the tribal leaders to power in post-Taliban Afghanistan, the role of the mullahs was now unclear. Where there is confusion, there is profit. Where there is discord, there is exploitation. The Taliban used this wedge against the government and tribal leaders. Oh, you've lost power and status under the Infidel-supported puppet regime? We can help you regain it. . . . In addition, the Guv wasn't funding the mosques and wasn't paying the mullah's salaries. The PRT was just figuring this out. Yet another wedge the Taliban could use.

The government of Afghanistan was reestablishing the Ministry of Hajj-Awfak, or religious affairs. Its job was to coordinate the Hajj and to maintain religious buildings. In theory, it should also handle salaries, but it wasn't ready to do so in 2006. There was a national-level ministry and provincial branches, but the one in Kandahar was rife with corruption. Most of the money wasn't making it to Kandahar (just like money wasn't making it to the police . . . ).

The other religious institution was the Ulema Shura: it had a national office and provincial offices. It was not a government agency, however. It was an independent body but also a political appointment. To confuse the issue, the head of the national Ulema Shura was also the president of the Supreme Court of Justice. The Ulema Shura at the provincial level was the senior meeting of religious representatives, just as the Provincial Council was a meeting forum for elected officials. The Ulema Shura wasn't elected, obviously. It was a potentially powerful body, however, and could sway opinion in the uneducated rural areas. In a word, the Ulema Shura provided legitimacy to whomever they chose to bestow it upon. Notably, the Kandahar Ulema Shura usually dominated the national Ulema Shura, so it was a powerful link between national and provincial religious affairs. OEF, by the way, had overlooked the importance of almost all of this in their planning processes.

I also knew that the mosques had a role in education: they took up the slack when secular schools were prohibited under the Taliban. In many cases, in the areas where there were no schools or in areas where the Taliban had burned the schools, the mosques and their mullahs were the primary educators. By influencing the Ulema Shura, one could influence this particular branch of education. My thinking was that secular education would undermine the medieval Taliban thinking over time—if given a chance. The combination of secular education with moderate Islamic education was unbeatable: the Taliban had nothing to offer that could compete with it. And we haven't even touched on the gender issue. Moderate Islam, secular schools, coeducational environments—all this would undermine and destroy the Taliban ideology in a generation.

Suleyman was rooting through an individual meal pack (IMP) in the Bison, looking for a halal IMP, but this vehicle had none. He sighed. Everything seemed to have pork in it.

> I wanted to see the state of religious affairs here, so Major Liebert arranged for two local mullahs to meet with me at Colonel TJ's (Colonel Tor Jan, the PRT police commander) compound.[12] I was shocked. They were not that well educated. They kept asking me, "You are Muslim, right?" I recited some verses of the Koran and they were impressed. Nobody questioned my lack of beard, though. I attended a *shura* in Zharey district. One of the leaders said to me, "We wish we had you as our mullah. It would solve our problems." They weren't comfortable with Arabs, but because I was Turk, it was okay with them. When I met with the mullahs in town, they had a lot of questions for me. We had an amazing dialogue. I found out that they despised the bombings. The killing of civilians wasn't ethical. They especially don't approve of suicide bombings. I also found out they condemn air attacks that kill civilians. The biggest problem is that the government here doesn't support the Ulema Shura and won't provide funds. The governor is an openly unreligious man, which creates more bad will with the Ulema Shura.

The Bison bounced over a speed bump, throwing us around. "So it's no wonder that he won't fund them. He's worried about being condemned morally by the Ulema Shura, so he won't support them," I observed.

"Correct. The Ulema Shura's view of Canadians is interesting. They distinguish between us and the Americans. The Americans showed no interest in the Ulema Shura or its affairs. We apparently are gentle and polite compared to the Americans, who viewed all mullahs as potential Taliban. In the districts, however, they don't distinguish between us. The 'hit first, repair later' approach is causing problems."

I learned from other sources that the mullahs in the villages also had a relationship to the narcotics problem. The more money that was made locally from the harvest, the greater tithe, or *zakat*, they received. They had no incentive, particularly in the rural areas, to interpret Islam in a way that condemned poppy cultivation. Again, the coalition was completely missing this in its I/O approach.

We had to win over the mullahs in the rural districts if we wanted to make headway there, but first we had to maintain the positive relationship with the Ulema Shura in the city. That was becoming more and more problematic. Kyba TV in Pakistan, acting as a Taliban I/O tool, announced that members of the Kandahar Ulema Shura would be assassinated if they continued to "collaborate." In 2005–2006, twelve members had been killed in separate incidents, including the well-regarded Mawlawi Abdullah Fayaz in June 2005 and Mullah Mulavi in April 2006. Even Fayaz's funeral was attacked by the Taliban. Analysis conducted later indicated that these killings were selective: they not only were designed to intimidate those left alive, but also to advance the careers of infiltrators. At the same time, there was no governmental protection, police or otherwise, offered to the members of the Kandahar Ulema Shura because of the poor relationship with the governor. Pressure tactics were being employed by the Taliban on other members. It was a real battleground: if the enemy was expending this level of effort to influence the Ulema Shura, it was obviously important to him. Therefore we had to be in the fight too.

## THE CHENAR OPERATION: PRELIMINARIES

TF ORION moved from Operation Jagra back into the Operation Mountain Thrust planning cycle immediately. While we were arriving in KAF, however, word came in from the JCC that a civilian bus had been bombed in the eastern part of Kandahar City near the Golden Arches. The police were securing the site: coalition forces let the Afghans handle it. There were an estimated seven wounded and eight killed. These were locally employed personnel who worked at KAF. Clearly the enemy was hitting soft targets in order to deter the KAF workforce that in theory would degrade KAF's capacity and then degrade the economic benefits that KAF provided to the population as a whole. On the I/O side, however, this could piss off the people who were losing revenue and employment. It could cut both ways. CNN, incidentally, had a report on the news within forty minutes. They were reporting that five of our interpreters were dead, but we had no confirmation of that yet.

Ian, Kevin, and I went into the TF ORION TOC, where someone had put a graphic with Jessica Simpson as Darth Vader on the door of Mason Stalker's S-3 office. TF ORION's battle update briefing was already on, and had further info. The device on the bus detonated prematurely: it was supposed to have gone off inside KAF. There were, in fact, five terps killed, which reduced interpretation capacity. A new IED facilitation network was being set up in the Panjwayi–Zharey area, supposedly under the command of Mullah Abdullah Addi. Apparently there were two hundred suicide bomber trainees in Pakistan waiting to be "facilitated" into the province. Targets were going to be government officials, police officers, and particularly the Guv. This "soft targeting" had obvious objectives that included the undermining of government authority and ability to control Kandahar City. CTF AEGIS' I/O response was that the Taliban were targeting civilians *again* and that this was anti-Islam.

There was more fallout from Operation Jagra. The enemy was in trouble and was demanding water and medical assistance from the local population in both Zharey and Panjwayi. They were desperate enough to harass the locals, something the I/O people were prepared to exploit.

A SOF TIC ten kilometers north of Martello had a similar effect in Neish district: the locals were getting pissed off over Taliban impositions. The Canadian special operations forces (CANSOF) were now making noise about declaring a JSOA in the Chenar area, TF ORION's target area for Mountain Thrust. It would screw up all the planning, so much so that even Mason Stalker resorted to profanity: "Fuck off, it's our AOR [area of operations]!" He was seriously concerned about a "blue on blue" incident, especially if the planned operation involved helicopters and SOF without effective coordination with TF ORION's battle space. "When

I called over to AEGIS, they just blew fish kisses at me. They weren't aware," he said. The ongoing debate over SOF—conventional coordination or lack thereof was interrupted. "QUIET IN THE TOC!" Captain Keith Saul yelled. There was a Nine Liner medevac. A Canadian solider had contracted meningitis and had to be evacuated.

CANSOF wanted to hit two targets in Chenar and then hand over to TF ORION. These targets were deemed to be TSTs. But CANSOF had put the JSOA in not understanding that TF ORION wasn't anywhere near the area and wouldn't be for at least a day. Ian was annoyed. "What, there isn't enough enemy to go around? Send them into Panjwayi!"

Ian explained to me the problems he had with SOF. There were concerns about command-and-control relationships and ensuring access to intelligence resources.

To make matters more interesting, the existence of Operation Mountain Thrust was announced publicly by the international media—*before* TF ORION had even stepped off! Consequently, the media was banned by CJTF-76 from Operation Mountain Thrust. No media would be accompanying us when we went up north. This produced a rumor that the media was afraid to go out on the operation and another that they didn't want to spend five uncomfortable days in a remote district away from the comforts of KAF.

It was back to the JCC at the Governor's Palace for more coordination on the Chenar operation. When we pulled into the palace complex, a variety of police notables were on hand, including some from Khakriz district. Better information was available. About a hundred Taliban, including twenty to thirty foreign fighters, were operating out of Chenar and Tambil village complexes west of the Belly Button. They had observation posts (OPs) watching the Delenem and Khaltui Passes. The element of surprise would be difficult to achieve without access to helicopters. Ian had worked up an outline plan and Mason Stalker and his staff had tweaked it a bit. The problem was the open terrain between Khahkriz district center and the target villages: the enemy would have early warning if TF ORION made a beeline for Chenar and Tambil. Deception again was key, but there were limits as to what reasonably could be accomplished. Operation Mountain Thrust was to sweep these supposed sanctuary areas: the Chenar operation, now called Operation Axe Chop, could do that, but if the enemy dispersed, made no contact, and we left, they'd just come right back.

It didn't make sense to me at the time. Somebody at CJTF-76 firmly believed that there were sanctuary areas that needed to be rousted simultaneously. It was possible that that divisional plan was designed to generate information—that is, get the enemy to communicate, so we could build a picture. I learned later that the operations in northern Kandahar province were to act as a screen and deter enemy in Oruzgan from heading south when other OEF units swept in from the east. That wasn't clear at the time at CTF AEGIS or TF ORION. The Chenar operation wasn't designed to act as a block for these operations except in a very general way. It was to me a "small map–big crayon" problem—that is, broad planning unable to take into account local complexity and detail.

The TF ORION plan was to use two companies each augmented with an Afghan platoon. A firebase would be established for the M-777 guns, while a mobile police force supported with Coyote surveillance would act as a block to the south, just east of Khakriz. It was a "net." The two companies, operating on separate axes, would move toward the passes going to Nesh. Instead of continuing north, however, "C" company would abruptly turn east and roust Tambil, and "A" Company would turn west and go into Chenar. If the enemy headed south, he would get caught in the police net, which was why the operation needed a substantial number of police. Thus, that was why we were back at the JCC and why Ian needed to talk to the Guv. If there was no net, there was little point in the operation.

Then there was the Neish problem. This district north of Khakriz had unreliable police (well, less than normally unreliable) and it was certain they were in cahoots with the Taliban. As part of the deception plan, they were to be asked to set up blocking positions to the north of the two passes to catch anybody trying to get away. They were told to wait for a linkup . . . that wouldn't happen.

General Esmatullah and Colonel Paul Calbos came along to see how policing was working in Kandahar province. The provincial police general went over the numbers with the TF ORION staff. Khakriz district said it could spare twenty; Shah Wali Kot had another twenty. Each company would have ten police to act as guides. It wasn't enough. Forty guys in pickup trucks couldn't cover the distance that constituted the net. At least forty more were needed. Could Massoud's unit provide forty to fifty men? This was the rub.

Some of the Afghans at the provincial level favored keeping up the pressure on Zharey and Panjwayi: others went further and stated they didn't want to do operations up in Khakriz. This was conveyed subtly to us at the JCC and at the palace. For example, there was suddenly "new intelligence" that there were Arabs in Kandahar City who had been "facilitated" in from Quetta. There were requests to keep M-777 guns down south to support police operations in Zharey, requests for a platoon from "B" Company to go in Zharey. Relations between some of the Unit 005 police and "B" Company weren't good: 005 police beat a detainee, which prompted "B" Company to intervene, which led to a "Mexican standoff." The chief of police lost face in front of General Esmatullah and promised it wouldn't happen again, that his people needed better training, and so on. Ian saw this as an opportunity for partnership and was continually upbeat, "Together we can do these things! We will take the fight to the Taliban." The chief of police, in good Afghan fashion, used this opportunity to request more vehicles, weapons, and fuel. He also needed maps. I noted that this was a chronic problem in coordination between coalition forces and the Afghan security forces. They could navigate, but calling in support depended on common maps. The chief wanted helicopters. Hell, *we* wanted helicopters. . . .

Drawing on Massoud's experience in Zharey and Panjwayi, Ian also wanted to use the Chenar operation as an opportunity to establish an informant net using hand-out cell phones. That would set the stage for future ops. The best people to do this were the police.

While we were in the middle of these discussions, there was an incident just outside the Guv's palace. An ANA truck driving along the main drag outside the mosque struck and severely injured a mullah. People started gathering and it was possible that a riot was in the offing. Just when you thought things were developing into a routine. . . .

Then the next day Axe Chop hit a snag: the Guv. He didn't want the police to go on the Chenar operation, something he announced on the day we were supposed to mount the operation. Ian was called in and I went along to watch. In our departure briefing we were told that the mullah that was hit subsequently died and there was an I/O campaign on to let the population know that it was the ANA that hit him, and that the coalition used every possible means to keep him alive.

Niner Tac drove once again to the JCC where we met up with Major Harj Sajjan, Colonel Paul Calbos, General Esmatullah, and the chief of police. There was some speculation as to what the issue was. The Guv wanted to meet us in his chambers, so we went into the cabinet room. The meeting started with a excruciating discussion over police ammunition, the need for RPG rounds, RPK (machine gun) availability, and so on, technical and tactical detail a governor didn't need to be involved in. It was all very subtle. The message, apparently, was, "You need police for this operation, the police need ammo, therefore get us ammo." Oh, and the police need radios. . . .

Ian wasn't interested in playing games. "We'll take whatever you can give us in twenty-four hours," was his position. But he knew the issue wasn't ammo or radios or numbers. It was control. It was always control. The district police belonged to the districts and they ostensibly reported to the provincial chief of police who reported to the MOI. The reality was that the district police reported to the district leaders. Those leaders had a relationship with the Guv, a relationship that varied depending on the district. Indeed, this might even bypass the chief of police. Then there was Unit 005. It belonged to the MOI in Kabul, not to the Guv. The situation was complicated by the personal relationship between the Guv and Captain Massoud. They were old friends from the pre-2001 days, after all.

During this disorienting and confusing meeting, TF ORION learned that CANSOF had cancelled its operation in Chenar. The two leadership targets had apparently moved on, and one was being tracked heading east of the Belly Button past FOB Martello. It was now possible that there was nothing in Chenar.

The Guv was now arguing that Standby Police Unit 005 couldn't be used on the Chenar operation. He claimed that there were too many targets in Kandahar City that would be unprotected: UNAMA, the PRT, his palace. He needed 303 additional police, he told us. Yes, exactly 303. Kabul has four thousand police, he said, Where were *they*? Paul Calbos explained that they weren't ready yet, they weren't trained or organized for operations like this. The Guv was ready to hire eight hundred police on his own and then train them in Kandahar, not wait for Kabul to deliver. The ANHP were useless and should be converted to Standby Police, he said.

The clock was ticking. The pressure from CJTF-76 to get going, the time element vis-à-vis the enablers, and now the ostensible ammo issue all bore down on people in the room. Then it all came out. The Guv asserted adamantly that the police worked for him, not for the coalition forces. Somebody pointed out that the police technically reported to the regional commander, who reported to the MOI. The Guv argued that they shouldn't . . . and Paul Calbos finally locked horns with him. The Guv demanded two hundred RPG rounds and fuel, but Paul countered that the Guv had money and he should use it to buy the rounds himself. He recognized and accepted there was a disconnect between Kabul and Kandahar, but come on—we had an operation to run. "If you guys don't get a grip, the international community will leave and you will be back one hundred years." I could tell he immediately regretted saying that. Things were getting heated, never a good thing when it is 120 degrees F (50 degrees C) outside. . . . I could see how frustrating things were for Paul. He knew effective policing was key to the counterinsurgency effort, that the police should be the first visible security link between the government and the people, not the army. Legitimacy had to be conveyed by the presence of the police. Yet there weren't enough of them and the anti-Taliban effort had to make do with what was available, no matter what quality they were. The ANA had better relations with the people than did the ANP.

One of those present muttered to me, "He'd better be careful. Pushy people get whacked around here."

I asked, "You mean like Glyn Berry?"

"Yeah."

Ian adopted a conciliatory tone. "Okay, we can go with fifty guys instead of a hundred. We'll reduce the numbers of guides in the companies. But we have to go soon." The Guv deflated. "We will pray for you," he said. "There is some enemy up there, but they are hiding. They will be difficult to find. They look like normal citizens. Take fifty guys from Khakriz. Take Massoud, but not his police. No, take five of Massoud's guys." The negotiation had begun. Massoud and the Guv went into another room. It was becoming clearer that the Guv didn't think we should go up to Chenar. It was in part related to his belief, I think, that the threat was emanating from Zharey and Panjwayi, not Khakriz. There were no doubt other reasons, too, related to the Kandahar provincial power structure.

This was all theater, a power play over police control. Massoud vented to me later. He had been under considerable personal pressure in the meeting. The issue was national versus provincial control over the police. If the police were not nationalized, there would be no money for them from Kabul. He was for nationalization, but the Guv was his friend.

The Guv wanted a police militia, under his control. There were other issues between Massoud and the Guv. For instance, there needed to be legitimate, trained, MOI police, not just anybody who could wield an AK and wear a uniform. Massoud explained that there were tribal police in the old days, but Afghanistan had had to move beyond that. He explained that moving the meeting from the JCC was part of the game: the venue shift had turf overtones. The Guv, as he saw it, essentially horned his way into the process. In theory, General Esmatullah should have been the head honcho in these discussions, but he knew the limits of his power so he backed off. He was, after all, a Hazara and not a Pashtun.

Massoud's other concerns related to operational security. He told me that the palace was penetrated by at least two Taliban agents, but the JCC wasn't. He didn't want to hold operational discussions in the palace. Too much had been said.

My question was, Why exactly did the Guv need to control the police? Or was it somebody else that wanted police capability limited in Kandahar province? I learned later that there were elements in the Kandahar power structure that were trying to limit NDS operations in the province as well. Somebody didn't want too much police scrutiny in Kandahar province—or at least didn't want police that couldn't be controlled.

Two groups of people came to mind: obviously, the Taliban didn't want effective policing. Then there were those involved in criminal activity. They certainly wouldn't want outsiders from Kabul, especially police, poking around in their affairs down here. What was interesting was the possibility that both shadow entities were working together in an ambiguous fashion to exert influence. At what point did somebody who was Taliban use a familial or tribal connection who was non-Taliban to get something done that benefitted both? Or was the reverse possible: could non-Taliban entities get their relations who were Taliban to do things that were in *their* interests too? Like assassinate people? Naturally, all violence would be associated with Taliban violence by the coalition forces. That was the conundrum. How did you prove it? The Kennedy assassination was straightforward compared to all of this. It was nearly impossible for an outsider to peer into this complexity without local help.

As it stood on the eve of the Chenar operation, the Guv didn't want us to go. He didn't want to release Standby Police Unit 005. He wanted more equipment for the police in the province. Ian needed police as part of the operation because of the nature of plan and the terrain. Ian had to mount an operation to satisfy requirements for Operation Mountain Thrust. The open compromise position was that some police could be used. There was in turn skullduggery going on that we didn't know about when TF ORION launched north to the Khakriz district center. That skullduggery already had affected the outcome of the operation, but we didn't know it at the time.

I learned later that, in addition to its "official" activities, the 005 unit contracted out to UNAMA for security in Kandahar City. They received a substantial daily rate, some of which went to 005 police and the rest of which went to a number of power brokers. Another scam was that the whole USPI security force was essentially the entire ANHP in the province. These USPI personnel were trained, at our expense, in the RTC as police, but were used as a private security force. A similar levy extracted from the contracting agency also went into the pockets of Kandahar power brokers. The effect of this on coalition operations was that badly needed police were being used for private purposes to enrich certain people. They were doing mostly static security for nongovernmental entities in the City and were not under MOI control. The UN pays a lot of money for security—and somebody was profiting at the expense of helping secure the rural approaches to the City and supporting the counterinsurgency effort. This behavior on the part of a handful of greedy individuals directly undermined our ability to combat the Taliban, implement governance, and conduct reconstruction activities in Kandahar province. And if you think the population didn't see this, guess again. And guess who showed up to exploit it? You bet.

OPERATION TABER KUTEL ("AXE CHOP"), 17–21 JUNE, 2006

Corporal Neal Carswell, Captain Massoud, and I climbed into the 9-W G-Wagon for the drive up to Khakriz. It was reaching close to 110 F (high 40s C) and the drive took some time. I kept dozing off. The heat put off by the electronic gear cancelled out any benefit from the air-conditioning system. I struggled to keep awake and hydrated. Finally we bounced through the ANA checkpoint in the pass north of Arghandab and could see Khakriz in the distance.

Niner Tac arrived at the Khakriz district center late in the day. This was a new facility that replaced the one I had visited in 2005. I could see "splash" on some of the walls: the place had been under attack recently.

One of the police told us via Bashir that they had been hit the other night with RPGs fired from across the road. The Niner Tac vehicles laagered next to the Khakriz gate, which was made from three large Red Army antenna pieces lashed into an arch.

Captain Massoud explained that Khakriz was a resort town for the Kandahar leadership because it was slightly cooler and away from the city and that members of the Karzai family visited here. The chief of police of Kahkriz district and the district chief greeted us. We went inside to a lavish room with couches, carpets, mirrors, and gilt décor. I wondered how the Khakriz leadership could afford it, but knew that Khakriz had a relationship with the narco trade. The police chief explained to us that they were intercepting enemy communications. The Taliban were using a repeater, though, and the chief couldn't get a location. The enemy was complaining that they were under attack again, so the action was probably to the north, up in Oruzgan.

The police chief explained that there was criminal activity in the passes to the north and that the Taliban was retreating to the mountains north of Chenar. They were led by a Mullah Shukar, who was irritating the locals by appropriating their food. He had Punjabi fighters with him, too. The chief of police sketched out the enemy structure in Khakriz. Kari Fez Mohommad had two subcommanders and reported to Mullah Omar. They had around seventy-two foreign fighters, all told, with about four leaders for the estimated four hundred Taliban. (As usual, these estimates were high. It was probably around ten and forty, respectively.) The Khakriz enemy leadership was related to some of the Taliban leadership east of the Belly Button: Mullah Karim, Mullah Tahir, and Mullah Bul. TF ORION had nearly captured Karim, whose cell was responsible for the IEDs in and around Gumbad. This cell had killed Dave Fraser's close protection party.

The police chief, of course, needed more vehicles, weapons, ammo, and fuel. He only had two vehicles ready to go and ten police. He had a total of eighty personnel in the district but not all had their own weapons. Only forty of these were actually police; the rest were relatives and hired guns. The district chief cut in and recommended that we get Mullagol, a police district commander in Kandahar City who was from Chenar and knew Mullah Shakur by sight. Word was passed back to the JCC to find him and send him up.

I talked with the police chief to gain insight into how things worked in Khakriz. He sketched out for me how the Taliban came out of Tambil and Chenar at night and fired at the district center and returned. He didn't have the vehicles to chase them down, nor did he have enough heavy weapons. The disarmament, demobilization and reintegration program had limited what he could possess. Was he police, a militia, or the army? He just did not have the means to challenge the Taliban for control of Chenar and Tambil. The people there didn't like the Taliban. The enemy had cut the throats of three people in these communities to terrorize the rest. There was, he explained, a symbiotic relationship between the small teams in the villages, which consisted of three to four men each, and the larger groups up in the mountains. If the small team was harmed by the locals, or if the locals didn't resupply them, than the larger group would come down and terrorize everybody. He could not project force into the hills that was enough to offset that threat, so there was no point in taking on the small teams. He didn't have enough vehicles to patrol or even exert a presence throughout the district. The enemy used the attacks against the district center to challenge government authority, even if the attacks didn't cause too much damage. It was clear to me that the enemy possessed a better understanding of Afghan psychology than we did. The police chief lamented that if he had 180 men with enough weapons and vehicles he would be self-sufficient and he wouldn't even need the ANA. But the problem was Kandahar—they wouldn't allow him the resources. They were blocking him, but he didn't understand why.

Ian got word that the police, the ones needed for the net, would not arrive. Other information indicated that the enemy in Chenar and Tambil had been tipped off about the operation and were preparing to run for the hills. The assumption was that there was a leak back in Kandahar, but that didn't explain the lack of police.

Niner Tac was up at first light. "C" Company was already moving up the wadis and roads, heading north. The Chenar "subject matter expert," Mullagol, had arrived during the night in a pickup truck with five of his guys. Niner Tac moved north following "C" Company, but soon shifted to an east northeast direction using the wadi system as cover, heading toward Chenar. When the appointed time came, "C" Company and "A" Company retraced their routes from the passes and turned toward Tambil and Chenar without warning. Niner Tac had been hung up by a UN-funded dam in the wadi that wasn't on the map, so it took

## Operation Taber Kutel, 17–21 June 2006

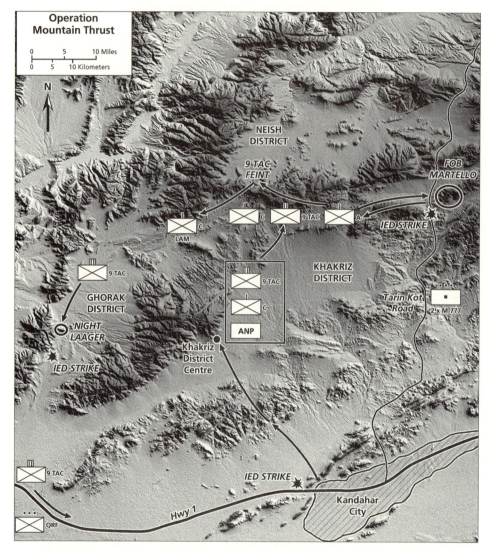

longer to find a route out of the arid waste and into the Tambil–Chenar green zone. Instead of waiting for "A" and "C" to fully deploy, Ian took seven Niner Tac, two Coyotes, and two ANP vehicles and, working along paths, tracks, and a road, moved north of Tambil and Chenar to a bowl-shaped feature that overlooked both communities. It was an unexpected and gutsy move, but a necessary one because of the compromised net. Niner Tac looked like half an infantry company and moved so rapidly that any enemy in the villages wouldn't have had time to react. The bowl was between the communities and the mountains, which seemed to tower above us. Niner Tac was now an armored "hedgehog" blocking any enemy retreat to the hills, while the companies conducted cordon and searches and *shuras* with the Chenarians and Tambilians. I noted as we drove through that there were no smiles, no waves. Everybody was wary. Then the district chief of Khakriz showed up in a pickup truck with a group of armed guys. This was unexpected. Why was the district chief coming along? The Khakriz police chief wasn't impressed.

One of the Afghan leaders suggested that the enemy needed water from the mountain streams. Could we send people up there to keep them from getting water? It was hot, after all, now pushing 120 degrees F (50 degrees C). Ian agreed and told the snipers to prepare a plan to interdict any attempt to get water. The sniper group, 64B, had three people in it. They were equipped with AR-10s, a 7.62-mm version of the C-7 assault rifle, and the Macmillan .50-caliber sniper rifle.

Then we started getting information from ISTAR resources. There were four separate enemy leaders communicating. They were in an arc to our north, roughly from west of the Belly Button, through the hills, and then somewhere near Lam, far to the west. They were confused as to what was going on. Then someone within five hundred meters of Niner Tac was trying to pass information to these leaders on our operations.

Mullagol, the Chenar subject matter expert, was with "A" Company. Major Kirk Gallinger was conducting a cordon and search, but Mullagol wouldn't let his guys into a particular compound. Captain Massoud got on one of his phones and was trying to figure out why Mullagol was being so obstructive. Then Taliban were detected moving to the Hogum Valley, which was up in the mountains to the north of us. It wasn't clear if there was a relationship to this movement and our activities yet.

Information from "A" and "C" Companies came in: Mullah Shakur had been in the Chenar area but not for some time. The enemy did send small groups down and the locals confirmed what the police chief had told us. Massoud then told us that Mullagol was obstructing the search because he claimed it was his mother's compound. Ian told Kirk to back off—for now. He instructed Kirk to send two platoons north into the Hogum Valley area where three streams originated. The snipers were moving to cover a collection of streams to the northwest. The snipers cammed up and put on their Ghillie suits. They were to deploy into OPs and use TI to watch these four areas and develop pattern-of-life analysis so that enemy activity could be distinguished from civilian activity. One of the snipers, Billy B, had a dark ball cap with a subdued bit of kanji on the front and a green and black infrared Canadian flag patch stitched on top for identification, friend or foe, purposes.

The LAV smelled like oil, canvas, hot plastic, and dirt. Davis and Whitey had rigged a lean-to off the LAV and the guys who weren't on duty went to ground. I recalled a conversation Nick Grimshaw and I had at PBW: "The enemy moves up into the caves in the winter and they brainwash each other in order to get their Jihad face on for the spring." I could see it: the place had a monastic air about it. The mountain above us had brown rock spires like something out of Lord of the Rings. "I still think it looks like Rohan," Neal said. "I don't know—with all the Taliban up here it could be Mordor," I joked.

ISTAR information came in that there were enemy within five hundred meters of Niner Tac; they were in contact with some of the hill groups. They were trying to assess what Niner Tac was and what it was doing. The intelligence people estimated there were two hundred Taliban in and around the hills of Chenar. Then ISTAR reported that someone *inside* the Niner Tac area was communicating with two "persons of interest." That someone was Mullagol. It was like a game of Whodunit or Clue. Mullagol, in the compound, with the AK-47. Why exactly had Mullagol blocked a search of what he claimed was his mother's compound? Why was Mullagol communicating with two known Taliban commanders or Taliban sympathizers? Who recommended Mullagol to us in the first place? The district chief. Did he know Mullagol was dirty?

The most likely scenario was this. First, the district chief probably had a deal going with the Taliban in Chenar and the northern part of the district: I won't bug you if you don't bug me. This probably related to the transshipment of narcotics through the district, which Khakriz was known for, and the Taliban probably got a cut of the money to support its operations if they didn't interfere. It looked like the police chief was out of this loop, therefore the district chief needed a "reliable" cop to watch things for him, thus Mullagol. Mullagol had familial connections with Chenar and the Taliban, so he was perfect for the task.

But then there was the leak at the palace. Somebody had already warned the enemy we were coming exclusive of what the district chief was up to. There were other motives for this and they related to three separate but interrelated things. First, there were people in the Kandahar power structure that didn't want the coalition poking around northern districts: this related to the narco trade. Second, there were people hindering the development of the police force, again because they didn't want too much outside scrutiny. Third, there were those who believed the main enemy threat came from Panjwayi and Zharey districts, not from Khakriz, Neish, and Shah Wali Kot. They wanted to convince us of where the enemy came from, wanted to discourage us from wasting our efforts in the north, and couldn't convince the higher-ups to do so. Were these all the same people? Was it different factions that had reached an arrangement? Probably.

This situation was too complex for a divisional headquarters located in Bagram to grasp. It couldn't be addressed with any division-level plan, nor could it be addressed with a coordinated division-level sweep. It could only be addressed with a lot of local knowledge, a build-up of trust, and a detailed understanding about how power was wielded at the district and provincial levels plus a clear understanding as to what the coalition wanted to achieve, and where and when it would achieve it.

Operation Mountain Thrust was stymied in Kandahar province because of this state of affairs. Sweep the enemy sanctuary areas? Deny the enemy sanctuary areas? Sweep—maybe. Deny—not possible. Denial was dependent on occupation, and if the Afghans and the coalition lacked the capacity to occupy, then why bother? Beating the grass for the snakes up in Khakriz made sense but only to a certain extent. It didn't address our primary problem: how do we gain the support of the Afghan people at the local level in those areas? How do we introduce and then back legitimate governance? How were we supposed to convince the people that we weren't supporting corrupt provincial power brokers? As Colonel Steve Bowes and the rest of the PRT discovered back in 2005, the people in the rural areas were caught in the middle. They would sit on the fence until they saw who was going to prevail—or until somebody offered them a third option that provided them with what they needed.

It was Day Three of Taber Kutel. Massoud, Ian, and I discussed the situation. We mulled over the lack of helicopters: even two Chinook loads, dropped here as the two companies swung in, might have caught the enemy as they pulled out of Tambil and Chenar.

"Why won't the enemy fight here like they did in Zharey, Massoud?"

"The Taliban here in the north are different from the ones in Panjwayi," he said, "These are local people, with fewer foreign fighters. The people here know who the enemy is."

We discussed, in academic terms, what the best approach should be. In a place like Chenar, was killing or capturing the enemy leadership the answer? We wanted to get the people of these communities on our side, but they were uncommitted because some of their own were Taliban. A better approach was to convert the leadership here, take away cached weapons, and then set the conditions for expanded government: provide medical and commercial access. Killing the local leadership might in fact be counterproductive. Killing the foreign fighters, however, was not. They were the ones most likely encouraging resistance. Selectively killing leaders that weren't from Chenar or Tambil would sever the ties between the Taliban here and in Quetta. Some means had to be found to remove the Quetta influence from Chenar and Tambil before other measures could be used.

Massoud and I were deeply involved in conversation, sitting on cots in the shade of 9-W, when Massoud broke off midsentence and suddenly exclaimed, "*Aiiiiiii!* Get away from it! It's poisonous!" and scrambled off his cot. I looked down and saw this huge, multi-legged creature that appeared to be half scorpion, half spider aggressively—and I mean aggressively—moving toward us. I jumped back and Massoud's bodyguard slammed the butt of his AK-47 down onto it repeatedly until it was squished. The abdomen detached.

"What the hell was that??"

"A Rondak, very dangerous!" Massoud said.

I'd never seen or heard of it before. It was apparently a species of camel spider.

The search continued. Then "C" Company found a cave in the hills to the south of Tambil. The district chief was now up and about and asked Ian what he was going to do. Ian told him we were going to move up to Mienishein and upper Shah Wali Kot. The district chief then tried to convince Ian to go to Lam, which was west of Tambil and in a valley that led to upper Ghorak district. He was adamant, for some reason, that we'd catch the enemy in Lam. No, no, Ian insisted, "The enemy has gone to Neish and we're going to follow him there. No, I can't go to Lam. I have to ask the generals first. I think Mullah Tahir is in Neish."

I'd like to thank the Academy. . . . Ian had every intention of going into Lam, but not when the district chief thought we should.

I saw two A-10s overhead circling. Our Slayer call sign, the forward air controllers, asked them to take a look in the mountains to the north. This obviously concerned somebody in Chenar. An old man approached the police and asked if he could go up into the hills to look for a donkey and two fifteen-year-old kids that hadn't come home yet. The ANP said it was okay, but only if he reported what he saw up there. Before he could depart, however, the party rode out of a reentrant.

Ian made up his mind to have the compounds that Mullagol had not wanted searched yesterday examined. He made sure there were no ANP around when he contacted Kirk. Then Major Nick Grimshaw down in Zharey passed on a follow-on report from Operation Jagra. The enemy had wounded hidden around the district, but now was using false-bottomed Jingle trucks to evacuate them. For a bunch of die-hard jihadis, it was interesting to see how many of their resources they put into their medical system. That ratline, by the way, went all the way back to Quetta and I'm sure to some places in the Gulf where money was no object.

The more pressing issue was what was motivating Mullagol. How was a police officer from Kandahar City mixed up with the Taliban in Chenar? It was probably a familial or tribal connection. Massoud explained that support for a family enterprise could look like support for the Taliban. But in his view there might be a private problem that we were overlooking and it might have a bearing on the Lam issue. Some police trainees from Lam who were at the RTC had left before they finished their training. Mullagol, apparently, wanted revenge on those deserters and he apparently wanted to go after the fathers of those who deserted. So it was possible that he had overlapping agendas: dilute the coalition effort in Chenar, but use them to go after personal enemies in Lam.

Then "A" Company found Mullah Shakur's compound. There was ammo in the nicely furnished rooms. The neighbors claimed he had last been seen ten days ago and that he had left for Pakistan. Too bad he wasn't home. "C" Company, conducting a *shura* in Tambil, developed more information. There were two Taliban groups each consisting of fifteen to twenty men with the usual mix of AK-47s, PKMs, and RPGs. They were retreating east . . . and Mullah Shakur and Mullah Malang were with them. Aha! These had to be the CANSOF targets from the cancelled mission the other night. The locals also explained that the four Taliban leaders in the hills around here were Mullah Abdul Akim, Mullah Tahir, Hajib Karim, and Mullah Sardar. These guys were all known Taliban subcommanders from Shakur, and each had his own group and moved in and out of the area as necessary, even down to Zharey.

Major Kirk Gallinger called in. He was concerned. Mullagol and his ANP from Kandahar were talking to people—and the locals were frightened. Kirk thought they were being deliberately intimidated, so he asked one of his terps to discreetly see what was up. It turned out that Mullagol was known here and that he had a shady reputation. He was, according to a local person, even *related* to Mullah Shakur! The district chief, on the other hand, seemed to be only interested in eating. Kirk's search of Mullagol's mother's compound produced some ammo and a warm fireplace. The neighbors claimed that nobody had been there in ten days.

ISTAR reported that the enemy was watching. "Here they come!" "I'm moving to the trees!" There was at least one identified enemy repeater, so it wasn't clear to me where this was coming from, but it later turned out the enemy was using a police repeater for its communications.

Ian and Kevin were working up the next move. Given that the whole mission was compromised, what could be salvaged from it? The compromised police thought TF ORION was going to move north to Neish, and they had already contacted (legitimately) the Neish police to prepare a net on their side of the passes. The scheme of maneuver now was to have "A" Company feint north to its assigned pass, then move east and back to FOB Martello to prepare for future ops. "C" Company would also head north, and then swing west and go into Lam.

Until then, Ian was content to sit in the bowl and wait. It was like keeping a submarine underwater so it couldn't get air. It was blazing hot, and the enemy in the hills didn't have access to water or food—and hadn't for two days. They knew we'd leave eventually, but for the time being TF ORION could keep the pressure on. They might even move north and get caught up in the action in Oruzgan, where American, Australian, and Dutch SOF task forces were scouring the province.

To encourage some movement, Ian decided to have the M-777 guns fire into the hills. This was done in a controlled fashion into empty areas that were under Captain Howie Nelson's observation. It wasn't a random event and safety considerations regarding the civilian population were taken. If the enemy started yakking, the FOO was ready to adjust the fire onto their locations. I called my Dad, who is ex-Canadian Army, on the satellite phone. (It was brought into the field for morale calls on multiday operations.) One had to be careful about operations security.

"Hi, Dad. I'm somewhere in Afghanistan."

"What's going on?" he asked.

"Well, you're about to hear Canadian artillery fired in anger."

"What??"

The guns boomed from their firing position off the Tarin Kot Road. The rounds crashed into the rock above us. Lo and behold, there were excited Punjabi speakers up here yakking with somebody who had eyes on the M-777 gun position . . . and somebody else closer to Niner Tac. Without any prompting, four ANP showed up and asked us what was going on. Then Mullagol arrived to ask what was going on. Hmmmm! Ian ordered up two more rounds for Mullagol's benefit. The snipers reported that they could see numerous prepared positions, rock sangers really, up there but they were unmanned. They may even have dated back to an earlier period. Mullagol was now deep in conversation with Captain Massoud. ISTAR reported that enemy orders had gone out to plant IEDs because they thought TF ORION's operation had started.

Massoud explained to me that other Taliban cells had laid IEDs along the routes elsewhere in the province to disrupt movement that might support whatever coalition operations were ongoing. It appeared that if one cell or network was attacked in one district, others could provide support in this fashion. He believed that the Taliban signalers carried repeaters on their backs, and that they weren't necessarily static repeaters.

"What did Mullagol want?"

"He says he heard from the locals that a cousin of Mullah Shakur and twelve Punjabis are moving south. I think they are trying to draw us away from the group in the hills here to the north." ISTAR reported otherwise: it looked like there was some dissension amongst the four groups up here. One group wanted to get its equipment, lay an IED to the west of Tambil, and ambush "C" Company, while others wanted to disperse and leave the area in four-man groups. A Taliban leader of unknown rank demanded that he be picked up and escorted out . . . but it wasn't clear where he was or who he was. I could see that some of the ANP in the Niner Tac camp were clearly agitated. We all made sure we had weapons at hand just in case.

"A" Company detained three individuals who provided new information. There were forty to fifty Taliban moving to the south. Shakur had been in the area in the past week. One explained that there had been a beheading in a nearby village: the murdered person had refused to give the Punjabi (!) Taliban food. With no net to the south, there was nothing to stop them from getting into Arghandab or Zharey districts. It was as if they knew it was clear. Two Platoon then found a cave in the southern hill line; it was large with stored water. We knew it recently had been occupied because it had fresh human waste in it.

It was now Day Four. The plan was to use a JDAM from an orbiting B-1 to seal up the cave. The B-1B was supporting Operation Mountain Thrust in Oruzgan and had a spare munitions. It was something to see the big B-1B with its wings splayed out fly over the Chenar valley. Ian was demanding "hockeyrep" from the TF ORION TOC: the Edmonton Oilers were playing North Carolina in the Stanley Cup:

"Niner—send updates whenever there is a score, over."

"Niner to net—2–1 Carolina, over."

A patrol was dispatched to the town of Petaw where the reported beheading had taken place. Lieutenant Alcock from "C" Company then reported he had information from a *shura* indicating there were caves north of his search area. The locals also told him that there was food in the hills, mostly almonds, so it was possible that the enemy could sustain themselves for a time if they had access to water.

There was more bad news. The Oilers lost, 3–1. There was despondency and morale dropped. This caused more damage than the Taliban. The 12 RBC guys didn't care. They just yelled, "Go Nordiques!"

The cordon and searches continued. I figured that if a soundtrack was available for this place, it should be the theme from *The Good, the Bad, and the Ugly* or *For a Few Dollars More*. I could almost hear Lee Van Cleef adamantly tell people, "This train *will* stop at Tucumcari!"

The enemy's early warning net was pretty good. They had agents in the city, they had OPs in the hills, and they had locals who assisted them with movement information. For a place like Chenar, the only means to get in here unobserved would be at night and by helicopter. Deception, surprise, and operational security have always been and remain elusive and paramount in any operation in Afghanistan.

The district chief then told us his police had a contact in Lam. They had wounded one enemy and captured him, but others had escaped. In an unrelated operation elsewhere, it was reported that the notorious Toor Naquib, the Taliban commander from northern Shah Wali Kot, had been captured by the ANP down in Damand district. But there was no confirmation. Naquib's IED cell was responsible for seven deaths and twelve woundings.

Niner Tac mounted up and followed "C" Company toward the northern pass to Neish district. "C" Company feinted away and unexpectedly moved east. As they did, fifteen people, some talking on cell phones, dispersed into the green areas. ISTAR reported that an enemy leader from Chenar was retreating into this area. The local elders said this group wasn't openly armed and, since there was no cutoff group or net to the west, there was no way to actually fix them. They essentially "bombshelled"—that is, split up and went in fifteen separate directions. Without weapons and wearing civilian clothes, it would be next to impossible to run them all down. The feint had worked—to a certain extent. It allowed ISTAR to collect and add to their picture.

Niner Tac continued north, through incredibly rugged country. The road here was unpaved. When the Neish ANP checkpoint was in view, Ian turned west and then south to Lam to meet up with "C" Company. Major Bill Fletcher's guys had already started a search of the green area. The district chief was already there and announced he had a prisoner. Niner Tac deployed into a wadi next to a compound complex. The district chief was lying on a blanket drinking chai with the local mullah and local leadership under a tree. Williams, Davis, Massoud, and I joined Ian. There was an emaciated young man squatting, with a bandage on his arm. He had that "woe-is-me, I've-been-caught" look. He was scared. Especially when the district chief looked at him. I got the sense that they were related or at least knew each other.

During the course of the conversation, the district chief told us that the prisoner had been in custody three times, but the local mullahs vouched for him and insisted that he be released, and he wouldn't get involved in the insurgency again. The district chief was sick and tired of apprehending him and wanted to kill him, but for some reason couldn't. I suspect that if he did kill the prisoner, some aspect of Pashtunwali would kick in and there'd be a blood feud or it would otherwise interfere with some local logrolling deal between those in upper Khakriz and those in lower Khakriz. If the jail in Kandahar was operating properly, the chief said, he'd send him there. Instead, if he did he knew he'd be arresting him again. The implication was if coalition forces killed him, the district chief's problem would be solved. Of course there was no way in hell that was going to happen. As usual, this was implied. The district chief didn't come out and say this, but Bashir conveyed it.

The detainee issue remains sensitive in the West and achieved much more prominence later in 2007, so the context should be firmly established so that critics understand what was going on. The policy in early to mid-2006 was to turn over detainees to the Afghan security forces. It is their country, after all, and in any event TF ORION did not have the means to handle detainees. I'm not sure what ultimately happened to the prisoner. He was already in the custody of the district chief, not TF ORION. It was not our affair. It was local politics. The human rights mavens, safe in their comfy offices in Toronto or New York or London always scream bloody blue murder about this kind of thing. Without the full legal apparatus in southern Afghanistan—that is, functional police, judges, defense lawyers, jails—there was no way that Western standards could or should be applied in this case. This was frontier justice, and it used different rules. Italy was in charge of the judiciary pillar.

The Lam green zone stretched along the wadi system west to east. "C" Company was searching, so Niner Tac moved to a road that paralleled the wadi but ran along a hill. One of the LAVs lost a tire, so we stopped for the repair. Somebody from "C" Company urgently radioed that a black SUV was traveling at speed through the wadi, heading toward us. It had ignored an ANP checkpoint, but the checkpoint didn't have time to engage. The adrenaline started to pump. Stitch turned his LAV around and Davis was tracking with the 25-mm. Kevin Barry, Neal, Massoud, and I were talking, and then Kevin and Neal assumed shooting stances. The Echo LAV had reversed its turret and prepared to engage. The SUV came around the corner on the road: Was it a suicide bomber? An ANA pickup intercepted the vehicle, and then the district chief's white SUV arrived. It was all a false alarm. These were the Lam ANP—or at least they claimed to be. None wore uniforms and all were heavily armed. The district police convinced the ANA to let the SUV continue on its way.

The hiatus in the action allowed Ian to consider the next move. It was possible the enemy figured "C" Company would continue east and might reconstitute east of Lam or back in Tambil, thinking we'd left for good. Ian decided to take Niner Tac west and make it look like "C" Company for deception purposes, then "C" Company would head back east, then south and back to KAF. Niner Tac would continue through northern Ghorak, then south through Ghorak to Highway 1, and then back to KAF. This sudden and unexpected move might force the enemy to start communicating, especially in northern Ghorak, which was terra incognita to TF ORION and was a known ratline that ran from Helmand, to northern Kandahar province, to Zabol, and then to Pakistan. More information was required and this move could generate part of it. I knew from 2005, though, that there was an IED cell operating in Ghorak: they had taken out a PRT G-Wagon . . . on a trip I was supposed to be on and in a vehicle I was supposed to be in. I had skipped out at the last minute.

THE IED ATTACKS

It was getting late in the afternoon and we'd just finished with clearing Lam. Niner Tac's organization remained the same: Neal Carswell drove 9-W, I was sitting in the codriver seat, and Captain Massoud was the passenger in the back. As usual, it was real hot, damn hot. We moved west along a wadi system and into northern Ghorak district. We knew this was "Indian country" now: the people in the compound complexes didn't wave and even went indoors when we passed by. The mental image I want you to have here is of a wadi, with gravel interspersed with flat hard mud with a trickle of moisture running down it. There were banks on either side, with cuts where appropriate to bypass the more rocky bits. In some places a vehicle-wide track paralleled the wadi. The light brown hills were a few klicks on either side, and darker mountains were to the front in the distance. These hills went on for some time. The wadi was wetter and wetter as we moved west.

In time we came to a confluence: it was like a three-way "crossroads" with hills all around: part of the wadi continued west, to Helmand province, and the other branch went south into Ghorak district. Ian called a halt when one the LAVs shredded a tire. Everybody went into watch mode covering all arcs while the damaged wheel was replaced. I cracked the door on the G-Wagon and so did Carswell, and cooler air flowed through the vehicle. It was 104 degrees F (40 degrees C) outside. . . .

Massoud mixed Gatorade into some water bottles and we rehydrated. I noticed there were three compound complexes nearby: there was no movement, no "Hadji TV." Nobody working the fields. Yet there was habitation. I could see the smoke from cooking fires. We pressed on, heading south. Then the RG-31 bogged down in a soft part of the wadi. A LAV moved to extricate it. The sun was starting to wane. I knew Ian wanted to make Highway 1 before nightfall and then get back to KAF. That was starting to look less and less likely. We moved off again onto a parallel track, which then crossed over the wadi again through a ford that was full of water. The two LAVs and the RG-31 up front of us each raced down the bank and accelerated through the water to gain maximum momentum and traction. The RG-31 looked like it was about to tip over but negotiated the stream. Then it was our turn. Carswell knew what he was doing and hit the water running. The G-Wagon lurched to the left, water spraying in all directions but he fought with the wheel and righted us, the tires clawing at the mud on the bank. We cheered.

The column continued. Our "ears" were listening—no contact so far. The enemy was not communicating via those means. We hit another rocky part of the track and the artillery LAV shredded its tires. It was starting to get dark. Ian made the decision to laager for the night and conduct repairs. The original idea to deceive the enemy by moving a small force into northern Ghorak, making it look like it was the main effort while "A" and "C" Companies continued with their missions. Ian assumed that the enemy had eyes on us and was still hoping that rattling their cage in Ghorak might stimulate precipitous activity elsewhere that could be monitored. Remember that Ghorak was terra incognita, just as it had been in 2005. I knew from my experiences then that there was an active IED cell in Ghorak. It had attacked a PRT patrol in December and later on targeted ANP forces trying to establish some order in the area.

The column continued on until the terrain opened up into a valley. There was a cluster of high ground to the left, and another cluster to the right. There was plenty of stand-off range for the 25-mm, and with the TI sights nobody could get within three kilometers of us without being seen. The vehicles were dispersed: some LAVs on the high ground above us, with the artillery LAV, Kevin Barry's RG-31, the sniper's G-Wagon and trailer, and the 9-W G-Wagon facing west in an arc to watch the track to the reentrant. Again, we assumed that the enemy was watching in some way, so Ian gave permission to test-fire the 25-mm as a deterrent. After ensuring that the area was clear using the night vision equipment, we took turns firing the 25-mm in the artillery LAV across the valley. Whitey test fired his C-7, and Massoud hauled out his Kalashnikov.

Carswell set up the cots, but we weren't ready to turn in. Kevin Barry and Billy B came over and we prepared some MREs. It was getting pitch dark, but our eyes were adjusting. I made sure my red-filtered Maglite was at hand. One of the sniper teams deployed into an overwatch position. I had one cigar left in my portable humidor: it was a Romeo y Julietta Churchill. I offered Kevin half and cut it in two with my multi-tool; we had a good smoke and looked at the stars. It was dead quiet, once the shredded tires had been replaced. This was the calm before the storm, but of course we didn't know that at the time.

Everybody was up packing at 0430. There was no enemy activity during the night: nothing from the snipers. No comms traffic. Nothing on the TIs. Nada. "A" and "C" Companies continued with their tasks, but there was no contact. Mountain Thrust was turning into a bust. Niner Tac mounted up and we were on our way, headed south. We passed a huge graveyard on our left. "That's an old one," Massoud told us. "See how the graves face north-south? That's how the locals tell what direction they're traveling."

It was a significant grave site. "Who's in there?" I asked.

"Probably people killed by the Soviets in the 1980s. But the Battle of Maywand was fought near here, so some could be from 1880."

It was light. The order of march was two LAVs, our G-Wagon, the RG-31, the sniper G-Wagon, and two more LAVs. The terrain had completely widened out and the mountains and hills were distant in all directions. There was a wrecked pickup truck, one probably taken out by the Ghorak IED cell. I said to Neal, "I hope there isn't an IED ahead." I looked at my watch: it was 0555 hours. I looked up and the LAV in front of us disappeared in an evil, black cloud.

In these circumstances, a whole bunch of things happen simultaneously. It takes more time here to describe what happened than the actual elapsed time.

I knew instantly that we were under attack. I knew that Carswell would be anticipating orders on where to go with the vehicle, but that he might just react to the attack. I knew that the drill was to bypass, move out of the strike zone, reconstitute with the others, then respond. I knew that we had to be prepared to operate independently if necessary, just the three of us. And this is where instinct took over. I had been a crew commander in a previous life after all. . . . Neal jammed on the brakes. The radio yelled, "Push through, push through!"

"Driver left! Left! Get around the cloud!"

Carswell swerved left. Ian's LAV loomed in front of us.

"Driver right!" Carswell avoided the vehicle, then swung the G-Wagon in behind as it raced off the road to the right. We followed, our hearts pounding, adrenal glands pumping. I looked to the right (our vehicle was on an angle to the road now) and I saw a LAV dashing off toward the wadi. The radio was an aural blur. There was some 25-mm fire.

"I think it's the buttonman!"

"Can we take the shot?'

"He's reached the wadi!"

Another LAV had moved to the left of the road and was scanning in case there was an ambush from a low wall.

At the RV the vehicles were in an all-round defense: the sniper G-Wagon (its occupants pulling out their sniper rifles and scanning their arcs); 9-W; Kevin's RG-31 with the remote firing unit scanning back and forth; and Ian's LAV. Massoud and Carswell were lying on the ground finding cover and observing their arcs. Someone handed me a 9-mm pistol. We waited. One of the snipers saw movement in the nearest compound complex. I could see the stricken LAV in the distance: another LAV was moving to assist it. How many dead and wounded did we have? Were we going to have to fight our way out of northern Ghorak? There was no air cover available: it was busy elsewhere. We were on our own for the time being.

Ian instructed Kevin to assess what was going on in the strike site. I went with him. The two of us walked from the RV, carefully checking the dusty, gray-brown ground for signs of other devices. It was possible that a secondary device had been planted to catch those assisting the effort. Fortunately, the assisting LAV was the Echo call sign, the combat engineer LAV with Major Webb and his guys. The engineers had assessed the strike site as "clear."

I saw Digger, the driver, standing up in the stricken LAV's hatch: he was shaken up but unwounded. There were bits of LAV lying around. The front axle was lying on the ground. Fluids poured out of the wounded vehicle like blood. Nobody was hurt. The engineers were looking at the crater: they assessed that it was an IED, not a mine. It appeared as though a nearby sanger had been the buttonman's hide. The crater was a dark gray hole surrounded with a ring of burnt sand and dust. The device had gone off under the front axle, but had not penetrated the hull.

On reflection, I realized the mortal danger Carswell, Massoud, and I had been in. If the buttonman had waited to hit us as little as two or three seconds, it would have been a different story. The G-Wagon would not have survived the attack as the LAV had. It would have killed me and Carswell and severely injured Massoud. A matter of seconds, the choice of a terrorist to go after one vehicle and not another. This could have been a lot to take in if I'd taken time to examine it at the time. But I didn't: I was busy. The troops were picking up the pieces of the LAV: "Don't leave anything behind for these assholes!" The G-19 crew was shook up but more pissed off than anything.

The nearest village was a place called Blagh. I mean, come on. How improbable was that? The Castle Arrrrggghhh and the Village Blagggghhhhh.

"I'm going into that village and I'm going to give the elders a piece of my mind! Let's find out who did this!" Ian angrily said over the radio. Kevin and I remounted our vehicles and pressed on with Ian to establish a laager outside this complex. Ian jumped off his LAV with his rifle. "Who's with me?" Massoud and I joined him. The three of us walked slowly line abreast down the track into the village.

I looked around. "This is like that scene in *Kelly's Heroes*. Holy shit, did I really just say that out loud?"

"Yeah. You have the beard and pistol and you used to be Armoured Corps: you get to play Oddball," Ian said. "I'll be Clint Eastwood."

Carswell who was guarding the vehicles with the LAV and RG-31 crews told me later that he thought it was the bravest thing he'd seen in his life: three guys going into a potential Taliban nest to parlay with the leadership man to man. We were quickly joined by Kevin, Whitey, Bashir, and Massoud's man, who was toting his AK. Massoud's man checked out one alley, while Massoud, Ian, and Bashir called the local leaders to the village square for a chat. I saw a young man sprint around a corner.

"Doc, we're short of people," Kevin said. "You and Whitey cover this approach here. I'll go across the square and cover the boss from there with Carswell."

"Watch it: I saw a young guy run over there."

Kevin moved off. Then there was shooting. I heard barking and a fusillade of shots from around the corner where I was stationed. I had eyes on the mini-laager and the guys were preparing to come in to support us. Massoud called out, "It's just a dog. My man was attacked and he wounded it then he shot it again."

"Okay." I shouted this along to the others.

Then there was automatic fire from an AK down in the wadi.

Kevin called out, "Doc, get us more dismounts!"

I yelled to the laager that we needed two more soldiers. Two guys came running down to the village.

"Sir, where do you want us?"

"Captain Barry's covering the square, the boss and the terp are talking to the locals, and the ANP are over there. Cover these two alleys and try to get eyes on to the ANP."

More shots rang out. Kevin came over. Then Massoud appeared with his guy.

"There were two of them, young men. They ran away from us. I ordered them to stop but they didn't, so we shot them. When we went to go after them, they got into the green area and across the wadi. There might be more. I don't like this place, Dr. Sean. They are all Noorzai. They are all Taliban."

Kevin positioned men on the roofs. One LAV reported that they chased somebody they thought was the buttonman into the wadi, but he disappeared so they broke off the search. As I was crouched down covering the ally, a white-bearded old man with a stick walked out of a doorway: I pointed to the mini-*shura*. He nodded and waved. I kept an eye on him, then Whitey and I checked the room that he came out of. Nothing.

Ian, Bashir, and Massoud were discussing things with the elders. Massoud was browbeating them. He was angry and it was tense. He knew something we didn't. The locals meekly denied any involvement. Ian told them he would station police here if there were attacks. Did they want that? No, they didn't: then they'd be harassed by the Taliban.

"How could they *not* know about the people that did this?" Massoud said. "The attack is less than three hundred meters from here. They *have* to know something."

Kevin then arrived: "We've got somebody." Massoud gave the elders a withering look. "We'll be back!" We found out from one of the other locals that there had indeed been several men in white and black turbans in Blagh the night before.

The guys at the laager had one young, portly, bearded fair-skinned individual wearing a white turban. He had been spotted on a motorcycle minutes ago and been apprehended by one of the LAV crews. This was suspicious: why was he moving around so early in the morning? He just didn't belong here. He was out of place, and too well fed for northern Ghorak. Massoud questioned him. He denied, of course, any involvement in the attack. He admitted to being a mullah and was evasive about admitting he was from Pakistan. He was discreetly photographed. Massoud wanted to kill him outright, asserting he was Taliban, but we couldn't prove anything.

So who was he? We strongly suspected him of being a "wandering mullah." These guys were Taliban and worked in the rural areas of southern Afghanistan proselytizing remote villages that had uneducated and even illiterate mullahs. Wandering mullahs were one-man I/O weapons: they could cause a lot of damage, even though they were unarmed and operated alone. They could deal one-on-one with the local leaders: cajole, subtly intimidate, convince, manipulate. All in the name of Allah. Allah wills it. . . . Who are you to go against Allah's will? Extremely dangerous. This one denied that he had anything to do with Taliban activity in Ghorak and denied that there was *any* Taliban in Ghorak. Ian invited him to sit on the hood of his LAV for the trip out of the district, but the mullah declined. He offered to ride ahead of the column on his motorcycle, but it was unclear how sincere he was about the offer. He was let go.

There was no movement with the village elders, who refused to provide any information on the youths who were shot, on any Taliban activity, on anything at all. They were pretty resolute. Massoud confirmed that they were Noorzai, which in his view meant they were all Taliban sympathizers. There was little we could do: we weren't the Soviets and they knew it. They knew Ian wasn't going to call in an airstrike and wipe the place out, something the older ones no doubt had seen done in the 1980s. Then Massoud's people picked up some iCom (radio) chatter: the enemy was putting another IED into a wadi crossing to the south.

Then we heard over the radio that "A" Company had been attacked with an IED up in Shah Wali Kot. There were no details other than that the crew of a LAV was severely wounded and the vehicle destroyed. The drama continued on the radio: helicopters were scrambled, recovery resources deployed. We were not the priority. Niner Tac was ordered into a defensive posture. We were grouped with the Echo call sign and the snipers and put out front to provide overwatch to the south, while the rest of the troops surrounded the damaged LAV from all sides. Everybody settled down to wait for the recovery team.

The sun climbed in the sky and it got hotter and hotter. We were running out of food and especially water. The water we had was the same temperature as the water one shaves in: not palatable, but you need to stay hydrated, so you drink it after mixing in Gatorade powder. Most of us tried to get some sleep. I used the shady side of the G-Wagon, with my pad on the ground leaning against the wheel. I vaguely recalled people pissing on the wheel hubs at halts, but I was too hot to care. Massoud was in the back with his AK cradled, the doors open for some ventilation. Neal joined the engineers in recce'ing a nearby hut.

What we didn't know was that "B" Company was undergoing its own odyssey during the recovery effort. A recovery low-bed had to be escorted from KAF to Maywand, where Nick Grimshaw was holding a *shura* with Haji Saifullah. Nick convinced Saifullah to escort the force north to the strike site, but then an engineer LAV broke down and it had to be towed back to Maywand district center before the force turned around again and headed north to where we were.

During the next twelve hours, Neal, Massoud, and I talked about the usual things that disparate people in desperate circumstances talk about: sex and religion. Massoud's a pretty switched-on guy and was massively curious about Western society. "So why is you people worship three gods?" he asked.

"What do you mean, three gods? There is only one God."

"But you have this djinn god, too."

Neal figured it out. "Oh, you mean the Holy Ghost."

"Yes. What is this all about?"

For the next hour Neal and I struggled to explain to Massoud the concept of the Trinity. We had to reach a little bit.

"So: what are lez-biens?"

"Well, you know in your culture you have men . . . who get together. It's the same thing, only with women."

"I don't understand. There are three types of this activity here in Kandahar."

"Three?? Like the Trinity?" How was that possible? I could see Neal trying to work out the permutations.

"No, no, no. First, there are the Dance Boys."

"OK. What do they do?"

"Well, they dance for the men. Sometimes they dress up as girls when they dance. They just dance. Nothing happens to them. Most of the time, at least."

"OK. What's the second?"

"Then there are the Fun Boys. Some touching is allowed but they don't go all the way. Finally, there are the Touch Boys. Everything is permitted."

"Is this all consensual activity?"

"What does 'consensual' mean?"

I hasten to point out, by the way, that Massoud is married with kids and lives in the northern part of Afghanistan. It was embarrassing for coalition troops to get into these discussions, but at times it could be inadvertently funny. Indeed, some coalition soldiers were offered boys at some social events just to yank their chains. The Afghans knew we found it culturally disturbing and it was part of their sense of humor to poke fun at us. I developed a theory about it. Recall that Alexander the Great spent some time in Kandahar a few thousand years ago. The Greek city states practiced pederasty. I understood that some of the political figures we dealt with had been given over as young men to older, more powerful men to be similarly mentored in a variety of ways. It was conceivable that this one "deep time" effect on the culture here that has survived. I always suspected that the *shura* system at the community and district levels resembled ancient Greek city-state participative democracy to a certain extent. It was entirely possible that visages of ancient Macedonian culture, however distorted, had survived.

The situation vis-à-vis sexual relations with boys was so bad in the rural areas that the intelligence people had intercepted orders from Mullah Omar to the Taliban forces that their personnel could not have sex with boys that were not yet able to grow beards. Omar apparently was concerned about losing hearts and minds . . . and worried about our I/O effort to portray the Taliban as "not Islamic" to the population using this theme. Pat Benatar was right: love is a battlefield, and sex is a weapon. Incidentally, Massoud's pronunciation of "fuck" came out as "fack," as in, "the facking Taliban."

"So what animals does Canada have? Do you have monkeys? Lions? Tigers?"

"No," Neal explained, "but we have scary things like bears. We have three types: brown, grizzly, and polar bears. The polar bears are white and live in the Arctic. We have mountain lions and lynx. They kill people all the time. And smile when they do it."

"And the most dangerous animal in Canada is the moose," I added.

"Mooze?"

"Yeah. Transport trucks can be destroyed if they hit them. They have antlers like tree branches."

Isn't cross-cultural dialogue fun?

Some more information on the LAV strike came in. A triple-antitank mine stack had been detonated as the vehicle passed over it near Pada between Gumbad and FOB Martello. The crew commander was severely injured and the gunner was going to lose both legs. Then the JCC called in another threat warning: there was a white Toyota Corolla (surprise!) that was a possible suicide IED car operating in Highway 1, somewhere in "B" Company's area of responsibility—that is, between Zharey district and Kandahar City.

Then word came down around 1415 that the low-bed recovery vehicle had a fuel leak. The guys from the Echo LAV used the term "Gong Show" and "Goat Fuck" for awhile.

The look-out on top of the Echo LAV then called out, "Here they come!" and we could see dust in the distance. The advance LAVs from "B" Company, followed by the recovery team, skirted a compound complex, staying off the road to avoid IED attack. In time, they linked up at the strike site. Massoud was getting antsy: "I am flying home to Kabul tonight. I still need to get a haircut and see the governor," he said. We were all tired and dehydrated and ready to get on with it. As we left, Massoud announced, "Goodbye, boring place!" and he waved.

"Facking right," I said.

On the way out, we bypassed several crossing points at successive wadis: I noticed that there were the remains of a blown-up and stripped pickup truck at each one. Somewhere along here in December 2005 a PRT G-Wagon had been blown up. It was very systematic: the IEDs had been planted on the slope of the ford of each wadi so that when the vehicle slowed down and shifted gears to climb out the buttonman blew it up. I learned later that this attack on us was conducted using a pressure-plate

IED. The contact point was armed by the buttonman, and the vehicle rolled over the contact point, which then detonated the explosive. It was clear that the IED cell doing this was used to using just enough explosive material to destroy a SUV-like vehicle. They had never attacked a LAV before that survived. No doubt they would be figuring out how to increase the charge to take out the new vehicle.[13] It was evident that the Ghorak IED cell had both experience and sophistication.

We made Highway 1 in the late afternoon. Massoud called his guys and ordered them to send a vehicle to meet him at the Maywand district center so he could make his flight. It was a relief to be on a real highway again, no more bouncing around at slow speed. We stopped briefly at the Maywand district center to confab with the police, who generally didn't like going north of the highway into Ghorak for obvious reasons: most of the blown up SUVs were theirs and they had lost about fifteen people in there. We stopped again east of Maywand to hand off Massoud to his party and they were off at speed toward Kandahar. The sun was setting—and we weren't at Zharey district yet. Ian was concerned: Zharey was a known ambush area and he expected we would be engaged with small arms and possibly RPG fire as we passed by the eastern end of the district. The order of march was changed to Ian leading in his LAV, followed by the RG-31, us in 9-W, the snipers in their G-Wagon that had a .50-caliber mounted in the cupola, then another LAV, the low-bed, and the remainder of the LAVs from "B" Company.

The rest of "B" Company was deployed to cover our move through the area. I was still apprehensive, like everybody else. I knew the reputation of the district and I kept a sharp lookout on the right side of the vehicle for possible ambushers. The LAVs had their turrets traversed right and left. The RG-31 in front of us had the weapons turret sweeping back and forth. Any RPG team would be human meat if they tried anything. There were police checkpoints. The sun was going down and it was a perfect time to hit us. What was that shadow? Was there movement? I waited for the radio call of contact. Nothing. The tension built up and built up with each passing kilometer. Were we going to make it out unscathed? It looked like it. No contact. Nothing. Bated breath. Then we hit the bridge and saw the ANA FOB, the 530 Compound. Neal and I let out our breaths as we passed into the western part of Kandahar City. But we knew that we were not home yet. There was still the city with its dangers.

Then suddenly, without warning, there was a bright orange light. Flame suddenly enveloped the G-Wagon, turning everything orange. The vehicle we were in shook. I couldn't see out of any of the windows. Then the shock hit: it was like jamming on the brakes hard. I instinctively knew we'd been hit again and that it was our vehicle this time. Neal kept going but was forced to stop when the RG-31 halted in front of us. "Are you all right?" he yelled and banged me on the front plate of my body armor.

"Yeah!" I yelled. "You? Here we go again!"

"Yeah!" The vehicle lost power as the electrics went. The radio was dead.

A whole bunch of things happened simultaneously. We couldn't maneuver and everybody else was stopped. The drill was not to exit the vehicle: a German officer had done so in Kabul in response to a car accident and had been blown into pieces when he left his Dingo. I was prepared to stay put, but the big hatch on the back of the RG-31 opened up and a soldier jumped out. He started waving to me madly as if I should urgently get out of the G-Wagon. I cracked the door and he was yelling, "Get out! It's going to blow!" Neal and I scrambled out of the G-Wagon with our weapons. I looked at the rear of the vehicle and saw a pool of fuel spreading rapidly over the ground. I looked at Neal and we ran forward to the front of the RG-31. As I was running I saw Ian in the turret of his LAV. He was yelling at me, but I couldn't hear what he was saying. He told me later that somebody was firing at me as I ran forward and that the splash from the rounds was kicking up dust to my right. I misunderstood and thought he was telling me to go back to the vehicle, so I yelled up, "The G-Wagon's N/S [not serviceable]! It's not going anywhere!"

Neal and I had taken cover at the front of the RG-31. Kevin dismounted. "Let's go back and check," Kevin said, so we moved back, carefully scanning the flanks. The soldier who had yelled at us to get out was panicky—not hysterical, but on the verge. I knew that hysteria was contagious so I fought down any flight reaction and focused on the immediate situation. There would be wounded: they'd have to be taken care of. We might get hit with a secondary IED or an ambush or both. Neal and I were okay and functional, but others might not be. "Doc, assess 9-W for me. I'm going to check on the snipers," Kevin said in an extremely calm voice. I looked around: there was a "strip mall"-like marketplace full of people to the left (north) of the road, and a wall to the right.

It was tough to look at it: 9-W was in rough shape. The explosion had holed the fuel tanks. I now realized the G-Wagons were diesel, so the chance of an explosion from the fuel was negligible. There was a deep penetration in the hull armor—exactly where Massoud would have been sitting. The ECM antennas were all messed up in a spaghetti tangle, spilling out of the ruptured housing. The rear window was starred: that glass is armored and at least two inches thick. The tires were slashed and flat. What looked like sprayed mud along the side of the vehicle was in fact splash from the explosion, shrapnel that hadn't penetrated. This G-Wagon wasn't going anywhere on its own. The sniper's G-Wagon was in similar shape: it was about twenty meters behind us. I looked around and saw the blast had gone into the marketplace. I heard later there were nine civilian dead, but I must have blocked out images of the remains. When I recall the event, I recall everything in detail except that: it's like there is a black "censored" spot covering up that part of the picture.

I do recall seeing a severed human hand lying in the middle of the road between our vehicles. For some reason, or unreason, I thought it was the suicide bomber's hand. I got extremely angry looking at this hand, a blinding anger I hadn't felt before. I came very close to urinating on that severed hand to demonstrate my anger and contempt for the bomber. I resisted this urge successfully.

Then the eeriest, most surreal thing happened. It was now dusk. There was carnage, destroyed vehicles, and human pain. In the midst of this, the people in the marketplace pulled out rugs, faced Mecca, and started praying in rows; we could hear the call to prayer.

Kevin walked up and I told him the 9-W G-Wagon was toast. "Okay. The crowd is starting to encroach up front and the ANP isn't here yet. Try and keep them back." Again, calm as calm can be. Neal, me, and another soldier moved forward . . . and I could see Master Corporal Greg White lying in the back of the LAV, bleeding profusely. Williams, Stitch, and Davis from the Niner Tac LAV were working on him. Ian was getting a grip on the situation and calling for assistance on the radio. Whitey, who had been acting as Ian's air sentry on the left-hand side of the LAV, was in agony: his left arm had been shattered. His head was lolling around unfocused while he was being worked on. I thought he was blacking out.

"Whitey!" I said loudly. "Master Corporal White!" I got his attention.

"Is this how your book is going to end?" he said. Which I took to mean, am I going home after this?

"No fucking way, baby! I'm going to immortalize you!"

Whitey held up his bloody right fist and I dapped it to mine.

"Right on, Doc! Fuck, man, they messed up my ink!" His elaborate Haida tattoo work was on his left arm. "*Owwww*! Goddam it, that hurt!" They had at least three tourniquets on him, but everything, including the seat of the LAV, was soaked in his dark, red blood that clashed with his arid CADPAT uniform. It wasn't stopping. The medic worked harder. Whitey kept complaining, "No, no, do it *this* way! That's not right. No, twist it *left*!"

(Whitey: consider yourself immortalized.)

Kevin Barry was moving up and down the column calming people and assessing the situation. At this time, Ian was on the radio arguing with KAF about medevac. The Americans from TF KNIGHTHAWK wouldn't bring in a UH-60 to the strike site: there were legitimate reasons. It was a confined area and it wasn't secure. If the bird went down, there would be more carnage. It would be like *Black Hawk Down* except worse.

The decision was made to use the PRT LZ as the pickup point. The problem was, the PRT was on the east end of town. Whitey was bleeding out. Ian passed control on the scene to Kevin and told Stitch Hayward to get ready for the drive of his life. The LAV was buttoned up and Stitch drove that huge vehicle within an inch of its tolerances to get Whitey to the PRT. It's dark. It's Kandahar, which has no traffic lights. There is minimal street lighting and lots of debris from construction. Stitch made it to the PRT in record time and the UH-60 Black Hawk was waiting. They loaded Whitey up . . . and then the bird took off. It narrowly missed some obstacle and nearly crashed, then Whitey was on his way.

"Doc, I need you to debrief one of the snipers. He saw it all happen and I'm concerned he won't remember the details later. You got your notebook?" asked Kevin Barry.

The sniper was Billy B. Billy couldn't hear very well: he was the .50-caliber top gunner on the sniper G-Wagon right behind us.

"Ok, Billy," I said loudly, "Tell me exactly what happened in as much detail as possible." He was groggy and singed, but I could see his pupils weren't dilated. He was still holding his weapon.

"It was a red Mercedes. It was traveling in the opposite direction. I had the gun shield cranked over to the left. It just didn't look right to me. Something was odd about seeing a red car here. The driver was a light-skinned guy. He looked Pakistani, not Afghan, and had short, short black hair. He looked like he was about twenty. I looked into his eyes—we made eye contact. Then he made a gesture with his hand." Billy tried to replicate it. "Then the vehicle detonated, there was a huge fireball, some kind of incendiary. I was able to duck down just in time. The flame flowed through the hatch into the vehicle and stuff inside caught fire."

"Sketch it for me."

Billy drew it out.

"Where did the car detonate in relation to your G-Wagon and mine?"

"It detonated between the left rear quarter of your vehicle and the front left quarter panel of ours."

"So this guy sees a LAV, an RG-31, then two G-Wagons, and then goes for the softer targets," I speculated.

"Yeah, it looks that way."

I was concerned about Billy—he was still stunned by the attack and his hearing was affected, obviously, but the overpressure from the blast could have produced a brain injury. He needed to be seen and as soon as possible. I handed him off to the medic, passing on what I suspected to him. The situation, however, was getting more chaotic on the ground.

Captain Massoud, sporting a new haircut, arrived on the scene with his men. I showed him the 9-W G-Wagon and pointed out the penetration where he would have been sitting. The friendly Captain Massoud I had been dealing with for the past five days was now replaced with a cold, remote, resolute man. "Thank Allah that you and I have been spared, Dr. Sean," he said. I think he was a bit shocked too . . . and a bit pissed that he'd be missing his flight home. Or he had just had another dust-up with his friend the Guv. He set about organizing the police cordon. First, there was a fuel truck parked right alongside our damaged vehicles: it was the proverbial elephant in the room and we'd all missed it. What if it was a secondary? Massoud's people found the driver, who moved it. There were problems: the ANP that arrived first were not Massoud's people and interfered with the strike site: they picked up the car axle, and poked around the remains of the Mercedes. Any forensic data was now lost. Massoud was annoyed. Two guys from TF IED DEFEAT arrived from somewhere. I passed on Billy B's information and my own so they could assess the attack. They started taking pictures.

The main issue that Kevin now had to deal with was that this road was the main east–west highway through Kandahar City, and traffic was backing up in both directions. Then the QRF arrived, part of "B" Company from the PRT. Then the recovery team from KAF arrived. Then another coalition convoy came in behind that. The situation was generating a bigger and bigger target. One of the newly arrived mobile recovery team (MRT) guys insisted that 9-W and the sniper G-Wagons could drive back to KAF on their own. Kevin told him they were not serviceable and needed to be towed. It looked like a debate was going to start. I worked with some of the soldiers from the Golf and Echo call signs to keep the increasingly large Afghan crowd back: the police weren't doing a good job of this. I have no idea what was going on at the back of the column at this time, but I gather there was a series of heated exchanges between our people and the ANP. I heard later that there were bad guys in ANP uniforms trying to get into the strike site, perhaps to photograph it. We learned later that an Afghan stringer for a Canadian media outlet filmed the attack and the aftermath, which begs the question, How did he know something was going to happen?

Kevin finally prevailed: hook up the G-Wagons, mount up, and we're getting the hell out of here. After five days and two IED attacks, everybody was tired, hungry, pissed off, and dehydrated. It was time to go back to KAF.

Neal and I climbed back into the stricken vehicle as a tow bar was attached. We were dragged home. Neal, not having to do anything, looked wistfully from the driver's side as we went through Kandahar City. We passed the new cafés with their pink and blue neon lights. The people sitting at small tables with tea all looked at us like this was some type of anti-parade. Here were several shattered, leaking, wrecked Canadian Army vehicles being towed or low-bedded right by the population of the city. This wasn't the message we wanted to send.

There was more confusion when we got to KAF. Neal and I were towed to the EME shops, where there were sparks flying, welding flashes, and metal-on-metal noise as the mechs worked on various refitting tasks. Neal and I weren't sure what to do. We took our personal kit and told the mechs we'd strip the vehicle later. Where the hell were we? It was dark and we were in KAF, someplace on a base that I'd never been to. There were just the two of us. It was weird. We had to navigate "home" on our own airfield! And it was still hot. . . .

As we walked along, a LAV passed us then stopped. "Doc, do you guys need a lift?" I think it was Sergeant Hurleburt in the Echo call sign. They headed to the TF ORION TOC and dropped off Neal.

"Where's the CO?"

"I think he's headed for the Role 3. Do you want to go there?"

"Yeah." I was exhausted and didn't really want to walk the five klicks anyway.

I guess I was a sight to the nurses at the Role 3. I still had my body armor on and I was carrying my helmet. I was filthy. And I was having problems making myself intelligible, I was so dry.

"Are you okay, sir?" the medic asked.

No, I wasn't. I was dehydrated and I felt like shit.

"I need rehydration solution and water *right now*, please."

I pumped a couple of liters of water with the solution into my body, but I still felt awful. A nurse came out into the plywood lobby, which was decorated with the painted images of various OEF medical units. "Are you *sure* you're okay? What happened?"

"I was involved in the IED attack this evening. I'm just meeting Colonel Hope here to see how our guys are doing." Then Ian came in. He was still wearing his body armor, too, and looked about the same as me. I handed him some water and we went inside.

The thing is, no matter how bad you feel, there is always somebody in worse shape. Corporal Ryan Elrick was the LAV gunner who was severely injured in the other IED attack that day. Ian and I approached the bed. The tubes and monitors were all hooked up and he looked like a cyborg. I noticed immediately that the stumps of his legs below the knees were wrapped in beige bandages. He was coherent. Ian greeted him and introduced me. "Good to see you, sir," he said as he shook Ian's hand and mine. I told him it was a privilege to meet him. What else can you say? Words are always inadequate in such circumstances. Always.

I was astounded at the conversation. Here was a man who had lost both legs hours ago—and, as he explained to us then and there, he already had a plan to continue weightlifting, to get back into shape, to get prosthesis. To continue his life! He was almost upbeat. I have never seen such a positive mental attitude in such dire personal circumstances short of Corporal Paul Franklin! This was real strength. I have recounted that story to people later and some just write it off to the medication(s). I think not.

We found out that Whitey had already been airlifted to Germany for treatment, that he had kicked up a fuss with the Role 3 staff, but that he would keep the arm. Whew! Then there was Billy B. Billy was in the ward tent. He still was having problems hearing but insisted to Ian that he was okay and wanted to get back out into the field.

Ian and I went to Green Beans and got some cigars. It was nearly midnight. We sat out on the deck and lit up. It was finally cooling off—maybe down to 95 degrees F (35 degrees C). I stared into space for a while.

"Helluva day."

"Yeah, it has been."

The war continued.

## OPERATION TABER POLAD: INTO THE CHENARTU VALLEY, 23–25 JUNE

It was time to get back up on the horse again. Niner Tac was reconstituted, refueled, resupplied, and ready to leave KAF. Ian had a talk with everybody concerned. The reactions to the attacks were across the spectrum from cynical, quiet stoicism to emotional and open discussion of the details. Each of us handled it in our own way. Ian reminded everybody that there was no evidence that the enemy was targeting Niner Tac specifically as the headquarters element and there were indications that the unanticipated move through northern Ghorak had its intended effect: the enemy thought it was the advance guard of an infantry company and revealed a variety of details to ISTAR. They thought, until Niner Tac turned south, that TF ORION might go all the way into northern Helmand province. Niner Tac was soon off headed north up the Tarin Kot Road through Shah Wali Kot to FOB Martello.

The state of play in Kandahar province after the IED attacks really didn't change dramatically. The NDS reported that the enemy was reconstituting in Zharey and that they were getting support from Helmand province. The stricken "A" Company LAV III up in Shah Wali Kot was recovered, while "B" Company prepared for a VMO operation in Zharey and Panjwayi. This operation was delayed. SOF was about to go into Zharey and Panjwayi. It wasn't clear exactly what they were after, but they had a U.S. Special Forces ODA and its associated Afghans, all in local dress, mounted up. This was a no-notice gig, so they must have had some time-sensitive information. A Sperwer TUAV was tasked to patrol the periphery of the districts to see what the enemy was up to and to see what CJSOTF wasn't passing on, just in case TF ORION had to go back in.

TF ORION was slowly moving resources to FOB Martello to avoid the impression that there was a surge on in support of Mountain Thrust in Oruzgan. Recce Platoon, led by Captain Jon Hamilton, was operating north of FOB Martello; they were starting to get indicators that the enemy might make a play for the FOB. The bulk of "A" Company was already there, then some Coyotes from 12 RBC showed up. A det of two M-777s was moved into range and then to the FOB. A contingency plan was under production by Mason Stalker's staff in the TOC. They had identified a possible sanctuary area that actually had bad guys in it this time and they were working up how to get at those guys. The contingency operation (CONOP) was called Taber Polad.

Taber Polad had several objectives. First, there was the Gumbad Platoon House issue. The decision had been made to withdraw from this location, but a surge of resources into the Gumbad region wasn't a good idea given the forbidding terrain. A snap operation to the east of FOB Martello would focus enemy eyes elsewhere and get them moving away from Gumbad to support their own. Since they were slower to move and couldn't react as quickly, they might not be able to react to both operations at once. If they did call in resources from outside Shah Wali Kot to reinforce from Oruzgan or elsewhere in Kandahar or Zabol provinces, so much the better: those players could be identified and killed too. That might benefit "B" Company down in Zharey, because there was a known link between the cells in both districts, and fighters from up north had been used down south before. The "B" Company VMO, already planned separately, might gain "bonus points" from Operation Taber Polad. Could the enemy react effectively to all three movements?

The Gumbad VMO was also going to be used as cover as part of the hunt for Mullah Tahrir, who may have been in the area. It was possible that information developed during the VMO might lead TF ORION to Tahrir, so part of the plan catered to that option.

Taber Polad, as we will see, was dependent on the availability of CH-47s from TF KNIGHTHAWK. That airlift was still under discussion. The limited number of birds and the maintenance situation placed restrictions on how helicopters could be used. KNIGHTHAWK had to approve the plan. They had strict criteria about going into hot LZs. If certain requirements weren't met and the risk matrix was too high, they'd say no, so TF ORION had to make sure its ducks were in a row.

While these evolutions were in progress, the SOF mission into Zharey and Panjwayi went in. In effect, "B" Company was told to stay out of the temporary JSOA, so they did. The SOF team then ran into trouble in Pashmul and started taking casualties—two U.S. dead and one ANA

Operation Taber Polad, 23–25 June 2006

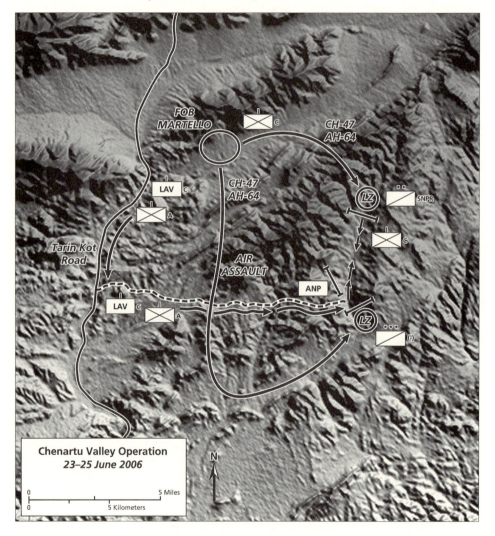

wounded. They called for help, but because there had been no coordination with CTF AEGIS nor with TF ORION, there were no control measures in place. Why was that important? Conventional forces reacting to support unconventional forces at night was a prescription for disaster. SOF blended in with the population—and with the enemy. Without agreed-upon recognition signals and passwords, TF ORION could wind up gunning down SOF operators. Or what if SOF called in their own airpower—and they hit TF ORION on the way in? "B" Company had to wait for those measures to be formulated, and then had to pass them on to their deployed forces, while at the same time being under pressure from higher headquarters to go in. This took time. There was not enough time. SOF had to pull out with their casualties, with "B" Company covering their withdrawal. The excessive secrecy and compartmentalization again placed barriers to an effective partnership between CTF AEGIS, TF ORION, and CJSOTF. Like the British helicopter medevac incident in Part 1 of this book, it generated a certain amount of friction between CTF AEGIS and CJTF-76.

The enemy was trying to reconstitute in Sha Wali Kot and Mianeshien. The opening of FOB Martello was a real affront to them and they needed to be seen doing something about it or they would lose the allegiance in several important communities. ISTAR indicated that Mullah Shakur, Mullah Tahir, the notorious Toor Naquib, and Sayed Mohommad were still on the loose and might be planning to meet in a region called the Chenartu Valley. Killing or capturing these leaders would have an obvious benefit. Even if they were unable to meet and coordinate, that would be a positive though less-satisfying effect on what TF ORION was trying to accomplish.

Ian had other objectives too and they related to TF ORION's morale. He realized that some of the troops were pissed off that they had to wait around at FOB Martello and possibly be ambushed, rocketed, or IED'd. They couldn't see that what they were doing was part of a larger effort across RC South—and that the effects of what they were doing weren't always tangible but were important in other spheres. Ian believed that continuous maneuver prevented a "FOB mentality," and that it instilled the belief that TF ORION retained the initiative and could go where it wanted, when it wanted. Maneuver, in Ian's view, was disruptive to the enemy, and if the enemy couldn't be pinned down, he could be kept moving so he wasn't able to consolidate control over a particular district. I pointed out that the Taliban had no true parallel government so they couldn't really control any seized district anyway, even if they took it. The enemy had to continue to resort to trickery and intimidation, and that control could only be extended so far. Ian wanted to demonstrate to the enemy that the Taliban's freedom of movement was over. Okay, TF ORION couldn't be everywhere, but neither could the Taliban. I parenthetically noted that the enemy then chose to use IEDs to counter TF ORION movement and to resort to greater IED usage—which in turn had a high chance of killing civilians, which in turn could be exploited for our I/O purposes to convince the people to side with the government and support coalition forces.

There hadn't been operations in Chenartu Valley for months and it was possible that the enemy thought the valley was safe because Mountain Thrust forces were all tied up elsewhere. Building on the last operation, the JCC would be used as part of the deception plan. People would be told that operations would commence in Shah Wali Kot and then without warning TF ORION would swing into Chenartu Valley. If anybody blabbed, ISTAR would be onto them. No ANP would be used: they were considered compromised.

One version of the plan was a completely airmobile raid, but the helicopters weren't available to lift the whole force. Another aspect of the plan using the helos was to demonstrate to the local population that TF ORION could drop in anywhere without warning. The message was supposed to be, "We can reach out when we want to." In theory, this would reassure the progovernment people, be part of an effort to move the uncommitted to the government side, and generate some anxiety in the pro-Taliban part of the population.

Ian and the staff explored several options, all dependent on airlift. There were also constraints on the use of the helicopters. The outline plan was to insert Jon Hamilton's recce platoon to secure the LZ at 0100 hours. The main problem in an air assault was the enemy's early warning system, so the CH-47s would do the pickup at FOB Martello, fly south down the Tarin Kot Road, and then double back through the mountains to Chenartu. The LZs would be two blocking positions: the northern part of the valley and the southeast part. This, in theory, would deter "squirters" who would hide and then be found during the more extensive cordon-and-search operations. One problem that emerged was that if the recce insert was detected, the enemy might run for the hills before the blocking force could get in. TF KNIGHTHAWK insisted that the LZs be secured with vehicles, so Jon's platoon would establish a patrol base, send in the snipers and move in on foot; their vehicles would follow. Artillery would be dropped on possible enemy evacuation routes to demonstrate that TF ORION could put fire anywhere quickly and thus deter egress. Once the blocks were in, "A" and "C" Companies in their LAVs and the ANA would deploy from the Tarin Kot Road as a feint, then move east into the southern end of the Chenartu Valley. "C" Company would secure the route in and out while "A" Company searched the whole valley. Both companies would be augmented with CIMIC and PSYOPS.

It reminded me of the operations that were conducted by the 82nd Airborne back in 2003, except that now the blocking force was airmobile and the ground force did the search. Staying in place for a couple of days was also part of the plan, again to demonstrate to the population that the force could stick around if it wanted to.

In effect, Ian wanted to present to the enemy three options: go to ground, egress, or fight.

I loaded up with Neil Carswell into the brand-new 9-W G-Wagon: it was just us since Captain Massoud was on leave. Niner Tac departed for FOB Martello. It was the time of the Chuck Norris joke craze. Neal had the best: "Chuck Norris' tears can cure cancer, but he *never* cries!"

There was a four-fifths moon above the FOB and I was introduced to a new crew. I'd be going in with "A" Company's headquarters LAV, call sign 19. The gregarious Pete Leger, who reminded me of the actor Clancy Brown (in *Starship Troopers*, not *Highlander*) sporting a Red Devil tattoo on his arm, was the CSM. When you shook hands with Pete, you just knew you were dealing with somebody who knew what the hell they were doing. Corporal Brian "Gibby" Gibson was the driver, and Corporal Gerald Strong was the 25-mm gunner. Master Corporal Steve Pichovich crew-commanded 19, while Corporal Chris Raike handled signals. These young guys, barely in their early twenties, knew the multimillion dollar LAV inside and out like it was their own private sports car. They were always smoking and joking, and their high morale and humor were infectious, especially when they went on about their exploits involving something called the "Dirty Sanchez" and the "Angry Dragon."

The quiet-spoken and introspective Major Kirk Gallinger was officer commanding (OC) "A" Company. You didn't always know what Kirk was thinking, which could be an advantage. His outward calm was compromised only by his chain-smoking, but I could tell Kirk was a guy who gave a damn and wanted to make sure all of his guys got home in one piece. He and Pete complemented each other in having opposite temperaments but the same objectives.

The night recce and sniper insert was successful, so at 0455 "A" Company departed. Kirk and Pete had only two Canadian infantry platoons, but an ANA platoon in its pickup trucks, plus a Canadian CIMIC team joined the column. There was an engineer LAV, E-11, and an artillery LAV, G-11. While we were en route south, word came over the radio that the airmobile insertion of the blocking forces was successful. "A" Company turned off the Tarin Kot Road and headed east. This "road," if I could call it that, was a goat track canalized by hills and rock formations on either side. It was one long defile, perfect for ambushes, IEDs, mines, and whatever mayhem could be brought to bear. It was the only way in and out of the valley for vehicle traffic and I saw three burnt-out wrecked jingle trucks pushed off the road and into a gully. I reflected on that fact: if the road could be paved, then the Chenartu Valley wouldn't be so isolated. Trade could flow out better, and ideas would flow in. The police could patrol. The enemy wouldn't want to use it because it wouldn't be isolated anymore.

Then things started to go wrong. As "A" Company approached a green oasis-like area, G-11 blew a drive shaft. Pete looked around: "It looks like the *Planet of the Apes* set here!" All we needed was to see Charlton Heston pounding the sand with his fist, yelling about "damn dirty apes." It was still cool out, and the blowing heat hadn't started yet. I could see hoses lying all over the place; they were part of the irrigation system. The children weren't waving. The LAV up front was silhouetted in the haze, with the turret traversed left.

ISTAR reported that the enemy had seen us move in. There was a sniper position just east of Chenartu, and about five guys were hiding nearby. But no contact. Kirk moved the vehicle and the enablers to an overwatch position east of Chenartu village. The valley was elongated and ran north to south. The dwellings were all along the greenbelt that followed a wadi, also north to south. We were on a small ridge that bisected the valley itself and the support vehicles occupied a bowl behind us. ISTAR reported that the enemy was close and communicating from a nearby building, which looked like a small fort. Jon Hamilton sent two of his

RG-31s to search it. The road was rough and by the time the search was completed, Jon figured the enemy had got away. ISTAR kept reporting that the enemy was there, however, and it turned out that the Taliban had put a repeater into the dried mud wall of the place.

The shadow of an AH-64 passed over the suspect compound and the bird made a loop, using its sensors. There was also what the guys called a "Houdini bird" present—that is, something that was there but wasn't: a Predator UAV. Still nothing. It was now 1130, hot as a furnace. Kirk used the same tactic that had been used at Chenar: interdict all the water supplies and wait for the enemy to come up for air.

By the afternoon, there was still nothing. A Harrier conducted a recce in a valley to the east, but saw nothing. Kirk was getting pessimistic: "The enemy had sophisticated overhead cover for their spotters. They know about Pred and they know about TI so they position near hot rocks when they're up in the mountains. You need plunging fire to get the OPs: direct fire won't work if it's dug in. They do need to come down for water, though. That's when they're vulnerable."

Cordon-and-search operations that turned up nothing were always hard on the troops. Kirk's platoon leaders had to keep the guys motivated in the 120 degree F (50 degrees C) heat, wearing body armor and carrying weapons, to go into compounds time and again, always at the alert for ambush or booby traps, always having to be careful to avoid shooting civilians. It was stressful, hot, sweaty work. They had to be polite to people who obviously didn't appreciate being searched. Each man would drink almost a box of water bottles in a day doing this. Some even carried two CamelBaks. It would be easy to get frustrated and lose it, and that's where the discipline came in. The soldiers were professionals doing a job that had ambiguous results, at best, and that had no "instant gratification" payoff. And they did this for days at a time.

Kirk looked at the map. To the southeast of the valley was a cluster of communities collectively called Karez in what looked like a small subvalley. The cordon-and-search ops hadn't been in there, but instead of just barging in Kirk decided to send a CIMIC and PSYOPS group down to meet with the local leadership. Warrant Officer Mark Pickford would lead the team in: Pickford, a sarcastic guy who shaved his head and wore a black T-shirt in the 120 degree F (50 degrees C) heat, was another outstandingly competent soldier. Like Pete Leger, with Pickford you knew you were in good hands.

I was attached to Master Corporal Chuck Prodonick's team. I walked up to Chuck, who also had shaved his head:

"Quintus Varus, give me back my legions!" I roared and lifted my arms to heaven.

Chuck lifted his arm up, with "SPQR" and a shield from the 19th Legion surrounded by a tattoo of the skeletons of two Roman Legionnaires.

"For those about to die, we salute you!" he exclaimed and checked his weapon. Chuck had special skills: he knew when people were lying, so he was going along too.

The group included a LAV and about seven G-Wagons, some of which towed trailers carrying PSYOPS material. It was a short but bumpy drive from the "A" Company laager to Karez. The vehicles stayed grouped together outside the village complex. It was a green zone with trees and a stream, surrounded by hills. There were fields to the north. It looked like around one hundred people lived there. Flanking sections went to cover the fields, while a section scaled a small hill for observation purposes. Once both were in place, Pickford led a delegation slowly down the road into the trees. A three-man delegation of elders, all wearing white turbans, emerged onto the road and the terp, "Lucky," went to work. We were invited to sit amongst the trees next to the irrigation ditch.

There was an "excitable" gent, a "distinguished" gent, and a "calm and smiling" gent. Captain Walter Martin, a CIMIC officer who in civilian life was a wheat farmer from western Canada, asked questions about the state of the crop, what Karez produced, and so on. He learned that the harvest was on, but the elders expected the Taliban would take a portion of it for themselves. One of the elders talking to Pickford explained that their leader had been killed last year by the Taliban. The last time the Taliban had been here was four or five days ago and the soldiers demanded water. If the village didn't provide it, they said they would kill people.

The other elders were gesticulating and there was some rapid-fire talk. They weren't sure how much they should tell us. We understood. The Taliban were in the hills in the day and came down at night. Like in Chenar, they implied that there were more of them than there actually were to intimidate the locals.

"Lucky" was able to explain to us that the people in Karez were progovernment but not openly so. They would be killed if they had been open. If they put up a government flag, they would be killed. There was no permanent ANP presence, though there had been a patrol that came in a week before.

ANP? Way in here? That didn't make sense. Pickford asked where they were from.

"Khakriz district."

What the hell were the police from Khakriz doing way over here in eastern Shah Wali Kot? The name they gave Pickford matched a name in Khakriz. . . .

Was there a local Taliban commander that they encountered regularly? No, the three men explained. There were different guys all the time. How did they know for sure they were Taliban? The elders explained that they could tell from their facial expressions, that they were far from home, that they were in their late teens and led by twenty-somethings, and that their turban colors didn't match those around here. Some had long beards, others had shaven heads. Most were wearing black makeup, they explained.

Black makeup had been used by the Taliban when they took the place over in 1996. It made them look like raccoons with black turbans. That these fighters were using that makeup was interesting. The elders explained they were heading northeast and had stayed in a school in Chenartu. The locals had been told that if anybody else used the building as a school, the Taliban would burn it. They used it for training.

The CIMIC team was distributing radios, tools, and seed. They explained to the elders that this was for the community, not for the Taliban. The elders explained that, yes, they understood that, but without security they couldn't guarantee anything. If we had security, they told Walter, everything would be okay. Pickford told them that security was linked to information: if we knew where the Taliban were, we could take them out and improve security.

"But if we give you information and you leave, they will come with rifles. The Taliban is the enemy of our country, but when we saw the 'birds' [helicopters] we were scared."

"We were hunting Taliban with the 'birds,'" Pickford said. "But we need to be able to distinguish the people from the Taliban so nobody gets hurt. We can only do this with information." The excitable gent then blurted out, "If you see people with rifles, kill them. They are the enemies of Afghanistan. If you don't help us, the Taliban will kill us."

It was getting circular, so Walter stepped in and asked more questions. How can the village be helped? What was the most pressing need here? The elders were still very animated about the Taliban and security, so it was difficult to get answers. Did the community have enough food? Was the crop significant? Taliban, Taliban, Taliban. They just didn't want to stop venting about the enemy. The distinguished gent told Walter that the government sent agricultural assistance to the village and the Taliban ambushed the three trucks and killed the drivers.

The community of Karez, like the other communities in northern Kandahar, was caught in a dilemma. If they supported the Taliban, they wouldn't get government support. If they supported the government, the Taliban would kill them. The calm smiling man told us that the community did have an electrical generator. The Taliban told them that if they used it, they would blow it up. They were forced to use old methods for the crops. He wanted a generator to run pumps to irrigate his crops. It emerged in further conversation that one of the Taliban leaders was from a rival tribe, the Tokhiy, and didn't like his rivals being prosperous.

One of the PSYOPS team asked how the community got news. We were surprised when the distinguished man told us they had a hidden transistor radio and they listened to the BBC in Pashto. It reminded me of occupied France in the 1940s: code stuff like "Jean has a long moustache." The Taliban also provided counterinformation, and told everybody they met that OEF was there to take over the country and that they were popular resistance against the invaders. It was all perception management. So when the left-wing BBC used Taliban reports without vetting them, they reinforced the Taliban message with the weight of the BBC's reputation behind it! This was troublesome.

Pickford asked them if the Taliban was recruiting local men. No. Well, how many local men have joined the ANP or ANA? Well, none. Pickford used this as an opportunity to explain that if the community didn't get involved in its own defense, nothing would change. We wouldn't be there forever, and they had to take some responsibility. The elders didn't like this one bit. They explained again they were afraid of the helicopters.

This helicopter theme kept coming up again and again, so Pickford asked if the village had lost people to gunfire from a helicopter. They said no. As far as I could tell, this fear may have gone back to the 1980s in the Soviet era. Soviet use of Mi-24 HIND gunships firing indiscriminately into villages may have been the source of this fear.[14]

Everybody took a break for lunch. I spoke with a CIMIC operator about her experiences. She had been a gung-ho CIMIC person, ready to help, very positive, but had become disillusioned. That of course, was easy in Afghanistan, as I knew myself. "What happened?"

"One of our 10-ton trucks damaged a wall by accident moving through Gumbad. I insisted that we stop and compensate the people. A hundred meters away, one of our LAVs hit a huge RCIED [radio-controlled IED], the one that wounded Corporal Elrick and Captain Larose. Those people we stopped to help had to have known that an RCIED was placed there. They could have told us. Elrick would still have his legs." She was so turned off with the place she didn't want to come back. It was this killing of hope that was a real evil, not just the evil inside the twisted sadistic soul that occupied the man who built, placed, and detonated that RCIED. How did we care for the damage caused to her idealism? Elrick would get prosthesis. He would power lift again, and thank God he was alive. But this CIMIC operator—would she ever be able to see the good she accomplished in this place? Or would the RCIED episode override all of it?

Pickford and I talked about Karez. "I've seen this before. When there are three leaders in a delegation, that means that the real leader fears being singled out and killed. They think that the Taliban won't kill off three leaders and alienate the community."

"So what were we seeing there?"

"I think Mr. Distinguished is pro-Taliban. He didn't say much and let everybody yak on. This is a village caught in the crossfire, remote from government influence. The people here will side with whoever is in control—the government or the Taliban. We see this all the time up here."

We departed Karez and headed back to the "A" Company laager.

The move into Chenartu Valley had provided ISTAR with new information on what the enemy was up to in the northern part of the province. Locally, the enemy was frustrated. They laid several IEDs on the route we took into the valley from the Tarin Kot Road, but none had gone off! They were frantically trying to figure out what countermeasures had been used and they were openly discussing how to counter what they suspected those countermeasures were. It appeared that they had even set an IED to bring down a huge boulder on us, gloating "If this thing falls on them, their mothers will be destroyed!" But . . . nothing. And they were pissed off, like sadistic children who stuffed a firecracker into a frog's mouth and couldn't light it. They kept calling us "the witches." I think the prospect of fighting armed female soldiers disturbed them and they thought they were satanic.

ISTAR also reported that the enemy was tracking call sign 6, that there was still enemy somewhere around Chenartu. They were going to try again to IED the exfiltration route. "C" Company, however, had eyes on the whole route and was prepared to take anybody out. The Taliban didn't try. "A" Company packed up, mounted up, and we left Chenartu Valley and headed back to FOB Martello. There were no incidents during the exfiltration nor were there any on the Tarin Kot Road.

## RECCE PLATOON GETS A CONTACT

With all the focus on infantry companies maneuvering hither and yon, it's easy to overlook Recce Platoon, call sign 69. Led by the quietly confident Captain Jon Hamilton and mounted in G-Wagons, Recce was employed as an "economy of force" subunit in the Shah Wali Kot and Mienashin districts by TF ORION. Jon's platoon spent a lot of time operating from FOB Martello and maintaining a presence in the villages in the surrounding area. A Dutch mechanized platoon moved in to help with road security.

Jon's boys were feeling a bit left out of things—their buddies in the companies seemed to be getting into all the TICs they wanted. With their numbers cut by home leave and augmentation to other subunits, Jon was down to three six-man sections, his headquarters section, and an ANP detachment—eight guys with AK-47s crammed into a Ford Ranger pickup.

Chalibar village hadn't really been visited by coalition forces for some time, and was considered to be enemy controlled. Jon wanted to find out what the real deal was.

> I had to conduct a route recce anyway, from FOB Martello to Zamto, where the district headquarters were and back. We were looking for alternative routes in the area because of the IED attacks around Gumbad.
>
> When we got near Mien village, we saw a roadblock made of rocks, but it was deserted. We asked the local people to move the rocks and they told us that the Taliban had been there the night before. The rocks were positioned so that the Taliban could get

their leadership out of town while a patrol was hung up at the block. We did a leadership engagement with the people and explained what the PTS program was and moved on.

The plateau turned into a valley as we headed north: the road curved to the right. There were hills on both sides, with a wadi branching off to the right past a high feature to our right; the wadi was essentially a gully at that point. There was a compound at the juncture of the road and wadi.

As we came around the bend, we saw people moving in the compound. They were Taliban—they were wearing black turbans—and had been resting in the compound. They grabbed RPGs and AKs. Our turreted C-6s [7.62-mm machine guns] and C-9s [5.56-mm machine guns] opened up. The G-Wagons were stopped on the curve, so all the guns could be brought to bear on the compound. There was a heavy volume of fire. We then dismounted. I sent one det to the left and they advanced along to the road to the compound. I sent another det up onto the high ground to the right. The enemy was still firing back but it was ineffective. Sergeant Macdonald got one of them with a C-8. He had an EO Tech sight [holographic weapon sight] and it's pretty good.

The enemy took off so quickly that he left running shoes behind. There were dropped AKs too. They tried to break contact and tried to use three to four men to hold us off. By then our FAC [forward air controller] had called up an A-10 that was on its way. We swept the compound and found an old man and three kids, who were unhurt. We told them through our terp to go back to the vehicles and get down so they wouldn't get hurt. We then started combing the wadi methodically. The det I'd sent up on the high ground had eyes on; they saw the enemy and opened fire as they moved through the wadi. One of the enemy went to ground and holed up in a rock sanger—we used an M-72 on him. In the sweep we found an RPG, AKs, RPG warheads, clothing, rations. The ANP looted the site. As we pushed farther up the wadi into the hills we found more running shoes (Reeboks) and bundles of clothes. There was another enemy guy—dead from small arms rounds. There were blood trails everywhere. We found another guy three hundred meters away holed up under a tree alone. It took great personal restraint not to kill him. There was yet another site with another guy—the artery in his leg had been cut by a small arms round and he was bleeding out. We said, "Don't move, we'll help you." I went and personally checked that he didn't have a grenade or an IED on him. We cuffed him and gave him first aid. He'd been shot through the left buttock and it exited out the front. He'd been running when shot.

I asked him some questions. He admitted to being Taliban and that there were more wounded about four hundred meters away. We were now almost eight hundred meters from the vehicles, and there were more blood trails. I didn't have enough manpower, so I decided to get the guys the hell out of there. We did a back sweep and found another dead guy and another wounded guy. We waited three hours for a UH-60 to evacuate the wounded enemy. I was worried about a counterattack. We got into a defensive fire position and were prepared to lay down harassing fire and break contact if we were hit.

The ANP and our terp conducted the proper Muslim burial rites for the dead enemy and they got the local people to bury them before sundown. It was great I/O. 69 mounted up and we headed back to the district center. This TIC was a big morale boost: after months of hearing our peers getting hit by IEDs, we finally got payback. It was in rough terrain, the enemy proved they were cowards, lacked the will to fight, and could only IED us up there. It was the first major TIC for Recce.

Jon's eighteen-man platoon probably killed or wounded ten Taliban in this engagement.

## THE GUMBAD VMO
One of the most interesting counterinsurgency operations conducted by OEF was the Village Medical Outreach. The theory behind the VMO was straightforward: it was an attempt to counter Taliban influence in the rural areas of Afghanistan using part of Maslow's hierarchy of needs as a weapon. The Taliban brought violence, intimidation, and a distorted perspective of Islam to the rural people. The VMO brought medical, dental, and veterinary assistance to improve their daily lives.

After the Chenartu Valley operation, "A" Company redeployed to FOB Martello. It was evening when we pulled in and the battle staff was working on the next operation. One of Ian's issues was the Gumbad Platoon House problem. Gumbad Platoon House was established by TF GUNDEVILS sometime in 2005 in a remote valley area adjacent to the Belly Button complex. There was an unpaved track that ran virtually wadi to wadi off the Tarin Kot Road to the northwest, then north through rugged terrain to Gumbad, then to a large wadi system, and then east to a point north of MARTELLO and back on to the Tarin Kot Road. When I was in Kandahar with the PRT in 2005, the Gundevils seemed to be in constant TICs up around the Belly Button, so the platoon house was established to give the Gundevils a "foot on the ground." Later, a district center was established to get some governance going. The Americans wound up playing a cat-and-mouse game with an individual who became known as the "Gumbad Sniper." These stories were still floating around when I came back, but, like fish stories, the number and sophistication of the "kills" grew.

As the Taliban exhibited better organization in the area, Gumbad Platoon House increasingly became a liability. TF ORION inherited the facility, but the paucity of helicopters meant that resupply went in by road, which in turn increased the number of opportunities to attack Canadian convoys with IEDs. The attack that killed four of Dave Fraser's close protection party occurred north of the platoon house where the road exited the hills into the wadi. Another deadly attack took place on the southern road.

There was no reason that operations in the Gumbad and Belly Button area could not be handled from MARTELLO, which was more secure and more easily resupplied. There were not enough forces to man everything. Could the ANA take it over? Hopefully, but they were stretched thin. Ian decided to pull out. It was a tough decision: Canadians had died in there. Blood had been spilt. There was a psychological attachment, however unhealthy, to the place in certain quarters. If TF ORION pulled out, the enemy would claim a propaganda victory: "We drove the White Cancer out of Gumbad! See? Here are the pictures of their base!" and sure enough this would be on hand-out DVDs in Kandahar City, and then in Pakistan . . . then maybe on Al Jazeera and on the Internet. The Taliban could mock up battle damage, set fires, strew captured kit around, and make it look like a big battle had taken place and that we'd lost it. Perception would become reality with no fighting at all.

The plan was to deploy part of "C" Company with its attached Afghans and an RCP in the early morning into the Gumbad area and tear down the whole facility: no graffiti-covered outhouse plywood, no food scraps, no bits and pieces of uniforms, nothing. Not even the barbed wire would be left behind. The intent was to do it in one day and get out before nightfall.

The concept for the extraction of the Gumbad personnel took into account social as well as military factors. TF ORION could not just walk away: there had to be some basis for a future coalition return, even if it was just an operation passing through; someday Afghan and coalition forces would be back to stay and govern in force. The population became accustomed to a coalition presence and did not appear to outwardly support the Taliban cells in the area. I suspected, like in so many areas, they tried to remain as uncommitted as possible because security could in no way be guaranteed. A VMO would be deployed by helicopter during the extraction operation to help the community and leave just before the convoy pulled out. Hopefully the people would remember the help that had been provided and compare that with the lack of assistance the Taliban didn't provide. This would hopefully bolster support for the small ANP and ANA presence in the valley. Those guys were in for a rough ride, but there was no choice, given how thinly spread forces were in the province.

Another nonkinetic weapon was the containerized delivery system drops into remote areas. These drops included pallets of food, seed, water, tools, and so on. Sometimes the parachutes didn't work. Captain Keith Saul in the TF ORION TOC called it the "Anvils for Afghans" program. (Keith, incidentally, also came up with the idea of bacon flechette rounds, an idea that wasn't implemented. I reminded him about the Sepoy Mutiny.)

I hadn't seen a VMO before so I wanted to go in with the ground extraction force to watch. I asked Bill Fletcher and he had no problem with it. It was dark as I grabbed my kit and humped over the hill to "C" Company. I hadn't had any time with "C" Company and an unfamiliar face was greeted with some wary suspicion by the quiet CSM. Bill launched into his briefing: the convoy would be led by an American RCP. This was a series of three vehicles: a four-wheel tractor with wing-like sensors called the Husky, a huge six-wheeled angular vehicle sporting a large articulated arm for lifting explosives called the Buffalo, and a vehicle identical to our RG-31. These vehicles were called "The Funnies," with a tip of the hat to World War II's 79th Armored Division by the more historically minded troops.[15] There were four ANA International trucks and their drivers. The Canadian part of the force consisted of "C" Company HQ, 3 Platoon, engineers, and a FOO/FAC LAV. A CIMIC det in its G-Wagons and trailers was also part of the operation.

Bill put me in with Captain Marty Dupuis, the LAV captain for "C" Company. Marty reminded me of the actor C. Thomas Howell. His driver, the spunky Corporal Laidlaw, had more tattoos than I did—and her hair was shorter. We all went to ground for a few hours.

The convoy must have been nearly thirty vehicles. This concerned me because it would be slow going and thus vulnerable in the complex terrain around Gumbad. I figured that the enemy wouldn't pass up a chance to go after something so big that would be difficult to extricate if it started getting cut up. Oh, and by the way, we didn't have air cover: the British and American AH-64s were busy in Helmand, and the Dutch wouldn't relinquish control over their AH-64s that were providing top cover for their convoys. A det of M-777 guns was moved north so they could cover the operation.

Bill also had a deception plan that involved an early morning departure in the dark. Instead of taking the obvious direct route to Gumbad—north to the wadi, west in the wadi, and south by track to Gumbad—he took the whole caravan south along the paved Tarin Kot Road, abruptly cut west into a fertile wadi system, then cut north into the Gumbad area. The enemy would be anticipating the easiest move and put his forces in place there. Anything leaving Martello going south was obviously going to Kandahar and would become the responsibility of somebody else's cell. The southern move might even draw off enemy resources to cover the southern end of the Tarin Kot Road, but they would be waiting for a convoy that wouldn't arrive, leaving an empty uncovered center. The enemy's ability to redeploy rapidly in the district was limited: once he was committed, he could melt away but could not move to another part of the district quickly. He had only so many resources, too: he wasn't everywhere, no matter what he wanted people to think.

Coincidentally, an American ODA was working with its associated Afghans north and northeast of the Gumbad area, on the seam between Oruzgan and Kandahar provinces. Intelligence indicated that the enemy was moving forces away from the ODA to the east and away from the

Gumbad–MARTELLO area. This would serve to draw off any enemy reserves that were not already in northern Kandahar province itself.

It was nice and cool in the dark at Martello as we mounted up. I occupied one of air sentry hatches. The move down the Tarin Kot Road was smooth as silk. There was no civilian traffic that time of morning. Then we veered off into a wadi system that paralleled a dark brown and red cliff face. The vehicles splashed through some water. The wadi was flat and was mostly gravel-like rocks. The turrets traversed to cover all arcs and we moved at a good clip. Then the wadi became more like a ravine, and then broke out into a compound complex with a road running through it. The kids waved—always a good sign—and everybody stopped to see the caravan. I could see people working the fields. I didn't have that bad vibe, that anticipatory feeling here, though I was wary. I couldn't help feeling Russian. I had read one too many Les Grau ambush vignettes from *The Bear Went Over the Mountain*.

The wadi narrowed significantly until it was only as wide as a LAV. The open-air sentry hatch scraped the muddy bank here. There were trees! It was lush, in complete contrast to the blue sky and the brown hills and mountains in the distance. A winding path with a hairpin turn slowed things down as the LAVs, G-Wagons, and International trucks struggled to get around it. We were starting to climb. The antennas bumped into low-lying tree limbs. Still no contact. We were now up a plateau. It was grassy, and there was a dirt road. The vehicles were now kicking up dust: a signature. When would they hit us? It had to be only a matter of time. Laidlaw negotiated a tricky part of the road where the dirt ends and a random collection of large worn rocks begins before the dirt started again. I looked to the right and saw an intricate hill that appeared to be made up of individual rocks—not a mass of stone, but individual worn rocks. I made out a number of small caves as Marty slewed the turret right to cover the entrances.

There was some staticy communications. The RCP, with the Husky leading in front, found something. I could see the column stopped like a snake draped over two bounds. Turrets and crews were scanning all arcs. The Buffalo moved up, but I was too far back to see the action. It was an IED, mine or mine stack, so it had to be dealt with. We waited. Air sentries, including me, peered over the sides of vehicles looking for disturbed earth or other signs of IED or mine placement. Nobody dismounted. It was odd. Normally an enemy spotter would be watching the proceedings and communicating with the buttonman or ambush group. Nothing. We moved on.

Marty was nervous. I didn't blame him: so was I. He was jiggling his knee constantly. Everybody in these circumstances has a nervous tic of some kind, I don't care who it is: with some people it's physical, with others it's mental. An image. A song. A vibe. A feeling. A mantra. A lucky charm. It's a human reaction to death and extreme violence. It actually enhances survival. It provides a calming effect. It allows a certain amount of pent-up energy to escape without compromising the integrity of the mission. Energy is neither created nor destroyed and some of it must leak out, a steam valve. Better knee jiggling than something else. We were all keyed up.

The column moved through more of this rock-hill terrain, but I could now see the eastern edges of the Belly Button feature more clearly. And then we were into another greenbelt and wadi, except this one ran perpendicular to the road. We stopped again. The Husky detected something else. Bill had everybody dismount for a piss break because we had been on the road for a couple of hours.

I looked around as Bill approached. I saw bits of metal around, and what looked like part of an axle.

"This was one of the IED strike sites," Bill explained. He gestured at a plate that looked like it had been part of a LAV. I saw some white silvery insulation in the grass. It reminded me of Halloween cotton batting. I was looking at a perfect ambush site: canalized terrain, lots of potential positions from which to fire down on it. The historian in me wondered how many Soviets had been wiped out here. Bill smiled: he knew what I was thinking. We pressed on.

Into another greenbelt. A LAV III stood guard at the district center. The crew commander sat on the turret wearing a Tim Horton's ball cap scanning a line of Afghans who were waiting to get in through the gates. (Tim Horton's is a Canadian doughnut chain that had a place open up at KAF.) The platoon house was down a slight hill. It was a small fortress surrounded with barbed wire, OPs, and mortar pits containing 60-mm mortars. The column pulled in and the teardown started immediately.

The field between the platoon house and the district center was the designated LZ and in due course an RAF Chinook helicopter arrived, escorted by an AH-64 attack helicopter. People and equipment poured out the back and were loaded onto trucks. I greeted Julie Roberge as she was helping put some boxes onto an International truck.

"I thought you weren't a 'combat chick'!"

"I wanted to get out and see a VMO in action! And get out of KAF."

Julie, who had a couple of kids of her own, really wanted to help the Afghan kids on a personal level, too.

Once the VMO was established, I wandered around to get a sense of its moving parts. A small mobile clinic had been established in Gumbad. There was triage in one large room; people were seen there and then ushered to more specialized people. The crew in the main room included three civilian Afghan doctors and medical assistants, two ANA medics, a U.S. Navy corpsman, two U.S. Special Forces medics, and Captain Marilynn Chenette, the health services support boss from TF ORION. They did the initial exam. The dentist, an Afghan from Kandahar City, had his own bailiwick. Another separate room was established for women and small children; two Canadian female medics worked out of there. The intent was to keep the coalition people in the "second row" and have the Afghans handle things first.

It was all very systematic. The VMO wasn't merely a tool for addressing health-care needs, but was a larger I/O weapon. Our ring of security for the VMO was ANA, not coalition forces. The first people the locals saw were smiling friendly ANA troops with clean uniforms, some with weapons, others unarmed. They handed out information leaflets to those who were literate: the message generally was that there was a legitimately constituted government in Afghanistan, the Taliban wasn't part of it, the ANA was a legitimate army, and that they were here to help. For those who were not literate, the ANA soldiers (in berets, not helmets and body armor) would read out the leaflets to small groups and answer any questions. There were a lot of questions from what I could tell. They were equipped with paper and pencils for the children. Traditional Afghan music played in the background.

I recognized one of the intelligence guys that arrived on the Chinook; he was with an NDS man in a separate room. At some point in the presentations, people were asked if they had any information, no matter how minor, on enemy activity. Those that chose to pass it on could do it discreetly with the NDS, who seemed to be loaded down with tea and cookies for these discussions. Nobody was coerced and the NDS certainly weren't rubber hosing anybody in private. I learned that this type of information collection was extremely valuable.

I saw a line of boys and men sitting down in the shade waiting to be seen. A couple of kids, toddlers really, had minor scrapes and one had a cut finger.

"Come on, tough guy," Julie egged me on, "*You* can help put bandages on too." She handed me a pack of Elmo Band-Aids. "Get to work!" Then she had one of the photogs take a picture when I wrapped the red bandage around a kid's finger. "I'm going to blackmail you with the other tough guys at work!" she joked. Everybody had a good laugh. For the most part, the level of hygiene wasn't good but when I talked to the dentist he explained that there was a basic understanding of how to take care of teeth in Pashtun rural culture. "See? They don't have 'Austin Powers' teeth here."

The terps were really busy; some of them had to bone up on Pashtun medical terminology. It wasn't easy for the docs and medics. They had to deal with a language barrier and a cultural barrier. The Afghan docs and medics were critical members of the team. Indeed, in theory, the whole VMO should have been made up of Afghans. Dr. Arun Abdullah, MD, explained to me that he wished all of his colleagues in the south would participate in VMOs, but many were afraid of retaliation from Kandahar City–based cells. He was from up north and wasn't concerned. He enjoyed the VMOs in part because he got to improve his skills working with different coalition contingents. Everybody had something to learn from everybody else. There were maladies common to Afghanistan, he explained, that Canadians and Americans didn't see at all in their native environments. He passed on knowledge that in turn improved the heath care of the coalition forces operating here. It was all very symbiotic.

Captain Chenette and I compared notes. We didn't see any pregnant women and we didn't see any teenagers older than thirteen. "We've seen this on other VMOs," she said. "We think the women are scared, so we have to ask the men to bring them here. We get the usual excuses: it's too hot, they're too tired, it's against their religion to leave home, and so on."

The U.S. Special Forces doc was Lieutenant Colonel Tony Littell, who had come all the way from BAF to join the VMO. An experienced man who had worked at U.S. Army Medical Research Institute of Infectious Diseases (USAMRIID) and throughout the SOF community, he and I talked about the role of the VMO and ANA training. "It gives us an opportunity to implement the 'train the trainer' philosophy. These ANA medics here will take all their experience back to their units. It also serves the dual purpose of showing the people that they have an army, and that it is active. The ANA medical system is just starting now and it has some catching up to do with the combat forces. There is about a two-year lag in service support training by comparison."

Tony also explained to me the higher-level operational concepts underlying the VMOs. There was a larger program called Cooperative Medical Assistance (CMA). CMA brought together several partners, as the VMO did, but operated at the regional level to establish a health-care system starting in the urban areas and then dispersing out from there. In theory, the CMAs were the basis for regional health-care committees that would work with the provincial governments and the line ministry reps from Kabul. There was a coordinating link between the provincial-level committee and the military commanders, in this OEF. VMOs were "targeted" using this process so that it wasn't only military operational considerations that dominated VMO deployment. The operative word, once again, was "effects." What effect did the commander want on the ground? What effects did the provincial leadership want on the ground? If the Afghan provincial leadership was disengaged and overly focused on security issues, as the situation in Kandahar, the military commanders (OEF, by default) handled VMO "targeting." One major issue, we agreed, was how to hand over this sort of construct to a civilian authority and transition to Afghan control.

Master Chief Rick Wilson, U.S. Navy, was also working hard in the heat of the day alongside Rashid, an ANA medic. "I've done several VMOs. We think we might even get some Taliban wounded coming in to be treated, pretending to be civilian locals. We've anticipated that and we use it," he explained. See? The coalition isn't so bad after all. Go tell your friends. "On my first VMO, we got hit. But we turned it around and used it as I/O with the message, 'The Taliban don't want you to be healthy.'" I watched as Rick, Tim, and Rashid worked on a malnourished baby, who was wrapped up in a blanket. "This poor guy has a 50 percent chance to live," Rick told me. Rashid explained in Pashtun to the mother how to use formula. The level of ignorance vis-à-vis basic infant care was nothing short of heartbreaking. And it was perpetrated by the Taliban. "Allah will provide." Well, "Allah" was here wearing CADPAT, ACU, ANA gray, and medical smock green.

The separation of the sexes among the Afghans was noticeable: the girls tended to come in the back gate. They were striking because of the colorful veils they were wearing: not burkas, but veils. Then I heard some screaming. The Canadian medics ran into the women's room and closed the door. A couple of the younger kids started to cry and a sympathetic detonation of tears was likely. Julie quickly calmed them down.

I asked Marilynn Chenette what was going on.

"Well, we've found one of those things about rural culture that isn't very nice here."

"What's that?"

"There's a twelve-year-old girl in there."

"Yeah. So?"

"She's suffering from rectal bleeding. She was married last night."

The medical staff did what they could to relieve her suffering, but technically nothing illegal had taken place, so there was little that could be done by our people beyond that.

I needed some air, so I went out back to check out the security. There were some ANA guys with American OMLT mentors showing them how to lay in arcs for a .50-caliber machine gun mounted on a tan pickup truck.

"What's doing?" I asked.

"Not much," the American sergeant said. "We don't want to alarm anybody but we're being watched."

"We are?" I said in mock surprise.

"Yeah. Without being obvious or pointing, look at that high feature. To the right of the pile of rocks there's an OP." And sure enough there was.

"So why don't they do something? Like snipe at us?"

"Well, you heard about the Gumbad Sniper? I hear they used the ammo from an entire AC-130 to get that guy!"

Attacking a VMO, I reflected, wouldn't make sense anyway. The beauty of the VMO was that if the enemy attacked it or stole the items from the people, they lost. They lost in the eyes of the population, which the VMO helped, and they would lose strategically in the information warfare sense if they massacred female medical personnel and children. If the enemy *didn't* attack the VMO, they lost too. The VMO still helped the people. It was the perfect weapon: it was lose-lose for the Taliban, and win-win for us. "Inshallah" and "Allah provides" didn't work, really. And the more contact the rural population had with us, the less they would rely on "Allah provides" and thus the less they would rely on Taliban perception management. The people could see that our people cared about their health and welfare. The local women could see other women with short hair and guns working alongside the men as equals. That seed alone would take root somewhere, with some of the girls someday starting to undermine the local theocracy. It was a long-term effort. It was not measurable. But it could start just like that.

Next to the district center was a large enclosed area loaded with livestock. There were about ten kids squatting down like "Hadji TV," watching something going on. I rounded a truck and saw two women in U.S. Army ACU uniforms injecting the livestock using a pile of injectors on a folding table. One mule was thrashing away, hee-hawing and making a ruckus. "Whoa, boy! Easy!" one of the soldiers said. She fed the mule something and inspected an infected flank.

This part of the VMO team was made up of reservists from the U.S. Midwest. They were all curvy and had names like Bobby Sue and spoke with that relaxed wheat-belt drawl of experienced farmhands. They were right in their element, though they all carried M-4 assault rifles and were no doubt adept at using them, like they were probably adept at using their daddy's Winchesters back home to take out groundhogs. One of them showed a curious Afghan kid how the process worked, though there was an obvious language barrier. She let him inject a cow, to his great delight. Could the Taliban do that? Could they help keep the livestock healthy? Or would Allah just "provide"?

Once individuals were taken care of by the medical staff, they were funneled to a series of sheds where American, Canadian, and British CIMIC personnel worked with the ANA soldiers to hand the women a blanket bundle and the men tools. Each bundle contained seeds, rice, vegetable oil, a crank-powered radio, and some other items. The tools included saws, hammers, picks and shovels, and water hoses. Everything was done with a smile and good-byes said with a hand over the heart, Afghan style. Small groups of local Gumbadians wandered away to use the booty, chatting animatedly.

Is it possible to combat Taliban ideology with Maslow? That concept bugged me as the VMO packed up, moved to the LZ, and waited for the Chinook. We returned to KAF flying evasively at low level through Kandahar airspace and landed at the PRT to drop off the terps and the Afghan docs. The machine popped flares on approach to KAF to confuse any enemy MANPADS. This particular VMO treated nearly four hundred people and I don't know how many animals on that one day. The lack of local medical facilities meant that access to protracted medical care was limited for the Gumbad community. What happened when the meds ran out? The VMO was itself a Band-Aid of sorts. It could address short-term problems, but the community really needed its own clinic and doctor. It could whet the appetite for more, but to get more there had to be a higher level of security. I think these underlying psychological aspects of the VMO could play out in two ways among the local leadership. Some would be conservative and argue that things didn't need to change. Others would see the possibilities on a number of levels and might demand change. That is the important cleavage. And, just as important, each community would have to make the choice: did they want health care and other benefits or not? Then those who wanted change might migrate away to communities where they could get what they wanted. Those who didn't want change would just stay in place. This all assumes, of course, no external influences. In districts that the Taliban moved through and districts that had little security, the local communities who wanted change might in fact be blocked from getting it by Taliban or other coercive elements. There had to be security, there had to be governance from outside the communities present to allow people to make the choice. And that was the conundrum in Gumbad. The mainstay of security was pulling out.

I left Gumbad on the Chinook with an unsettled mind and thought what might happen to those people we helped today if the Taliban groups in Shah Wali Kot came back into the area. That is the human cost of a choice that had to be made. The greater good of getting the Dutch into Oruzgan province, the need to reduce the psychological effects of the horrific IED attacks on the media and population and politicians back in Canada, the fact that at this point some provincial districts were operationally more important than others, meant that the people we had just helped might be revictimized by the enemy despite our best valiant efforts to help them. It was a sobering state of affairs and it disturbed me greatly—especially when the Gumbad district center was attacked by the Taliban later that summer and burned to the ground.

It was after Gumbad that I started to seriously think about what to do with an area after it had been cleared by our forces. The conversations I had with Ian Hope in Zharey and Erik Liebert at the PRT led to an idea for the progressive clearance and then holding of the districts. I sketched it out in my field message pad and, in time, this became known in Canadian organizations and later in ISAF campaign plans as "Clear-Hold-Build."

## OPERATION ROCKET MAN

I was in the process of getting the tour of the Sperwer flight line when at 2035 hours two rockets screamed overhead and exploded with a loud *"CRUMP"* somewhere on the base. The siren went off and we headed for the bunkers. The TUAV crew was in the process of preparing a bird to launch: it was perched on the foldable catapult rail that extended from the back of a 10-ton truck, Skidoo engine revving. With a *"BANG"* it was off. The TUAV flight had to be careful and coordinate with the air space management people: two GR-7 Harriers had taken off and were looking for the Rocketman. Word filtered in that the DFAC near the TF AFGHANISTAN HQ had been hit and there were six casualties. The TUAV flight personnel were really concerned. The roll call indicated that there were people away eating and then there was further information that a member of the flight was in the Role 3 fighting for his life.

This attack was unusual. It was on a Friday—that is, the Muslim holy day—and it was early. Normally the attacks took place between 2200 and 2400 hours. The updated casualty information came in. Eight Kellogg Brown and Root employees were injured, and two Canadians, one seriously. The center tent in the DFAC had been hit. Parenthetically, this was the DFAC where I usually ate and I had a nodding relationship with some of the staff. The "all clear" was given and I drove over to CTF AEGIS to find out what was going on. I passed the crew who were doing their CSI thing on the attack. There was shrapnel gouges everywhere around the DFAC. The main sign was splintered and the tent itself had collapsed. People were mopping up blood. A Canadian soldier had been seriously wounded and, as the hours wore on, his prognosis looked better and better. It was a close call. Apparently, he nearly bled out but was saved by the fact that the Role 3 was about five hundred meters away. An American JAG officer was hit while he was getting ice cream, and a U.S. SOF flight surgeon was seriously wounded. Overall six members of the Kellogg, Brown and Root (KBR) kitchen staff and four military personnel were wounded, some seriously.

The next day I was at Canada House having a coffee with Lieutenant Commander Mark Macintyre, the public affairs officer (PAFFO).

## Maloney Sketch: Clear-Hold-Build

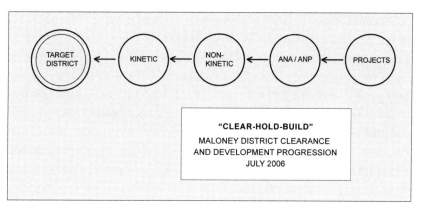

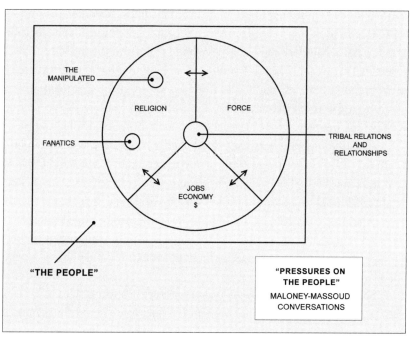

We were both in a surreal mood. Tim Horton's was filming a commercial with the troops and Macintyre was riding herd on it. The producer wanted footage of the soldiers and their weapons so he could film the bullets that would be used to kill the enemy later. I mean, this was less than twelve hours after the rocket attack on the DFAC and the producer of the commercial was trying to emulate the "Normandy" commercial Tim Horton's did on the anniversary of the invasion. Tim's had widely distributed ball caps that had the old American "chocolate chip" desert cam pattern on them. I'm not sure if the good people at Tim's knew that or if it was coincidental. Dave Fraser was wearing one when he was interviewed by the media, who promptly asked about the rocket attack from last night. Macintyre had to remind General Dave to remove the ball cap before the interview could commence. It was surreal: Tim Horton's, doughnuts, rocket attacks, war. An American corporate-war conspiracy theory would feature oil and avarice and a Canadian corporate-war conspiracy theory would feature doughnuts and smiley-faced people.

It reminded me and Macintyre of *Catch 22* and the conversation got into Milo Minderbinder-isms. We had both heard the latrine ("That's LA-trine—from the French") rumors that KBR paid a bonus to its employees every time they had to put body armor on and go for the bunkers. Therefore, the theory went, KBR employees were paying Rezik Sherzai to have his people launch the rockets so everybody could make money. An alternative version was that Rezik had a stake in the cement plant that had the contract to pour all of the concrete antirocket bunkers, so it was in his best interest to ensure there was a steady rain of rockets against KAF. Of course, none of this was provable and it probably wasn't true—but hey—anything could happen in Afghanistan. I knew there was a rocket attack–betting pool at KAF. People bet on the number of rockets and the number of casualties. Maybe they were fixing the pool by paying off the rocketeers. . . .

So who was using whom? Was Tim Horton's using the CF, or was the CF using Tim Horton's? Lieutenant Colonel John Conrad was quoted by the media saying that Tim Horton's was part of Canada's social fabric, just like the CF was. Knowing John, it was all tongue in cheek, but then people started repeating it and it took on a life of its own. When he heard what was going on, Mark retracted into the fetal position and let out a primal scream that only a PAFFO could let out under such circumstances. Then somebody in Ottawa got upset. . . . John's response: "So now what?

We're going to get sued by Second Cup? I'm in AFGHANISTAN."[16] I blamed the war correspondent Chris Wattie. It was Chris' media exposé of corporate stupidity at Tim's that shamed them into deploying a Tim Horton's franchise to KAF to support the troops in the first place. My theory, which I related to Macintyre, was that Canada did this strategically to counter the American fast-food dominance in KAF that consisted of Burger King, Subway, and Pizza Hut. But it took American C-17s to lift the Tim Horton's trailers to KAF . . . so was the USAF co-opted by Tim's corporate influence? Hmmmmm . . . the doughnut-military-industrial complex. Tim Horton's versus the Taliban. Tim Horton's: A proud supporter of counterinsurgency. I thought that the troops could use empty Tim Horton's cups to replace the Vietnam-era "death card" on enemy bodies—or what was left of them. Macintyre retracted into a fetal position and begged me to keep my voice down.

But I digress. Captain Kevin Barry was annoyed. Or at least irked. I could barely tell since Kevin is the consummate professional. We had a coffee at this old hut that served as a "rest easy" in the middle of the old USAF tent compound. Kevin explained that he had been assigned to Operation Rocket Man duty, along with a composite platoon drawn from TF ORION. He'd rather be out in the districts killing Taliban.

Rocket Man was a vital but incredibly frustrating job. The purpose was to deter rocket attacks against KAF, but it was like trying to squeeze Jell-O with your fist. It was one of those jobs—like taking out the garbage—that just had to be done. Julie Roberge explained to me that the rocket attack issue operated on a number of levels. There was the immediate impact of the attacks on the base and its personnel, which was comparatively minimal, but there was an I/O dimension that reached back to Canada. The media reported every rocket attack, just like it reported every IED attack. The perception was generated by the media back in Canada that KAF was somehow under siege, that the rocket attacks were constant, that the enemy held the initiative and, by implication, we were losing because we weren't "doing anything" about it. The government, in this case the prime minister's office, started to intervene and ask detailed, tactical questions and demand detailed, tactical answers. These people were trying to micromanage the issue so they could respond to the media. The Department of National Defence was trying to stave off these people and stop the interference, but then we were into civil-military relations issues that were in the upper stratosphere.

How does one explain that rocket attacks on one hand really aren't a problem, and then explain ten seriously wounded in action? It is exactly this gray area that the media were unable to grasp effectively. On the operational level, the attacks accomplished very little. They killed and wounded a comparatively small number of people. But each wounding or death was considered by the media to be a massively horrible national tragedy *each time* it took place. Yes, there was the human dimension and it was indeed tragic—especially if you or your family was on the receiving end—but in the overall scope of the campaign, it was minor. How do you address the complexities of this proportion?

Kevin and his QRF had to labor under these conditions. They were caught between two stools at this time. The Romulans were pulling out of the KAF defense task and were going to be replaced by the RAF Regiment, but there was a gap in the coverage and TF ORION was going to help cover it off. The Rocket Man QRF actually was a divisional asset; it reported to CJTF-76 in Bagram and had to be "cut" to support the Joint Defence Operations Centre (JDOC) the organization in charge of KAF's defense. The JDOC was responsible for the defensive "bubble" surrounding KAF, or the range of a 107-mm rocket to the camp. The JDOC had a number of tools at its disposal, including a UTAM radar that tracked the point of origin (POO) and the point of impact (POI) of a rocket attack. JDOC also controlled a number of cameras that could see at night.[17]

Kevin's Rocket Man QRF platoon was kept at a high state of readiness right next to the helicopter flight line. The platoon also kept their LAV IIIs there, too, in case they had to respond on the ground. In some cases, the QRF had access to AH-64 and even B-1 support.

There was a report that during the attack the previous night two men were seen running from the POO. Two AH-64 Apaches were launched, but one crashed and killed its crew—nobody knew why. So the tally from this attack was really two dead, ten wounded, and a multimillion dollar AH-64 destroyed, not just ten wounded and a bunch of canvas ripped. The QRF and an EOD standby detachment jumped on board two CH-47s and took off for the POO. On landing, Kevin did a sweep of the area that turned up two men, a boy, two women, and two girls. They were all afraid and claimed, when Kevin sat down with them, not to know what was going on. Nothing was found when the compounds were searched.

While the QRF searched the POO for clues, the Romanian Immediate Reaction Team found the downed AH-64. EOD was dispatched to secure the unused ordnance on the helicopter, while the RAF Regiment mortar teams fired illumination rounds.

I met with Squadron Leader Macintyre of the RAF Regiment who explained some of the aspects of Rocket Man. "We see two types of 107-mm rockets here. There are the stake-launched ones, where the enemy sets up an 'x,' lays the rocket on it, adjusts the stakes, and attaches a timer and battery and leaves. We also are seeing a buried, tube-launched version that is completely hidden underground." I learned that there were two suspected rocket cells operating around KAF and they had their own signatures. The stake-launched and tube-launched rockets weren't used together.

The 107-mm rockets were made in China and came into Afghanistan from Pakistan in packs of twelve.[18] The pack would usually be fired over the course of three days, then there would be a lull until the cells could be resupplied from their dumps near Quetta, Pakistan. This could take up to twenty days, depending on several factors. Shane Schreiber explained to me that the J-2 shop conducted every possible form of pattern analysis and it got weird—they tried to correlate the new moon, the time of month, religious holidays—and came up with nothing tangible except the time of the evening. The pattern analysis apparently found some correlation to Ian Hope's presence in KAF. If he was in from the field, rockets would be fired that night. In the old days, rockets never, ever fell on camps I was in, but this changed in 2006. A new correlation?

"It's just like *Catch-22*, baby!" Shane Schreiber exclaimed. "The local merchants and trucking companies have to have something to do with this to get the rockets in here. And those people also support KAF operations. General Fraser is going to close the market until we get some good intelligence on who's doing this." Closing the market—that was severe. More than one hundred vetted local merchants held a market weekly in a carefully guarded and swept compound where the troops could buy souvenirs. It was a major source of hard currency for a lot of people, especially the carpet dealers. Shane and I speculated: Would this move trigger a spike in proxy violence between the merchants and KBR? Were the coalition forces and the Taliban in fact being manipulated by KBR and the local merchants? Were we *their* proxies? Or had Shane and I been in Afghanistan too long?

Kevin and his QRF would still have to deploy at night into uncertain and unknown situations, regardless. A number of lessons had already been learned. Early on in the tour, TF ORION deployed sniper detachments to positions northeast of KAF: they were promptly mortared by the Taliban as they crawled in their Ghillie suits into their hides. That particular area was just too populated and too unfriendly. The cluster of villages there had a number of grievances that had not been addressed. Back in 2001 an airstrike went astray and killed a number of civilians. The locals hadn't forgotten. Then it looked like commercial expansion along Highway 4 (including what I heard but couldn't confirm was Colonel TJ's new SUV dealership!) was encroaching on their land. Both grievances were ripe for Taliban exploitation. One cell operated in this area. The other cell fired from positions north-northwest of KAF. It took advantage of the ratline coming in from Panjwayi district to the southwest suburbs of Kandahar City, but skirted Dand district, which was controlled by a very anti-Taliban policeman who wasn't afraid to get heavy-handed.

There was a break in the case, however, and it related to the PRT. Our old friend Colonel Tor Jan, whose crew handled PRT security, was subjected to a grenade attack that wounded three of his guys. One of the perpetrators was apprehended by the Dand ANP—and he offered to give up one of the rocket men. The ANP, with apparently little or no coalition assistance, raided a compound complex in a village north of the KAF runway. They bagged a four-man rocket cell: a father and his three sons. The possibility that the grenade attack against Colonel TJ was some form of payback for his land expansion issues couldn't be discounted, nor could the linkage between that issue and the grievances in that area and the rocket attacks. The larger question in terms of dealing with counterinsurgency warfare was how exactly could coalition forces influence this sort of problem? How could coalition forces influence this sort of problem replicated in, say, a hundred different locations? Or were we merely bystanders who sustained collateral damage that resulted from somebody else's muscular dispute resolution mechanism?

PART *Three*

# EXECUTION

In the wake of the northern Kandahar operations and the multiple IED attacks, CTF AEGIS' attention shifted to events unfolding in Helmand province. By this point in late June, the British HELMAND TF was getting into position, its "laydown" from FOB Bastion to Musa Qala. SOF operations continued in the northern part of the province and 3 Para moved into platoon houses and FOBs in the Sangin Valley. Two problems emerged. First, belligerent forces—and it wasn't clear whether this was the tribal dynamic, Taliban, narcos, or all three—started to move on Musa Qala. Then somebody started firing mortars at the USPI contractors handling security at Kajaki Dam. This reverberated up to CJTF-76 and higher. Kajaki had once supplied almost all the electrical power to Kandahar City and the region. To improve output, a vast USAID program to refurbish the turbines was in the works and that program demanded a higher level of security in the area. It was a showcase aid project and, as with anything put up in a showcase, somebody will try to break the glass just for the hell of it.

Musa Qala seemed to be an enemy focal point, but then there were reports that the Sangin police had done a power-sharing deal with the Taliban. Then there was a flurry of threat reporting around Geresk and then Garmser. It looked like all of the main population centers along the northern Helmand river valley were about to be attacked, perhaps simultaneously.

It was around this time that ISTAR reporting increased over in Zharey and Panjwayi districts. Reinfiltration of Zharey district was assumed after Operation Jagra, but now enemy leadership targets were moving from Helmand into Maywand through Band-e Timor and into Zharey and Panjwayi. On 23 June "B" Company got into a firefight in Mushan while conducting a recce for a VMO. The .50 calibers in the G-Wagon gun trucks sang their song and four enemy were killed; numerous blood trails were found. The next night SOF went into Pashmul after a leadership target. This operation reportedly resulted in the death of a significant leader who was trying to unify Taliban groups still suffering the combined effects of the elimination of the Baqi network, Operation Yadgar and Operation Jagra. We also heard that Mullah Dadullah Lang was near Pashmul and that the SOF job was probably meant for him.

"B" Company and the PRT then reported that local civilians in Zharey were told by Taliban sympathizers to stay off the roads and to stop clearing brush away from the sides of trails and in the irrigation systems. The local Taliban cells were instructed, after several leaders met, that they were to be prepared to establish permanent checkpoints throughout the district and to be prepared to defend them. The combination of Mullah Dadullah Lang's presence and these kinds of defensive preparations was a significant indicator that the enemy was changing his approach. More reports flowed in that Taliban from Helmand were moving into Maywand and that Mullah Dadullah Lang was moving back and forth between Helmand and Zahrey.

All the while, KAF was showered with rockets and "B" Company was trying to keep order on Highway 1. On the night of 4 July, "B" Company heard firing from an ANP checkpoint west of PBW. "C" Company had a platoon of LAVs in a discreet overwatch position on counter-ambush duty. As a platoon left PBW, it was ambushed with RPGs from rooftop positions along the road. LAV III 25-mm guns swept the roofs, while Nick Grimshaw's guys called in an AH-64. A "B" Company patrol found four sets of body parts and weapons on the roofs. The patrol had to count the parts and divide by four because the 25-mm high-explosive (HE) rounds had fragmented the bodies. The Apache got on station and tracked the retreating enemy to a compound. A patrol later found twelve more dead bodies. The compound had been used as an enemy casualty collection point.

The situation in Helmand deteriorated further after 3 July. HELMAND TF reported to the JOC a significant and notable increase in enemy activity. Their police contacts told them they hadn't seen anything like this in the previous year and they were concerned. Then the USPI contract security at the Kajaki Dam deserted, nearly to a man. TF HELMAND wanted to rush into Sangin and Kajaki, but the Helmand governor wanted coalition forces to stay put in the south. He was worried that any movement of coalition troops might add to the panic that was developing in the province and add to enemy information ops.

There seemed to be a relationship between the Helmand buildup and the Zharey buildup, but at the time it wasn't clear exactly what that relationship was. It looked like the enemy was fortifying Zharey district as a precursor to interdicting Highway 1. At the same time it looked like they were going to pressurize the partially deployed British forces in Helmand. Or maybe the Helmand buildup was a feint and the Zharey buildup would serve as a base for operations into Kandahar City. Or both in sequence. The effects were potentially catastrophic for RC South. Seizure of multiple population centers in Helmand, however temporary, coupled with the severing of Highway 1, however temporary, would be a huge I/O victory. Bonus points if they got into Kandahar City and wreaked havoc.

What was clear, however, was that Zharey was crucial to whatever it was that they were up to. The presence of more and more MVT leadership, including the possible presence of a HiG leader in there, seemed to be something beyond the mere replacement of attrited bosses and commanders. The enemy was displaying a level of sophistication not yet seen in 2006. What emerged later was that there was a Taliban *shura* in Nahlgam sometime in June between Mullah Daduallah Lang, Mullah Ramatullah, and Mullah Mansoor at which they reshaped operations vis-à-vis Zharey and Panjwayi districts. It looked as if a number of ORION and SOF TICs in the area had "bumped" these leaders' close protection parties.

CTF AEGIS was carrying out contingency planning to deal with the Helmand issues and CJTF-76 was keeping a close eye on progress. Lieutenant Colonel Mark Brewer and his staff worked up what they called Operation Hewad, which apparently meant "Homeland" but was subject to differing and humorous pronunciations—*he*-wad, *hew*-ad. No two people pronounced it the same way. CJTF-76 thought it was Heward. American, Australian, and Canadian accents mangled it even further.

Hewad was designed to address the Sangin buildup problem. At the same time, various SOF organizations were eyeing the region and slavering, waiting for leadership targets to develop. Several started to pop up within the Sangin–Musa Qala–Kajaki triangle, and they now wanted in too. It was a virtual Taliban leadership convention: There was Koo Agha, the architect of several sophisticated ambushes. He had been wounded in a Predator strike in May, but was back, tanned and fit after recuperating in Pakistan. And there was Haji Matin, suspected of being killed, still alive and moving around. He had a team with money and a facilitator and had a grudge against the town of Musa Qala. A recruiter named Tor Jan was collecting the faithful in Musa Qala district. There were two weapons facilitators in Kajaki, and there were disaffected members of the Akenzudah family who were in contact with Taliban leaders.

After some debate, the decision was made to mount a suboperation of Hewad, called Operation Augustus. The British HELMAND TF was itching to have a go with an air assault, but that would be useless without enough blocking forces, so AEGIS agreed to concentrate the bulk of TF ORION and TF WARRIOR in Helmand to support it. TF BUSHMASTER, the combined 2-87 Infantry and U.S. Special Forces task force involved in the Bagran Valley operations, was also brought in, courtesy of CJTF-76 and CJSOTF. The general idea was to position the blocking forces (Hewad) and then mount Augustus with 3 Para. SOF could track and kill any MVTs trying to exfiltrate the area of operations. AEGIS was able to get CJTF-76 concurrence by associating the Helmand operations with Operation Mountain Thrust.

Dave Fraser's purpose, then, was to attack and destroy Taliban command and control in Helmand province and deny enemy influence in Sangin district in Helmand, and Panjwayi and Zharey districts in Kandahar. He also was able to secure a boatload of CERP money—more than $1 million—from CJTF-76 for effects mitigation and aid projects. AEGIS also framed these operations as an I/O campaign. The target audience was the governors of Helmand and Kandahar provinces, and, not incidentally, President Karzai. The president had been publicly critical of coalition operations in RC South of late. As for the population, the I/O plan was going to "message" that the Taliban could not provide aid projects, but that the coalition and the government could.

CTF AEGIS had to accept risk. Ian Hope pointed out that he couldn't guarantee the security of the Tarin Kot Road and that the Dutch DTF deploying into Oruzgan would have to take care of itself. FOB Martello would have to be virtually stripped for the operations. The Dutch and the Australians were engaging the Taliban in the Chora Valley and might have to stop to take care of their supply lines. The possible spillover effect was that Stage III Expansion might be delayed if the Dutch didn't think they were ready in time. There were other pressures: The ANA from 209 Corps had to return to northern Afghanistan at some point. CJTF-76 was preparing to launch Operation Mountain Lion in RC East, enablers were tied up hunting HVTs in RC East. . . . It was all interconnected.

Pam Isfeld was involved with an interesting piece that was called Operation Rana, also known as the mega-*shura* or super-*shura*. The idea was to hold a massive *shura* in Sangin or Musa Qala after the operations were completed. The national PTS coordinator, the legendary Dr. Mojaeddedi, would be flown in from Kabul to KAF and then by Afghan Mi-17 helicopter to the mega-*shura* where he would link up with Governor Daoud. There were two objectives: PTS as many Taliban regional leaders as possible, and allow local grievances to be expressed and recorded so they could be addressed by the government. The potential I/O effects were tremendous, so Dave Fraser agreed to incorporate Rana into the planning.

In the middle of all this, Shane Schreiber and his staff were confronted with problems that were developing in Kandahar City. Information was coming in from the JCC that the enemy was meeting openly with people in a mosque in the Loy Wala neighborhood, which is in the "cone," the northern part of the city. There were reports that local people were not comfortable with the presence of the enemy so close to home; subsequent reports revealed that there was a network of safe houses and caches located in a number of mosques. There was some SOF activity in the southwest part of the city, in an area that used to be the terminus of the Zharey–Panjwayi–Kandahar City ratline.

On the heels of those developments, Shane learned that six UN deminers had been kidnapped in the city. The Afghans had been handling this without coalition support, which itself was significant. They were now frustrated by their inability to track the kidnappers and were asking for help. NDS, police, the intelligence community, and CANSOF were all spun up, CANSOF because of their expertise in hostage rescue. The assessment was that this kidnapping was specifically designed to intimidate the UN and NGO community and keep their activities suppressed. Then Major General Freakley started reaching down with a lot of good ideas. In effect, CTF AEGIS formed an ad hoc Crisis Action Team to handle this problem and the intricate coordination issues between the Afghans, AEGIS, SOF, and the JCC. It was impressive.

"What is the historical background on kidnaps here?" Shane asked the intelligence people.

"Well, they don't end well. There was an Indian engineer kidnapped and beheaded. There was also a kitchen worker from FOB Gheko kidnapped and beheaded. UNAMA is new, it's big, and is therefore a big target."

That was at 1100 hours. At 1355 hours, word was received at AEGIS from the Afghans that the kidnappers had released the deminers, but kept their vehicles, IDs, cell phones, and equipment. So now we had an enemy element in the city that could behave in "Trojan Horse" fashion at a time of his choosing. That was worrying.

Less than an hour later, a 3 Para call sign in Helmand reported a TIC near Sangin. You could hear the gunfire over the radio in the JOC. They were taking RPG and small arms fire and were requesting air support.

"What have we got?" Shane asked. Staff Sergeant Clayter from the U.S. Air Force calmly checked his computer lists. "We have two AH-64s. There is a B-1B bomber available with twenty-four JDAMs that has playtime. He wants planes, he's gonna get planes!" The staff went through a procedure so that the B-1B knew where to drop. "We have to do that procedure ourselves," he explained to me. "In 2001 some guys here in the field put their own grid into the system and not the target grid. They bombed themselves." In five minutes it was all over and 3 Para was doing its BDA.

Then the rocket warning siren at KAF went off. I slept through it, but it produced a flurry of activity on the base. Apparently, the NDS had a source that ratted out one of the rocket teams. This source came forward because his people were employed on a project funded with CERP money and he wanted to show his appreciation. A police patrol in Kvosh Ab north of KAF also received information that there were rocketeers nearby. The police engaged some Taliban, who were in the process of setting up a rocket, with an RPG. Blood trails were found in the morning. The two 107-mm rockets that were recovered were made in China but had English markings—that is, they came from Pakistan. A PKM and an RPG were also found.

I went over to the ORION TOC to see what was up. "Do you want to sit in on the ROC [rehearsal of concept] drill?" Mason Stalker asked me. "Sure. I like war games," I said.

"Oh no. ROC drills go beyond war games. We use them as a coordinating tool, to synchronize the flow of events, and to make sure the groupings and tasks are balanced."

All of the "players" were present in the planning room. Almost all of them were in their twenties or early thirties. As the process played out in the course of the morning, I was duly impressed by the maturity and the knowledge that this group brought to bear. These weren't the grizzled older staff officers I remembered from the 1980s. This team was energetic. They maintained a healthy level of cynicism. They knew it was real and that the lives of their men literally depended on what they were doing.

"OK, we're going to go into a series of compounds in Pashmul, disrupt enemy operations, and destroy any caches. We'll then project to Maywand and then up to Ghorak in preparations of coalition operations in Helmand province. Keep in mind, people, this is still considered part of Mountain Thrust," Mason reminded everyone.

"The sequence of events is as follows: Clear out Objective Puma." Mason pointed to the map. "Transition to Maywand and Ghorak. Consolidate Zharey, then block the Ghorak passes into Helmand. Wait for a series of operations to go down, then extract from the passes. The Zharey part will be called Operation Zahar or 'Sword.'"

The idea was to have the ANP establish vehicle control points on Highway 1, while a British force consisting of two troops from the Household Cavalry Regiment in their Scimitars and a Estonian light infantry platoon moved west of Maywand to act as a screen. Then the whole battle group, all three companies and recce, would converge on Objective Puma. Assessments of Puma indicated it was the most likely concentration of enemy resources and personnel. Unlike Operation Jagra, where there weren't enough resources to surround the enemy, Operation Zahar would have everything that could be brought to bear. Objective Puma would be hit from three sides at once, with Recce Platoon screening what would look like a gap but was in fact a trap. To make things even more interesting, Operation Zahar would be initiated at night for maximum surprise and deception.

The TF ORION planning staff knew that there were many eyes and cell phones in Kandahar City, so the trick was to get the battle group into position in assembly areas at night before the operation was launched. The deception plan was a choreographed production. PBW and the Panjwayi district center were the assembly areas. "B" Company was at PBW, "A" Company was up north at FOB Martello, "C" Company was in Spin Boldak, while Recce Platoon was in a number of locations with its sniper dets. How do you move a whole battle group—artillery, engineers, logistics—from all these locations to the assembly areas without the enemy realizing what was going on?

The first move was to have "B" Company leave PBW and head east into the city, while "A" Company and Recce Platoon drove south from FOB Martello. The forces would essentially intermix in the western part of Kandahar City. "A" Company and Recce would proceed to PBW so it would look like "B" Company returning to base. "B" Company would then shift to blackout drive and head south to Route Fosters, move west, and hole up in the Panjwayi district center. "C" Company would move in small groups to KAF, into the city, then follow "B" Company into the Panjwayi district center. "B" Company would meet at the PRT in the day to link up with the ANA.

The American RCPs would follow later. Their job was to keep the routes from Objective Puma back to the assembly areas clear once TF ORION had gone in. The guns and the mortars would move at night from FOB Martello to a presurveyed gun position north of Highway 1.

The leaks in the ANP revealed by the Chenar operation had to be addressed. For Zahar the only police involvement would be along Highway 1—and the police weren't going to be told what was going on. They were to be kept on the perimeter and out of the objective area, just in case the enemy was wearing ANP uniforms. As for the ANA, they were going to be part of the operation. An infantry company from 209 Corps was positioned in the 530 Compound, which was an ANA FOB in the west end of the City. One Afghan platoon would be attached with American mentors to each Canadian company. All three Canadian companies were down approximately a platoon anyway because of the leave plan.

There was the issue of enablers. Captain Chris Hunt, who worked with ISATR, was concerned that the presence of UAVs, particularly the loud TUAV, over Zharey or anywhere near Zharey might give the game away. The U.S. liaison officer nodded and explained that Predator support was available but would be kept away until required. Canadian Coyotes would accompany the British–Estonian screen to the west to catch any "squirters."

Once the Puma sites were exploited, the whole kit and kaboodle minus "B" Company would recock and head west. The idea at this point was that TF ORION would support Operation Augustus in Helmand by blocking the two passes that ran from Ghorak to Helmand with a company, and then by moving another company to FOB ROB to backstop the British operation. TF ORION also had to protect TF MAURAUDER, an American logistics unit that would be transiting along Highway 1 to resupply TF BUSHMASTER operating in northern Helmand. When the British operation was complete, ORION would redeploy to its positions throughout Kandahar province. At least, that was the plan.

## Operation Zahar: The Battle of Pashmul, 7–10 July 2006

Dave Fraser had given me standing instructions that when Major General Ben Freakley was around, I wasn't to be. I understood that the CG didn't like media; even though I wasn't media, Commander CTF AEGIS didn't want any misunderstandings. When the CG's arrival was imminent, I went over to TF ORION's TOC where I bumped into Ian Hope. "You're coming with us on this one. Get your kit and move to the marshalling yard by 1400." I collected my body armor and my pack from my quarters and enough moderately priced cigars from Green Beans to last a couple of days in the field.

As usual, it was blazing hot in the middle of the day. Even the crushed gravel looked like it wanted shade as the Niner Tac and "A" Company vehicles roared into columns. The mechs had a couple of tents with refrigerators under them. In time they were empty of water. Kirk Gallinger and Pete Leger pulled up. Gibby, Strong, Raike, and Pichovich all dismounted the LAV.

"Hey, Doc! You're going with us? Right on!" as we shook hands. I pulled mine back at the last second with Strong. "Not doing any Dirty Sanchez's lately, have you?" I inquired.

"We've made room for you in 95-E, the CIMIC G-Wagon," Pete told me as sweat dripped off his sunburnt nose. "You know the plan?"

"Yeah. We deploy to PBW, laager, then go in around midnight."

Someone passed me a Browning 9-mm pistol. I checked the action and the mag, strapped it on, and trudged over to the CIMIC G-Wagon where a familiar Captain Walter Martin and Sergeant Dan Guillaumme greeted me. I slung my kit inside and hydrated. It was still that old Army game of "hurry up and wait" as the departure timings faded away. Again. And again.

"Damn brass," someone groused. One of them wanted to say goodbye and good luck, I guess. Then Major General Ben Freakley, Brigadier General Dave Fraser, and entourage entered the marshalling area. The "A" Company guys and Niner Tac lined up in ranks and the CG went up and down talking to every other soldier. Then the CG came over to me where I was waiting with the terps. Dave's eyes got wide when he realized I was present. The CG walked up and gripped my hand.

"Errr, General, this is Dr. Sean Maloney. He's a military historian who is joining us."

The buzz-cutted General Freakley looked up at me, waaaay waaaay up (in a *Friendly Giant* sort of way) with a strange expression—and didn't let go of my hand. "Good to have you with us," he finally said.

"Good to be here, general," I said. "I wouldn't miss it for the world." So much for keeping me away from the CG. . . .

The general called for a huddle and he gave the troops an American-style pregame pep talk. One of the more seasoned "A" Company guys was wearing shades and his floppy CADPAT hat, chewing gum with his arms crossed in an attitude of, "Let's just get on with it, eh?" And we did. I climbed into the G-Wagon behind Walter, Dan started the engine, and we were off.

The column deployed very late in the afternoon taking a meandering route through Kandahar City, what some of the guys called the Crane Route because of the rusting remains of a giant crane that stood beside an unfinished building in a southwest district. It took forever. Everybody kept a close eye out for suicide bombers. We didn't need that kind of delay, not now. Walter fiddled with the air conditioning, but it was a futile battle. As we exited the more built-up part of the western city, I could see the partially smashed grain elevator to the right of the road. It still boasted some rotting Cyrillic letters in the setting sun. Then we passed the ANA compound where the gate guards waved at us.

We rounded the curve near the mosque and community center right before the bridge over the Arghandab River and slowed down. Without any warning, I heard a deep "plunk" sound and the armored glass right next to me instantaneously transformed into a broken crescent that went from the top of the window frame to the bottom. My heart contracted as my brain in a microsecond made the connection between the nonpenetrating round and where I was sitting.

"Shit! We're being shot at!"

Walter had his headset on and the air-conditioning fan was going full blast.

"Hey! We're taking fire!" I yelled. Walter turned around languidly.

"What?"

"They're trying to kill us, Walter!" I yelled.

"Oh!" he exclaimed and struggled to call in a TIC, but by that time the intrepid Dan Guillaumme had accelerated across the bridge to get "off the X" and the column just kept on going. It took a few klicks for my heart rate to return to normal.

"Those *fucking assholes!*" I yelled, and exhaled a lung full of air. "*Fuckers!* Trying to kill me *again, goddamit!*" I felt better.

"A" Company deployed as it moved down Highway 1, waiting for the ambush that didn't come. We pulled into PBW and I dismounted from the G-Wagon to get some air.

"What's this about a round?" one of the guys from another vehicle asked with a skeptical tone of voice. I showed him the window.

"It's just a rock!"

"Bullshit. It's an aimed shot."

"No it isn't." And the debate started. Denial is an interesting thing. I pointed to the indentation where the round hit. "What the hell is this, then?" I asked. A bunch of guys had a CSI-like discussion of whether it was a 9-mm, 5.56-mm, or 7.62-mm. "Nah, 7.62 would have penetrated," one of the guys said. "It had to be a rock." I backed off to calm down.

Billy B. was standing in the shadows, a cupped hand over his cigarette as I walked by.

"That wasn't a rock," he said quietly as he spun the butt away. "They're full of shit. I was the top gunner behind you guys. Nobody threw a rock. It looks like they fired down the river or from the community center. Pretty good shot, too."

Major Mason Stalker and part of the TOC had deployed forward to PBW and were preparing a briefing. As it turned out, Lieutenant General Mike Gauthier, command of Canadian Expeditionary Forces Command, happened to be at PBW . . . and the show was on. The room was humid and airless When it was full of the command staff, we all dripped sweat. It had to be 105 degrees F (40 degrees C) in that room with no air-conditioning. I kept passing water to Lieutenant Colonel Simon Hetherington; the water came from a fridge without power. Mason and Ian walked through the plan one last time and General Gauthier was assuaged. Until the Sigs guys explained that there was a forcewide crypto change scheduled for 0430 hours or so . . . right when we would be fighting the battle! Every vehicle and manpack radio would have to change crypto. A workaround was devised.

Everybody was keyed up. This was history in the making, as I knew more than most. Operation Zahar was the first full battle-group deliberate attack for the Canadian Army since the Korean War. Yes, since 1953. There had been a couple of actions during the "peacekeeping" era, but nothing like this at all.

The ISTAR indicators were still in the green. The enemy was unaware. The deployment to the assembly areas had gone off without a hitch. Even the enemy's usually efficient spotter network was confused and reporting only fragments that night. It looked like a series of routine moves to them. Major Gallagher's guns made their way down from Shah Wali Kot and passed PBW, heading for their position. As he explained to me later, "We knew it was in the middle of an old Soviet minefield north of Highway 1. We'd recce'd it before. Part of it was clear in the center, and we figured that the mines would deter an enemy attack on the firing line. We did it all under blackout conditions, deploying the guns from the tractors, piling up the rounds, and doing the survey. Right in the middle of a minefield!"

It was pitch black. Everybody who could had gone to ground. Pete Leger was smoking and I could see Kirk pacing in the gloom. Dan had set up one of the cots for me and I crashed more or less immediately.

Suddenly, Dan shook me awake. I woke up feeling as if I hadn't nodded off at all. It hadn't occurred to me yet that I could lose my life on this operation, which was just as well. I had the same feeling I used to get when I was in competitive swimming, when I was young and knew nothing about nothing, just the exhilaration of exploding off the starting block, cleaving the cold water and sprinting for the finish to beat the hell out of the other competitors.

It was time.

The vehicle crews taped empty water bottles on their antennas and put infrared glow sticks into them for identification, friend or foe, purposes. Kirk and Pete had already sorted out the order of march. This was critical, as Kirk explained in the briefing: "The approach route off Highway 1 had been carefully recce'd. We know which routes will take LAV and which ones won't. It'll be dark, and we'll be in blackout drive. Don't get hung up! The roads are narrow and have walls on either side, just like the bocage country in Normandy. Keep moving but keep the speed down. We don't want too much dust." 1 Platoon (1-1) under Captain Kevin Schamuhn and Warrant Officer Justin Mackay would lead with its LAVs. The Bison ambulance would be up front, too. 2 Platoon (1-2) led by Lieutenant Ben Richard and Warrant Officer Mark Pickford was next, with the command group following. The command group had Kirk and Pete's LAV, the Engineer (E-11E or Echo) LAV, and the artillery (G-11 or Golf) LAV with the Slayer 11 JTAC on board. The CIMIC and PSYOPS G-Wagons were interspersed between the three command group LAVs, so Kirk and Pete were in front, and the Echo LAV was behind us. The ANA platoon was behind us; their task was to move up in daylight and link up because they had no night vision capability. "OK. Everything clear?" Kirk asked. There were a few "Roger Ds" and thumbs up.

I had to hand it to Ian and his planning staff. This operation took guts: a night approach in severely restricted terrain. The enemy wouldn't anticipate it. TF ORION would be right on top of the Objective Puma before the enemy even realized what was going on. If we were lucky. It would only take one antitank mine, one IED to stall an advancing company.

It was around 0000 hours when we left PBW. There was a bright, bright quarter moon as the Red Devils motored west along Highway 1. Ten minutes later, the column turned south onto a dirt road and I could see a white schoolhouse shining in the moonlight to the left of the road. Within five minutes, 1 Platoon called out "Contact!" on the radio and I saw streams of red 25-mm rounds going out and sporadic enemy shots in our direction. It was on.

The night battle was a series of discrete events that, when lashed together, looks like a narrative but is far more disjointed. I was sitting in the back of the 95-E G-Wagon, so I had a pretty good view forward and to the sides. Dan and Walter were using night vision goggles but with the moonlight I could get a sense of what was going on. I had an crooknecked Army flashlight with a red filter that I rigged from the handle on the back of the codriver's seat so I was able to keep track of what was happening in a field message pad. Dan already had the radios set to the right nets so I could hear what "A" Company was doing. There was also the ORION

Operation Zahar, 7–10 July 2006

battle-group net. We could hear Nick Grimshaw's and Bill Fletcher's companies calling in contacts. It was immediately clear that we had put our fist into a hornets' nest. After crossing the Arghandab River, Nick's guys began taking serious fire as they made their way west paralleling the river, where the enemy had an observation post line. Bill was hung up as his lead LAV pumped out the 25-mm northwest of the Pashmul School.

We were moving slowly along the road when I saw an RPG round streak red over the artillery LAV in front of us. Tracer from an enemy automatic weapon twisted into the sky. Kevin Schamuhn had his LAV's antenna shot off and was having comms problems up front.

"This is 1-1. Contact left, in the field!" LAV turrets with their 25-mm guns traversed left and poured red fire over a wall into the field. The night vision equipment made it like daytime for the gunners.

"ORION 1-9, there are too many TICs in progress and the terrain is too constricted. Close air support not advised, I say again, close air not advised."

There were four shots from the nine o'clock position that ricocheted off our vehicle. Walter called it in to the Echo and Golf LAVs, but they were having problems locating the source. It was only 0117 hours.

Then there was firing from the west, to our right.

"One Niner, there are kids fleeing the area." The civilian population was now on the move—not good for us or them. The enemy might even try to exfiltrate among them and then get in behind us, but that is what the trailing ANA platoon was for.

"One Niner, this is 1-1," 1 Platoon called in. "We've missed the turn onto the planned route. We're turning around. There is sporadic civilian population moving north to Highway 1. We see kids on people's backs."

"One Niner, roger, over."

A section from 1 Platoon dismounted from a LAV to search for the road. They startled eight civilians with children and, wearing night vision equipment, scared the kids, who probably thought they were monsters.

"One One. More kids and parents heading north."

By 0140 it was quiet again in the "A" Company route, but "B" Company to the south was having a tough time. Our column inched forward. I dozed off but bounced awake at 0225 hours when 2 Platoon called in a contact. "Light 'em up!" Ben Richard called over the radio. More 25-mm firing on targets to the right. "One enemy KIA, over."

I heard a LAV from "C" Company call in an RPG hit.

The horizon in front of us was lit up with flash after flash. Then the trailing LAV from 2 Platoon spotted two enemy RPG gunners. There was a flash and a *"Bang!"* but the LAV shrugged off the RPG rocket, which deflected in a streak of red without detonating. There was a stream of red tracer from the C-6 machine gun: "Enemy neutralized."

"There's more of them! RPG teams right!" The artillery and engineer LAVs in front and back of our G-Wagon traversed their turrets and started firing three-round bursts: *Bang-bang-bang!* There was a small ditch next to the road, a low wall, and a field with a grape hut in the distance.

"Echo, he's behind the wall!"

"Echo 1-1 Echo, roger." *Bang-bang-bang!*

Dan drove the G-Wagon forward to put a small building between us and the RPG teams in the field.

"Shit! There's three of them, and they all have RPGs!" one of the LAV commanders called out.

*Bang-bang-bang!*

*Bang-bang-bang!*

"This is One Niner. Watch your arcs. Watch your arcs." Kirk saw what the problem was. 1 Platoon had made the turn in the road. If 2 Platoon and the command group weren't careful with the fire, they could hit 1 Platoon when they tried to get the enemy teams in the fields.

"Fire at the flashes only."

*Bang-bang-bang!*

"This is 1-1. I'm under RPG fire, but it's ineffective."

"Echo 1-1 Echo. I have enemy dismounts. They're popping up and down along the wall." The column edged forward.

*Bang-bang-bang!*

"1-2. Contact."

"This is Echo 1-1 Echo. Enemy is trying to flank us to the right."

The enemy was in trouble and didn't even realize it. He was focused on the command group and 2 Platoon, which were both firing back, but now 1 Platoon had its bearings and was bringing enfilade fire to bear that caught the Taliban in a cross fire. It was now 0255 hours. And I had to take a piss badly. This was always a problem with overhydration. Somebody should come up with a catheter system, something like in *Dune*.

"Walter, I'm going to hop out and piss. Don't shoot me."

"We've got to keep moving!"

"Yeah, but we're down to a walking pace anyway." I cracked open the door. Unlike civilian cars, there was no interior light. I walked beside the G-Wagon urinating as the tracer arced over the road.

It was 0310 now. We had stopped and I had dozed off for a catnap. "C" Company was in a series of contacts at this time and we could hear Bill's guys over the radio. Kirk was getting concerned about a "blue on blue" with "C" Company as the companies converged. I could hear him trying to contact Bill.

At 0327 hours we stopped at a holding position. ISTAR picked up enemy movement. The battle-group net blargled that ISTAR from higher detected enemy three hundred meters away from us. Without a direction that was a useless piece of information. We then heard traffic between an A-10 and a Predator controller who was marking a building. Kirk instructed G-11, the artillery LAV, to mark our position with infrared and to tell Slayer to tell the A-10s it was us. Just in case.

"Niner, this is Six Niner. The block's going in now." Captain Jon Hamilton and his Recce Platoon were now set. It was 0346 hours.

"This is 2-3. Contact! I have dismounts throwing grenades over the walls!" "B" Company was active again. At the halt, another vehicle, a G-Wagon from "A" Company, reported a nonpenetrating RPG hit after the round hit and deflected off a mud wall. Then there was a lull in the action for a time.

The situation as it stood at 0515 hours had the first enemy capture, by Jon Hamilton's Recce Platoon. All three companies had been in contact, but the situation was quiet. An initial BDA in the dark by "A" Company found three enemy bodies, one of them in pieces. It was now first light, but sunrise wasn't upon us yet. I could now see Objective Alpha Puma, a collection of compounds about four hundred meters away across an open field. "A" Company was already dismounting and deploying.

"A" Company was at a crossroads of sorts. We passed over a small bridge. To our right was a compound complex, and to our left were ruins. The main road ran south. It had a shoulder-high wall running its length on one side on the right, and there was a shallow irrigation ditch on the left. The road T-junctioned and then ran southeast into Objective Alpha Puma. The southwest leg ran into Objective Bravo Puma, the "B" Company area. The "T" was caused by a collection of compounds surrounded with walls directly to the south. There was a huge open field between us and Objective Alpha Puma. To our left, a road ran past the ruins, past a huge grape-drying complex, and to another compound complex in the distance to the left of Objective Alpha Puma.

1 Platoon's LAVs moved down the road to the left and dismounted. 2 Platoon continued south and interspersed its LAVs and G-Wagons on the road. The G-Wagon top gunners had their machine guns aimed at Objective Alpha Puma. The Afghan platoon in its tan pickup trucks moved behind 2 Platoon and its U.S. woodland pattern–cammo'd guys with AK-47s and RPGs jumped out. Kirk took the command group over the ditch and into the field next to the tree line. The LAVs moved up and stopped, traversing their turrets. The G-Wagons and the Bison ambulance parked slightly behind them. We dismounted. In effect, the command group was a fire base or a hinge between the maneuvering platoons.

2 Platoon was already at the T-junction. Kirk and Pete Leger plus Chris Raike and Nathan Dart, the signalers, were sorting themselves out when the firing started. It was now nearly 0600 hours. Kirk, Pete, and the signalers crouched down, scanning the objective area. Dan Guillaume cocked his weapon and used the hood of the G-Wagon as cover, while Martin and I ducked behind the G-Wagon's left rear quarter panel.

The Taliban opened up with PKM fire, probably because of the range. They fired short bursts that were ineffective against the command group. Two of the LAVs started firing at Objective Alpha Puma. *Bang-bang-bang!* I could see the dust kicked up as the rounds hit the mud walls of the compounds.

1 Platoon was out of sight, somewhere on the left, so I couldn't see what they were doing, but we could hear what 2 Platoon encountered. As Ben, Mark, and their men moved into the southern compound complex, they ran into enemy AK fire at close range. This area was a tangle of compounds, walls, huts, and trees. 2 Platoon started firing back and lobbing grenades, trying to dislodge the Taliban and moving forward to clear the complex. The Afghan platoon with their American ETT mentors moved up to join 2 Platoon and soon we could hear the *"Boom! BOOM!"* of RPG fire. From where we were, it sounded like an RPG dual back and forth between the ANA and the Taliban. 2 Platoon started to clear the complex, wall by wall, courtyard by courtyard.

Enemy fire dropped off temporarily across the field. Pete waved us over. "We're going to move along the wall and hook up with 2 Platoon."

"Okay!" Pete jumped over the ditch, but Chris Raike sank up to his ankles in the blackish mud, the radio on his back. We got up to the road—Kirk and Nathan were behind us. Some of 2 Platoon's vehicles were halted along the road: up front was a LAV, then two G-Wagon gun trucks, then another LAV, and then three more gun trucks. I was following Pete when the firing started again. He and I ducked behind the G-Wagon back from the lead LAV. Everybody else took cover.

"Can you hear that?" Pete yelled "It's the rounds going supersonic!"

*Crack! Crack! Crack!* It sounded like they were right overhead. I was using the frame of the G-Wagon as cover, looking through the glass at Objective Alpha Puma.

"Let's hold here." Pete and I saw the LAV turret traversing left, looking for a target.

"Sure."

Then I heard a ricochet next to my head. Rounds were ricocheting off the roof of the G-Wagon. I ducked down. *Bweeeeee!* Then I realized what was happening. These rounds weren't coming from Objective Alpha Puma—they were coming from *behind* us. *Bweeee!* Another one.

"Pete! We're in a cross fire!" Pete looked around, trying to identify where it was coming from. He moved in a crouch to the wall and I joined him there.

"It's coming from that compound over there," he said, indicating a spot about three hundred meters away. Sure enough, whenever the Taliban fired, it kicked up puffs of dust near their firing positions.

Kirk and the signalers were taking rounds too. They were taking cover behind the G-Wagon behind us and I could see Kirk on the radio. Chunks of adobe wall sprayed around us.

*Crack! Crack! Crack!* More firing from the objective area. Then the gun truck G-Wagons that were at the back of the column started taking fire from another compound to the west. The lead LAV then traversed its turret to the right (it was hull-down to the compound, using the wall as cover) and started to fire on the enemy-held compound with three-round bursts. I brought my camera up for a shot when I heard the *BOOM!* of an RPG launch. The round impacted on the adobe wall, which disintegrated in a plume of dust. The LAV was unharmed and continued to fire. The gun truck G-Wagon behind us opened up with a C-6, while the second LAV traversed its gun over the wall and poured fire onto the compounds.

2 Platoon and the ANA were still at it, moving east through the complexes. The danger here was the unknown size of the force the vehicles

were engaging, but "A" Company was in the better position. If the enemy fighters moved and tried to engage 2 Platoon from the rear, they would be cut to pieces as they moved forward by the LAVs and gun trucks. However, it looked as if they were trying to get into the area near the culvert or, at the very least, put fire down onto it and interdict it. That would interfere with resupply. 1 Platoon was still clearing out the compounds over on the left, making headway toward the objective area.

Kirk decided to break contact and bring 2 Platoon and the ANA back down the road. There were A-10s orbiting at this time. The idea was to move the command group back over the culvert to a laager in an open space between the road and a large compound. 2 Platoon and the ANA would retrograde to a hasty defense that would run from the ruins, across the road, and along a wall. The enemy might believe they were succeeding and move into the abandoned 2 Platoon positions. Then the A-10s would strike, and 1 Platoon would hit them from behind. The preliminary moves were implemented. Slayer 11 contacted the A-10s and set up the strike. I saw a line of ANA pulling back along the wall where we had just been. It was 0722 hours and it was already hot. Cheryl, the medic in the Bison, was handing out rehydration solution and water.

I was with Chris Raike when ISTAR reported that the enemy in Objective Bravo Puma was withdrawing in groups of two to the west. As I looked up, I saw what could only be described as several black flowers silently blossom above us.

"Airburst!" someone shouted. It looked like mortars. Shrapnel pinged off the G-Wagon and the Bison. It was completely ineffective. (I learned later it might have been an airburst version of an RPG round, but then again 2 Platoon found 60-mm mortar rounds in its sweep, so who knows.)

Then "C" Company saw airbursts as well.

A hasty defense was put in and we waited for the air strike. Slayer had an A-10 ready to go. We had eyes on the compound just vacated by 2 Platoon, anticipating the bombs to drop. I could visualize the jihadis jumping up and down with glee, weapons thrust into the air, then dissolving in a 1,000-pound bomb detonation. And then nothing.

We were hit with a blast wave, but not from our front. A black pillar cloud slowly climbed into the sky about four hundred meters to the left of the target area, and to the left of Objective Alpha Puma.

The bomb had been dropped onto 1 Platoon as they were maneuvering onto the objective. Everybody held their breath.

Minutes later, the radio crackled.

"One Niner this is 1-1. I need the ambulance, over."

"Oh, shit! It's gonna be Tarnak Farms all over again!"

"*Jesus fucking Christ!*"

A feeling of dread leapt from man to man. The implications were unthinkable.

The artillery FOO didn't let the situation faze him: he called up the guns and was able to bring down a rain of 155-mm rounds onto the area the bomb was supposed to drop into.

The medics reported in.

"One Niner, there's one case. He's bleeding from the ears but otherwise he's okay." Kevin Schamuhn explained later that the bomb dropped into soft ground in front of them and the ground muffled the blast. The guys from the lead section were thrown around and stunned, but nobody was seriously hurt.

Mark Pickford and Chuck Prodonick were at the laager rehydrating from the last batch of water, pouring the stuff over their bald heads. Their arid CADPAT was dark from the sweat. (I never understood how Mark could wear a black T-shirt in the heat. . . .) Everybody had debloused their pants long ago to get air circulating. The 2 Platoon sections were in a line running east to west. Then we heard firing again.

It was sporadic and not concentrated. From where we were, it sounded like one guy with an AK-47 had winkled his way into the ruins and was taking pot shots. Ben Richard sent a section to track him down and sort it out. Kirk then told Richard to get ready to take 2 Platoon back in and move on Objective Alpha Puma.

2 Platoon moved back down the road, but a LAV broke off and moved in the field, putting down fire on the objective area. The other LAVs, with the dismounted infantry behind them using the vehicles as shields, advanced down the road and then into the field. A Taliban fighter was spotted on the roof of a compound building and then the firefight started again in earnest—small arms and RPG. The RPG rounds were being lofted instead of being fired on a flat trajectory, probably to increase range. The artillery LAV was lasing the guys on the roof and working up a fire plan to isolate the enemy positions. Rounds of 155-mm started to land in and around the objective area. ISTAR reported that the enemy

leaders were complaining that they were running out of ammo, that they were expecting to die and begging for help as the LAVs advanced on them.

It was around this time that some bad guys infiltrated the compound next to the "A" Company laager and started to fire on us. There was the Bison ambulance, and Kirk's LAV, plus the CIMIC and PSYOPS G-Wagons. It wasn't clear how many enemy there were, but the laager sat right next to the main road that went back to Highway 1 and PBW, where the logistics Bisons were loading up a vital water resupply. If the road was cut, "A" Company would have to back off and reopen it.

Pete Leger put together a team that included Gerald Strong, the One Niner gunner, and Chris Raike, the signaler. Kirk took over the gunner position while Corporal Gibson (Gibby) drove the LAV into an overwatch position. Pete and his team crept from wall to ditch to compound in an effort to find the shooter or shooters and take them out, while Kirk swung the turret back and forth, covering the open ground. Pete and crew stealthily moved from room to room and courtyard to courtyard in the building heat. The battle could be heard in the distance, but the only sound close by were hens clucking. After some time, Pete concluded that the shooters had bugged out to the west. The team returned to the laager.

ISTAR reported at around 1030 hours that enemy fighters were moving to a mosque to take cover from the onslaught. This was where the ANA came in: they could enter and search it without causing problems with the locals. The fact that the enemy was firing from the mosque meant that the structure was no longer a legally protected facility, however.

"We have a Predator overhead. Do you want to use it?" Slayer 11 asked.

Kirk shook his head. "No, 2 Platoon can deal with it." Ben Richard's guys and the engineer LAV opened up.

By 1330, it was quiet again. Recce Platoon reported a number of enemy captured in their net as 2 Platoon conducted a BDA in their part of the objective area. 1 Platoon, which had assaulted into the northeastern end of Alpha Puma, linked up with them. They found the intact remains of three enemy dead, plus a gooey brain pan that was merged with an equally gooey AK-47. The BDA continued. There were AKs, PKMs, and RPGs strewn about the objective, but not much ammo. Three more dead were found—intact. The parts of approximately four more bodies were discovered in various places.

It was impossible to get an accurate body count, however. There was no way Kirk was going to send his people back along the route in and check. We all knew the Taliban had a covert CASEVAC system and actively policed up body parts to deny us casualty information. They also put blankets under the PKM machine guns to catch the links.

"A" Company continued to secure the part of Alpha Puma they controlled. It was hitting 120 degrees F (50 degrees C) by now. A siesta was ordered and Schamuhn and his signaler came up. Kevin took off his helmet and wiped the sweat off. "Man, if we had been fifty meters closer we'd be dead. I expected the guys to be in pieces, but they climbed out of the dust—it was really thick—and we were good to go!"

"Yeah, it was a close one!" an engineer named Stadler said as he dusted off his shoulder. He had the Combat Engineer map symbol on a patch with the words, "More Bang for Your Buck" on it.

The radio was going again: a Slayer JTAC was bringing in an A-10 in support of "C" and "B" Companies. We couldn't see the plane, but we heard a 500-pound bomb explode about a kilometer to the south. Then the gray plane flashed by and we heard what sounded like heaven being ripped apart by a chainsaw. *BRRRRRRRRRP! BRRRRRRRRRRRP!* The GAU-8 Gatling gun spat death. The A-10 looped around and repeated the process twice more.

It was around 1450 hours when Ian called on the radio net. Kirk, the ETT commander and Ben, the ANA platoon leader, were drinking lukewarm water mixed with Gatorade powder.

"All stations, this is Niner One. We have been told that the enemy is fighting hard because this is a large drug production facility. Search for evidence that drug production is under way or if poppy is stockpiled. Two. When you conduct a cemetery search, do not photograph. Have the ANA conduct the search. ("So what?" said the ANA captain. "They're already dead!") Three. The enemy in Bravo Puma is talking about surrendering. Niner Seven is to disarm them and move them to Pashmul School. Out."

Nobody believed that the enemy was fighting this hard for narcotics. Not in Pashmul. "A" Company searched the area again and found only a bundle of dry, dead poppy stalks. Not enough to get a Toronto street junkie high. Anyway, the harvest season for opium poppies was long gone.

2 Platoon had driven through a marijuana field, but these were baby plants, not ready for harvest.

"You know," I said to Pete. "We might need to add to the post-ex declaration. I have no live rounds, empty casings, or marijuana in my possession, sir!" Pete and I had a good laugh.

By this time the command group had moved up to a field just outside the Bravo Puma compounds. The three platoons were still searching. I looked around. There was a huge grape-drying hut behind us to the north. There were grape trenches full of vines. The field we were in was probably used for poppy, but it was bare this time of year. There were small culverts over an intricate irrigation system.

Cheryl, the medic, reminded everybody to keep hydrated. "Either you orally rehydrate, or we'll rectally rehydrate you!" she said ominously. "You *promise*?" one of the soldiers asked. The resupply Bison dumped off pallets of bottled water. The search turned up no stockpiled opium, no labs, and no Colombian drug cartel members. Somebody was smoking rope, just testing a pet theory that this was all drug related. This defense was too well organized. The Red Devils had passed through a layered defense system consisting of listening posts, a covering force, all armed with RPGs, and forces in a main defensive position that stayed and fought. And maneuvered.

It was 1900 and the situation as it stood had all three companies completing their searches and then reorienting for an all-round defensive posture for the night. Not all the objective areas had been cleared yet, however. That would have to wait for first light. The troops were exhausted. They had been fighting since 0100. It was insanely hot.

"B" Company hadn't cleared Bravo Puma yet. They had made slow progress after passing the Pashmul School—contact after contact after contact—before swinging onto the objective area. Ian had Kirk reorient 1 Platoon to the southwest of Alpha Puma so the LAVs could cover any possible escapees from Bravo Puma as "B" Company moved west like a piston through their objective area. There was speculation that some enemy were able to squeeze out in ones and twos before 1 Platoon was able to get eyes on. Word was passed that a B-1B was available with JDAMs and that the Sperwer TUAV was going to be providing top cover. Ian, Kirk, and Nick communicated: in the morning, 2 Platoon would move south and squeeze Bravo Puma from the north, 1 Platoon would still cover the west, and "B" Company would continue to move west.

The "B" and "C" Company fights that day were different from "A" Company's but just as arduous. The deception plan had "B" Company move from PBW back to Camp Nathan Smith (the PRT) while "A" Company moved into PBW from the airfield. "C" Company joined up at Camp Nathan Smith. Then "B" Company moved at dusk to Panjwayi District Center. Ian Hope's Niner Tac moved from Camp Nathan Smith to the positions we'd occupied back during Jagra, behind the Panjwayi District Center. At the last minute "C" Company departed Camp Nathan Smith and deployed directly to the river-crossing site on the Arghandab south of the White School. The idea was to have "B" Company effect a forward passage of lines through "C" Company, move past the school to an unpaved road, and then turn west, cross an irrigation system in Haji Musa, and turn north into the western part of Pashmul. Because "B" Company knew the ground, their engineers prepared expedient means to cross the irrigation system: each G-Wagon carried a wooden box that was to be dropped into the ditch. Nick knew he wouldn't be able to get his LAV IIIs in there, but they could provide fire support. "C" Company, at the same time, was to head north into its objectives in southern Pashmul.

At least, that was what was supposed to happen. The whole operation was nearly blown. Out of nowhere arrived Haji Saifullah from Maywand district with a supposed Taliban "informant" in tow, wondering why so many coalition vehicles were in Bazaar-e Panjwayi. They were fed a ration of bullshit and the fact that Saifullah was inordinately interested was recorded.

Once "A" Company got its first contact back up near Highway 1, "C" Company moved into the riverbed and "B" Company mounted up. "We could see the tracer from the 'A' Company fight," Nick Grimshaw told me later. One of the problems with the southern part of the attack force was that the ANA didn't have blackout driving capabilities, and they were driving with white lights on. One of "B" Company's platoons made it to the crossroads up from the White School with some of "C" Company's engineers and then all hell broke loose. "B" Company's vehicles were moving forward from the riverbed, firing on the move against enemy positions on a long wall. The air sentry from the artillery LAV III spotted an RPG team as it prepared a broadside against the vehicle, and killed the fighters. "B" Company still was nowhere near its attack positions at Haji Musa—and the fight was on.

Nick Grimshaw took his column left down the unpaved road, while Bill Fletcher moved a platoon up to the crossroads, where they were engaged from the north and started firing back. "B" Company moved caterpillar fashion west, skirting the big open area to the south when they were engaged from three directions at once: a series of RPG fusillades were fired from some observation posts to the south that were along the river, PKM and RPG fire came from behind a wall from the north, and PKM and RPG fire from two large compounds in Haji Musa where the crossing was to take place. As the fire erupted, "B" Company vehicles blazed away using their night vision to seek out targets.

The enemy withdrew west from the southern posts, while the ones to the north behind the wall pulled farther north. The compounds kept fighting for some time before they faded west. It was now first light as "B" Company went in to clear Haji Musa: 5 Platoon left, 6 Platoon right, heading north. Shots were fired from the west. While 5 Platoon reoriented to deal with this new threat, an enemy force of fifteen fighters maneuvered in between the two platoons and attempted to exploit the "seam." The battle broke down into a series of engagements at ranges closer than fifteen meters, with the enemy pouring over the compound walls. It was during these actions that a corporal from 6 Platoon was seriously wounded in the neck and had to be medevac'd. 5 and 6 Platoons held firm. Nick, not having a third platoon because of the leave plan, had no maneuver force. The accompanying ANA, as he put it, was "less than effective." Fortunately, there was an A-10 on station. It spotted an enemy force of some fifteen fighters and engaged in two gun runs with its GAU-8, which essentially obliterated the insurgents.

"C" Company also hit the RPG-armed early warning network, which was arrayed in a tree line that enfiladed the route from the river northeast to Pashmul. Bill Fletcher had his forward elements in the Arghandab River bed, with a platoon forward, when they started taking fire. The gunners spotted at least five people not wearing traditional Afghan clothing, equipped with some sort of combat vest and weapons. They were moving confidently through the trees. The Canadians used 25-mm to rake that tree line and pushed a platoon forward to cover a crossroads so that Nick Grimshaw and "B" Company could pass through on the road and head west.

At first light "C" Company sent a dismounted sweep through the area that turned up two enemy dead and one wounded, who later died.

They had been fragmented by the 25-mm fire. Once "B" Company had moved off, Bill Fletcher kept one platoon mounted and one dismounted and moved to secure the southern part of Objective Charlie Puma. "Right away as they broke in, we came around a corner and they started taking fire. The enemy was maneuvering and trying to outflank them. It was aggressive," Bill told me later. "C" Company conducted some dismounted assaults against the closest compounds to the north, but the enemy started to push back from the west, so the FOOs called in artillery. 8 Platoon called in "Check fire! Check fire!" because of a large explosion that was first thought to be artillery, but might have been some other explosion. The enemy broke contact and headed west, disappearing into the congested area. "C" Company then conducted a methodical clear-and-sweep of the area it had under control. Nothing was found. A link-up with "B" Company was established as "C" Company consolidated the southern part of Charlie Puma.

Back to "A" Company. By the end of the day, people were too tired to set up cots. Many of the guys just went to ground where they were in the field, propped up against vehicles, or stretched out under them or in the backs of LAVs—wherever. The sun was down and it was still unbearably warm. I slept fitfully and was awakened by a burning, itching pain that ran all the way down my arm. I had my jacket rolled up as a pillow and had crooked my arm under it. I looked around. The soldiers on the ground were writhing and scratching away, trying to sleep. In the morning I checked my arm. It was covered—and I mean covered—with bites. My shirt had pulled up during the night and I had bites above my belt line. Everybody in the field was bitten by what turned out to be sand flies. Anybody who has been nailed by these little bastards can sympathize. The guys were scratching away and Cheryl told them to knock it off because they could get infected with Leishmeniasis, a parasitic disease. One of the guys exclaimed, "Fuck *that!*" and ripped the scabs away furiously, seeking relief. The ambulance Bison quickly ran out of antihistamine.

Around 0550 we heard bursts of machine-gun fire. "B" Company had a contact. It turned out to be an ANA negligent discharge, but when "B" Company started its move west, one of the sections stumbled across a cache that had crates of ammo and artillery shells for making IEDs. A more detailed search uncovered ammo on the roofs of many of the buildings in Bravo Puma, including crates of 60-mm mortar ammo that formerly had belonged to the U.S. Army.[1] "B" Company also found numerous blood trails from casualties that had been generated by yesterday's artillery strike.

By early morning all three companies were conducting detailed searches of the compounds in their areas. "C" Company then got a contact at 0810 hours, somewhere southeast of our position. They reported enemy holed up in a compound. One of their men had been shot and wounded and was Pri-1—seriously life threatening. We had to wait for the details because this bit of drama unfolded at the same time that a whole bunch of things happened at once.

First, Ian called up Kirk with information that the enemy wasn't cleaning up his dead at night, which was unusual. He didn't want the media taking pictures of them and TF ORION wasn't in the enemy casualty collection business, so he directed Kirk to conduct a local leader engagement at a village to the north to see what they knew and if they could help recover the corpses and dispose of the remains according to Islamic customs. CIMIC was tasked with this, so Walter and Dan took off with a protection party from 1 Platoon and the ANA.

Major Webb from E-11 reported in. His engineers were finding enemy kit and ammo all over the place, but rather than just blowing it all up, he recommended a sensitive site exploitation (SSE) team because it looked like there was IED-making equipment in some of the locations. A search also uncovered what looked like a leadership lair: it was hidden, it had radios, and there were motorcycles concealed nearby, presumably for a quick getaway.

The firing started up again in the "C" Company objective area. There was something serious going on, but the details weren't available yet. The suspense was killing us as the volume of fire increased.

The local leadership engagement gave ORION insight into what was going on with the population in the Pashmul area. The elders explained that the Taliban arrived after a JDAM strike from fifteen days ago killed a cow and calf (the elders displayed the skulls as proof). About "four thousand" Taliban came into the area and demanded food. When they realized the locals couldn't provide, they brought their own food in and many of the locals fled the area. The elders explained that when coalition forces came in, the insurgents usually fled to Mushan, Sangsar, and Taloquan if they didn't have enough ammo, then came back later when the coalition forces left. This particular community was pissed off with the Taliban. Four days before, the Taliban had shot an elder because he used his water for crops and not to support Taliban operations.

"They really don't care about the Taliban dead," Walter Martin passed on. Another elder told the CIMIC team that the Taliban planned to burn the Pashmul School, but elders tried to stop it. The Taliban burned all the "unholy" books they found and trashed the place. As for allegiances, some of the villages had been progovernment three years ago, but the Taliban came in and warned against anybody joining the ANP or ANA, discouraging any contact with the Zharey district center.

At 0905 hours a radio message went out. A Canadian soldier wounded in the "C" Company area was now VSA (vital signs absent). He was dead.

From our vantage point at Alpha Puma, we couldn't tell what was happening in Charlie Puma. We heard over the radio that two AH-64 Apaches were inbound; minutes later, they flew over us. I saw the 30-mm gun track and fire. We were sprayed with hot casings. A second Apache came in line astern for its gun run.

"This is Aces High. Do you want to use Hellfire?"

"Negative, Aces High." The target was in a built-up area. Hellfires fired horizontally on a slant and had an elongated egg-shaped "foot print." If the missile missed, it would hit something other than the target either in front of it or behind it. "C" Company's guys must be really close in to something.

There was some chatter with a FOO about using 155-mm artillery.

"This is G- Three Niner. Negative. We'll hit the cordon."

"This is Three Niner. I concur, over."

More chatter. I could hear that Ian was getting frustrated. "Three Niner, this is Niner. We have a Predator with top-attack Hellfire. We'll use that. We can't do anything else until you get on with it, over."

"Three Niner. Roger. I'm trying to get a LAV in to put fire onto the target."

"This is Niner. I'm going to vector a Predator in until you do that. I'll use the Predator, then if necessary 155. Be prepared to go in."

At 1145 hours the Predator strike went in. I saw the explosion in the distance.

What happened was this: As the lead section from 8 Platoon rounded a corner, they bumped into an insurgent who beat feet. 8 Platoon gave chase. This guy made it onto the roof of a building and with a buddy sprayed the section from elevation as the platoon was about to enter the compound. Corporal Anthony Boneca was shot in the neck. The section evacuated him. Bill moved his forces along with the ANA in to surround the compound complex. The problem was that this building was elevated, and it had a series of curved domes that formed a second story. The insurgents had cover from the ground and the mud was essentially concrete. They had a lot of ammo available to them, which they used anytime anybody moved for the stairs area.

The Hellfire strike blew one jihadist off the roof and wounded the other. Bill pulled back and dropped artillery onto the building, and then the AH-64s did their gun runs. This all generated a fire that set off ammo and weapons that had been stored in the building. The explosion was massive and took the air out of the lungs of the troops for a couple of seconds. An American ETT guy got hit with some of the shrapnel and had to be evacuated. It turned out Corporal Mooney, Bill's signaler, also was hit—in the upper thigh with shrapnel. Concerned that he had lost his genitalia, Corporal Mooney asked Bill to check and make sure it was all there . . . which it was. Mooney was evacuated.

A Canadian platoon fixed bayonets, scaled a wall, and got into the compound. During this assault, the third on the structures, they discovered another insurgent who had multiple shrapnel wounds. He was in a culvert curled up in a ball. The ANA wanted to shoot him, but 8 Platoon interposed themselves between them and the detainee and prevented it. One of the platoons found blood stains, tactical vests, ANA ammo boxes, and ID cards, but no bodies. We heard over the radio the detainee was a "higher asset."

At the same time, new information was coming in, some of it from Captain Massoud. The Taliban reported that they were near a LAV sitting next to a particular location, and that they couldn't recover ten bodies and weapons because of the vehicle's presence.

"This is Niner. Are there any LAVs next to a graveyard right now?"

"This is 1-1 Lima. Yes, we were there fifteen minutes ago."

Everybody thought it was a setup, that there was an ambush waiting for ORION forces if they rushed in, so eyes were put on the area but 1-1 Lima was moved away from the site. The cemetery issue was still hot when it turned out other vehicles were near other cemeteries and the enemy was reporting that they had dead in multiple cemetery locations. Ian wanted this sorted out so ORION wasn't chasing its tail. 2 Platoon was ordered to sweep dismounted with the Zulu LAVs providing overwatch. ISTAR assets were being focused on several locations. TF KNIGHTHAWK ordered the two AH-64 Apaches to help.

Major Webb was working with the other engineers doing SSE. The guys from 11 Field Squadron found what they thought was another IED facility or a leaders hide. It was the same pattern as the last one—radios, ammo, and motorcycles tucked away in a compound.

More reports were coming in about what we had been fighting in Pashmul. ISTAR reported that some of the dead were Chechens, and that at least two MVT leaders were dead. They apparently had been hit, extracted somehow during the fight, and died later elsewhere. One was a verified named person of interest and the other was a new guy, possibly one of the leaders sent in to replace Mullah Baqi. Those of us clustered around the One Niner LAV cheered.

"Two of them! Fucking A-right!" High fives all around.

The presence of the Chechens was interesting. It was like they were being used as a close protection party for somebody important. It looked like the layered defense was set up to protect a leadership meeting or nest. We learned later from ISTAR that "A" Company clipped the close protection party for another MVT just as we went in off Highway 1. That MVT fucked off at the high port to the west and, apparently, was telling his peers that he was lucky to be alive. Three Taliban leaders in the Pashmul area. Something had been up. Other reporting indicated the enemy was squawking about the loss of ammo and the expenditure of scarce medical supplies. I guess some jihadis just weren't as hard core as we thought. Not all of them wanted to die a glorious death by being torn apart by 25-mm HE rounds.

ISTAR now reported that enemy was regrouping to the southwest of the Puma objective areas, an area code named Lion. "B" Company fought through Lion on its way to Objective Bravo Puma, but it looked like the enemy had reoccupied it. This didn't make sense. The assumption was that the Taliban would un-ass the whole area, flee west, go to ground, and come back after we'd gone. The enemy also was reporting that he had dumped off ten dead fighters in the cemetery near Lion. Ian was wary and smelled a trap. It looked like the enemy was using the dead as bait, waiting for ORION to rush in and do an SSE. He put together an outline plan: If he could get a UAV, he'd take a look with that. If he couldn't, Recce Platoon would go and do a dismounted recce at night. The 155-mm guns would be prepared to fire west of Lion to cut off any enemy trying to get out of those compounds. This plan developed as the day progressed.

Aces High was back again at 1410, using Hellfires against another compound. Kirk, meanwhile, had dispatched 2 Platoon to check out a compound slightly east of the Alpha Puma objective area. It was a singular set of buildings, with what looked like open fields around it. Richard and Pickford got their guys ready to go. Pickford looked at the open terrain and said to Richards, "I feel like a Red Shirt in *Star Trek*." But there was no contact. 2 Platoon found that the compound was fortified but empty. There was a madrassa graduation photo and some ID cards, but little else.

At 1645 hours Kirk sent the logistics Bisons back to PBW to get more water. Then *they* had a contact on the road. Some Taliban were withdrawing with a body. The logistics guys pulled up and zap-strapped the bunch. Three captured. To make matters more interesting, the RCP working the resupply routes found and disarmed two IEDs.

It was around 2020 hours on day whatever. It was all starting to blend together—General Freakley's send-off, the briefing at PBW, the night action, the assault on Alpha Puma, night again, the clearance of Alpha Puma, "C" Company's clearance of Charlie Puma, and now night again and the problem of what to do with Objective Lion. Everybody was dirty, sweaty, and tired.

There was a meeting of the company commanders planned over where Alpha Puma and Charlie Puma met, so I followed Kirk's LAV in the CIMIC G-Wagon through the dark maze of walled roads and compounds. There were LAVs at the intersections, and an ANA checkpoint. We pulled over. There was a wall to the right of the road, and interspersed trees to the right. We dismounted and I followed them down a road past an Afghan sentry. The moon was bright and would be full in a few days, but the trees and walls cast deep shadows in here. The ANA pickups were laagered and there were a couple of crackling red cooking fires that made our shadows on the wall flicker as we walked along. Bearded men in watchkeeper caps and American woodland camouflage were slumped all over the place. Some were cleaning their weapons. Most were asleep on rugs. I noticed that we were in a graveyard. The Afghan soldiers were sitting with their backs on the stone footers and headers of the graves, with their kit on top of rock piles in between. They silently stared at us as we passed by. It was surreal. I felt like I was in Dante's seventh circle of hell.

The path dipped down into a ditch and we emerged out of the shadows into the "C" Company laager. Cigarettes were cupped in hands, and there was light discipline. Some of the troops were lined up at the back of a Bison replenishing their ammo. Nick Grimshaw tapped me on the shoulder and said quietly, "Over here." There was Bill Fletcher, with a lopsided grin, Kirk Gallinger puffing on a butt, and Nick consuming the contents of a water bottle. Jon Hamilton was wiping sweat off his neck. I pulled out a cigar, nipped off the tip, and offered more to the guys. "You're out here too???" Bill exclaimed.

"Hell, yeah. You guys just made history. I'm the historian, right? Gotta be here to see it."

There was a contained jubilant mood. The guys all sort of looked at each other and around the graveyard in disbelief, like they couldn't believe they'd made it this far alive, and smiled. I puffed on the Romeo y Julietta Short Churchill. My favorite. I'd held on to this one for an occasion like this. It was one of those split-second moments of collective satisfaction. It doesn't last long, but it's the kind of thing you remember forever.

"Bill, sorry to hear about Boneca."

"We did what we could but those bastards were using the roof as cover."

I asked them what they thought we were up against and there was a consensus that it was a layered defense—outposts, covering force, main defense. There were some surprising revelations. Some of the enemy dead were Pakistani, others were Chechen. "We saw something really interesting," Nick explained. "The enemy regrouped to the west when we hit the objective and *came back at us*. We haven't seen that before. Usually they just withdraw in the face of superior firepower." The guy caught in the tunnel turned out to be another leader.

The graveyard meeting was to determine how to approach Objective Lion. The presence of Chechens on the battlefield was cause for concern, particularly the possibility that they had snipers with them. The presence of Pakistanis and IED equipment indicated there might be suicide bombers in the area. Everybody agreed that the enemy was setting a trap at Lion and they were concerned about overextending ORION after nearly three days of battle. Rather than waiting, Ian decided to mount the preliminary moves for the Lion clearance in less than four hours and see if the enemy would react.

Objective Lion was the Haji Musa community, consisting of eight or nine compound complexes to the southwest of Objective Puma and west of the Pashmul School. Building on the outline plan, "C" Company would secure Charlie Puma. There would not be enough forces to surround Lion and converge on it, so the "squeeze" would consist of several moves. Recce Platoon would move toward Lion from the north but offset to the east of the objective. Any enemy in Lion would focus on this move, while "B" Company moved south, shifted west of Recce Platoon, and applied pressure to Lion. "C" Company would act as a tunnel for "A" Company, which would move through Charlie Puma, south to the school, and then west, following the same route "B" Company had taken on the first night. The guns would be used as a cutoff force of sorts: they would fire into a field to the west of Lion, and then walk the fire east toward the compounds to discourage any exfiltrators. The only problem was covering the gap to the south. This was a dense treed area with ditches that ran to the Arghandab River wadi. The idea was to put air assets to cover it but it wasn't clear if those assets would be available. "A" Company could put some direct fire onto the area, but it was more discouraging fire.

It was equally possible that the enemy was exhausted and might be susceptible to persuasion. The decision was made to try PSYOPS with the "A" Company move from the school to Lion. The plan was twofold: "A" Company would be making an open, magnanimous, and ostentatious move that would attract the enemy's attention, while Recce and "B" Company pressed in from the north. The hope was that the PSYOPS would act as a distraction, at the very least. If they gave in, so much the better.

The meeting ended and everybody said their goodbyes. Lion would not be like Puma. TF ORION had surprise on its side when Zahar started. The enemy was already alerted to our presence in Zharey, so they had time to prepare in a general sense. They probably wouldn't anticipate a snap night move, but on the other hand "A" Company would be transiting a route already used by "B" Company, a route the enemy had defended before over terrain the enemy knew. If they had time to reoccupy Lion then they had time to lay out new defenses. TF ORION was prepared for a hard fight if it came to that. Kirk, Pete, and I walked back through the surreal graveyard scene, mounted up, and headed to Alpha Puma.

Kirk held an orders group back in the sand fly field. I could feel a level of apprehension—barely discernable, but it was there. "H" Hour was first light, at around 0430 hours. After "A" Company passed the school, it had to move across west nearly a kilometer of open ground that had sinkholes and small wells randomly placed in it to get to Lion, which was a built-up area. There was a built-up area with grape-drying huts to the north on higher ground; to the south was the higher ground that ran along the river. It was studded with buildings and trees. Kirk would have to clear or screen both flanks before moving on to Lion. If things deteriorated, the whole approach route could become an RPG kill zone.

I prepared my kit and moved to the CIMIC G-Wagon. I looked at the door and just had a bad feeling.

"Hey, Walter. I'm going to shift the frag blanket from the left-side seat and curve it up the side of my door."

"Why?"

"To prevent spall in case we get hit with an RPG." I was feeling vulnerable on this one unlike on the first night.

"It won't do any good."

"I know that, but I'll *feel* better if I do."

Word came over the radio: "C" Company's "tunnel" was moving into place. Bill Fletcher's guys were marking out the route and would guide "A" Company through the confusing maze of walled roads and compounds to the Pashmul School.

We departed at 0230 hours. We were all keyed up as the column moved slowly through Charlie Puma. It took a lot longer than I anticipated. Kirk halted everybody behind the school. It was burnt out but still standing.

"This is 1-2A. I think I see tracer fire."

We heard a pair of A-10s communicating with the JTACs. TF ORION was marking with infrared to avoid friendly fire.

"Stop lasing my ass!" exclaimed an unknown call sign.

Around 0400 hours the A-10s spotted three vans or trucks moving west away from Lion. Ian temporarily delayed H Hour and was trying to vector a UAV to the west of Lion to see what was going on. It was confirmed: there was vehicle movement to the west, but it wasn't clear exactly who it was. The A-10s were put on a leash.

Just after first light, at around 0440 hours, the operation commenced. The 155-mm guns fired to the west of Lion. Kirk pushed 1 Platoon to the left and 2 Platoon to the right, with the command group and the PSYOPS G-Wagon and the ANA pushed to the middle. The two platoons' LAVs halted in a defensive posture and the dismounted infantry started to clear the high ground and the buildings. One G-Wagon gun truck and the PSYOPS G-Wagon with its loudspeakers advanced toward two compounds directly to our front.

"Come out or die!"

"PTS and be saved!"

I expected the enemy to shoot at the PSYOPS vehicle out of spite. The terp continued with his litany. The artillery crashed again, somewhere west of these compounds.

"See? We have artillery. Come out and be saved!"

ISTAR reported no movement in the "A" Company sector, but that both 1 Platoon and 2 Platoon were under enemy observation. It was a bit disconcerting. We were in an open area, and it was light. Nothing was happening. Then word came over the radio that a helicopter was inbound to pick up Bill Fletcher and Ian so they could attend the ramp ceremony for Corporal Boneca. Nick Grimshaw was now in command.

At 0615 somebody called in saying he'd seen four people with a white flag. This didn't correspond to the PSYOPS surrender instruction that was for surrendering enemy to hold their weapons above their heads. The Taliban, however, did use white flags to mark their territory. There were more reports of individuals moving about, but no weapons. Recce Platoon called in a contact, but there was no further information. We heard 84-mm rounds and 40-mm grenade launchers being used to the north. "B" Company was breaching a compound. The UAV above us was keeping a close watch. Recce Platoon confirmed they'd engaged two to three enemy who had RPGs.

More radio traffic: "I witnessed a dude hiding next to the tree. The bushy tree." Clearly, fatigue was starting to set in. We had a good laugh.

"Higher is reporting. They see six or seven people fleeing down a creek bed to the west. We think they're spooked by the UAV."

"Roger. We now see fifteen people in the ditch engaging call sign 6-1."

"Check fire. Those are our forces."

"Roger."

Jon Hamilton was talking to one of his sections: "Don't get engaged. Use indirect fire."

At 1039 hours Kirk was satisfied that the flanks were clear and that the PSYOPS was having little or no effect. The two compounds to the front looked formidable and we knew from the map there was a stream with a bridge behind them that would impede LAV movement. Kirk mounted everybody up. He sent a LAV at top speed into the space between the compounds and had it fire its smoke dischargers. The LAV then pulled back. 1 Platoon moved up on the left as a fire-base, and 2 Platoon and the ANA charged forward and assaulted the compounds.

"Clear!"

"Clear!"

The command group moved up and I joined Kirk. The platoons were conducting a detailed search with the engineers, so I went with Ben Richards to watch. "They've bugged out. Nobody home." Ben put some of his guys in overwatch positions on the walls looking south and west.

The search turned up some interesting things. There was a bed with restraints on it. There were medical supplies strewn about, so it was likely this was a casualty collection point or clinic. One of the guys found maps—military maps of Croatia and Bosnia. I recognized the coast near Zadar and Backovici where I had visited the UN Protection Force (UNPROFOR) back in 1995. There was graffiti all over the place. It was photographed for analysis. The other compound was empty.

Kirk then pushed a LAV over the stream and followed it with 2 Platoon and the engineers. There was a field to the south, and the Objective Lion complexes to the north. 2 Platoon set about clearing these. I followed Mark Pickford who leaned over and pulled a 9-mm Browning out of a bush. The owner had discarded it because it was jammed.[2] We went through a doorway and a passage into a courtyard. There were medical supplies strewn all over the place. Whoever had been here had scarpered. There was a pile of RPG rounds, including types of rounds even the engineers hadn't seen before. And then there was hair. There were piles of shaved hair stuffed into nooks and crannies in the walls, piled up on the ground. It looked like Vince McQade's Barber Shop on Johnson Street in Kingston. There were used plastic safety razors and shaving cream.

"What the hell is this all about?" one of the soldiers said.

"They were probably foreign jihadis. This is a prebattle cleansing ritual."

The search uncovered an ammo crate full of cassette tapes. I poked around and saw something unusual. What looked like a clothesline really wasn't: it ran into a small room and terminated with dangling wires. There was a grounding spike. It looked like an antenna. I had seen something similar in Hokumate Shinkay district back in 2003.

"What's that?" one of the guys exclaimed. He pointed up to a ledge and we could see what looked like a CamelBak. He got something and pulled it down. The canvas bag thudded to the ground and three dark green RPG rounds spilled out. The engineers who was examining a well jumped back with a start.

"Jesus *Christ!* Don't *do* that again! It might be booby-trapped!"

These rounds weren't like the ones in the pile. These were new: no scuff marks, and with a plastic cap on the nose. There were no markings. It was as if they had just come from the factory. Further searches on the roofs uncovered several RPG rounds prepositioned in threes in similar shoulder bags. Even the bags lacked exposure to dirt and oil.

Searches of the adjacent compounds turned up similar items. The guys found a burning section of compound that had been hit by the artillery cut off. But no enemy. No bodies. Nothing. Whoever was here left—with their wounded, dead, and weapons. They left behind ammo and scarce medical supplies. The southern end of Lion was a dry hole. There was nothing in the mosque, nothing but buzzing flies in the community square. It was, as are many things in war, anticlimactic.

There were several postscripts to Operation Zahar, but one that was of particular historical interest was the Predator engagement on 9 July. Captain Howie Nelson from "A" Battery, RCHA, was on duty in the fire coordination cell in the ORION TOC that day. When Corporal Boneca was shot, the Apaches were thirty minutes away and the A-10s had departed. The only precision asset in play was an MQ-1 Predator, which was being used to get eyes on the situation. A forward air controller with G-19, Sergeant Jeff Dickson who was call sign Slayer 1-9, called the TOC to ask if the MQ-1 was armed and then if the TOC could take control of the engagement. The problem was that there was no secure link between the American Predator unit, which was located far, far away, and the ORION TOC. The only link was regular telephone landline. So the communications path was from G-19 by radio to Howie Nelson in the TOC, then by phone to the 62nd Expeditionary Reconnaissance Flight, who vectored the MQ-1 over Pashmul.

Major Bill Fletcher described the compound, communicating with a sniper who was hidden in a haystack in a field. The MQ-1 controllers identified the shooter on the roof with the aircraft's camera, then called the TOC, who called back to Bill. Bill also confirmed that there were friendly forces fifty meters away and called them up to tell them to get their heads down. Slayer 1-9 then authorized the release of the Hellfire. The AGM-114 dropped vertically onto the roof, blowing the shooter away. This was the first time a Canadian JTAC released a Hellfire from an MQ-1.

## After Operation Zahar

"A" Company withdrew to PBW where a press event had been arranged to exploit the success of the operation. Lieutenant General Mike Gauthier greeted us as we came in. COM CEFCOM was somewhat taken aback as I exited the LAV. "Dr. Maloney. What are you doing here?" he asked quizzically as he shook my hand.

"Uhhhh, research." (Yeah. That's it.)

"*This* is the kind of research you're doing over here???" He looked me up and down.[3]

"Well, the only way to get it done right is to go up front here," I answered as I scratched my right arm.

"The doc was right in the middle of it with us, sir." Pete Leger interjected.

"Well . . . all I can say at this point is, be careful."

"We take good care of him, sir," Pete said.

"Carry on, Sergeant Major."

The press conference had a few high rollers including Major General Raoufi, the Guv, and so on. I wandered away and hooked up with Major Todd Strickland, Lieutenant Colonel Simon Hetherington, and Major Steve Gallagher who were quaffing water and examining a pickup truck with a 12.7-mm machine gun mounted on it like a Mogadishu "technical." They wanted to know how it went so I gave them all the gory details. I found out that Recce Platoon grabbed a few people but one escaped. He was wandering around Zharey still zap strapped. All of the other captured people were tested and had gun powder residue on their hands.

"How many rounds did the guns fire, Steve?" I asked.

"One det fired about thirty HE rounds in three missions. The other was supporting 'B' Company and expended about forty-five in seven missions. Plus some illumination. That's not bad for four M-777s. 'B' and 'C' Companies called in most of it. We also had a B-1 orbiting the first night in, but we didn't have a good target for them."

The guys explained that there had been some excitement in Kandahar City. The Guv gave orders for the police, including Standby Police Unit 005, to raid all the mosques suspected of supporting enemy activity. They pulled in around 150 people and released about 100 of those in twenty-four hours. It wasn't clear yet who they had, but it sounded like they had bagged a couple of facilitators, although the main purpose of the exercise was to disrupt enemy I/O in those mosques. I wondered if the Guv was getting collateral payback on members of the Kandahar Ulema Shura for their criticism of his lifestyle and what effects that might have.

One of Nick's platoons on a patrol down Highway 1 had a little drama. They pulled up to a police checkpoint and things just didn't seem right so they looked around. Just off the road they found bloody clothes and piles of used medical supplies—empty lactated ringer bags and so on. The police denied any knowledge, but the patrol leader wasn't buying it. It looked like elements of the police had been bribed into assisting with Taliban CASEVAC.

The press conference wrapped up and we were heading back to KAF. Kirk and I were talking in the intercom.

"I saw the enemy casualty estimates," he said. "They're pretty low."

"What're the numbers?" I asked as we hit a bump at speed.

"Only five enemy KIA and one wounded enemy, and five captured."

"That can't be right. No way. 'A' Company took out that many in the first five minutes."

The numbers game was always a problem. Everybody knew we couldn't use body count as a measurement of effectiveness. On the other hand, our sports-based culture is measured by the number of goals, so it is extremely difficult to not lapse into this way of thinking. The TOC I think lowballed the numbers just to make sure. And we all knew it was impossible to get an accurate BDA unless the whole battle area was swept more or less immediately—which wasn't happening. On other operations our people caught the enemy using wheelbarrows to collect the body parts of their comrades fragmented by our weapons systems, and saw people kicking dirt onto blood trails.

What were the effects of Operation Zahar? There was a collection of enemy leadership targets in the Pashmul area. They had a planned defense system and stockpiled stores. TF ORION engaged at least a company-sized force. I initially estimated the enemy took, at a minimum, twenty-five KIA and at least that many WIA, if not more. He lost his ammo and medical stashes, plus two command posts with communications gear and what looked like one or two IED-preparation areas. He was forced to expend a lot of ammo. He was clearly shocked that TF ORION could mount such a surprise attack at night. But more importantly, those leadership targets were killed or wounded severely enough that they died later. And there were three or four of those taken out, possibly including Mullah Baqi's replacement. If this was the base or a planned forward command center or waypoint for fighters that were to be infiltrated for operations in the city, it was thoroughly disrupted. Nick Grimshaw's later analysis, using the "B" Company connections in the district, estimated that there were two hundred enemy present during the fight, including support personnel in Sia Choy. Around fifty were killed, including wounded who died later in the enemy's CASEVAC system. I'll go with Nick's numbers instead of my own.

The Zharey district Taliban were now incapable of conducting operations into Kandahar City (the police raids also shut down their mosque sanctuaries in Kandahar City) and the Taliban were incapable of interdicting Highway 1 during the entirety of Operation Hewad in Helmand province. Operation Zahar had succeeded in its aims.

Ian and I discussed the problem of Zharey district. We were looking at a map, tracing out the movements of Operation Zahar and comparing it to the previous ops.

"That's the third or fourth time you've been in there. Have you tried *quadrillage* and cleaned it out?" I was referring to a technique used in Algeria.

"No, we don't have the forces. I'm spread out from Spin Boldak, to FOB Martello, to PBW, and now we have to go into Helmand again."

We looked at the map. "It looks to me like the ANA should put a FOB here instead of sitting in Sherzai." I pointed to the open area west of the White School in Pashmul that we'd been through on the way to Objective Lion. "It could serve as a patrol base, police could be brought in to patrol the area between there, Bazaar-e Panjwayi, and PBW, then the PRT can get involved helping the population. As that area was secured, you could move west progressively through the district and start to get a grip on it."

"I thought about moving PBW there for that reason," Ian explained, "but the powers that be won't let me. They say Highway 1 security is more important because of the deployment of HELMAND TF. Anyway, there isn't enough ANA yet. It makes sense. We need a presence there. Hell, I wanted to move my whole headquarters into the City but they didn't want that big a coalition presence in Kandahar. Maybe it should be in that bowl north of the Panjwayi district center where we watched Yadgar."

Ian knew we weren't done with Zharey and Panjwayi districts and I knew he wanted to get back in there. I knew looking at the pattern of operations that the fight was here—not Shah Wali Kot, not Khakriz—and that the fight was going to be here, given the area's proximity to the city and the terrain.

But I was in trouble. Major Dave Buchanan ominously told me General Fraser wanted to see me in his office.

"You went into Pashmul with an infantry company???" Dave exclaimed. He was really mad.

"Yep. It was awesome to watch our guys in action. You should have seen it!" I started to describe the night action. Dave cut me off.

"People are getting hurt out here!!!"

My first thought was, "No shit," but I didn't say anything. Dave was really, really mad.

"I can't afford to lose another civilian!"

"Oh come on! There aren't any civilians here! We're all the enemy. It doesn't matter what we're wearing! Hell, we get rocketed every night here! You said it was okay if I came over!"

"I didn't think you'd be going into the fight, goddamit!"

I sat down. I was tired and I itched.

"You know that everybody deep down wants to know what it's like. Everybody who's here. Nobody's going to admit it. I'm a historian and I know that this a constant in human nature. I'm no exception. How the hell can I write and lecture about this stuff if I haven't been exposed to it too???" Now I was getting emotional.

"You've been here how many times before! You've already done that!"

"Not like this. Not with my own people! Canada's at war, and I don't see any other military historians over here watching and recording it. I have an obligation to do this. It's historically important! The Canadian

Army just fought its first battalion-sized *battle* in *fifty years*."[4] I didn't need to explain that that's *half a century*.

Dave sat down.

"Okay. You've scratched that itch. Don't do it again. I'm restricting you to battle-group and brigade headquarters. You can go into the field but I don't want you at company or platoon level. You've done your part."

I got up to go. Dave looked up. He was pretty tired, too.

"If you do this again, I'm going to call your mother and have a chat with her!"

Like she could stop me from going to Afghanistan.

## Operation Hewad and Operation Augustus

There were concurrent events in Helmand province as the "moving parts" were getting repositioned for the next operation. TF BUSHMASTER, commanded by Colonel Ed Reader, was nominally under CJSOTF's control and not CTF AEGIS'. BUSHMASTER had moved into northern Helmand as part of Operation Mountain Thrust in late June and early July. BUSHMASTER was a hybrid organization consisting of two companies from the 2-87 Infantry in Paktia province (TF CATAMOUNT), and several ODAs and their associated Afghan forces from TF-73. The concept of operations involved the seizure of a high feature (called "1999") by a company-sized air assault. The idea was to stir the pot south of the Bagran Valley, which was a designated "sanctuary," while the other 2-87 Company and the SOF ODAs moved into Bagran and rooted around. The airmobile insertion was to interfere with any north–south movements from the insurgents in the Musa Qala–Sangin area to Bagran Valley and hopefully stimulate the insurgents to attack the positions on the 1999 feature. Tier I SOF and MQ-1 Predators would kill any emergent leadership targets while Tier II SOF would move south from Bagran in mobile groups and engage any insurgent concentrations. This is approximately what happened in northern Helmand from 1 to 10 July.

TF BUSHMASTER also had a logistics site (the "FLEE") situated near Musa Qala, and that link went down Route 611 to Highway 1 and to KAF. On the night of 6 July, a resupply convoy was hit by a sophisticated 150-man ambush, similar to the one conducted against the French earlier that spring. Only one American was wounded, but the extraction drew in a significant amount of ground and air support that was scheduled for other activities. This had "knock-on" effects elsewhere in the AEGIS operating area.

For forty-eight hours from 9 to 10 July, when ORION was clearing Objective Lion in Zharey, KAF was hit multiple times with rockets, wounding at least two people. At the same time the police in Garmser over in Helmand came under small arms fire. Fragmented reports flowed in that Garmser was having problems—and then the British and Afghan positions near the Kajaki Dam were mortared. There was ISTAR reportage that Mullah Dadallah Lang and Mullah Naim were orchestrating these operations, and that they were on the move somewhere in Helmand. The relationship between these operations and what was going on in Zharey was obscure, but it is likely the insurgents were trying to apply pressure in one area to draw off our pressure elsewhere. On the night of 10 July, a Tier I SOF operation went in somewhere near Sangin, and an MH-47 went down during the course of it. I understood at the time that the target was Koo Agha.

It was time for Operation Hewad. The Hewad plan had developed to the point where there was now a subplan, Operation Augustus, the air assault. Hewad would set the conditions that Augustus would take place in. The objective was to take out the insurgent command and control node that had already been identified northeast of FOB ROB. While Zahar was in progress, Mark Brewer, Shane Schreiber, and their staffs refined Hewad. TF BUSHMASTER would move south from Musa Qala to the river between the Kajaki Dam and Sangin. TF ORION would block the passes between Helmand and Ghorak, while other forces, including a squadron of the Household Cavalry with Scimitar light tanks, would block south of Sangin. 3 Para would air assault into the triangle formed by those forces and cordon and search everything, with an eye to getting Koo Agha and friends. Left unstated was that the uncoordinated higher-level SOF would probably make a play for any leadership that was flushed out, but there was no way that could be controlled at the AEGIS level. TF HELMAND was left to come up with the Augustus portion of the plan since they owned their own helicopters.

There were some ongoing issues. First, the British commanders wanted a Canadian LAV III company cut to them to be part of the block. There were concerns that "C" Company from 2-87 Infantry was short on men and its vehicles had been in the field without maintenance for some time, and that the British cavalry squadron might not be able to cover all the ground it was assigned to. Incidentally, too, there was part of one of their companies besieged in Sangin. Ian Hope resisted these moves, based on what had happened back in the spring. This is how TF ORION's role in the operations evolved away from just doing the Ghorak pass block to having an increased role in the Sangin area.

But other problems cropped up. Another issue was where the Afghans fit into all of this. The AEGIS staff wanted maximum Afghan participation but the numbers of effectives were low. Major General Raoufi was frustrated: he wanted to use the handful of Mi-17 helicopters that were at KAF but couldn't get Kabul to release them. He wanted to be part of the air assault, too. Raoufi cajoled Major General Esmatullah to try to get the 250-man Standby Police Unit 005 released as well, but, as we have seen, that unit really belonged to the Guv. The units from 209 Corps that fought alongside TF ORION in Zharey had to return north and were unavailable. This reduced the numbers of troops assigned to Hewad even further and increased the case for more TF ORION involvement near Sangin.

Third, there was a developing problem in Sangin itself. A 3 Para company occupying its patrol base in the town was taking a lot of harassing fire, including recoilless rifle attacks that produced multiple casualties. It was about to be cut off. An airdrop of water and supplies missed the target and it was starting to look like some kind of *A Bridge Too Far* situation was developing. I heard later that the paras were down to drinking river water at one point. (I once fell into the river out there. I wanted to sterilize my entire body afterward, let alone drink any of it.)

Fourth: the French SOF down in Spin Boldak pulled out of their positions much earlier than anticipated. The original plan was to have "C" Company from TF ORION redeploy to Spin Boldak after Zahar. When Bill Fletcher and his recce crew got down there, they found that the French were gone—no handover—and there was nothing left in the FOB. The French had taken everything. There was a platoon of American Military Police and that was about it.

TF ORION was stretched thin. Ian Hope still had to assert a presence in Zharey, so Nick Grimshaw and "B" Company's task was to continue to operate from PBW and keep Highway 1 open. There was still FOB Martello in Shah Wali Kot with a skeleton crew of Canadians (the B echelon and the battle group ops warrant officer, about twenty people) and Dutch. The decision was made to turn Martello over to the Dutch and ANA. Kirk Gallinger's "A" Company was prepped and ready for Helmand, but Ian anticipated that more forces would be needed, so he readied "C" Company, too. Spin B would have to take care of itself. The divisional QRF task was also taking up one of "C" Company's platoons. The PRT—well, Erik would have to make do as well. There were no forces available to escort the OGDs around. Reconstruction and development was all but stalled out by this point in the tour.

TF ORION was running into command-and-control problems vis-à-vis "C" Company and the British. "C" Company was now not going to secure the helicopter landing sites for Operation Augustus—that was finally confirmed. The terrain was just too complex for that, with its orchards, fields, and trenches. That changed again as the British commanders decided to use their engineers and fascines (like in Normandy) to help the LAV IIIs cross the ditches to get to the landing sites. There were, however, so many communications issues that Ian Hope waited to the last minute to cut "C" Company to the British commanders. Then the plan changed again. . . .

Eventually, when "C" Company, TF ORION, went into action in Helmand it actually consisted of "C" Company headquarters, a platoon from "C" Company, and two platoons from "A" Company.

AEGIS was also able to get a company from 1-2 Infantry (TF WARRIOR) in Zabol attached to TF ORION for the Helmand ops. This Hummer-equipped company rolled into KAF, refueled, and made ready, just hours before TF ORION crossed the start line.

On the eve of Hewad (12 July) a "dust event" (dust storm) saturated the southern Helmand area and spilled into Kandahar province. It was so bad that a conditions check was conducted at CTF AEGIS. Could the operation continue? TF ORION had already departed Zharey and headed west to Helmand. Ian saw that the dust was obscuring the enemy's early warning network in Maywand and altered the plan. He sent part of "A" Company and M-777 det and engineers up to handle the two Ghorak pass blocks, and established a log det at Tactical Assembly Area (TAA) Spear north of Highway 1 in Maywand. The rest of TF ORION, "A" Company group (the headquarters, 2 Platoon, and Recce Platoon), "C" Company, the American company from 1-2 Infantry (TF WARRIOR), the other two guns, and the logistics trail then plunged into the swirling darkness generated by the storm, traveling down Highway 1, and then up route 611 into TAA Dagger south of Sangin, all without incident—or detection. It was a masterful stroke.

# Operation Hewad/Operation Augustus, 12–17 July 2006

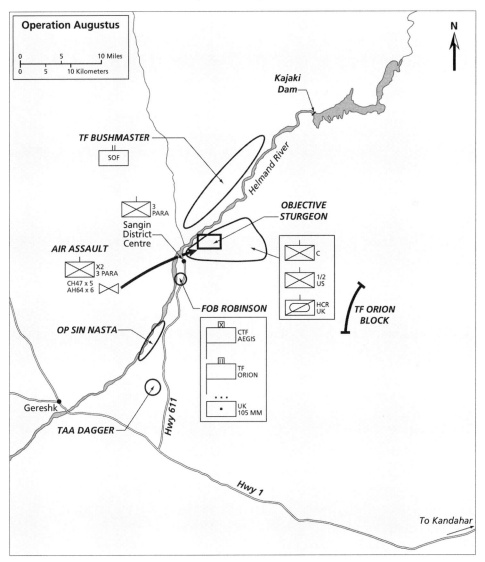

Since Operation Augustus was delayed and detection of TF ORION by the population was inevitable, Ian mounted a series of local operations. "We got our first target pack in the field from the ASIC," he told me. "There was a compound of interest about three kilometers from the laager, so we decided to generate some feints to the west into the greenbelt as a deception, be a pain in the ass, then go after the leadership." As it turned out, the target was an IED cell of around ten to twenty people. They were responsible for targeting coalition movements on route 611.

TF ORION aggravated the insurgent network south of Sangin, waiting for the delayed airmobile operation. Ian, however, was under increased pressure to send "C" Company in to resupply the besieged British forces in Sangin. Nobody else seemed to be in a position, or to be equipped, to do the job.

It was time for me to get out into the action again. Lieutenant General Andy Leslie, the chief of the land staff, was now on the ground and getting a series of briefings in KAF from Dave Fraser. The original plan was to fly him out to the assembly areas, but the dust event interfered with air movements. The decision was made to deploy out there on the ground using part of Niner Niner, Dave Fraser's tactical headquarters that had LAV III, a Bison command variant, and RG-31 vehicles. Since I couldn't go with TF ORION (Dave's orders), I went with Niner Niner, in the close protection party's RG-31. It was a rough ride. We stopped at PBW, where the chief of the land staff (CLS) got a detailed briefing by Harj Sajjan on what was really going on the criminal, policing, and political fronts. We then moved to TAA Spear, located north of Highway 1 in the Dasht in western Maywand district. This was where the TUAV handover detachment had set up its mobile relay equipment so that the Sperwer could operate in Helmand and feed data back to the terminals in KAF. It was getting hotter and hotter, and I wasn't feeling so hot.

The convoy progressed down Highway 1. Would we get hit? *When* would we get hit? Did the enemy know we had a three-star general, the head of the Canadian Army, on board? It took some guts for everyone to just get in and drive west, given the IED threat. If Canada had her own helicopters, this level of risk wouldn't have been necessary. We held our breath all along Highway 1 till we could turn north onto the black track that was Highway 611. Niner Niner moved in parallel to the "road" and covered every compound with remote-controlled weapons systems, 25-mm cannon, and air sentries. Everyone was prepared for anything—

except me. I was deteriorating. I felt like crap but couldn't localize what was wrong. Niner Niner stopped in at a logistics laager that lay between Highway 1 and TAA Dagger and then continued.

In time we got to TAA Dagger. It was amazing: we were moving along what amounted to a prairie, the Helmand River greenbelt way off to our left, mountains way off to the right, a few scattered compound complexes. The column crested a dune—and there was TAA Dagger with more than 150 vehicles in lines spread out below us! It was perfect. You couldn't see Dagger unless you were right on top of it. I could have been in the Western Desert in 1941 with Crusaders and 25-pounds instead of LAV IIIs and M-777s.

I dismounted and immediately bumped into Mason Stalker and Ian Hope, and then the Niner Tac crew from TF ORION who wanted to know why I wasn't with them this go-round, and then the boys from "A" Company HQ who asked the same thing! I had to explain why, and they were all disappointed. "We miss you, Doc!" Pete Leger told me. "You're good luck!"

I sat in on the briefings that Mason was giving everybody. "The plan has changed because of the dust event." He pointed to the map. "It has delayed the Augustus portion of the plan." There were also concerns that the failed Tier I operation near Sangin could have compromised the operation, but nobody was sure. Mason summed up the past twenty-four hours: TF ORION, I learned, had got into some action once it arrived in the area, generating at least twenty enemy killed on 13 July and another fifteen on 14 July.

At this point "A" Company had two platoons (another was attached to "C" Company), Recce Platoon and the snipers, plus an engineer section. Ian instructed Kirk Gallinger to conduct a series of diversions in order to apply pressure on the enemy south of FOB ROB. Kirk was to probe the greenbelt along the river. This series of skirmishes was dubbed Operation Sin Nasta by the planning staff. Target packs from the ASIC finally started to arrive in the field. The packs included info on "compounds of interest," where enemy activity was historically evident. It wasn't clear at the company level *who* was in the compounds, however. The identities of the target personalities were held higher.

One of these operations was a cordon-and-search mission conducted at Hyderabad. "A" Company was to conduct a silent approach on an objective that was, problematically, on the other side of the canal. This complicated things. Kirk and John Hamilton decided to infiltrate the area, set up an inner cordon, then conduct the search. However, when "A" Company led by Recce Platoon made it to the bridge, the enemy detected the force just before first light and opened up. Kirk had 2 Platoon dismount, while the LAVs used their 25-mms at range against the enemy. The firefight was fierce. Kirk later told me what happened.

> We could see the enemy RPG backpacks detonate when we'd hit them. Then things started going south. I had sent some guys north as a diversion. We fired illumination up there to confuse the enemy, but there was no effect. At one point we weren't 100 percent sure where all our forces were. Then there was a lull, so we sucked back and consolidated. A sniper det was missing. It was off on a flank and we had no comms with it. Eventually the snipers made it to the rally point.
>
> At the rally point, I sent 2 Platoon and Recce Platoon into the objective area, and pushed vehicles across the bridge. The enemy broke contact. We secured the area and there was no resistance.

"A" Company found about five enemy dead, all of them in pieces. There were cell phone parts, $3 million worth of opium paste, notebooks, and Taliban propaganda strewn everywhere. "I got that tingling feeling," Kirk said, "and I decided to extract." "A" Company went back to the laager. A helicopter eventually arrived to take the material back to the intelligence community for assessment. It was a significant "take," we found out later.

"A" Company continued with its probes each day. In every case the enemy would fire a few rounds and break contact. It was evident from ISTAR reportage that the enemy's attention was being drawn down to the Hyderabad area. Then on 14 July the American company, Devil 6, got into a scrape near the community of Pasab and requested assistance. Kirk sent Kevin Schamuhn and 1 Platoon in its LAVs to help, where they conducted an operation similar to Hyderabad: cross a bridge and a significant water obstacle while under fire, enter a built-up area, and force the enemy to withdraw. "We must have conducted at least three assault water crossings in Helmand," Kirk joked. In this instance, the platoon second-in-command Warrant Officer Justin MacKay charged across the bridge to help with the extraction of the American force. He was Mentioned in Dispatches.

During the briefings, we heard there were concerns in the British chain of command about using the British Chinooks to resupply Sangin. These aircraft were set to air assault on Operation Augustus. If something went wrong with them, either enemy fire or a maintenance problem, the air assault would be canceled. It was the belief of some of those observing the proceedings that somebody elsewhere desired an air assault for the sake of an air assault, but it was one of those things that couldn't be proven one way or another. The argument was made that American helicopters couldn't be used for the air assault or the resupply mission, apparently, because TF KNIGHTHAWKS rules stipulated that the LZs had to be secured by vehicles that had weapons mounted on them. The British Joint Helicopter Force had no such restraints. But somebody was still going to have to relieve the Sangin platoon house.

Meanwhile, there was a formal request on the table from the British commanders to have "C" Company escort a resupply convoy to the besieged Sangin platoon house. But on 14 June the British resupply convoy that "C" Company was supposed to escort in dumped its supplies at TAA Dagger and told TF ORION it wasn't going, that it was a Canadian job. They had been instructed not to do the escort by someone in their chain of command because of the vulnerability of their vehicles. Mason Stalker came up with a (barely armored) Canadian ten-ton truck at the last minute to move the supplies.

On the plus side, the U.S. Air Force intelligence staff liaison to AEGIS pulled, as Shane Schreiber put it, "a rabbit out of its ass," and secured continuous Predator coverage for the operations. Furthermore, the possibility of AC-130 Spectre coverage for the air assault existed, something that was unprecedented because these were usually SOF-only resources. As it turned out, another Tier I SOF operation was laid on for the Sangin area but was cut off at the pass by Major General Ben Freakley. Thus the Spectre availability.

As the day progressed it was clear to others that I was getting worse. Billy B noticed first, and so did Kevin Barry. "You're really *not* okay," Billy said. This was coming from Billy, who had a brain injury from the suicide attack in June. I was having problems, and my brain felt like it was in a fog. I could see things and identify vehicles and people, but something was interfering with my ability to link them all together. I was getting listless. Kevin got the medic, who gave me a checkover. "Your temp is okay, and you're hydrated," she said. "I'm sending you back in to KAF to find out what this is. Did you get bit by something? Snake? Scorpion? Spider?"

"Yeah. Lots of fucking sand flies in Pashmul." Having been bit by a scorpion in 2003, I already knew what that felt like.

The resupply convoy was headed back to KAF, so Billy and Kevin made sure I was on it. When I got back, I checked in to the hospital. When all was said and done, the chemical cocktail that I had in me, particularly the antihistamine I had taken for the bug bites, was at war with itself and I was losing. "Give it twenty-four to forty-eight hours," the doc said. "Keep hydrated to flush it from your system, then you can go back out. You'll be fine."

Once I had been cleared by the medical people, I had to figure how to get back out to Helmand. I was stuck at KAF but was not without resources. The close protection party told me that the rest of Niner Niner and a resupply convoy was deploying out to FOB ROB in preparation for Operation Augustus, so I got some cigars from the Dutch PX, slung my kit into the back of an RG-31, and was off down IED Alley.

We had to stop to the north, out in the middle of nowhere. There we met a single man wearing CADPAT, swarthy with a beard, carrying an assault rifle that was spraypainted tan and black. He had a small pack, and nothing else. He hopped into the vehicle and we were off. It was a little surreal, but given who he was and who he worked for, it was par for the course in Afghanistan.

It was a long, slow, hot ride up to FOB ROB. The RCP out front found an IED and decided to blow it in place as the column altered course. I saw a huge yellow excavator lying on its side like a dead dinosaur, along with the remains of a low-bed trailer. "This was the site of the French ETT ambush," Major Darcy Wright told me. In time, I saw the low-lying FOB way up on a high feature.

At this time, FOB ROB had a U.S. ETT/ANA compound; FOB ROB also had a British compound, separate but connected. The HESCO Bastion walls surrounded a one-story compound that served as the British command post. A pair of British 105-mm light guns sat on circular pads so they could be wheeled around and brought to bear 360 degrees. I saw the 3 Para Land Rovers and shuddered. They had virtually no protection against IEDs whatsoever. This was disturbing. I asked a bearded para who was cleaning the general purpose machine gun and he smiled and shrugged: "We drive as fast as we can to mess up their targeting." The British stationed at FOB ROB were the "wild men" from the OMLT: they were short, bearded, tough, tattooed, and friendly. They invited me in for a chai.

It was clear to me they were professional but underequipped. Some wanted to lynch whoever came up with the "platoon house" idea, and the people in London who thought operations could be done on the cheap. It was, frankly, shocking. My hosts were cognizant of and vocal about these things and were hoping for better days.

The crew from Niner Niner and the AEGIS tac staff were setting up the command post tents. I could see Major Randy Graddic of the U.S. Army and Major Darcy Wright making sure everything was in place so that Dave Fraser could monitor the battle from here. It was very different from the JOC in KAF. It reminded me of the Cold War, like something out of West Germany in the 1980s, since Niner Niner didn't have vehicle-mounted flat screen TVs or direct ISTAR feeds. It was all radios. There was, for example, no way to look at Predator or any other UAV imagery. I wasn't sure why AEGIS needed a forward command post for this particular operation. There was better situation awareness back at KAF with its ISTAR feeds, but it could have been justified on the grounds that Hewad was a significant brigade-level operation involving Afghan, American, British, and Canadian forces. Indeed, all AEGIS' battle groups, except the Dutch, were represented in Helmand.

I climbed up the ladder to the roof of the adobe building. There were antennas and guy wires everywhere, and cam nets and canvas flapped in the wind as the hot sun was setting. It was in every way a commanding view. I could see the whole upper Helmand River valley, including the greenbelt. I could hear sporadic gun fire in Sangin directed at the platoon house there. The roof was home to a couple of English-speaking Afghans who worked for the British. They were conducting ISTAR activity.

"How are you, my friend?" one asked. "Please join us." I broke out a cigar.

"Better now! What's going on?"

"Well, the enemy knows we're here!" We all laughed. I got a cook's tour of the Sangin Valley and we had some chai.

"So, where have you been and what have you been doing?" I sketched out the ops in Kandahar, including the IEDs in Ghorak and the battles in Zharey. One of the guys struck a match, put it to his cigarette, and waved it out.

"You, my friend, are beloved of God."

"Well, I'll try to keep it that way."

I had just climbed down the ladder around 2200 hours and was nearing the Niner Niner command post when the mortars struck. Two rounds went plus of FOB ROB and exploded outside the fort. There was machine-gun fire to the east. Dave Fraser was standing behind an RG-31. I offered him a cigar and we stood there and lit up as people scurried in the dark for cover. I breathed in my last Romeo y Julietta Short Churchill that I had in this operation as Dave cupped the lighter. He turned to me and said, "So: have you experienced *this* yet?"

I started laughing hard but it was drowned out by the crash of more mortar rounds bracketing the FOB and then the British 105-mm guns firing back, which included a fire mission that killed the mortar position that was firing at us.

I assembled a cot and situated it between the command post tent and the RG-31. I wanted the vehicle's armored bulk as protection in case we were mortared again. Darcy Wright and our bearded friend with the CADPAT had done the same down the row of vehicles. It was still dark when Dave Fraser stuck his head around the corner: "You guys sleep like elephants! You're missing the war!"

In the course of the night elements of 2-87 Infantry from TF BUSHMASTER had moved into the screen running in an arc from Kajaki Dam over to Sangin. TF ORION's forces covered the passes to the east, while a Scimitar squadron from the Household Cavalry, the company from 1-2 Infantry, and "C" Company from TF ORION, screened the comparatively open ground to the south. This "triangle" was designated Sturgeon, and was broken down into Objectives Claudius and Tiberius and several subobjectives: compound complexes that were search targets. (All we needed was Objective Caligula to round it all out.) In the air above Sturgeon were several UAVs of various types: two B-1Bs, two AC-130s, and two A-10s. All of this was in place around 0300 hours on 15 July.

Five British Chinooks (not four as planned) carrying a mix of two companies from 3 Para and their AH-64 attack helicopter escorts were now thumping their way from Camp Bastion toward Objectives Claudius and Tiberius.[5] They were significantly late, by twenty-five minutes, but it was unclear why. And instead of reporting their movements to AEGIS or responding to requests from the same, the helicopter force was communicating exclusively with Brigadier Ed Butler's BRITFOR HQ. This, shall we say, caused some angst at AEGIS.

We listened intently to the radio traffic in the command post. As the helicopter force approached its landing sites, the first two CH-47s were engaged more or less ineffectively with small arms fire on the way in; it was impossible to see where it was coming from. There was one para wounded. ISTAR reportage came alive as the enemy's early warning net reported it had eyes on the helicopter force as it was coming in. The Chinooks disgorged their paratroopers and lifted off, heading back to Camp Bastion. "C" Company with some attached ANA troops was prepared to cross the water obstacles to get in and provide overwatch and fire support to the air-assaulting company once it was on the ground. "C" Company, meanwhile, had problems crossing a culvert, which collapsed after several LAV IIIs crossed it. An enemy observer from a mosque excitedly reported "C" Company's movements, particularly the presence of the LAV III vehicles.

The ISTAR reportage flew hot and heavy. As the paras combed through the compounds, they were coming up with nothing. The insurgents brought in reinforcements in a column of civilian vehicles but changed their minds when they heard LAV IIIs were in the area and turned around.

But there were no "squirters" from Sturgeon. The three Predators overhead saw no movement from the objective areas. Other ISTAR resources were brought into play—nothing. Nada. Dave Fraser reached back to Shane Schreiber who was manning the joint ops center in KAF and instructed him to spread out the ISTAR resources and find out where the enemy had gone.

It was around 0425 hours when somebody or something picked up movement of about twenty people around a compound of interest; it was unclear who they were, so there was no point in engaging them. By 0430 "C" Company had linked up with the 3 Para companies on the objectives. Detailed searches of the objectives turned up nothing of value. ISTAR analysis indicated that some of the enemy had split up and headed north, while others were just moving around and not fighting. At 0537 the search teams found two bodies hidden away . . . and four lightly wounded females. They refused treatment from the ANA medics but claimed they had been wounded and their men killed by a Hellfire hit. This concerned Dave Fraser greatly. "All of the Predators from last night were equipped for surveillance, not attack," he said, mystified. Shane Schreiber confirmed this. Nobody could account for the strike at the time but it was later confirmed that somebody else who owned another Predator launched on something or somebody without CTF AEGIS knowing about it.

Breakfast was eaten on the run. Darcy Wright showed Randy Graddic and me how to make blueberry cake out of the contents of an Individual Meal Pack.[6] There was more ISTAR reportage from the objectives areas or nearby, but no contact. Operation Augustus was turning into a bust. Niner Niner packed up in preparation for its return to KAF after driving Dave Fraser around the outskirts of Sangin. I went with Dave Fraser and his key staff to the pickup zone, where we awaited a pair of UH-60 Black Hawks. It was *Dr. Strangelove* time again. After we left FOB ROB, a B-1B dropped five GBU-31s on a TST four kilometers south of Sangin that was estimated to consist of an enemy leader and fifteen to twenty personnel. We had just overflown that site minutes earlier. Then FOB ROB was mortared again.

The leadership strike occurred when there was a problem evolving back on the objective areas. 3 Para mounted up on the Chinook helicopters, leaving "C" Company behind sitting on the objectives. AEGIS was unaware that the paras were returning to Camp Bastion and, after the problems between AEGIS and BRITFOR earlier, there was some gnashing of teeth again. I found out later that Dave Fraser had told the paras to stay in Sangin, but 3 Paras' CO wanted them to go back to Bastion, so that the 3 Para CO went to Brigadier Ed Butler using his chain of command to bypass CTF AEGIS. This left "C" Company to go into Sangin alone.[7] To make matters even more interesting, orders then came down from CJTF-76 to AEGIS to go to the site of the B-1B strike south of Sangin and do an SSE mission. Ian now had two tasks and three infantry platoons to do it. Oh, and the paras in the Sangin platoon house were still besieged....

Ian sent "C" Company with its "A" Company platoon in the lead to the SSE site, where they encountered between fifty and a hundred insurgents and a volley of ten RPG rounds. It turned into a major fight. Whoever had been in that target complex was important and the insurgents were prepared to fight and die in place if necessary. Indeed, the enemy even tried to outflank the Canadian platoon and did not just fight from positions. The enemy could not, however, deal with the 25-mm fire from the LAV IIIs. One British AH-64 arrived on station and, according to Bill Fletcher, "Just started lacing the tree lines." Bill withdrew his company headquarters and Ben Richard's platoon around 1800 after killing an estimated forty to fifty insurgents. Ben told me, "I decided that a dismounted fight across 1800 meters of grape and poppy fields against a numerically superior foe to see a hole in the ground was not worth it. The CO agreed." Again, it looked like Koo Agha or other high-level enemy leadership got away.

One thing that Ian's people noticed was that eight vehicle antennas had been shot away during various actions in Helmand. Glow sticks usually were attached to the antennas as a control measure. Did the enemy forces in Helmand have night vision equipment? And the machine guns were well sited on the flanks during this operation. That, coupled with maneuver, meant that this enemy was different from the one in Kandahar province. Indeed, ISTAR reportage indicated that the enemy had introduced MANPADS into Helmand, but were having problems getting whatever system they had to lock on to our aircraft. (Good.)

The rest of the TF ORION forces still in the area linked up with the Household Cavalry and prepared to go into Sangin. Armored vehicles and Recce Platoon took up overwatch positions above the city while the Canadian infantry moved on to the platoon house. There was some firing but not a lot of resistance. Canadian artillery was called in to fire onto the west side of the river to disrupt enemy reinforcements, which they succeeded in doing. In time the paras were brought back in to clear the bazaar; Pam Isfeld's super-*shura*, Operation Rana, was conducted by Dr. Mojaeddedi, the national PTS coordinator, at the Sangin district center. Unfortunately, the *shura* was not as well attended as had been expected so the anticipated postoperation restorative impact was lessened.

A number of major issues emerged in the aftermath of Operation Augustus. There was a perception among some AEGIS elements that 3 Para was disobedient in its behavior during the operation. There were particular concerns about the helicopters, the twenty-five–minute delay in the insertion, and the ninety minutes to get in and clear the compounds. The U.K. staff at AEGIS, I found out later, was perplexed at this behavior, so it wasn't just the Canadians and Americans being hypercritical. The critics believed that the enemy was able to slip away during that time. Others believed that there were leaks in the Helmand governor's office that provided the enemy leadership enough warning to escape before or while the blocks were going in. A lot of ISTAR resources had been brought in for this operation. Some of them even had been diverted from Iraq, which was an indicator of the high-level interest in the enemy leadership that must have been present in the province. Ben Freakley backed the operation, but he was clearly annoyed at some of the British commanders. "If the Brits want to run their own show, fine," a frustrated senior American officer told me with potentially ominous implications. It was AEGIS' first brigade-level operation on the road to the similarly sized Operation Medusa that took place later that fall.

On 17 July TF ORION accompanied by the American company moved south of Sangin to TAA Dagger to rebomb and refuel. AEGIS packed up and headed back to KAF. Another critical piece of battlefield orchestration had to be coordinated, however.

The 2-87 Infantry elements of TF BUSHMASTER that had been operating for nearly a month in northern Helmand had to head back to RC East. Their vehicles needed maintenance. The most direct route was down 611 to Highway 1, past Zharey district, through Kandahar City, through Zabol, and into Pakitika and Paktia. AEGIS and TF ORION, with their forces spread out all over the place, now had to ensure that this American battalion got home safely. Moving a hundred or so vehicles along that route and not taking casualties from IEDs and ambushes wasn't going to be easy—and Ben Freakley was watching carefully. There were elements in CJTF-76 that didn't trust allies to take care of Americans and were vocal about it from time to time. The destruction of 2-87 Infantry could have a catastrophic effect on coalition relations, so a lot of effort went in to creating a protective "tunnel" that 2-87 could pass through.

There were minimal resources to cover the whole route. It was clear that 2-87 Infantry could pass through TF ORION down to 611, but there was nothing until they reached "B" Company operating along Highway 1 from PBW and into the City. The run from Kandahar City to Zabol was straightforward, but TF WARRIOR was depleted for Operation Hewad. It was down to two companies, which were operating in the hills. On the plus side, there was a lot of ANA along Highway 1 in Zabol. A variety of ISTAR and RCP resources also were diverted to this task.

Sometime late on 17 July, 2-87 Infantry struck out and, incredibly, made its way back to RC East with little or no incident over the course of the next twenty-four hours. There was a Canadian and American SOF strike in Kandahar City, but it was unclear as to what its relationship was to the 2-87 Infantry redeployment. It may have taken out an IED cell or other insurgents that were positioning to interfere with 2-87 Infantry.

By this time I was back at KAF and sitting in on the postoperation discussions watching the intercoalition infighting and finger-pointing, which I won't go into here. Suffice it to say, there were people who didn't want a historian, particularly a Canadian historian, taking notes because it might poorly reflect on them or their institution or their nation with subsequent career implications. This was not my first encounter with ego and reputation bumping up against lessons learned, and it would not be my last during subsequent trips to Afghanistan. Excessive personal ambition and historical reality seldom go hand in hand. No names, no pack drill.

Once again, word came from the JOC that a TST situation was developing, so I followed a number of ops staff in to watch. Back in Helmand, elements of the Pathfinder Platoon had eyes on five insurgent leadership targets including Haji Mateen, Tor Jan . . . and Koo Agha! Bingo!

The Pathfinders were at the limit of human endurance in their hides. They had run out of water and were drinking their piss to stay in position. They knew who they had and they wanted them bad, but there were just too many insurgents around protecting these five guys. The Pathfinders were requesting one JDAM—just one. One bomb would take out the targets that a multinational brigade had been after twenty-four hours ago. One bomb would do it.

And there were plenty of planes. But somebody higher up wanted confirmation. They wanted to conduct some activity in the area and generate ISTAR confirmation. That would take time. The target(s) might move or disperse. It was now or never.

Then the lawyers got involved. The targets occupied a particular structure. Any weapons directed at that particular structure had to go allllll the way to CENTCOM for approval! CENTCOM. In *Florida*, half a world away. I couldn't believe it. One bomb would take out the key enemy leaders for Helmand province and dramatically reduce insurgent activity for months, buy us time to get in there and exploit the vacuum—and there were concerns about collateral damage estimates. But this situation encapsulated the dilemma, the cul de sac, that the coalition in Afghanistan found itself in, given the apparatus it possessed, the insane nature of bureaucracies, and the media environment the military forces had to operate in.

One bomb.
Not approved.
Artillery?
Not approved.
Is there a Predator available?
Not approved.

I can't imagine what those Pathfinders were feeling when they got back in. It must have been white-hot incomprehensible rage. After all the bombs that were dropped and artillery rounds fired during the course of the summer, the destruction of this particular structure wouldn't have been noticed. Even by the locals who would have enthusiastically taken reconstruction money to build another and inflated their estimates to get even more money out of the coalition and the Afghan government. Once again, misunderstanding the culture limited the coalition's ability to accomplish its objectives.

### Operation Cauchemar: Saving Garmser and Nawa, 17–19 July

Just when we thought things couldn't get any more dramatic, they did. It was 2105 hours on 17 July and I was at AEGIS talking to Shane Schreiber. Dave Fraser was in a meeting somewhere, away. He might have been downtown, he might have been in Zabol. Word came in that Major General Ben Freakley was on the VTC—and he was pissed off. Shane motioned me away from the camera and nonverbally told me to take notes. Finally, I was going to see—no, *hear*—Ben Freakley in action and see what everybody made such a big deal about.

"I've just got word that the district centers in Garmser and Nowzad over in Helmand have fallen to the Taliban. [Governor] Daoud's made panicked calls to Karzai, who's called [General] Eikenberry. Butler's painted [Defense Minister] Wardak a rosy picture, that everything's okay in Helmand province. It's not. We need to move *now*, not eight or twelve hours from now. We're at war, not on a union schedule!" He was adamant. AEGIS had to retake Garmser and Nawa at all costs. "You want staff, you got it. You got close air support, Predator, whatever you need."

"There are special forces ODAs at FOB Gheko. Can we get Afghans from 209 Corps back down here?" Shane asked. "I'll call [Colonel] Reader and find out. Send TF ORION in now. They have at least a company and some ANA," Freakley instructed.

"They're still up in Sangin. We could do an air assault with a para company and an ORION company. We have a CONPLAN [contingency plan] at the company level to do something like this."

"Okay. Abandon Sangin and get in there now."

Shane got hold of Mark Brewer and headed for the JOC. "The police have abandoned Garmser and Nawa district centers and they've fallen," the duty officer told him. "We have no intelligence, and no eyes on, nothing."

"Well, get it!" Shane told him.

I followed Shane and Mark into a side office that had a whiteboard and they started to game out a selection of responses.

"Okay, what have we got?" Shane asked Mark. "We're under massive political pressure by the government and the governor to retake the district centers."

Mark went through the forces available. "Operation Talon, the contingency plan, requires too many resources. It'll take too long to line it up." Mark, as usual, had already anticipated this angle. Shane sketched out CTF AEGIS: There was the Romanian battalion at KAF. There was one company from TF WARRIOR with TF ORION in Helmand. There were two companies of TF WARRIOR in Zabol. There was a full Dutch battle group deploying to Helmand. 3 Para was spread out between Camp Bastion and Sangin. TF CATAMOUNT, the 2-87 Infantry companies, were almost back to Paktika and Paktia. There was an ANA brigade in Zabol. There was a couple of ANA kandaks in Helmand.

The ANA units in Zabol didn't have the mobility to get over to Helmand. Indeed, the kandaks as a whole and especially the ones in Helmand were not really capable of anything above platoon-level operations anyway. They could accompany coalition forces but were incapable at this time of independent maneuver.

The Dutch? "No way. They will not conduct operations until they have fully deployed—and they have not fully deployed. They have been adamant about that since they committed," Mark explained. Especially about deployments out of their area of operations. Turning around TF CATAMOUNT was out: their vehicles and their troops were fatigued. Reestablishing the "tunnel" to get them back wasn't viable at this time. There was a Danish armored recce squadron just coming in to KAF but it wasn't ready to sortie out yet. The Romanians were responsible for

KAF security—removing them from the task was completely out of the question.

Shane got an evil smile on his face and summoned the British liaison officer from the floor.

"Did 3 Para bring parachutes into theater? And palletized equipment delivery systems?"

The British liaison officer nearly had multiple orgasms as he ran off to consult with the BRITFOR log staff about the possibility of a combat parachute jump, maybe the first since Suez in 1956.

Mark looked at Shane. "Are you serious?"

"Who knows? Let's see." We all laughed.

"Maybe we can land some Hercs full of paras on the roads outside the towns," Mark deliberately mused out loud as the British liaison officer came back in. As it turned out, there were no parachutes available.

Remember *Band of Brothers* episode 2 verse 23: "No jump tonight."

C-130s, however, could be used to move forces to Camp Bastion, which had an airfield. It was about twenty minutes by air from KAF. The problem was that 3 Para was spread out holding down real estate in the platoon houses. The para company in Bastion had no ground mobility. It could conduct a snap air assault on the district centers, however. This was not seriously considered by Shane and Mark because of what had just happened on Operation Augustus, I think.

The whiteboard's order of battle now had a lot of red Xs on it crossing out the NATO symbols used for battalions. There was one symbol that was not X'd out: TF ORION with a TF WARRIOR company attached. I looked at the big board: TF ORION was sitting near Sangin on the map.

"An air assault is out," Mark said. The British leadership had determined that Lashkar Gah, the provincial capital, would have to be reinforced first, before Garmser and Nawa could be retaken, so 3 Para was preparing to race to Governor Daoud's "rescue." The situation, as it turned out, was believed to be generated by, as one staffer put it, "a mad governor trapped in his compound, dictating what is going on without knowing what was going on." The political pressure was really on. Shane was now getting calls from Governor Daoud, Eikenberry was about to call—and Dave Fraser was on his way back. There was still a lack of information on what was happening in Garmser and Nawa, so the contingency planning continued.

There was an Estonian mechanized infantry platoon. They could go into Lashkar Gah. Would that satisfy the British? Maybe. Maybe not. TF CATAMOUNTS reported in: their logistics trail consisting of fifty jingle trucks was now not available. Two months of constant operations had taken their toll. They were out of the equation.

"This is called RAPP planning," somebody in the JOC said to me. "Run around and piss pants."

What about the divisional QRF? It was too small—a single platoon. Then the meteorological guys chimed in: "We are tracking another dust event." That would ground the helicopters. "No air assault tonight." Oh, and it turned out that the British helicopters were reaching the limits on their monthly number of flight hours allowed . . . so they might not be available.

Shane and Mark were still working the problem. "I'm going to call this one Operation Chimera . . . because it just isn't there," he grumbled. Then there was CASEVAC. "What happens if this gets really ugly?" one of the air reps asked. "I have to preposition my CASEVAC and medical resources." That was another dimension that had to be considered.

"What we have here," Mark noted, "is that the whole brigade is committed to Helmand province, right now. There is a major risk here, and this is being Daoud-driven. We have an unknown enemy, and nobody knows what's there. We need Predator in there. That's going to take a couple of hours, given what's going on." There was talk about getting SOF to go in to do a special recce mission, but there didn't appear to be the channels of communication available to ask the CJSOTF at this time.

Back in the whiteboard room, Shane looked at Mark, and then me. "You know what the only real option is here," he said, turning to the board. "I've already checked," Mark said. "'C' Company is nearly out of fuel. 'A' Company is short of ammo. They'll need resupply before they can move anywhere." The meteorological people were now predicting blowing dust, which made any helicopter movement high risk.

The risk assessment in those early hours of 18 July went like this: no close air support, no intelligence, no CASEVAC, and exhausted, logistically depleted troops.

"We have B-1s, you know," the U.S. Air Force rep said. "We could bomb the district centers."

"What about the police?" an agitated voice asked. "Do you want to kill them or save them?"

"They're probably part of the problem."

"I've finally got a code name for this operation," Mark Brewer interrupted. "I'm going to call it Operation Cauchemar. That means 'nightmare.'"

"We can't use it. It has to be understandable by Dutch people," somebody objected

"But you're the *Dutch* liaison officer. You understand it!"

The historical record will now reflect that the level of cynical humor in the JOC was high at this point.

"This is definitely a *Sum of All Fears* scenario," Shane admitted.

Dave Fraser came into the room and looked at me. I was seated perusing the whiteboard with its plethora of Xs and taking notes with some of the staff around me. "Hey, give me the chair. *I'm* the general!" I put up my hands in mock protest. Shane brought him up to date. Dave told us, "I heard what was going on when I was at the governor's dinner. Asadullah wants to mount a thirty-day operation into Zharey and Panjwayi. There aren't enough ANA, and the ANP are crap. They abandoned their posts and I gave Esmatullah shit for it. Now we have this." Then Major General Freakley called back on the VTC around 2235 hours. The CG raised the possibility that this was police-on-police violence in Helmand. He was going to mount several aerial shows of force as soon as it was light and keep flying missions until the ground force showed up.

Following up on the earlier points, Freakley was going to press Colonel Reader for the release of a kandak from 209 Corps. He wanted this to be a coalition–Afghan operation and wanted it to be seen to be a coalition–Afghan operation. He told Dave Fraser to compel the Afghan security forces to get their act together, that they—not us—had to be seen to be in front. He was not happy with the British commanders at all. He dedicated more ISTAR assets to Helmand. "Good luck, baby!" the CG said to Dave Fraser. "Butler painted Wardak a rosy picture and there are multiple reporting chains out there. What the hell? The PRT is busted. If you get pushback from any of the Brits, I need to know about it." He signed off.

Dave instructed Mark Brewer to sort out the next phase: how to conduct a relief in place (RIP) for TF ORION in Helmand when this was all over. That had to be planned concurrently with the other operations. He then instructed the aviation staff to contact TF FALCON in Bagram and request more of their AH-64s to cover the convoys that would be moving around. "Run the blades off the Joint Helicopter Force," he said. The whole flight hours thing was beyond ridiculous at a time like this.

It was now around 2330 hours and time to contact Ian Hope and TF ORION. AEGIS instructed TF ORION to stay put and await orders, that the Garmser and Nawa district centers were under attack. "I got quick radio orders, which had never happened before," Ian later told me. "I was almost asleep when the duty officer came in and said that there would be orders in five minutes. I thought we were going back into Sangin at first. The Taliban had taken Nawa and Garmser. We were to recapture both ASAP. The order came from President Karzai to CJTF-76 to CTF AEGIS. We had until 1630 the next day. The political pressure was massive."

The problem was that nobody at TF ORION had any idea exactly where Nawa and Garmser *were*. They weren't on any of the maps. Canada had deployed no satellite-based data systems—there was no Falconview or Blue Force Tracker available in the field to TF ORION at this time. The task force had to wait for maps. Fortunately, Steve Wallace, the Devil Company commander, was able to secure on his means in his vehicles two very grainy Predator pictures of the district centers, both of them on fire. Ian's staff started sketching possible routes on their field message pads based on the image. TF ORION mounted up and headed south to the logistics laager near Highway 1. When they arrived, maps were there.

There wasn't much time to spare. Orders took about ten minutes. "A" Company under Kirk Gallinger would take Garmser, and Devil Company would go for Nawa. Niner Tac would be in the middle. "A" Company detached a LAV III platoon to the Americans for fire support: they were in uparmored Hummers and had no long-range heavy weapons.

The staff were concerned to see where the two towns were situated and what the terrain was like. It was nothing short of a tactical nightmare. The southernmost objective, Garmser, was nearly 150 kilometers away to the southwest. To get there, TF ORION would have to move southwest to the capital of Lashkar Gah. Nobody knew, exactly, what was happening there. Ostensibly it was under Afghan control, but Daoud's reportage made it seem like it was under siege. Then the task force would have to cross the Helmand River to the west, then head south through the greenbelt more than twenty-five kilometers to Nawa, then another fifty to

Operation Cauchemar, 17–19 July 2006

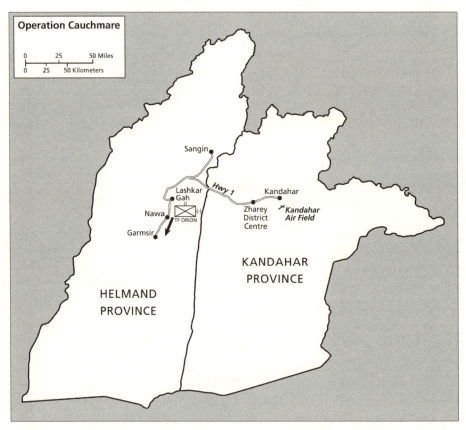

Garmser, where the force would have to cross the Helmand River *again*, headed east to get into the city of Garmser.

The greenbelt, incidentally, was not only festooned with compound complexes and communities, but also was crisscrossed with canals—not just irrigation ditches of which there were a lot of too, but proper canals. At least five canals went northeast to southwest, but then there were sub-canals that went in the opposite direction. There were so many that the maps just stated "numerous ditches" and provided little detail in places because the area was so congested. If the coalition forces came down the eastern side of the river, they would be seen for miles because it was all desert.

In other words, this was a major challenge, and not to be taken lightly. Whichever insurgent leader selected Garmser as a target had thought this out.

Kirk Gallinger and "A" Company had a head start, since Garmser was farther away, followed by Devil Company. As Kirk put it,

> We moved to a night laager. I had two mech platoons with LAV III—Recce was on RG31—engineers, a FOO, and an echelon. A UH-60 arrived. Colonel Hope and I got on, and we went and picked up the OC of Devil Company. We refueled at Camp Bastion, and then proceeded to Nawa. We were watching the approach terrain carefully. It was full of canals and vegetation. Nawa was like a Bosnian village—affluent but deserted. There was no fire, no ANA, no ANP. We then moved on to Garmser. Garmser was on the other side of a significant high-span bridge. There were a lot of irrigation canals, but not much greenery. The village was tight, tight terrain, like Pashmul. It looked like this was going to be ugly.

When the UH-60 made it back to the laager, maps had finally arrived from the Helmand PRT, but they were only route indication maps with very little detail. They were next to useless. "A" Company and Devil Company then moved to Highway 1 for replenishment. A truckload of ANA, less than a platoon, joined "A" Company. An American RCP arrived. It was given to Devil Company because they were mounted in Hummers, which had less protection than the LAVs. "It was the quickest battle procedure we'd ever done—all on the fly," Kirk explained. "If it hadn't been so serious, it would've been comical. We had a pdf file from the AEGIS J-2 that was this rudimentary drawing. We moved through the Lashkar Gah area like greased lightning and RV'd with the Helmand ANP. Or we were supposed to. Nobody showed up, so we carried on alone.

"Sean Ivanko from 3 Platoon was leading, with Sergeant Prescott Shipley commanding the lead vehicle, and we didn't get lost. It was a classic mechanized force movement. They started to report that there were enemy observers using signaling mirrors from the high features. We had been detected as we went through the villages south of Lashkar Gah. I put the company into an extended line and rolled up to the bridge to assess the area. Then the enemy opened up with everything they had." The firefight, according to those who were there, was "a company commander's dream, a live-fire range." There were two platoons in LAVs in an extended line, able to bring their weapons to bear. The enemy fired mortars, RPGs, and small arms fire back. "There were mortars and RPGs everywhere," Kirk said, "but the sandy ground stopped them from detonating. There were airbursts, though. The enemy held their ground but it was a turkey shoot for us. The JTAC, Sergeant John Furber, brought in JDAMs and A-10s, then the FOO brought in M-777 fire once they were in range."

Master Corporal Chuck Prodonick and his section even broke out their 60-mm mortar and started lobbing shells back. Jon Hamilton and Recce Platoon were guarding an open flank with nothing to shoot at and were pissed off they were missing the action. "The shooting went on forever," Kirk explained, "and we were running out of daylight. It eventually grew dark." Kirk estimated that "A" Company was up against a force of one or two platoons. It was in a built-up area, and it was getting dark. He decided to hold off. "I was not comfortable about crossing the bridge in a night action. I was concerned that it might be rigged for demolition, so I wanted to picket the area and cross at first light." 2 Platoon was left to keep eyes on the bridge and the village, while everybody else pulled back to a laager. "We were bagged and we needed ammo replen. Then one of the ANA had a negligent discharge and had to be medevac'd." There was also some night action when 2 Platoon killed a small enemy patrol as they attempted to penetrate west.

"A" Company rolled out in the morning. 3 Platoon and the engineers dismounted and checked the bridge. It was clear. They secured the eastern foot of the bridge, then 2 Platoon rolled across and established a second block in the village. 3 Platoon moved through 2 Platoon and so on until the whole area was cleared. There was no resistance, no IEDs, no booby traps. There were pieces of enemy—and lots and lots of blood trails. "A" Company, however, found massive caches. There were tons of machine-gun ammo, substantial RPG ammo, and, more importantly, a significant number of remote-controlled IEDs and parts to make many more. "We were surprised. That could have really screwed us up," Kirk said. The village was intact, the district center was intact—only the flag had been torn down. "A" Company spent several days probing around with numerous contacts. ISTAR reportage indicated that there were or had been leadership MVTs and HVTs in the area but they had to go to ground and were frustrated because they couldn't do anything.

"We handed over to a platoon from 3 Para. When they got to Garmser, they were wide-eyed. They had ANA and ANP with them, but the Brits had orders not to become engaged. They were there to provide overwatch on the Afghans. When the Afghans found out we were preparing to leave, they probed south and got into a big fight and took some wounded. We thought it was done deliberately to keep the Canadians in Garmser," Kirk explained. "Mark Pickford from 2 Platoon was helping patch them up and a U.K. Chinook arrived to medevac them. The Afghans also had American ETTs with them. We had a real ethical issue here. Do we leave or not?" In effect, the British platoon was there for cosmetic purposes and if they had been engaged they would probably have left. The Afghans were disorganized. The ETTs would be on their own. Orders came down from TF PHOENIX for them to stay with the Afghans. Consequently, Kirk's people passed on as much water, food, and radio batteries as they could to the ETTs and arranged for fire support from the Canadian M-777s. Then orders came down from TF ORION for "A" Company to withdraw.

The withdrawal from Garmser was conducted without incident. "A" Company linked up with the rest of TF ORION and headed back to KAF. That road move was not without incident, though: a Bison was hit with a suicide car IED as it got into the outskirts of Kandahar, killing Corporal Francisco Gomez and Corporal Jason Warren.

## Deadly Day for TF ORION: 3 August 2006

It was time for me to go home once again, unfortunately. After the Cauchemar affair, it looked like things were winding down. The RIP was starting, so to ensure I had space on the Herc out I had to book a time. I selected the morning of 2 August. I dropped by the TF ORION TOC. It was tough leaving—very tough. I said my goodbyes. Mason Stalker and Ian Hope presented me with a TF ORION coin in front of the staff. I was taken aback. "Don't forget what happened here," Mason said. "I won't," I replied. "I'm a historian!" Ian asked me, "You're sure you don't want to come out on this one?" I declined—I knew from previous trips I needed time off to decompress, and I had to start teaching again in September, so that gave me a month to sort myself out. I also knew I was pushing my luck and I had to back off. It was just a feeling I had. It was time for me to go.

If I had known what was about to transpire, I would have delayed my departure and joined Ian and TF ORION despite the risk. Knowing me, I would have gone in with whoever was in the lead, like in Zahar. When I saw the plan it looked like a routine company-level sweep, just another "maneuver to collect" and maybe a VMO. Like all the others "B" Company had done. There was little anticipated enemy resistance, according to the TF ORION TOC staff. Boring.

Right. It's Afghanistan. It's never boring.

After Operation Zahar and while Hewad, Augustus, and Cauchemar were in progress, Nick Grimshaw and "B" Company remained in Zharey district. Their task was to secure Pashmul, which was impossible given that there were two depleted platoons available and almost no Afghan security forces. Ian Hope instructed "B" Company to maintain a presence, and reestablish contact with the local population. Two VMOs were laid on 15 and 16 July, one in Bazaar-e Panjwayi and the other near the Yellow School. Nick wanted to conduct some reconstruction projects, like replacing a bridge near Lakhokhel. ANA engineers were brought in, and there were attempts to engage the locals in the project. "The idea was to improve the environment, and to establish and maintain a persistent presence," Nick explained. "We tried to get the police involved in the VMOs but it didn't work out."

Nick Grimshaw, Jay Adair, and Harj Sajjan also looked at conducting a series of village engagements in the Asheque area. The ambushes along Highway 1 seemed to come from there, and there was a sense that improved connections would improve the intelligence picture. Nick wanted to conduct a *shura*, find out what the grievances were, and gauge the level of support for the government. Habibullah Jan came to the fore to assist in these meetings. He candidly told Nick that in his view the coalition effort had to succeed in Afghanistan: "If we cannot make it work this time, it will never work."

Operation Zahar temporarily disrupted the insurgents in the area. "B" Company's analysis was that the coalition had demonstrated its resolve, and the locals had seen the ANA and the police work alongside the coalition forces. They knew more about enemy tactics and procedures. "There was a higher level of credibility among the locals, but it dissipated fast because of the low troop density after the operation," Nick explained. "We needed to maintain the initiative, so we conducted snap VCPs with the police on Highway 1, just to see what was on the road. People were happy to see coalition troops doing this instead of being shaken down by the ANHP."

Things changed, however. By the end of July, ambushes were up on Highway 1. They were more complex and involved more insurgents. One of these ambushes was two kilometers long. The convoy had to fight its way through. There were daily TICs. Habibullah Jan's people found a major weapons cache, with one hundred new Chinese rockets in it, plus piles of mortar bombs. RPGs were being fired or "lofted" against PBW.

Then the Zharey ANP commander, Wali Jan, was targeted, unsuccessfully, with some form of directional IED that nobody had seen before. And toward the end of July, more and more ambushes were taking place at Howz-e Madad, much farther west than before.

Harj Sajjan and Nick were in PBW one night when a series of explosions were heard closer to Pashmul. They checked and found that there was no coalition activity scheduled. They could see lights moving around Pashmul, but it was all very mysterious—until Harj checked in with his sources who told him the Taliban had dropped several small bridges and culverts in and around Pashmul. The consensus was that the enemy had figured out the LAV III's limitations and were canalizing the terrain in the event of a repeat of Operation Zahar.

With the increased contact and all the other factors, it was clear to "B" Company that somebody new was in town. AEGIS and CJTF-76, however, were nearly exclusively focused on Helmand, not Kandahar, and not interested or were unable to divert ISTAR resources to investigate further. Consequently, "B" Company mounted a series of "maneuver to collect" operations to confirm what they suspected. One of these netted an individual who led coalition forces to an IED factory. ISTAR reportage suggested that some Taliban leaders were meeting in the Pashmul bazaar, so another feint in the Ma'sum Ghar area was mounted and pointed toward Pashmul but was deliberately not launched across the river. This generated a level of ISTAR reportage that had not been seen for some time.

Operation Bravo Corridor, conducted on 1 and 2 August, employed two "B" Company platoons, a "C" Company platoon, a sniper det, and an artillery FOO. It was designed to keep Highway 1 open so that the incoming British forces could surge into Helmand and allow the RIP of the American units that had to return to RC East. In effect, "B" Company occupied the villages along Highway 1 and tried to push south to some extent, but there weren't enough forces to handle both Highway 1 and Pashmul.

Meanwhile, ISTAR resources, alongside "B" Company, worked hard to confirm the new enemy lay-down in Zharey district. At the same time, information came in from ANP sources that the new Taliban leadership were using the White School and the bazaar in Pashmul as a meeting point. A number of police leaders, including Captain Massoud, were trying to persuade Ian Hope to go in after them.

Ian Hope was interested in conducting an SSE of the school area to see what they might turn up. Indeed, he believed that the operation would throw the insurgents off balance so that the upcoming RIP would go smoothly. Ideally, he wanted an RIP in Pashmul itself so that Lieutenant Colonel Omer Lavoie's battle group would be situated on the ground right off the bat. At the very least, it would allow TF ORION to "bone up" on the latest intelligence in Zharey district. At the same time, there were the locals that had been evicted by the fighting earlier in July and there was pressure from the governor to get back in and establish control because it was grape harvest season. Promises had been made a number of weeks ago that the farmers could go back in, and the clock was ticking. This combination of objectives, development, governance, and security made the mounting of one last operation into Pashmul an attractive option.

The initial plan was to move in from the south and the north. The southern force would SSE the White School, while the northern forces would establish a presence on the road. The southern force would link up along the road and establish a defensive position, and then RIP from there. The problem was that the bulk of TF ORION was spread out all over Kandahar province again and forces were short—"C" Company in Spin Boldak and "A" Company up in Shah Wali Kot. This left "B" Company, Recce Platoon, and platoon from "C" Company to do the operation. "B" Company would come in from the north, while 3 Platoon and Recce Platoon would come in from the south.

TF ORION, incidentally, tried to get ANA troops for the operation, but the 209 Corps forces were gone. In fact, 205 Corps in Kandahar were in garrison, but there had been a significant change that prevented their use. On 1 August ISAF took over RC South from OEF. CTF AEGIS now reported to NATO ISAF and was subject to the conditions associated with that organization. What did this mean? First, OEF and not ISAF (who was still in a political tussle over the relationship between ETTs and OMLTs) controlled the ETTs with the ANA. Second, all the enablers that were previously available—American attack helicopters, Predators and other ISTAR resources, RCPs, and SOF—were no longer available because they belonged to OEF and had been moved to conduct an operation in RC East. Third, and this would play a critical role, the change to ISAF meant a change in how fires (artillery and close air support) could be employed. The rules of engagement and authorizations were completely different. All this occurred literally overnight on 1 August. The level of familiarity with these changes and their implications varied among staff and commanders.

An additional problem was that there were divergent opinions on the nature of the enemy in the Pashmul area. Some believed that the information from the police was faulty at best, a trap at worst. They noted the defensive preparations that had been taking place over the past couple of weeks, and the response by the enemy from the maneuver to collect near Ma'sum Ghar. They believed that the enemy was just waiting for TF ORION to make another go at Pashmul from the south. Elements in the intelligence world that were hostile to TF ORION's independent intelligence-collection efforts sided with this view. Another intelligence organization not related to AEGIS or ORION concurred. Others disagreed, and believed that the enemy was so disrupted with the goings-on in Helmand and in Zharey that they would avoid a fight and move away from any force coming in, flow west, wait for the coalition forces to leave, and then flow back in. There were attempts to take the matter up a level to CTF AEGIS and get the headquarters to postpone the operation. One option was to get SOF to do the job, but apparently that didn't work out. Eventually, Dave Fraser, who was in Kabul, came back to Kandahar, took a look at the arguments, and approved the operation.

Deadly Day for Task Force ORION, 3 August 2006

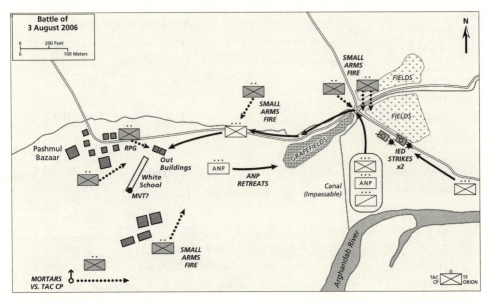

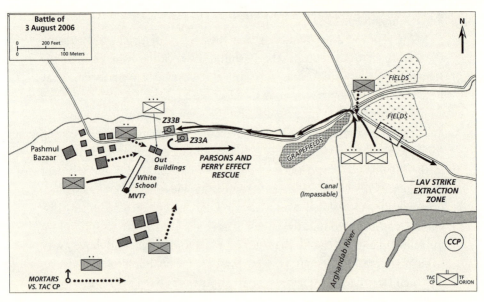

After a series of deception moves, the southern force, consisting of Recce Platoon, 9 Platoon from "C" Company, an ANP platoon, and Niner TAC arrived in Bazaar-e Panjwayi and deployed as TF ORION had before. Niner TAC was on the high ground overwatching Zharey district, with the assault force waiting at the district center. Jon Hamilton and Recce Platoon, followed by Sean Peterson leading 9 Platoon and about a platoon of ANP, moved under cover of darkness into the Arghandab River bed. 9 Platoon took over the lead, emerged onto the bank, and moved up the road toward the T-junction, planning on turning left on the way to the Pashmul White School. At 0415 hours one LAV hit an IED and was disabled, killing Corporal Christopher Reid and wounding another soldier, while enemy fire erupted from the same tree line that "C" Company had been engaged from during Operation Zahar. A second LAV, on the way to assist with the extraction, hit another IED, disabling it and wounding three more. The LAV crews fired back with 25-mm but had problems picking out targets this time. As it emerged later, the enemy had put loopholes in some of the walls to reduce their exposure. ISTAR reportage came in after the first IED went off. An enemy commander said to his superiors, "Thank God they're finally here. We've been waiting for this."

Ian Hope demanded M-777 coverage for the extraction of the two vehicles and their crews. After one round landed, the coverage was cancelled by the Fires staff at AEGIS. There was also a pair of Dutch AH-64s orbiting way, way up, but they didn't intervene, for whatever reason. Ian was furious and called for recovery assets to move forward anyway.

Then ISTAR reportage came in. There was a leadership target, Haji Lala, hiding in the Pashmul White School and he wanted to escape. Ian decided to make a play for him using dismounted troops. Ian wanted the ANP platoon up front to take him, with Jon Hamilton and Recce Platoon in support. As they moved off toward the White School, the enemy opened up from the walls and compounds north of the school, near the bazaar, and started dropping mortar rounds. The ANP fled, leaving fourteen Canadians going to ground in the outbuildings, subjected to a high volume of murderous fire from approximately sixty insurgents. A volley of RPGs and small arms fire hit the outbuildings at around 1240 hours, wounding Jon Hamilton and five others, and ultimately killing Vaughn Ingram, Bryce Keller, and Kevin Dallaire.

Ben Richard and 2 Platoon from "A" Company and Kevin Barry with the QRF (1 Platoon, as it turned out), had started moving earlier when the LAVs had been hit, and Lieutenant Colonel John Conrad dispatched a recovery team consisting of low-bed tractor trailers and recovery Bisons. These forces were moving into Bazaar-e Panjwayi while the firefight was in progress. By this time, the heat was intense and some of the subunits started talking heat casualties. Then the enemy mortar rounds started creeping up.

What was going on with the aviation and artillery support? The Dutch AH-64s were restricted from flying under a certain level by ISAF rules. This was a holdover, one of the Dutch pilots explained to me, from ISAF days in Kabul where they were concerned about *Black Hawk Down*–like incidents with RPGs. Well, those operations were stabilization operations in a built-up area in the north. This was troops in contact with enemy forces in a rural area devoid of civilians. As it turned out, the Apache crews had problems picking out where the enemy was because they were so high up, so they didn't engage.

As for the artillery that was a different matter. As Ian Hope vented to me, "We hamstrung ourselves." Not only had ISAF restrictions on the use of artillery been imposed on 1 August, somebody chose to impose Canadian peacetime safety regulations that were even more restrictive. That meant that the Canadian guns couldn't engage targets that were inside a specific distance from Canadian forces on the ground. Worse, they were forbidden from engaging targets within a specific distance of a civilian structure. Given the circumstances that TF ORION found itself in on 3 August, these restrictions may have been well intentioned to reduce collateral damage, but were clearly absurd. "The desire was to reduce the combative nature of OEF, to deliberately reduce the amount of combat as ISAF came in, and in turn to reduce the *impression* of too much combat in the media," I was told by a friend who had been with a coalition HQ in Kabul, "regardless of the circumstances on the ground."

On the northern front, "B" Company, with 5 Platoon leading, followed by the headquarters, 4 Platoon, 6 Platoon, and a cluster of ANP from Spin Boldak, headed south down Route Comox. The combat engineers led dismounted. Since there was no RCP, they swept for mines and IEDs the old-fashioned way, using hand-held detectors. Sure enough, at the first bend in the road, there was an IED that they then blew up in place. When Nick Grimshaw and his men reached Pasab, they were confronted with a deep irrigation ditch, with the bridge blown. Not only was the bridge blown, the ends of it had been removed by the insurgents so they could not be used as footings.

In the distance, they heard the first IEDs against the southern force go off with a series of "*Boom*s!" Then the forward elements from 5 Platoon were engaged in a volley of RPG and PKM fire. "Four Platoon went firm," Nick Grimshaw sketched out. "We believed that they would follow their tactical doctrine and withdraw, but they didn't. Then 4 and 5 Platoons started firing back and there was a tremendous volume of fire, and 6 Platoon on the right flank started taking fire from the White School, to the west." In effect, "B" Company was getting hit from three sides and couldn't cross the irrigation ditch with the LAV IIIs. "Chief Warrant Officer Rishchynski headed back to PBW and grabbed every scrap of wood, rebar, bricks, whatever, threw it all in a ten-ton truck, and drove back. The idea was to fill in the ditch and cross."

The problem was, the northern White School was a "civilian structure" and couldn't be fired on because of ISAF rules. This led to a debate between Ian Hope, Steve Gallagher, and Nick Grimshaw over the acceptability of shooting at the enemy in and around the school. This took some time.

TF ORION couldn't use artillery. It had no air cover. It was now up to the bravery of a few men. Kiwi Parsons, a New Zealander expatriate serving in "C" Company, said he'd go in with two LAV IIIs and extract the wounded in the school outbuildings. Ian Hope gave the go-ahead but warned him about the IED threat. The LAVs made it, put their ramps down, and started to extract Jon Hamilton's people, the living and the dead.

Back in Bazaar-e Panjwayi, Lieutenant Doug Thorlakson from the NSE was waiting in his Bison with the rest of the recovery column, which was stationary and spread out along the bazaar. Around 1300 hours a civilian vehicle approached the rear of the column . . . and stopped. The driver gunned the engine, mustering his courage. Dave opened up with his C-6 and walked the rounds toward the car as a warning to back off. Then the vehicle-borne improvised explosive device (VBIED) detonated, rocking everyone's world, wounding two Canadians, and killing twenty Afghans. There was no damage to the recovery force. The fact that a coordinated suicide attack could take place during a conventional battle was surprising, and yet was another indicator that things had changed.

On the northern front Nick Grimshaw was finally able to get some air support. A pair of A-10s arrived and expended their ammo loads covering "B" Company's withdrawal back to PBW. Farther south, a B-1B came screaming in at treetop level along the Arghandab River to bolster the morale of the TF ORION forces.

At around 1600 hours Ian decided that withdrawal was the best option. There were no ANA forces, and the ANP were unreliable. There was no reliable intelligence as to what his force was up against. "I would have to give back Pashmul in twenty-four hours anyway," he said. Not to mention that there were limits on the use of airpower and artillery, and the heat casualties were starting to climb.

TF ORION pulled back, consolidated, and awaited the RIP. Then there was the inevitable ramp ceremony, this time with four coffins instead of one or two.

In effect, the action in 3 August 2006 confirmed that there was a new enemy in town and he did business differently. It was an inadvertent recce in force. What was not known until later was that Mullah Dadullah Lang personally showed up with two hundred skilled fighters sometime after Operation Zahar to reestablish contacts with local leaders who were starting to shift their allegiances back in the Taliban's direction.

As Shane Schreiber explained to me, "It was worth trying it and in the end if we had not gone in early August, if we had not confirmed our suspicions, I think we would have been far worse off, probably in October. The Taliban would have further consolidated their hold in the area, the locals would have further slipped away. The Taliban might have achieved their operational objective of isolating Kandahar City by using their strong position in Zharey to cut off Highway 1."

Ultimately, the action on 3 August set the Taliban up for Operation Medusa in September and October. "We started to really take a look in earnest what they had there, so we started to focus more [ISTAR] assets and that allowed us to try to convince our higher headquarters, who didn't want to hear it, that we had a problem down south and that we were going to have to fight them," Shane said. "There was this biased view in ISAF that the Americans under General Freakley had done too much kinetic stuff, too much fighting, not enough reconstruction. The media was reflecting this." People in Ottawa, people in Brussels, and more importantly, people in Kabul didn't want to see the truth. It took the casualties of 3 August 2006 to convince people in various quarters that a deliberate fight was necessary in southern Afghanistan if NATO was going to succeed in getting anything done. The deaths and woundings of the Canadians from TF ORION on that deadly day in August underscored the situation, in blood. ISAF had to get serious. Or else.

Several power brokers in Kandahar City ensured that Ian Hope and Dave Fraser got the same message. Word on the street was that the vaunted Mullah Naqib over in Arghandab district, the man who handed the Taliban the city back in the 1990s, was now wavering on supporting ISAF, and was apparently permitting insurgents to transit his district. Ian Hope, with his replacement Omer Lavoie in tow, made a point of meeting with Naqib. Naqib was blunt: "You need to demonstrate strength. You have bought some time with this last battle, but you need to demonstrate strength."

In another meeting between Dave Fraser, Ahmad Wali Karzai, and those involved in security operations, Wali Karzai recommended that Taliban bodies be hung in the square, which appalled the Canadians. "You have to demonstrate strength!" he said. Consistent messaging. Identical language.

The implications were obvious. NATO had better get its act together, or it would lose public support in Afghanistan's second city. CTF AEGIS and TF ORION had bought NATO some time, but the situation in Kandahar province was extremely precarious by August 2006. It was definitely a Frijtof Capra-esque turning point. Preconceived notions had to be thrown out the window, despite months of staff work. A new paradigm was forced on ISAF and its commanders. Could the organization adapt? Or would it perish?

The Canadian government, which was a minority government at the time and therefore vulnerable to criticism on progress in Afghanistan, was going into an election in the fall. What happened in little old Pashmul at the tactical level suddenly had strategic implications for Canada. If the enemy could generate enough casualties to influence the opposition, those opposed to the war in Canada, and their friends in the media, Canada might get out of the war. It would be just like the Spanish pull-out from Iraq after the Madrid bombings, or the Belgian pull-out from Rwanda after their troops were butchered . . . or the Americans when they left Mogadishu after the *Black Hawk Down* incident. If Canada pulled out, what did that mean for the ISAF effort in Afghanistan? Would others follow? Those questions remained unanswered in August 2006 as the planning staff at CTF AEGIS went to work on a plan called Operation Medusa and 1st Battalion, The Royal Canadian Regiment attempted to adjust to the near-140 degrees F (60 degrees C) August heat. It was a no-fail situation. That particular drama, however, would play out in early September long after the men and women of TF ORION returned home to Canada.

# CONCLUSION

There was a lot of soul-searching and finger-pointing in the weeks and months following the events of 3 August. Coupled with the plunge into Operation Medusa, the opportunity to assess and place in context the performance of CTF AEGIS and TF ORION was deferred. Indeed, elements in the media and other analysts conflated the 3 August and the September operations, and in some cases even referred to these separate events together as "Operation Medusa." The hunt by the legalistically minded and by the aggrieved for alleged "negligence" combined with a lot of armchair quarterbacking blurred almost all the positive aspects of the AEGIS and ORION experiences. Personally, I found it all annoying. This isn't a car accident—it's a war. I Ching. Shit happens. The enemy gets a vote, to paraphrase a certain Michael Mann movie. What do we learn from it and how do we make it better next time? As the Japanese say, we needed to "fix the problem, not the blame."

What did AEGIS and ORION accomplish? The key objectives as stated before the mission started were achieved: NATO Stage III Expansion went forward, and Stage IV was even accelerated in the fall of 2006 in an attempt to get a singular coalition command in place throughout Afghanistan. Unity of command is a key principle of war and moving toward one command instead of two is better. In the long run however, this was never fully achieved and in 2009–2010 there were still far too many reporting chains. That, clearly, was beyond the ability of AEGIS and ORION to influence no matter how talented their commanders and staffs were. It is through no fault of AEGIS' and ORION's actions that other NATO allies were reluctant to join the fight for the south once it commenced. National governments will have to answer to history for that.

Ensuring the safe deployment of the arriving British and Dutch contingents through the Canadian sector to their respective provinces, another stated aim, was achieved. Without the lay-down of and the operations conducted by TF ORION, these substantial tasks would have been far more difficult and, if they had encountered serious resistance and casualties during the deployment phases, there would have been domestic political ramifications with spillover NATO alliance implications. This, thankfully, was avoided.

Achieving Canadian objectives related to governance and development were held in check by the expanding enemy activity in the province throughout the spring and summer of 2006. Systematic activities in those lanes could not be seriously contemplated throughout the province, given the deteriorating security environment. That said, when CTF AEGIS and TF ORION realized that the situation was evolving, they adapted with what they had to confront the emerging threat *and* continued to try to support the governance and development aspects of the mission within the internal and external constraints imposed. As the enemy expanded his operations further, and posed a serious threat to Highway 1 and Kandahar City itself, the plethora of aggressive TF ORION operations succeeded in thwarting any buildup that could have carried the day for the Taliban if left unchecked. The insurgency was definitely put back on its heels by this series of operations.

The actions of TF ORION, along with those of TF WARRIOR, TF BUSHMASTER, and the SOF task forces, saved the British position in Helmand until they could reinforce later that fall. Indeed, special mention must be made of TF ORION's flexibility, agility, and mobility. The precarious British position in Helmand was propped up on several occasions by both Canadian and American forces brought in from elsewhere. As we have seen, only a LAV III–based organization could have conducted the Cauchemar operation immediately on the heels of Operations Hewad and Augustus. It is increasingly evident that those operations would not have been necessary, however, if the United Kingdom had adopted a different approach to Helmand early on. No matter how you slice it, the problems were a combination of the U.K.'s counternarcotics policies coupled with a problematic command structure leading an inflexible force structure. That combination got TF HELMAND into trouble.

CTF AEGIS' problems tended to be attitudinal and structural. In particular was the Canadian intelligence apparatus and its Cold War peacetime mentality whereby Ottawa was a priority to be fed and information over-compartmentalized in a timely fashion to the field commanders during the crucial months in 2006. This problem carried over into the first days of the next rotation when an experienced operator, an officer, was physically blocked by an NCO from passing crucial information to a higher headquarters at a critical time during the September operations. The reticence of some within the intelligence world to accept nontraditional information sources and an unwillingness to accept other nonintelligence staff analysis stands out as particularly problematic. By 2008–2009, this situation dramatically changed for the better. It took these early challenges to get there.

Overbureaucratization with regard to rules of engagement and fire control procedures will remain staples of debate in this and any future conflict. There are a number of examples of this problem mentioned in the book and there were plenty more after 2006. Only human reasoning, trust, and communication can overcome such obstacles. Those characteristics are sometimes in short supply if the right team has not trained together intensively prior to deployment. CTF AEGIS, a multinational headquarters, coalesced under fire, so those characteristics were the inevitable by-products of that lack of common experience and training. Sometimes a commander just has to do the right thing, when it looks to everyone else like the wrong thing. That is what command is all about.

Another issue that stands out from the AEGIS and ORION experience are the numerous times whereby special operations activity was not effectively coordinated with conventional force operations. This state of affairs, incidentally, started to improve in some respects as early as August 2006, in part through the efforts of Major General Ben Freakley and of Brigadier General Dave Fraser and their SOF counterparts. Indeed, when I returned in 2007 and 2008, there had been dramatic improvements with dramatic effects. It is probable that the steep learning curve generated by the AEGIS and ORION experiences regarding SOF in 2006 contributed to this improvement.

Ultimately, the most important effects of the operations that summer were these: the Taliban were unable to physically isolate Kandahar City and they were unable to mount "spectacular" attacks that would have psychologically isolated the population in the city. Yes, they blew things up and killed people. Yes, they seriously challenged the coalition in the Zharey and Panjwayi districts. They threw off the development agenda. But they failed to generate a split in the alliance. They failed to interfere with the continuous expansion of NATO activity in RC South. The road through Zabol province to Kandahar remained open, as did the highway from Kandahar to Helmand and from Kandahar to Oruzgan. The main regional trade route from Spin Boldak to Kandahar and beyond remained open. The enemy failed to generate levels of dissent in Canada that would have interfered with Canadian operations in Afghanistan, or resulted in a outright pull-out.

All of this was bought with the limbs of the wounded, the blood of the fallen, the sweat of the command staffs and support personnel, the tears of the aggrieved, and the sanity of some of us. The odyssey of the men and women from CTF AEGIS and TF ORION is unique in military history and deserves to be recognized as such.

I have traveled back to Afghanistan many more times over the subsequent years to keep track of the war, but for me nothing will ever match the drama and the violence of that long, hot, dangerous summer of 2006. It was a privilege to have been there to bear witness to the good, the bad, and the ugly.

# TERMS AND ACRONYMS

| | |
|---|---|
| 9-W | 9-Whisky |
| ACU | Advanced Combat Uniform |
| ADZ | Afghan Development Zone |
| AEF | Afghan Eradication Force |
| AMF | Afghan Militia Forces |
| ANA | Afghan National Army |
| ANHP | Afghan National Highway Police |
| ANP | Afghan National Police |
| ANSF | Afghan National Security Force |
| ASIC | All Source Intelligence Center |
| BAF | Bagram Air Field |
| BDA | battle damage assessment |
| Bison | eight-wheeled armored carrier |
| BRITFOR | Senior British national headquarters in-theater |
| CA | Civil Affairs |
| call sign | designator for a given vehicle and its crew or passengers |
| CANSOF | Canadian special operations forces |
| CASEVAC | casualty evacuation |
| CENTCOM | U.S. Central Command |
| CERP | Commander's Emergency Response Program |
| CF | Canadian Forces |
| CFC-A | Combined Forces Command–Afghanistan |
| CG | commanding general |
| CIDA | Canadian International Development Agency |

| | |
|---|---|
| CIG | Confidence in Government plan or program |
| CIMIC | Civil–Military Cooperation |
| CIVPOL | civilian police |
| CJCMOTF | Coalition Joint Civil-Military Operations Task Force |
| CJSOTF | Combined Joint Special Operations Task Force |
| CJSOTF-A | Combined Joint Special Operations Task Force–Afghanistan |
| CJTF | Combined Joint Task Force |
| CJTF-76 | Combined Joint Task Force 76 |
| CMA | Cooperative Medical Assistance |
| CONOP | contingency operation |
| CSM | Company Sergeant Major |
| CSTC-A | Combined Security Transition Command–Afghanistan |
| DEVAD | development adviser |
| DFA | Department of Foreign Affairs |
| DFAC | dining facility |
| DFAIT | Department of Foreign Affairs and International Trade |
| DIAG | disbandment of illegal armed groups |
| DTF | deployment task force |
| EBO | effects-based operations |
| ECM | electronic countermeasure |
| EME | Electrical and Mechanical Engineers |
| EOD | explosive ordnance disposal |
| ETT | embedded training team |
| FAC | forward air controller |
| FLIR | forward looking infra-red |
| FOB | forward operating base |
| FOO | forward observation officer |
| GSK | the gun shield kit version mounting a 7.62-mm or a .50-caliber machine gun |
| G-Wagon | armored Mercedes patrol vehicle |
| HE | high-explosive |
| HiG | Hezb-I Gulbiddin |
| HIMARS | high mobility artillery rocket system |
| HTN | Haqqani Tribal Network (or Organization) |
| HUMINT | human intelligence |
| I/O | information operations |
| ICRC | International Committee of the Red Cross |

| | |
|---|---|
| IDP | internally displaced persons |
| IED | improvised explosive device |
| IMP | individual meal pack |
| ISI | Inter-Services Intelligence (Pakistani secret service) |
| ISTAR | intelligence, surveillance, target acquisition, and reconnaissance |
| JCC | Joint Coordination Center |
| JDAM | joint direct attack munitions |
| JDOC | Joint Defence Operations Center |
| JFECC | Joint Fires Effects Coordination Center |
| JOC | Joint Operations Centre |
| JSOA | Joint Special Operations Area |
| KBR | Kellogg, Brown and Root |
| KCT | Korps Commando Troops |
| KHAD | Khadamat-e Etela'at-e Dawlati, Government Intelligence Service |
| KLE | Key Leadership Engagement |
| KMTC | Kabul Military Training Center |
| LAV | light armored vehicle |
| LAV-III | eight-wheeled LAV with a 25-mm gun turret |
| LGB | laser-guided bomb |
| LZ | landing zone |
| M-777 | 155-mm artillery piece |
| MANPADS | man-portable air-defense system |
| MEWTS | Mobile Electronic Warfare Teams |
| MICV | mechanized infantry combat vehicle |
| MLRS | multiple launch rocket system |
| MOI | Afghan Ministry of the Interior |
| MRRD | Ministry for Rural Reconstruction and Development |
| MRT | mobile recovery team |
| MVT | medium value target |
| NCE | National Command Element |
| NDS | National Directorate of Security |
| Niner | commander, Canadian equivalent to "6" in U.S. terminology |
| Niner Niner | mobile tactical headquarters for the Brigade commander |
| Niner Tac | mobile headquarters for the battle-group commander |
| NSE | National Support Element |

| | |
|---|---|
| NSP | National Solidarity Program |
| OC | officer commanding |
| OCF | Other Coalition Forces |
| ODA | Operational Detachment Alpha |
| ODB | Operational Detachment Bravo |
| OEF | Operation Enduring Freedom |
| OGDs | Other Government Departments |
| OMLT | operational mentoring and liaison team |
| OP | observation post |
| PAFFO | public affairs officer |
| PAKMIL | Pakistani security forces |
| PBW | Patrol Base Wilson |
| PDC | provincial development committee |
| POI | point of impact |
| POLAD | political adviser |
| POO | point of origin |
| Pred | MQ-1 Predator UAV |
| PRT | Provincial Reconstruction Team |
| PSYOPS | psychological operations |
| PTS | National Reconciliation Program or Program Takhim-E-Sohl (Afghan government amnesty program) |
| QIPs | Quick Impact Projects |
| QRF | quick-reaction force |
| RBC | Régiment blindé du Canada (12th Armoured Regiment of Canada) |
| RC East | Regional Command East |
| RC South | Regional Command South |
| RC West | Regional Command West |
| RCAG | Regional Command Assistance Group |
| RCHA | Royal Canadian Horse Artillery (the regular field artillery units of the Canadian Army) |
| RCIED | radio-controlled IED |
| RCMP | Royal Canadian Mounted Police |
| RCP | route clearance package |
| RDZ | Regional Development Zone |
| REMF | Rear Echelon Mother Fucker |
| RG-31 | armored patrol vehicle with a remote weapons system turret |

| | |
|---|---|
| RIP | relief in place |
| ROC | rehearsal of concept |
| RPG | rocket-propelled grenade |
| RTC | Regional Training Centre |
| RV | rendezvous |
| SAS | Special Air Service |
| SBS | Special Boat Squadron |
| SFOR | Stabilization Force |
| SOF | special operations forces |
| SRR | Special Reconnaissance Regiment |
| SSE | sensitive site exploitation |
| TAA | Tactical Assembly Area |
| TAC HQ | tactical headquarters |
| TAG | training assistance group |
| terp | interpreter |
| TI | thermal imagery |
| TIC | troops in contact |
| Tier I | SOF controlled from way on high |
| TOC | tactical operations center |
| TST | time sensitive target |
| TUAV | Tactical Unmanned Aerial Vehicle, CU-116 Sperwer |
| UNAMA | United Nations Assistance Mission in Afghanistan |
| USAMRIID | U.S. Army Medical Research Institute of Infectious Diseases |
| VBIED | vehicle-borne improvised explosive device |
| VMO | Village Medical Outreach |
| VSA | vital signs absent |
| VTC | video teleconferencing |

# NOTES

INTRODUCTION: THE SITUATION
1. Amrullah Saleh, "Strategy of Insurgents and Terrorists in Afghanistan," 5 May 2006. This document was distributed in CTF AEGIS in June 2006. In effect, Saleh and his helpers identified all the major issues related to the political and religious fight that plagues us today. (I was told there was a Western intelligence agency that helped translate the final draft into English and there had been some modification.) These aspects continue to be ignored or, at the very most, are approached in an uncoordinated fashion.
2. For an ex-post facto elaboration on this, see Sean M. Maloney, "Taliban Governance: Can Canada Compete?" *Policy Options*, June 2009.
3. CTF BAYONET briefing to the author, Kandahar, December 2005.
4. Ibid.
5. Discussions with Canadian staff officers serving with CJTF-76 in 2006.
6. CTF AEGIS briefing to the author, Kandahar, June 2006.
7. As described in Sean M. Maloney, *Confronting the Chaos: A Rogue Historian Returns to Afghanistan* (Annapolis, MD: Naval Institute Press, 2009).
8. For the full story on the NSE and its operations during this time, please read John Conrad's excellent *What the Thunder Said: Reflections of a Canadian Officer in Kandahar* (Toronto: Dundern Press, 2009).

PART 1. MISSION: CTF AEGIS
1. This call sign's name has been changed to protect the innocent.
2. Air Force press release, 11 December 2006, "No Other Country Is Doing Airdrops," at www.airforce.forces.gc.ca/8wing/news/.

3. By 2008, MQ-1 had gone from "Black" to "Green." As of this writing, screens showing real-time Pred imagery are commonplace in Canadian tactical operations centers. Indeed, Canada–United States cooperation on UAV use in Afghanistan is an amazing success story. Some years will have to pass, though, before the details can be written.
4. CSTC-A was formally Office of Security Cooperation–Afghanistan; it changed its name in early 2006.
5. See Maloney, *Confronting the Chaos*, for a discussion of the various disarmament initiatives.
6. Major General Raoufi would become, temporarily, governor of Kandahar province in 2008. He was then ousted by the power structure in the province because he was trying to clean things up.
7. DIAG: a disarmament program and a verb.
8. For a more detailed explanation, see Sean M. Maloney, "On a Pale Horse? Conceptualizing Narcotics Production in Southern Afghanistan and Its Relationship to the Narcoterror," *Small Wars and Insurgencies* 20 no. 1 (2009): 203–14.
9. The U.S. and U.K. embassy representatives responsible for counternarcotics programs were, I am reliably informed, warned in February 2006 that there wasn't enough Afghan security force presence in Helmand and that the population would be annoyed, to put it mildly, at the AEF's presence and would shoot back.

PART 2. MISSION: TF ORION
1. Gazeau and Poulin weren't the first from TF ARES to get killed in 2006. On 4 March Premier maître Loïc Le Page was leading a French SOF unit pursuing a Taliban cell in Maruf district. During the climactic action, he was killed leading an assault that resulted in three enemy dead and ten captured.
2. Assassinated in July 2008 in Zharey District after visiting his girlfriend.
3. See Sean M. Maloney, *Enduring the Freedom: A Rogue Historian in Afghanistan* (Annapolis, MD: Naval Institute Press, 2005, 210–12) for more on the Sherzais.
4. See Maloney, *Confronting the Chaos* for a discussion of DIAG.
5. These issues were resolved by the fall of 2006.
6. Note that Route Summit, the paved road that runs from Highway 1 to Bazaar-e Panjwayi, didn't exist yet. It was built in the fall of 2006.
7. PRT origins and evolution in Afghanistan are covered in detail in Maloney, *Enduring the Freedom*, and in Maloney, *Confronting the Chaos*.
8. A pseudonym.

9. Sergeant Paul Bartlett of the SRR and Captain David Patten, Special Boat Squadron. See http://www.cnn.com/SPECIALS/2004/oef/casualties/.
10. This was "Phoenix" as described in Maloney, *Confronting the Chaos*.
11. See Maloney, *Confronting the Chaos*.
12. See Maloney, *Confronting the Chaos*, regarding Colonel TJ.
13. In 2007 a LAV-III was attacked in southern Ghorak and northern Maywand district with a large IED. It destroyed the back of the vehicle and killed six Canadians.
14. There had been an SOF raid into the valley in December 2005, and this may have had an impact on the population.
15. The 79th Armoured Division was a British division that served as the repository of specialized armored vehicles such as Sherman Flails, Churchill Crocodiles, and Ram Kangaroo armored personnel carriers.
16. "Second Cup" is a Canadian "Starbucks"—or "Starbucks" is an American "Second Cup." Take your pick.
17. This setup drastically changed by 2007 with the deployment of fully equipped RAF Regiment squadrons equipped with mortars, various forms of radar, snipers, mobile patrols, and augmented with USAF HUMINT collection teams.
18. In 2007 the RAF Regiment saw a change in 107-mm rocket types and identified Iranian-made 107-mm rockets. This indicated that there was a shift of suppliers that occurred sometime in late 2006–early 2007.

PART 3. EXECUTION
1. This is likely from the U.S. SOF unit's emergency ammo resupply from the abortive mission a few weeks earlier.
2. And, as it turned out, wounded.
3. This became a running gag between the COM CEFCOM and me for the next two years. Whenever I was visiting Afghanistan, I'd bump into him after every Canadian operation I was on, and it was usually on the ramp of a LAV.
4. I'd spent most of my time in Afghanistan with American, German, Romanian, and other forces before I visited the Canadian PRT in late 2005.
5. That is, the fifth helicopter could have been used to resupply the platoon house in Sangin concurrently. . . .
6. Take the blueberry dessert and open it. Shred the desiccated bread. Insert the pieces into the dessert sleeve. Add two coffee whiteners and

one packet of sugar. Mix. Put dessert sleeve into a heating pouch, add water. Wait till hot. Enjoy with instant coffee. Get back to the war.
7. Bill Fletcher told me later, "In all fairness, CO 3 Para left a platoon in a helicopter on station to act as a reserve if I needed it."

# INDEX

A-10 fighter-bomber, 205, 241, 244, 247, 250, 259, 302
Abdullah, Arun, 13
AC-130 gunship, 93–94, 215, 275
Achechzai, 101
Adair, Jay, 88, 91, 148, 294
Afghan Development Zones, 34, 35, 36–37. *See also* Regional Development Zones
Afghan Eradication Force, 71–72, 75, 86
Afghan Militia Forces, 55, 59, 60, 102
Afghan National Army, 10, 34, 53, 105, 113, 120, 207, 208, 212, 232, 285; 205 (Hero) Corps, 23, 53, 58, 265, 297; 209 Corps, 57, 73, 105, 229, 269, 288, 297; Op Zahar, 242–44, 256; training, 55–56
Afghan National Development Strategy, 11, 34, 26
Afghan National Police, 38, 59–61, 66–69, 88, 103, 116, 130, 140–43, 146, 157–60, 162, 208, 224; flee at Pashmul battle, 299. *See also* Standby Police Unit 005
Agha, Koo, 87, 95, 227, 268, 281, 283
Akenzudah family, 228
Al Qaeda. *See* Qaeda, Al
Alikozai tribe, 7, 103
All Source Intelligence Centre, 14–15, 106, 109, 147, 272, 274
Alozai, 101

Angus, John, 148
Arabs Taliban fighters, 118
Australian forces, 228
Azizi strike, 47, 93–95

B-1B bomber, 45, 78, 172, 230, 248, 280, 302
Bagram Air Base, 29
Baluch, Abdul Halla, 121
Baqi Network, Mullah Baqi, 90, 91, 122, 129, 226, 255
Barakzai, 102
Barry, Kevin, 111, 116, 154, 170, 174, 176, 178–81, 221, 275, 300; calmness in IED attack, 186–88
Bashir (interpreter), 100, 126, 129, 162, 179
battle damage assessment, 45, 241, 246–47, 264
Battle of 3 August, 294–304
BBC, 43–44, 202
Beare, Stu, 17
Berry, Glyn, assassination, 27, 32, 60, 88, 122, 132, 140, 141, 159
Biage, Marc, 139
Billy B (sniper), 166, 188–89, 191, 235, 275
bin Laden, Osama, 1, 4
Bishop, Tim, 21, 23
*Black Hawk Down* (movie), 116, 188, 300, 303

Blagh village, 179–81
Blatchford, Christy, 99
Boneca, Anthony, 252, 254, 257, 260, 262
Bos, Van Den, 21
Bowes, Steve, 167–68
Brewer, Mark, 21, 35, 227, 268, 285–87
BRITFOR HQ, 50, 70, 279
Buchanan, Dave, 21, 266
Buchin, Gavin, 140
Butler, Ed, 50, 73, 279–80, 284, 288

Calbos, Paul, 59–60, 106, 111, 140, 156–58
Callan, Michael, 32, 33, 132, 145
Camp Nathan Smith (PRT), 249
Canada and ISAF, 6; peacekeeping, 4, 5
Canadian Army Units: 1 Combat Engineer Regiment, 14; 1 Royal Canadian Horse Artillery, 14 (*see also* M-777 artillery); 1st Battalion, Princess Patricia's Canadian Light Infantry, 13 (*see also* Task Force Orion); 2 (EW) Squadron, 14; 12e Regiment Blinde du Canada, 14, 111–13, 193 (*see also* Coyote vehicle)
Canadian International Development Agency, 21, 31, 132–33, 140, 145
Carswell, Neal, 111, 162, 166, 174, 175, 176, 178, 179, 182, 190, 197
Casey, John, 15
casualty management, 80–82, 252
*Catch-22* (movie), 220, 223
Catton, Kelly, 148
CERP money, 27, 31, 32, 39, 66, 137, 139, 228, 230
Chechyns, 255, 257
Chenette, Marilyn, 212, 213
cigars, 17, 111, 171, 233, 257, 276–77
CIMIC, 24, 25, 31, 32, 39, 48, 84, 98, 137, 148, 197, 198, 200, 201, 203, 209, 216, 233, 252–53
Civil Affairs (U.S.), 31, 137
CIVPOL, 14, 59–60, 88, 139
clear-hold-build, 217–19

Combined Forces Command Afghanistan, 74
Combined Joint Prioritized Kinetic Target List, 47
Combined Joint Special Operations Task Force, 9, 10, 47, 65, 85, 86, 195, 228, 267
Combined Joint Task Force 76, 9, 11, 12, 22, 26, 29, 33, 120, 155, 158, 167, 225, 227, 280, 282; campaign plan 12, 156
Combined Security Transition Command Afghanistan (U.S.), 53
Combined Task Force AEGIS (CDN-led), 6, 9, 10, 11, 13, 24–26, 29, 33, 41, 57, 120, 225, 227, 229, 280; command arrangements, 12; development, 31, 145; fire control on 3 August, 299–301; helicopter issues, 49–51; organization, 21–23
Combined Task Force BAYONET, 9, 10, 102
Combined Task Force DEVIL, 9
communications systems, 117
Confidence in Government plan, 32, 33, 132–33
Conrad, John, 14, 58, 220
Co-operative Medical Assistance, 214
Costall, Robert, 87
counter-narcotics operations, 8, 74–77
Coyote vehicle, 14, 87, 99, 112, 113, 116, 117, 165, 193, 232
CU-116 Sperwer, 15, 87, 92, 114, 116, 148, 149, 192, 218, 232, 248

Dallaire, Kevin, 299
Daoud, Engineer, 37–38, 73, 284, 289–90
Dart, Nathan, 242–43
Davis, Greg, 111, 173, 188
Davis, Paul, 85
Davis, Ross, 139
deception operations, 172–73, 209, 231
Department of Foreign Affairs and International Trade, 21, 140
Deployment Task Force (Dutch), 38, 62–63, 98
detainee issue in Canada, 174

Dickson, Jeff, 262
Dimeray, Suleyman, 100, 149–53
Dinning, Matthew, 85
Duggan, Mike, 17
Duguid, Ian, 51–52
Dupuis, Mart, 209, 210–11
Durrani tribes, 7
DynCorp, 75, 141

effects based operations, 24–25, 27
effects mitigation, 47–8, 92–95, 143
Electrical and Mechanical Engineers, 19
Elrick, Ryan, 191, 203
embedded training teams (ETTs), 53–4, 56, 95, 113, 242, 254, 276, 293
Esmatallah, Major General, 60–61, 69, 106, 111, 156–58, 160, 269, 288
Estonian forces, 231–32, 287
explosive ordnance disposal, 45

Falconview system, 116
Fayaz killing, 153
Ferris, Dave, 146–48
Fisher, Matthew, 99
Fletcher, Bill, 13, 85, 87, 113, 120, 173, 208, 211, 239, 250, 254, 257, 259, 263, 269
foco-ism, 8–9
forward operating base mentality, 195
forward operating bases (FOBs):
    Gheko, 230; Martello, 53, 62–64, 84, 96, 98, 149, 170, 192, 195, 196, 204, 209, 228, 232, 269; Robinso, 86–88, 95, 268, 273, 276, 280. *See also* Patrol Base Wilson
Franklin, Paul, 191
Fraser, David, 21, 22, 26, 27, 45, 46, 59, 67, 73, 85, 96, 97, 99, 106, 108, 133, 145, 150, 207, 220, 223, 228, 229, 234, 266, 272, 277, 279, 280, 288, 297, 303
Freakley, Ben, 11, 26, 33, 46–47, 73, 93, 94, 114, 120, 233–34, 275, 282, 284, 288, 302
Furber, John, 292

Gallagher, Steve, 14, 85, 92, 110, 113, 236, 263, 301

Gallinger, Kirk, 13, 84–86, 165, 169, 170, 197–98, 199, 233; 236–47, 256, 257, 259, 261, 273, 291–92
Garmser, 225, 284–91
Gauthier, Mike, 235, 263
Gazeau, Joel, 95
Ges, Bert, 10, 83, 122
Ghorak district, 175–85
Gibson, Brian, 197, 233, 246
Goddard, Nichola, 82, 87, 92
Godefroy, Mark, 14
Gomez, Francisco, 293
GR-7A Harrier (fighter-bomber), 52–53, 114
Graddic, Randy, 21, 277, 280
Grau, Les, 210
Green, Christina, 21, 31, 32–35, 39–40, 137
Green Beans coffee shop, 192, 233
Greene, Trevor attack on, 85
Grimshaw, Nick, 13, 88, 91, 102, 103, 118, 120, 142, 144–48, 166, 169, 182, 226, 239, 248, 249, 250, 257, 260, 264–65, 269, 294, 300–301
Guantanamo Bay, 124
Guillaumme, Dan, 233, 235, 236, 237, 240, 242
Gumbad Platoon House, 84, 193, 206–18
Gumbad Sniper, The, 207, 215

Hamilton, Jon, 192–93, 196, 198–99, 204–6, 241, 257, 261, 274, 292, 299, 301
Haqqani Tribal Network, 6, 7, 47
Harold, Bob, 97
Hart, Bob, 139, 142
Hart, Darren, 104–5
Hayward, Dave "Stitch", 111, 112, 188
Helmand province, 10, 29, 35, 38, 57, 64, 70–77, 84–6, 226–27
Helmand Task Force, 43, 49–50, 70–77, 225, 227, 266, 268
Hetherington, Simon, 14, 236, 263
Hezb-I Gulbiddin, 6, 7, 71, 110, 111, 227
HIMARS, 45–6, 47
Hope, Ian, 13, 83, 86, 92–93, 95, 96, 97, 100, 103, 105–6, 112, 114,

119–20, 121, 122, 124, 125, 126, 130, 131, 144, 154, 156–58, 163, 165, 166, 168–69, 173, 176, 178–81, 185, 191, 185, 217, 223, 228, 234, 236, 249, 259, 265, 269, 273, 294, 296, 299–300, 303
House, Tim, 33, 34, 35, 53–54, 59
HUMINT, 96, 109–10, 112, 117–18, 120–21, 122, 123, 148, 254
Hunt, Chris, 232

Ibrahim, Mullah, 90, 122, 123, 124, 126–31
IED, suicide vehicle borne, 186–97
IED attacks, 81, 83, 85, 126, 144, 153–54, 177–92, 203, 207, 293, 295, 299, 301; and I/O attacks, 42
IED cells, 94, 122, 144, 252, 265; Ghorak cell, 175–85; Helmand, 272
IED facilitators, 48, 143, 144, 154
IED methods, 171, 184–85, 196, 203–4, 295
information operations (I/O), 24, 29, 31, 34, 39, 40–43, 93, 100, 109, 123, 130–31, 149–53, 157, 212, 215, 221–22, 228, 264
Ingram, Vaughn, 299
Innes, Quenton "Q", 40, 42, 98, 99, 123, 124, 130
intelligence "enablers", 23
intelligence processes, 105–9, 117, 143, 147–48, 166, 171, 173, 176, 181, 212, 241, 297
International Committee of the Red Cross (ICRC), 135–36
International Monetary Fund, 34
International Security Assistance Force, 1, 2, 4, 5; expansion, 5; implications of 3 August, 303–4; Stage III Expansion, 2, 6, 13, 28
interpreters, 43
Iraq war, 1, 4, 32, 282
Irwin, Anne, 18, 20
Isfeld, Pam, 21–22, 33, 61, 281
Ishaqzai tribe, 7
ISI, Inter-Services Intelligence, 122, 128, 129
Ivanko, Sean, 292

Jan, Habbibullah, 102, 103, 145, 294, 295
Jan, Kadr, 89–90
Jan, Tor, 140, 152, 224
Jan, Wali, 148, 295
JDAMS, 45, 47, 92, 172, 283
jingle trucks, 169
Joint (Provincial) Coordination Centre, 100, 104–8, 140, 142, 147, 149, 155, 160, 162, 229
Joint Defence Operations Centre, 222–23
Joint Fires Effects Coordination Centre, 24–25, 27
Joint Operations Centre, 23, 44
Joint Special Operations Areas, 10–11, 61, 93, 154, 193
Joint Special Operations Command (JSOC), 54, 93. *See also* Other Coalition Forces
JTACs, 169, 237, 244, 246–47, 259, 262–63, 292

Kabul Military Training Center, 55–57
Kajaki Dam, 225, 227, 228, 268, 278
Kakar tribe, 122
Kandahar Air Field, 9, 15, 18, 43, 44; 114, 123; rocket attacks against, 82, 95, 121, 218, 221–23, 226, 230, 268
Kandahar Provincial Reconstruction Team, 11, 14, 27
Kandahar Ulema Shura, 42–43, 151–53, 264
Karzai, Ahmad Wali, 303
Karzai, Hamid, 37, 38, 39, 47, 61, 228
Keller, Bryce, 299
Kelly, Wayne, 88
Khakriz district, 161–75
Khalid, Assadulla ("The Guv"), 33, 39, 94, 96, 97, 99–100, 103–6, 123, 151, 154, 156–60, 263, 264, 269, 288, 296
kidnappings, 229–30
Knaggs, Charlie, 72
Knudsen, S., 35

Lala, Haji, 299
Lalai (Destegeri), Haji Agha, 103, 123, 124, 126, 145

INDEX | 323

Lang, Mullah Dadullah, 43, 94, 122, 226, 227, 268, 302
Larose, Martin, 85, 203
LAV-III vehicle, 13, 19–20, 116, 174–75, 178, 181
Lavoie, Omer, 296
leadership targeting, 25–26, 124, 226, 283
legal system, 60
Leger, Pete, 84–6, 197–98, 199, 233, 236, 242–43, 246–48, 263, 273
Leslie, Andrew, 272
Liebert, Erik, 14, 134–39, 142, 145, 217, 270
Littell, Tony, 213–14
"Lucky" (interpreter), 200–201

M-777 artillery, 14, 84, 87, 96, 113, 148, 156–57, 171, 209, 232, 236, 251, 263–64, 292, 299
Maceachern, Errol, 55–56
Macintyre, Mark, 219–21
Mackay, Justin, 237, 275
Malang, Mullah, 170
manouvre to collect operations, 295–96
Mansell, Myles, 86
Martin, Walter, 200, 202, 233, 234–35, 237, 253, 259
Martin, Wayne, 139, 142
Maruf district, 10
Massoud, Zia, 88–89, 96, 101, 104, 106–7, 109, 110, 111, 112, 114, 117, 119, 120, 123, 147, 149, 156, 157, 158, 161, 162, 165, 166, 171, 173, 178–85, 187, 189, 254, 296
Matin, Haji, 28
McCambridge, Al, 139, 140–41
McGlaughlan, "Beave", 66–8
medical operations, 24, 50–51, 97–98, 113, 135, 145–46, 244, 248, 287. *See also* village medical outreach (VMO)
Ministry of Rural Reconstruction and Development, 22, 36–37
Mobile Electronic Warfare Teams, 14
Mohommed, Niaz "Junior", 125–26
mosques, 7–8, 109, 149–53, 246, 264
MQ-1 Predator UAV, 46, 47, 63, 96, 113, 116, 148, 199, 232, 241, 253, 262, 279–80

mullah, wandering. *See* "wandering mullah"
mullahs, 42, 151, 157
Multinational Medical Unit (Role 3), 123, 124, 126, 130, 191

Naim, Mullah, 268
Naqib, Mullah, 303
Naqib, Toor, 173, 195
narcotics groups, 7, 71–77
National Directorate of Security, 7, 105, 107, 123, 142, 143, 147, 148, 160, 192, 212, 229
National Police Reform Program, 59
National Solidarity Program, 32, 33
National Support Element, 14, 19, 190, 270, 301; and mentoring ANA, 58
Neild, Tom, 40, 98, 130–31
Nelson, Howie, 171, 262
"night letters", 85, 122
non-governmental organizations, 31, 32, 38–9, 68, 136–37, 229
Noorzai tribe, 7, 101, 109, 180, 181
Norris, Chuck, 197
Noseworthy, Randy, 139

Omar, Mullah, 121, 129, 162
Operation Augustus, 228, 233, 268–84
Operation Bator, 87
Operation Bravo Corridor, 296
Operation Bravo Guardian, 91–92
Operation Cauchemar, 284–93
Operation Counterstrike, 83
Operation Enduring Freedom, 2, 4, 5; command arrangements, 9, 11
Operation Hewad, 227–28, 265, 268–84
Operation Jagra, 110–21, 154, 169, 225, 231, 249
Operation Katera, 86–88
Operation Mountain Lion, 229
Operation Mountain Thrust, 11–12, 28, 34, 35, 63, 102, 149, 153, 154, 161, 167
Operation Rana, 229, 281
Operation Rocket Man, 84, 218–24
Operation Sin Nasta, 273
Operation Sola Kowel, 84–86

Operation Taber Kutel, 155, 157, 161–75
Operation Taber Polad, 192–206
Operation Yadgar, 91–92, 226
Operation Zahar, 231, 233–67, 295, 302
operational detachment alpha (ODA), 54–55, 86–87, 192, 209–10, 267. *See also* Special Operations Forces (SOF)
operational detachment bravo (ODB), 61, 73
operational mentor and liaison teams (OMLTs), 53, 54, 277
Oruzgan province, 61–63, 228
Other Coalition Forces, 47, 93–94, 267–68, 273, 275
Owens, Kevin, 9

Pakistan, 8, 23, 24, 37, 77–80, 122, 126, 154, 169
Panjwayi district, 47, 101, 115, 116, 118, 144, 147–48, 225; Taliban ratline, 121; terrain 118
Parsons, Keith, 111
Parsons, "Kiwi", 301
Pashmul, 112, 117, 120, 144, 193, 226, 239, 248, 249, 294, 296
Pashtunwali, 151, 173
Patrol Base Wilson, 90, 112, 134, 144, 148, 226, 232
Payne, Randy, 86
Peyton, Paul, 55–56
Pickford, Mark, 199–203, 237, 242, 245, 261, 293
Pichovich, Steve, 197, 233
Pistone, Renata, 140
Polain, David, 95
police corruption, 89, 102, 105, 142, 160, 161, 166, 201, 264
Popalzai tribe, 7, 102, 145
poppy, 7, 65, 89, 247
poppy eradication, 8, 71, 103. *See also* Afghan Eradication Force
Prioritized Kinetic Target List, 47
Prodonick, Chuck, 200, 245, 292
Provincial Coordination Centres, 34, 59, 88, 106–8
provincial development committees, 22, 33, 34, 36, 39, 89

Provincial Reconstruction Teams, 4, 9, 10, 17, 27, 32, 33, 35, 39, 40; in Helmand, 70, 75–76; and ISAF, 5; in Kandahar, 6, 60, 88, 100, 121, 131–40, 151, 176, 218
psychological effects of war, 81–83, 186, 187
PSYOPS, 24, 25, 40, 41, 65, 98, 124, 197, 199, 200, 202, 258, 260–61
PTS amnesty program, 47, 123, 124, 205, 229; Dr. Mojadeddi and, 229, 281
public affairs versus I/O, 41
Punjabi fighters (Taliban), 162, 171

Qaeda, Al, 1, 5, 6, 24, 116, 126
Quetta, 223
Quetta Shura, 6, 7, 42, 65, 94, 121, 122, 157
quick impact projects, 39, 137, 139

RAF, 51–52, 57
RAF Regiment, 40, 222–23
Raike, Chris, 197, 233, 241, 244, 246
Raoufi, Major General, 58–59, 263, 269
Reader, Ed, 267, 284, 288
Red Cross. *See* International Committee of the Red Cross (ICRC)
Regional Command (South), 5, 9, 31, 227
Regional Command Assistance Group, 53
Regional Development Zones, 34, 35. *See also* Afghan Development Zones
Reid, Christopher, 299
religious engagement, 149–53
RG-31 Nyala vehicle, 13, 20, 110, 176
Richard, Ben, 237, 239, 245, 261, 281, 300
Richards, David, 37
road paving, 101
Roberge, Julie, 40, 124, 130, 212, 213
rocket attacks against KAF, 82, 95, 121, 218, 221–24, 226, 230, 268; conspiracies about, 220–21
"Role 3" (hospital). *See* Multinational Medical Unit
Romanian Army, 65–66, 83, 222

route clearance package (RCP), 96, 109, 208–9, 210, 232, 276
Royal Canadian Mounted Police, 88, 139–40

Saifullah, Haji, 103, 182, 249
Sajjan, Harjit, 102, 103, 106, 142, 147, 148, 157, 272, 294
Saleh, Amrullah, 7, 8
Sarposa Prison, 101
Saul, Keith, 155, 208
schools, 7, 65–66, 102, 136–37
Schreiber, Shane, 21, 23, 27, 223, 229, 268, 275, 279–80, 284–89, 302
"Schreiber-Hope gram", 28–29
Seyyedin, 111–12
Shamuhn, Kevin, 237, 245, 247, 274
Sherzai, Gul Agha, 102
Sherzai, Rezik, 102, 220
Shipley, Prescott, 292
Shukur, Mullah, 162, 165, 169, 170–72, 195
Snipers, 165, 166, 176, 187, 224. *See also* Gumbad Sniper
Special Operations Forces (SOF), 5, 6, 10, 13, 24, 29, 35, 38, 43, 47, 54, 63, 70, 71, 92–95, 101, 109, 122, 124, 134, 154, 193–95, 212–13, 226, 227, 229, 282; British, 142–43; Canadian, 154–55, 158, 170, 229; Dutch, 10, 170; French, 10, 95; U.S. (*see* Joint Special Operations Command [JSOC], operational detachment alpha [ODA], operational detachment bravo [ODB], Task Force 31, Task Force 73)
Spin Boldak, 10, 269, 297
Stage III Expansion, 13, 28, 33, 35, 229
Stalker, Mason, 13, 97, 154, 193, 231, 235, 273, 294
Standby Police Unit 005, 59, 88, 101, 103, 104, 107, 114, 123, 147, 156, 158–59, 264, 269
State Department, U.S., 71, 75
Stone, John, 87
Strickland, Todd, 13, 263
Strong, Gerald, 197, 233, 246

Strueck, Frank, 61–62, 67
Stutchfield, Daniel, 51–52
sufism, 150
suicide bombers, 188–89

Tahir, Mullah, 84, 162, 170, 195
Taliban, 6–10, 24, 94–95, 96, 104, 147, 200–202; code-names, 116, 119–20; info ops, 44, 71, 85, 103, 122, 151, 156, 181–82, 207, 227, 242, 245, 295; intimidation, 172; medical system, 169, 247, 264; and mosques, 8; movements, 105, 117, 163; parallel government, 196; police infiltration, 146–47, 174, 232, 264; Punjabi fighters, 162, 171; sanctuary areas, 12, 156; types, 120; view of female soldiers, 204
Tarin Kot road, 62–63, 84, 98, 192, 198, 203, 228
Task Force 31, 10, 11
Task Force 42, 143
Task Force 73, 61, 86, 267
Task Force Bushmaster, 228, 233, 267, 278, 282
Task Force Catamount, 267, 285
Task Force Eagle, 75–76
Task Force Gundevils, 10, 83, 106, 121, 207
Task Force IED Defeat, 190
Task Force Knighthawks, 49–51, 64, 113, 193, 196–97, 255, 275
Task Force Marauder, 233
Task Force Orion, 6, 9, 11, 13–14, 27, 40, 41, 63, 82, 83, 94, 105, 121, 193, 195, 225, 269; and PRT, 133–34; TOC, 117, 122, 154, 155, 161, 170, 174, 227, 231, 285
Task Force Phoenix, 53–5, 293. *See also* Kabul Military Training Center
Task Force Warrior, 61, 64–69, 228, 270, 274, 282, 285
Task Force Whitesharks, 83
10th Mountain Division, 6, 11
Thayne, Andy, 40
Thorlakson, Douglas, 301
Tim Horton's, 211, 220
time sensitive targets, 43, 155, 280, 283

Tootal, Stuart, 74
training assistance group, 55–56
TUAV. *See* CU-116 Sperwer
Turner, William, 86

UK Army units: 3 Para, 73–74, 230, 268–9, 276, 279; Household Cavalry Regiment, 268, 278, 281; Pathfinder Platoon, 283–84
UK helicopter problems, 50, 195, 275, 279–81, 289
United Nations in Afghanistan, 31, 33, 68, 158, 161, 230
United States Protections and Investigations (USPI), 103, 161, 225, 227
USAID, 32, 66, 71, 132, 134, 145, 225

vehicle recovery ops, 19–20, 190
Vernon, Chris, 21, 23, 36, 38–40, 77–80, 108
veterinary operations, 216
village medical outreach (VMO), 65, 90, 136, 145, 192, 226, 294; Gumbad VMO, 193, 206–18
von Finkelstein, Konrad, 148

"wandering mullah", 180–81
Warren, Jason, 293
Wattie, Chris, 221
Webb, Trevor, 14, 110, 178, 252, 255
White, Greg "Whitey", 111, 177, 179, 187–88, 191
Williams, Nigel, 111, 112, 173, 188
Williams, Peter, 21, 24
Williams, Steve, 21
Wilson, Rick, 214
Wilson, Tim, 85
World Bank, 34
World Food Program, 137
Wright, Darcy, 81–2, 276–78, 280

Zabol province, 10, 27, 53–54, 57
Zabol PRT, 64–69
Zahir, Mullah, 87
Zhrarey district, 88–90, 96, 101, 104, 121, 144, 147, 168, 185, 225, 232; enemy build up, 227; enemy leadership disrupted, 91; terrain, 118
Zia, Ehsan, 36–40
Zimmer, Hans, 17, 19
Zoi, Yusuf, 142

# ABOUT THE AUTHOR

**Dr. Sean M. Maloney** is associate professor in history at Royal Military College of Canada and taught in the War Studies Program for ten years. He is currently the historical adviser to the Chief of the Land Staff for the war in Afghanistan. He previously served as the historian for 4 Canadian Mechanized Brigade, the Canadian Army's primary Cold War NATO commitment, right after the reunification of Germany and at the start of Canada's long involvement in the Balkans. Dr. Maloney has extensive field experience in that region, particularly in Croatia, Bosnia, Kosovo, and Macedonia from 1995 to 2001. His work on the Balkans was interrupted by the 9/11 attacks, and from 2001 Dr. Maloney has focused nearly exclusively on the war against the Al Qaeda movement and particularly on the Afghanistan component of that war. He has traveled regularly to Afghanistan since 2003 to observe coalition operations in that country.

The **Naval Institute Press** is the book-publishing arm of the U.S. Naval Institute, a private, nonprofit, membership society for sea service professionals and others who share an interest in naval and maritime affairs. Established in 1873 at the U.S. Naval Academy in Annapolis, Maryland, where its offices remain today, the Naval Institute has members worldwide.

Members of the Naval Institute support the education programs of the society and receive the influential monthly magazine *Proceedings* or the colorful bimonthly magazine *Naval History* and discounts on fine nautical prints and on ship and aircraft photos. They also have access to the transcripts of the Institute's Oral History Program and get discounted admission to any of the Institute-sponsored seminars offered around the country.

The Naval Institute's book-publishing program, begun in 1898 with basic guides to naval practices, has broadened its scope to include books of more general interest. Now the Naval Institute Press publishes about seventy titles each year, ranging from how-to books on boating and navigation to battle histories, biographies, ship and aircraft guides, and novels. Institute members receive significant discounts on the more than eight hundred Press books in print.

Full-time students are eligible for special half-price membership rates. Life memberships are also available.

For a free catalog describing Naval Institute Press books currently available, and for further information about joining the U.S. Naval Institute, please write to:

Member Services
U.S. NAVAL INSTITUTE
291 Wood Road
Annapolis, MD 21402-5034
Telephone: (800) 233-8764
Fax: (410) 571-1703
Web address: www.usni.org